New Essays on Thomas R

Thomas Reid (1710–1796) was a contemporary of both David Hume and Immanuel Kant, and a central figure in the Scottish School of Common Sense. Until recently, his work has been largely neglected, and often misunderstood. Like Kant, Reid cited Hume's *Treatise* as the main spur to his own philosophical work. In Reid's case, this led him to challenge 'the theory of ideas', which he saw as the cornerstone of Hume's (and many other philosophers') theories. For those familiar with Reid's work, it is clear that its significance extends well beyond his challenging the theory of ideas.

The variety of topics which this book covers attests to the richness and variety of Reid's philosophical contributions, and the persisting relevance of his work to contemporary philosophical debates. The work included in this book, by leading figures in Reid scholarship, deals with aspects of Reid's views on topics ranging from perception, to epistemology, to ethics and meta-ethics, through to language, mind, and metaphysics.

This book was originally published as a special issue of the *Canadian Journal of Philosophy*.

Patrick Rysiew is Associate Professor of Philosophy at the University of Victoria, Canada. His primary research interest is in epistemology, including its points of intersection with certain issues in philosophy of language and psychology. He has published a number of articles on Reid.

New Essays on Thomas Reid

Edited by
Patrick Rysiew

Routledge
Taylor & Francis Group

LONDON AND NEW YORK

First published 2015 by Routledge

2 Park Square, Milton Park, Abingdon, Oxon OX14 4RN
711 Third Avenue, New York, NY 10017, USA

Routledge is an imprint of the Taylor & Francis Group, an informa business

First issued in paperback 2017

British Library Cataloguing in Publication Data
A catalogue record for this book is available from the British Library

ISBN 13: 978-1-138-85928-9 (hbk)
ISBN 13: 978-1-138-08288-5 (pbk)

Typeset in Times New Roman
by RefineCatch Limited, Bungay, Suffolk

Publisher's Note
The publisher accepts responsibility for any inconsistencies that may have
arisen during the conversion of this book from journal articles to book chapters,
namely the possible inclusion of journal terminology.

Disclaimer
Every effort has been made to contact copyright holders for their permission to
reprint material in this book. The publishers would be grateful to hear from any
copyright holder who is not here acknowledged and will undertake to rectify
any errors or omissions in future editions of this book.

Contents

CONTENTS

Citation Information

The chapters in this book were originally published in the *Canadian Journal of Philosophy*, volume 41, S1 (July 2014). When citing this material, please use the original page numbering for each article, as follows:

CITATION INFORMATION

Chapter 7
Reid's moral psychology: animal motives as guides to virtue
Esther Kroeker
Canadian Journal of Philosophy, volume 41, S1 (July 2014) pp. 122–141

Chapter 8
Common sense in Thomas Reid
John Greco
Canadian Journal of Philosophy, volume 41, S1 (July 2014) pp. 142–155

Chapter 9
Thomas Reid on truth, evidence and first principles
Keith Lehrer
Canadian Journal of Philosophy, volume 41, S1 (July 2014) pp. 156–166

Chapter 10
Reid's First Principle #7
Patrick Rysiew
Canadian Journal of Philosophy, volume 41, S1 (July 2014) pp. 167–182

Chapter 11
Reason and trust in Reid
Nicholas Wolterstorff
Canadian Journal of Philosophy, volume 41, S1 (July 2014) pp. 183–196

Chapter 12
Reid on powers of the mind and the person behind the curtain
Laurent Jaffro
Canadian Journal of Philosophy, volume 41, S1 (July 2014) pp. 197–213

Chapter 13
Reid on the priority of natural language
John Turri
Canadian Journal of Philosophy, volume 41, S1 (July 2014) pp. 214–223

Chapter 14
Disagreement, design, and Thomas Reid
René van Woudenberg
Canadian Journal of Philosophy, volume 41, S1 (July 2014) pp. 224–239

Please direct any queries you may have about the citations to
clsuk.permissions@cengage.com

Notes on Contributors

Todd Buras is Associate Professor of Philosophy at Baylor University, Waco, Texas, USA. His essays on Thomas Reid have appeared in *Philosophical Quarterly*, *Philosophy and Phenomenological Research*, the *Journal of the History of Philosophy* and the *History of Philosophy Quarterly*.

Rebecca Copenhaver is Professor of Philosophy at Lewis & Clark College, Portland, Oregon, USA. Her research interests are in early modern philosophy, Thomas Reid, and philosophy of mind. Her work has appeared in *Philosophical Quarterly*, *History of Philosophy Quarterly*, the *Journal of the History of Philosophy*, the *British Journal for the History of Philosophy* and *The Oxford Handbook on British Philosophy in the Eighteenth Century*. She is co-author, with Brian P. Copenhaver, of *From Kant to Croce: Modern Philosophy in Italy, 1800–1950* (2012).

Terence Cuneo is Professor of Philosophy at the University of Vermont, Burlington, Vermont, USA. In addition to having co-edited *The Cambridge Companion to Thomas Reid* (2004), he has published widely on Reid's ethics. He has also published two books on ethical theory, *The Normative Web: An Argument for Moral Realism* (2007) and *Speech and Morality: On the Metaethical Implications of Speaking* (2014).

Lorne Falkenstein holds the rank of Professor in the Philosophy Department at Western University, London, Ontario, Canada, where he has been employed since 1987. He has written articles and books on a number of eighteenth century philosophers and has co-edited Hume's *Enquiries, Dissertation on the Passions*, and *Natural History of Religion*.

Giovanni B. Grandi is Assistant Professor of Philosophy at the University of British Columbia, Okanagan Campus, Canada. He is the editor of *Thomas Reid: Selected Philosophical Writings* (2012).

John Greco holds the Leonard and Elizabeth Eslick Chair in Philosophy at Saint Louis University, Missouri, USA, where he has taught since 2006. He has published widely on virtue epistemology, skepticism, and Thomas Reid, including *Achieving Knowledge: A Virtue-theoretic Account of Epistemic Evaluation* (2010), *Putting Skeptics in Their Place: The Nature of Skeptical Arguments and Their Role in Philosophical Inquiry* (2000) and 'How to Reid Moore,' *Philosophical Quarterly* (2002).

Laurent Jaffro is Professor of Moral Philosophy at Panthéon-Sorbonne University, Paris, France. He has published on the third Earl of Shaftesbury, George Berkeley, John Toland, and Thomas Reid.

Esther Kroeker is a Post-Doctoral Fellow at the University of Antwerp, Belgium. She has published papers on Reid's moral philosophy, moral perception, and agency. Her current research is concerned with Reid's moral philosophy, with morality and religion in the Scottish Enlightenment, as well as with issues dealing with love and practical reasons.

Keith Lehrer is Regents Professor Emeritus, University of Arizona, Tucson, Arizona, USA, and Research Professor, University of Miami, Florida, USA. His research focuses on aesthetics, epistemology, free will, rational consensus and Thomas Reid, and he has published books on these topics. He has been elected as a fellow of the National Science Foundation, the National Endowment for the Humanities, the American Council of Learned Societies, the John Simon Guggenheim Foundation, the Center for Advanced Study in the Behavioral Sciences, and the American Academy of Arts and Science. His most recent book is *Art, Self and Knowledge*, which attempts to combine his philosophy with his artwork.

Patrick Rysiew is Associate Professor of Philosophy at the University of Victoria, British Columbia, Canada. His primary research interest is in epistemology, including its points of intersection with certain issues in philosophy of language and psychology. He has published a number of articles on Reid, most of which focus on his epistemological views and their relevance to contemporary issues and theories.

John Turri is Assistant Professor of Philosophy at the University of Waterloo, Canada. He specialises in epistemology, experimental philosophy, philosophy of language, and cognitive science. He is the author of *Epistemology: A Guide* (2014) and holds an Early Researcher Award from the Ontario Ministry of Economic Development and Innovation.

René van Woudenberg teaches Epistemology and Metaphysics at VU University Amsterdam, the Netherlands. In addition he is the Director of the Abraham Kuyper Center for Science and Religion at VU University and of the 'Science Beyond Scientism' project. He edited, with Terence Cuneo, *The Cambridge Companion to Thomas Reid.*

Nicholas Wolterstorff is Noah Porter Professor Emeritus of Philosophical Theology at Yale University, USA, and Senior Research Fellow in the Institute for Advanced Studies in Culture, University of Virginia, Charlottesville, Virginia, USA. Among his most recent publications are *Thomas Reid and the Story of Epistemology* (2001), *Justice: Rights and Wrongs* (2008), and *Justice in Love* (2011). He has been President of the American Philosophical Association (Central Division) and President of the Society of Christian Philosophers. He is a Fellow of the American Academy of Arts and Sciences.

Introduction

Thomas Reid (1710–1796) was a contemporary of both Hume and Kant. Like Kant, Reid cited Hume's *Treatise* as the main spur to his own philosophical work. In Reid's case, this led him to challenge 'the theory of ideas', which he saw as the cornerstone of Hume's (and many other philosophers') theories. Indeed, late in his life Reid wrote, in a letter to James Gregory, that,

> "... there is some merit in what you are pleased to call *my Philosophy*; but I think it lies chiefly in having called in question the common theory of *Ideas*, or *Images of things in the mind* being the only objects of *thought*..."[1]

For those familiar with Reid's work, it is clear that its significance extends well beyond his challenging the theory of ideas. The present collection of papers attests to the richness and variety of Reid's philosophical contributions, and the persisting relevance of his work to contemporary philosophical debates. The original papers included here deal with aspects on Reid's views on topics ranging from perception, to epistemology, to ethics and meta-ethics, through to language, mind, and metaphysics.

The first trio of papers collected here addresses aspects of Reid's views on perception. Among the chief errors of previous theories of perception, according to Reid, was a failure to attend to the distinction between sensation and perception. The former have no objects distinct from themselves, according to Reid; but sensation is a normal part of the total perceptual act, which does take a presently existing external thing as its object. In his article, **Todd Buras** defends this type of 'dual component' theory against recent criticisms that have been made by A.D. Smith. Responding to Smith's criticisms, Buras argues, attests to the resilience, originality, and significance of Reid's theory. **Lorne Falkenstein** has a rather less sanguine assessment of the easy response Reid appears to offer to Hume's 'table argument' on behalf of the theory of ideas. According to Falkenstein, while Reid has shown that arguments from perceptual relativity do not tell against the view that our perceptions are caused by external objects, Hume's reflections on the role of color sensations in our perception of primary qualities undermine the case for direct realism of the sort Reid wished to defend. Color sensations are also at center stage in **Giovanni Grandi's** paper. Grandi carefully considers Reid's claim that our color sensations are neither extended nor arranged in figured patterns. Following John Fearn (1768–1837), Grandi suggests that Reid's views here may have been driven by his views about the immaterial soul.

Perception looms large as well in **Rebecca Copenhaver's** paper. Here, however, the focus is on whether there is a moral *sense*, according to Reid, and one which strongly parallels what Reid has said about our capacities to perceive both (non-moral) objectual qualities, and aesthetic properties. According to Copenhaver, the answer is an unqualified 'yes'. While Copenhaver is concerned with the manner of our acquaintance with moral features of the world, **Terence Cuneo** and **Esther Kroecker** consider aspects of Reid's views on moral thought and theory. Cuneo's paper addresses the question of how we should conceive of the role played by the 'first principles of morals' that Reid articulates. Certain passages in Reid suggest that they are supposed to serve as foundational evidential grounds for other (moral) propositions. Cuneo finds this suggestion problematic, and argues that the first principles of morals, or an adherence to them, are better thought of as being somehow constitutive of moral thought, albeit in such a way that moral realism is not compromised. Kroecker, meanwhile, is concerned with the role played by 'animal motives' (hunger, a desire for esteem, etc.) in our moral thought and development. Kroecker argues that Reid's view is a hybrid of sentimentalist and rationalist ideas: while animal motives, and the feelings associated with them, do not ground moral judgments, in their proper extent and directed towards their natural objects, they help us to live well and are guides to virtue.

The next cluster of papers deal with Reid's epistemological views. Common sense, of course, figures centrally in Reid's philosophy. However, some of the things Reid says about common sense and common sense beliefs have struck various people, both historical and contemporary, as problematic. **John Greco** discusses the latter criticisms, and suggests that they can be addressed by clearly distinguishing between two different types of priority that common sense beliefs are supposed to enjoy. **Keith Lehrer** and **Patrick Rysiew** are also concerned with common sense in its epistemological guise. But their focus is on Reid's 'First Principles of Contingent Truths'. Lehrer seeks to clarify the manner of these principles' justification, their evidence, and how the latter is both empirical and opposed to 'externalist' epistemological theories. The resulting view, according to Lehrer, combines elements of foundationalism, coherentism, fallibilism and nominalism. Rysiew's paper addresses the interpretive difficulty posed, in particular, by Reid's first principle #7 – '*That the natural faculties, by which we distinguish truth from error, are not fallacious*' (FP#7). Rysiew offers a novel account of why this principle is needed, and why it is (as Reid says) special, even though it's often taken simply to summarize some of the principles that precede it. Rounding out this group of papers is **Nicholas Wolterstorff's** discussion of the anti-rationalistic theme running through Reid's philosophical views. Given Reid's central place in the Scottish Enlightenment, that there is such a strand in his thought might sound paradoxical. As Wolterstorff explains, however, Reid's account of the etiology of certain beliefs, his response to the sceptic, and his conception of the philosopher's role, do all involve a marked downgrading of the importance of reason, understood as essentially involving ratiocinative processes.

The final group of papers addresses Reid's views on mind, language, and metaphysics. According to Reid, the active and intellectual powers – the powers of will and powers of understanding – are always conjoined in practice. **Laurent Jaffro** addresses the question of *whose* intelligence is implied by an individual's exercise of his/her intellectual powers, given that much of our intellectual activity is not up to us. Answering this question, Jaffro argues, brings Reid's theistic beliefs to the fore. A significant part of Reid's alternative to 'the theory of ideas' was his suggestion that we regard various operations (e.g. perception, language use) as involving the interpretation of 'signs'. Some of those signs, according to Reid, comprise a 'natural language', one that is prior to any 'artificial' language (such as English, or Japanese) that humans might invent. **John Turri** critically examines the latter claim, and places Reid's views on language within the broader context of Noam Chomsky's enormously influential linguistic theory. Lastly, **René van Woudenberg** seeks to clarify and defend Reid's 'design principle', which states, *'That design and intelligence in the cause may be inferred, with certainty, from marks or signs of it in the effect.'* While the thinking embodied in this principle has come under fire from both historical and contemporary figures, van Woudenberg argues that the *real* controversy concerns whether and when we do detect marks of design in nature. Van Woudenberg scouts the possibility that disagreements about the principle itself will persist, and considers Reid's views on the likely causes of such enduring disagreement. The latter, Van Woudenberg suggests, constitute a distinctively Reidian contribution to the current literature on the epistemology of disagreement.

Patrick Rysiew

Note

1. Wood, Paul (ed.) 2002. *The Correspondence of Thomas Reid.* Edinburgh: Edinburgh University Press, 210.

PERCEPTION

Reidian Dual Component Theory defended

Todd Buras

Department of Philosophy, Baylor University, Waco, TX

For Reid perception, broadly speaking, was a complex of two very different mental states. Calling such views dual component theory, A. D. Smith questions whether any such theory, and whether Reid's version in particular, is a viable theory of perception. The aim of this paper is to defend Reidian Dual Component Theory from Smith's critique. Answering Smith's critique reveals the depth and resilience of Reid's approach to perception, highlighting specifically the continued interest of his thought about the relationship between sensation and perception, the nature of illusion, the immediacy of perception, and the content of perceptual belief.

1.

Reid's thought has been the subject of some of the best one-liners in the history of philosophy. Upon reading a portion of Reid's *Inquiry*, Hume wryly wished that 'the Parsons would confine themselves to their old occupation of worrying one another and leave philosophers alone to argue with temper, moderation and good manners' (Wood 1986, 416). Kant surely pleased a very different sensibility with his fierce chiding of the appeal to common sense as a 'convenient way to be obstinate and defiant without any insight.' '[S]een in the light of day,' he jeers, 'this is nothing but an appeal to the judgment of the crowd—applause at which the philosopher blushes but the popular charlatan struts and triumphs' (2004, 66). James Mackintosh thankfully preserved Thomas Brown's barbed estimation of Reid's contribution: 'Reid bawled out, We must believe an outer world; but added in a whisper, We can give no reason for our belief. Hume cries out, We can give no reason for such a belief; and whispers, I own we cannot get rid of it' (1837, 346; quoted in Grave 1960, 109). Joseph Priestley hit closest to home, quipping that Reid's account of the mind required 'such a number of independent, arbitrary, and instinctive principles that the very enumeration of them is really tiresome' (1978, 5–6).

4

These epigrams make it clear enough that Reid's ideas have not always persuaded, but not exactly why. Reid has had his champions, not all of whom have been a credit to his legacy;[1] and there certainly have been piecemeal criticisms, often embedded in sympathetic reconstructions.[2] But carefully argued refutations of Reid's central ideas are surprisingly hard to find.

A. D. Smith's engagement of Reid in *The Problem of Perception* is, arguably, the high-point of this rare genre. Smith's project brings him into direct confrontation with Reid's account of perception, which, after thoughtful examination, he rejects as philosophically untenable. Those interested not simply in understanding Reid's views but in advocating for their abiding significance must confront Smith's critique. The purpose of this paper is to do so. My aim is to demonstrate that Reid's understanding of perception is sufficiently resourceful to parry all of Smith's attacks.

2.

One response Reidians will not be able to make is that Smith's criticisms rest on a fundamental misunderstanding of his account of perception. To the contrary, Smith's understanding of Reid's views is well-informed and deeply illuminating.

Smith engages Reid in search of an adequate direct realist response to arguments from illusion. In illusions we seem to be immediately aware of something that has a feature the mind-independent objects in the vicinity lack. The immediate objects of illusions thus seem to be something other than mind-independent physical objects. Given the similarity between perception and illusions, it is implausible to think the two have different immediate objects. Therefore something other than mind-independent physical objects seem to be the immediate objects of perception as well; or direct realism seems false (2002, 22–27).

Direct realists have challenged each step of such arguments. For reasons space does not permit us to address, Smith thinks the only promising response is to develop an account of perception that distinguishes it clearly from 'perceptual sensation,' which it has in common with matching illusions. Differentiating perception from mere sensation, then, is the central project for direct realism, according to Smith (2002, 66).

Enter Reid. Reid undertook the same project for different reasons. The tendency of philosophers to 'confound' sensation and perception – to treat these operations as if they were the same – was Reid's diagnosis of the deepest errors of his opponents (1997, 167; 2002, 210–211). For Reid an adequate theory of perception begins with a clear distinction between sensation and perception – a distinction he delineated as follows.

Sensations are feelings, simple affections of the mind. A sensation and the feeling of it are one and the same thing, for Reid. He distinguishes sensations from all other mental states in terms of their objects. Sensations, he says, are acts of the mind that have no objects distinct from themselves (2002, 36). He distinguishes sensations from one another with respect to their qualitative character (2002, 193–200).

5

Thanks to the principles of the constitution of our nature, sensations occur as a result of the stimulation of our sense organs. Similar principles ordain that sensations do not usually occur alone. In normal human beings they are accompanied by very different mental acts, acts which do have an object distinct from themselves (1997, 174). If the principles of our constitution did not ordain this pairing, Reid believes we would be merely sentient beings (176). No amount of cogitation on our sensations, in other words, would lead to or produce a mental act worthy of the name 'perception.' Indeed, we could neither form the conception of a mind-independent material world, nor ground belief in such a thing (57–58). Yet we are percipient; and for Reid this means that our sensations are followed by a second psychological operation, which he analyzes in terms of conception and belief (2002, 226).

By acts of conception we apprehend and characterize things (2002, 295 and 24); through acts of belief we give assent to the way things are characterized by our conceptions (2002, 406). Not just any act of representing with assent makes us percipient, though. Reid's account of perception also includes a restriction on the content of the constitutive perceptual acts. Perception requires conception of and belief in the present existence of mind-independent bodies and qualities (2002, 22).

Reid reserves the term 'perception' for this second act in the larger perceptual process. Perception, properly speaking, is simply content restricted belief acquisition, i.e., being inspired with conception of and belief in the present existence of mind-independent bodies and their qualities (2002, 22). Given the contingency of the laws pairing perception and sensation, not only could our sensations occur in the absence of perception but our perceptions could occur alongside very different sensations or none at all (1997, 176). Yet, sensations and perceptions are paired by the principles of our constitution. So normal human perception – perception broadly speaking – is a complex of two very different mental acts, feeling and conception-and-belief. Here are Reid's own words:

> The external senses have a double province; to make us feel, and to make us perceive. They furnish us with a variety of sensations, some pleasant, others painful, and others indifferent; at the same time they give us a conception, and an invincible belief of the existence of external objects. This conception of the external objects is the work of Nature. The belief of their existence, which our senses give, is the work of Nature; so likewise is the sensation that accompanies it. This conception and belief which Nature produces by means of the senses, we call *perception*. The feeling which goes along with the perception, we call *sensation*. In our experience we never find them disjoined (2002, 210).

Reid's attempt to distinguish perception from sensation is, for Smith, an early and lucid example of an instructive failure – which, for obvious reasons, he calls the Dual Component Theory (DCT). DCTs take perception (broadly speaking) to be sensation-plus – i.e., sensation supplemented by another mental process, characterized in cognitive or representational terms. Sensation contributes the phenomenal character to perception; the cognitive element contributes the object-directed, representational character.

Though, for Reid, 'perception' properly designates only the cognitive component of DCT, categorizing Reid's view as Smith does is not at all a misunderstanding. For Reid does hold the views Smith attributes to him of perception broadly construed – what Reid calls in the passage above 'the province' of the external senses. If Smith underestimates Reid's views, as I will be suggesting, it is not because of the things he attributes to Reid, but because of the things he does not. The issue will be whether the untapped resources of Reid's thought are sufficient to deflect Smith's criticisms.

Smith's characterization of Reid's view, I suggested, is also deeply illuminating. Seeing Reid as a dual component theorist places Reid on a clean conceptual map that relates his views to a variety of historic and contemporary options in the philosophy of perception.

The classification highlights the differences between Reid's views and those to which he is most strongly opposed, as well as those closest to his own. While sensations are a crucial part of Reid's story, he does not expect them serve as objects of perception as idealists do (cf. Foster 2000). Neither do they serve as representations of external objects as various representative realists require (cf. Jackson 1977 and Robinson 1994). While cognitive acts (conception and belief) figure prominently as well, his view can by no means be equated with contemporary theories which either eliminate or reduce any purely sensory components (cf. Armstrong 1961). Conversely, while representational content figures prominently in Reid's theory as well, his view can by no means be equated with contemporary intentionalist theories which treat sensations themselves as representations of externals (Dretske 1997).

Some versions of DCT (Smith calls them causalist) require the objects of perception to be conceived as causes of our sensations (e.g., Schopenhauer 1969; Smith 2002, 67–69). Not so on Reid's version; we need only conceive of perceived objects as presently existing mind-independent things. Some versions of DCT (call them conceptualist) require only that the immediate objects of perception be represented, thought, or conceived (e.g., Sellars 1975). Reid's version goes further, treating perceptual cognition as full-blown belief.[3] Similarly, dual component theorists may part ways with respect to what they say about the sensory aspect of perception. Like Reid they may say that sensations have no objects distinct from themselves, which is at very least consistent with the claim that they constitute awareness of themselves.[4] Or, they may like adverbialists claim something stronger, namely that sensations are referentially empty, taking no objects at all (e.g., Chisholm 1957).

For better or worse, Reid charts a path through these issues which Smith's characterization brings into sharp focus. But the particulars of Reid's version of DCT are not Smith's target. He aims to bring the framework down entirely. His objections are fourfold, ranging from the less to the more serious. The next four sections will examine them one-by-one.

3.

Imagine gently touching a table top with a single finger. According to Reidian DCT, you will experience a fleeting tactile sensation, a simple feeling which constitutes an awareness of nothing distinct from itself. Because it is neither especially pleasant nor painful, it typically passes through your mind completely unattended (which is not to say unconsciously). This sensation will then be followed by a thought about something completely different, i.e., a conception of and belief in the present existence of hardness in a body, a mind-independent, extended thing. What would make a person think of such a thing in this situation? Smith's first critique is that Reid's answer makes this movement in thought 'unintelligible.'

Reid's answer, we noted, appeals to the original principles of our constitution, which ordain a (loosely) causal connection between sensation and perception.[5] Reid arrives at this explanation somewhat reluctantly and only because no other explanation suffices (1997, 57–58). The movement in thought from sensation to perception is not, he thinks, established by custom or education, which can only reinforce connections that are already established.[6] Neither is the movement in thought the result of any reasoning or inference as Reid thought Berkeley and Hume made perfectly clear (1997, 61).[7]

How then shall it be explained? Reid's answer treats perceptual acts as the mental parallels of bodily reflexes. When certain stimuli are regularly followed by involuntary motions (e.g., startling), and when these motions cannot be explained in terms of other known principles of change in our bodies (e.g., autonomic processes and voluntary decisions), we posit original principles of our nature (e.g., reflexes). This is entirely as it should be. For Reid takes it to be a 'Rule in Philosophizing' that

> Whenever two things are constantly and invariably connected in the course of Nature, and where at the same time this connection cannot be accounted for by any known law of Nature: We ought to consider such a connection as being itself a primary law of Nature, or else a consequence of some law of Nature hitherto undiscovered (1997, 260).

For Smith this answer makes the cognitive element of perception no better than what he calls 'a blind hunch.' 'A headache,' he says,

> could make me think of my mother. Indeed, it is presumably possible that a headache should cause me to believe that my mother is present. I should not, however, thereby be perceiving my mother—even if she were indeed present, and even if she had somehow caused the headache (2002, 74).

What the answer seems to be lacking, from Smith's point of view, is something that makes the hunch less blind – i.e., something in the content of the sensation that gives us a reason to cognize the things we do upon having sensations.

Though he does not formulate his criticism as an explicit argument, the following seems to capture his point.

Premise 1: A theory of perception is acceptable only if it makes the connection between sensation and perceptual cognition more than minimally intelligible.

Premise 2: A theory of perception makes the connection between sensation and perceptual cognition more than minimally intelligible only if it assigns sensation more than a merely causal relation to perceptual cognition.

Premise 3: Reidian DCT does not assign sensations more than a merely causal relation to perceptual cognition.

Conclusion: Reidian DCT is not an acceptable theory of perception.

In framing this argument in terms of minimal intelligibility, I mean to do Smith a service. Smith himself speaks of intelligibility, full stop (2002, 75). But intelligibility comes in many varieties. An explanation in terms of subsuming natural laws is certainly an intelligible answer to the question, What would make a person think of such a thing as hardness upon having a tactile sensation? Such explanations are often all we have, and they clearly pass normal standards of intelligibility (as they do in the case of reflexes). We have, for example, no better answer to the question, what would make a sensation follow a certain brain-event? Or, indeed, what would make a certain brain-event follow the stimulation of nerve endings? These are patterns in nature for which we can give no deeper explanation (except perhaps in terms of still other patterns). Such explanations admittedly make events only minimally intelligible, since they simply appeal to the patterns rather than explaining why the patterns are there in the first place. But such causal explanations clearly aid intelligibility.

Smith, it is equally clear, wants more by way of 'intelligibility.' And Reid can give him more – though in the end Reid will no doubt reject the first premise of the argument sketched above, rather than the third. (The second is not in dispute.) Smith says of the perceptual cognitions that follow sensations on DCTs: 'Nor are such judgements perceptual in their own right: in themselves they are just judgements as to what is the case, differing from any non-perceptual judgement simply in their aetiology' (2002, 74). Reidian DCT certainly does better than this, in three ways.

First, Reid's account of perception appeals to content-restricted conception and belief. So there is more of a difference between perceptual and non-perceptual judgments than etiology. If sensations were followed only by conception of and belief in past events, mental states, or abstract objects, Reid would not count us percipient. Conception of and belief in the present existence of mind-independent physical objects will no doubt still seem like a blind hunch to Smith. For the appeal to properly content-restricted conception and belief still does not distinguish perception from the case of the headache-and-mother.

Second, however, Reid appeals to *law-like* connections between sensations and perceptual cognition – those based on the original principles of our constitution. The lack of a law-like connection between headaches and mothers provides Reid ample grounds to agree that Smith's case would not be an instance of perception. If Smith's headaches were connected with the presence of his mother in a law-like way, however, it would be quite appropriate to consider whether he possessed an uncanny sense. This is just what we do in cases of synesthesia, blind-sight and chicken-sexing. The catalogue of human sensory abilities is, after all, a contingent matter.

Third, as Smith notes elsewhere (2002, 79–80), Reid allows that sensations play a more constitutive role in some cases of perceptual cognition (Reid 1997, 62 and 2002, 201–203). Hardness is a primary quality. What distinguishes the perception of primary qualities is that they involve direct conceptions of bodily qualities. Direct conceptions characterize their objects as they are in themselves and not merely in terms of a relation they bear to something else. In the perception of hardness, for example, Reid thinks we conceive the quality as *the firm adhesion of bodily parts*. This way of thinking of the quality is wholly unrelated to the sensation that occasions it; we can think of the quality this way without thinking of the sensation at all. The perception of secondary qualities is another matter; these perceptual acts involve only relative conceptions of the qualities perceived. We understand them not as they are in themselves but in terms of a relation they bear to something else. Further, not only are the conceptions involved relative, they are sensational. We conceive of secondary qualities in terms of their relation to our sensations, as *something in a body that causes such-and-such sensations*. This way of thinking of the quality is not wholly unrelated to the sensation that occasions it; we cannot think of the quality in this way without, as Reid says, being led back to the sensation (2002, 204). In normal cases of perception, we perceive primary and secondary qualities together. So it is only rarely, in artificial cases, that the content of perceptual cognition is wholly unrelated to the sensations which occasion it.

Even so, all of the content of some perceptual cognitions (i.e., artificially isolated perceptions of primary qualities) is wholly unrelated to the sensations that occasion them. Likewise, some of the content of all perceptual cognitions (i.e., the part having to do with the primary qualities) is also wholly unrelated to the sensations that occasion them. So Reid's explanation of the connection between sensation and perceptual cognition certainly falls short of the sort of explanation Smith demands. In the end, Reid offers us nothing more than the principles of our constitution to account for the fact that sensations are followed by thoughts about something altogether different – which makes the connection between our sensations and perceptual acts only minimally intelligible.

Still Reid's explanation ends where it does for reasons. Berkeley and Hume convinced him – and many since (see Campbell 2002) – that sensations alone cannot make available conceptions of things wholly unrelated to themselves (much less justify the belief in such things). In the absence of a better explanation of the movement from sensation to perceptual cognition, a purely causal theory is the best we have. The best theory we have is surely acceptable. Reid would thus reject the first premise in the argument above.

The remaining issue between Reid and Smith is not whether Reid's explanation is intelligible, but whether a better explanation is available. Reid's rule of philosophizing makes his endorsement of a causal explanation tentative and open ended. He is obliged to consider all comers, and Smith may well have a better explanation to offer. But we need not settle such momentous issues to answer this first critique. Reid's account of the connection between the two components of DCT is not unintelligible.

4.

Imagine watching a white billiard ball quickly collide with a yellow and then a green ball. You have a series of visual sensations that accurately reflects the order of the collisions. Yet due to inattention (or simply slow processing) you may form a false belief about the order of collisions. Alternatively, due to unfavorable lighting, your visual sensations might not accurately reflect the order of events. But by some fluke you may nonetheless form the correct beliefs about the order of events. Call these *mismatch cases* because of the way they trade on variance between perceptual sensation and cognition. Smith's second criticism is that DCT's can give no account of what is amiss in mismatch cases (2002, 75–76).

In both the examples above something in perception goes well or badly – is accurate or inaccurate – other than the beliefs formed. In the first case sensations go well; they reflect the order of events accurately, even though one forms the wrong belief. In the second case sensations go badly; they inaccurately reflect the order of events, even though one forms the right belief. To account for mismatch cases, Smith thinks one must be able to assess the accuracy or inaccuracy of sensations themselves, which requires sensations to have cognitive significance or representational content over and above the content of the perceptual cognition they occasion.

Yet he thinks Reidian DCT deprives sensations of any independent cognitive value. For Reid sensations are mere feelings that have no objects distinct from themselves. If they have no objects distinct from themselves, they do not represent things distinct from themselves; *a fortiori* they do not represent things well or badly. Using 'see' to describe what takes place in sensation, he asks: 'What, however, can it mean [on DCT] to say that, despite your judgement to the contrary, you really did see the white ball hit the yellow one before the green?' 'On the dual component theory,' he notes, 'sensation is of no cognitive value whatever except in so far as it occasions a judgement, which alone can be accurate or inaccurate' (2002, 75).

The gist of the critique is that mismatch cases force DCT to say something about sensations that it cannot consistently say. We may summarize Smith's reasoning as follows – though, again, the explicit formulation is my own:

Premise 1: A theory of perception is acceptable only if it can account for mismatch cases.
Premise 2: A theory of perception can account for mismatch cases only if it attributes cognitive value to sensations (or assesses sensations for accuracy) independently of the perceptual cognitions they occasion.

Premise 3: DCT does not attribute cognitive value to sensations (or assess sensations for accuracy) independently of the perceptual cognitions they occasion.

Conclusion: DCT is not an acceptable theory of perception.

Smith is right to note that Reidian DCT endows sensations with no cognitive value independently of the perceptual cognitions they occasion. But Smith fails to appreciate the significance of the fact that sensations occasion perceptual cognitions in a law-like way. Smith thus underestimates the cognitive value Reidian DCT assigns to sensations in virtue of the fact that they occasion cognition about external objects. Reidian DCT, I will show, endows sensations with derivative cognitive value in terms of which Reid may frame a plausible account of mismatch cases. Reidian DCT, in other words, may reject premise 2 of the argument above.

Reid's sign theory of sensations is an attempt to characterize the cognitive significance sensations have by virtue of their law-like relations to perceptual cognition. Signs are roughly things that make us think of other things; less roughly they are things, the awareness of which, makes of think of other things. They are, in Reid's words, things we interpret. He means by this simply that 'the appearance of the sign to the mind' is 'followed by a conception and belief of the thing signified' (1997, 177).

Having independent cognitive significance is not a requirement for satisfying this condition. Consider the case of linguistic signs. Inscriptions and utterances have no cognitive value of their own; they are just noises and marks. But because of the 'laws' governing their use (i.e., implicit human compacts) these marks and noises have the power of suggestion. They regularly occasion cognition of objects. Thus we take 'gold' to be a sign of gold, even though the word has no cognitive value independently of the acts of cognition it regularly occasions.

The same is true in perception, on Reidian DCT. The only thing in the perceptual process with the relevant sort of cognitive significance is downstream from sensations, i.e., the conception of and belief in the present existence of bodily qualities. But the law-like relation sensations bear to these contentful acts endows them with a dependent cognitive value. Sensations naturally signify mind-independent material qualities. This does not mean that sensations represent external objects or take them as objects, but rather that sensations regularly occasion cognitive acts that do represent or take such things as objects. As Reid says explicitly in the case of hardness, the claim that a certain sensation is a sign of harness is simply 'other words' for the claim that 'by an original principle of our constitution, a certain sensation of touch both suggests to the mind the conception of hardness and creates the belief of it' (1997, 58).[8]

Derivative though this sort of cognitive value may be, it does provide Reidian DCT the basis of an account of mismatch cases. The account, however, looks very different for cases of original and acquired perceptions. To frame the account, then, we must first attend briefly to Reid's original-acquired distinction.

The movement in thought from perceptual sensation to cognition is grounded in two sorts of laws (Buras 2009, 343–347). Our original perceptions follow from sensations as a result of what Reid calls particular principles of our constitution (Reid 1997, 191). These laws unite particular sensation-types (e.g., certain tactile sensations) to particular perception-types (e.g., conception of and belief in the present existence of hardness). Acquired perceptions, by contrast, are underwritten by what Reid calls general principles of our constitution (Reid 1997, 191). General principles link any sensation-type with any perception-type, provided a certain condition is met. Reid's inductive principle is an example. This principle grounds our ability to conceive of and believe in the present existence of anything (e.g., roses) that has been constantly conjoined in experience with certain sensations (e.g., rosy scents). Particular principles are functions from sensations to perceptions. General principles are functions from sensation and something else (e.g., background knowledge of regularities, habits of attention) to perceptions. Particular principles explain the constancy of the content of human perception (i.e., all perception is of external objects characterized by the primary qualities). General principles explain the variation (i.e., the sommelier perceives, not just wine, but particular vintages).[9]

Smith's question, recall, is 'What, however, can it mean [on DCT] to say that, despite your judgement to the contrary, you really did see the white ball hit the yellow one before the green?' Reid sign theory allows him to answer as follows: you 'saw' things correctly in the sense that you experienced a series of visual sensations that are natural signs of the white ball hitting the yellow one before the green. These sensations are related to conception and belief by natural laws – in this case general laws. Because the laws are general, the cognitive acts occasioned depend on factors other than the sensations alone, e.g., background knowledge and habits of attention. Still the connection is grounded in laws, and the laws support counterfactuals. So we can speak meaningfully of the acts of perception that would have occurred, if the sensations had been coupled with greater habits of attention or fuller background knowledge. Thus Reid can explain what goes right in the first mismatch case: you experienced sensations that would have produced the true belief if you had been more attentive or knowledgeable. Likewise, he can give an account of what goes wrong in the second mismatch case: you experienced sensations that would have produced a false belief if you had been more attentive or knowledgeable. In both cases, sensations are misinterpreted, in the Reidian sense of the term; they are followed by less-than-ideal acts of conception and belief.

My answer to Smith's question takes mismatch cases to be acquired perceptions.[10] Accordingly, my answer mimics Reid's own response to cases of legerdemain and ventriloquism. These deceptions involve acquired perceptions; so the acts of conception and belief we perform depend on sensations and background factors. Inattention or imperfect knowledge may thus lead one to form beliefs which more careful attention or more perfect knowledge would prevent (2002, 248–249). Reid's discussion of 'the improvement of the senses' echoes the answer I have given to Smith's question as well (2002, 239–241). The fact that our knowledge, experience, and attention is limited means that, in acquired perception, our sensations rarely suggest the cognitive acts that, in ideal circumstances, they would. Our senses may thus be improved by enlarged experience, expanded knowledge and greater habits of attention. Reid's account thus not only accommodates mismatch cases, it makes them a pervasive feature of acquired perceptions.

Mismatch cases in original perception are possible not due to a deficiency in background conditions but because we do not always perform the acts of perceptual cognition we ought to. Reid's sign theory supports not only counterfactual descriptions of perceptual cognition, it supports a normative description as well. We can identify what one ought to think when a sensation is experienced, even though, considered in itself, a sensation ought not make one think of anything. The principles of our constitution endow sensations with a natural office or function. We ought to think of the things our sensations naturally signify. We ought to do this in just the same sense that our irises ought to constrict when exposed to light, and the valves in our heart ought to seal during constriction.

As Reid notes, the human perceptual system is fragile and imperfect, and like other bodily systems it may become unfit for its natural office (2002, 251–252). When bodily organs are damaged or manipulated, sensations ordained by natural law to signify certain qualities may actually be caused by other qualities. The laws linking bodily qualities, sensations, and perceptual cognition encode sufficient conditions only: if a certain quality stimulates one's nerve endings, one will have a certain sensation; and if one has a certain sensation, one will have (at least in original perception) a certain conception and belief. These laws do not rule out the possibility of deviant causal chains. Through such deviant causal chains, we may have sensations whose natural office is to signify bodily qualities when we are not supposed to; and likewise for acts of perceptual cognition.

Reid explains phantom limb cases in just such terms: a man who has lost a limb may, through a deviant causal chain, have the tactile sensations that contact between the limb and a hard object naturally produces (2002, 251). Other things being equal, this man will conceive of and believe in the present existence of a hard object. Whether this belief is true or false, something has gone wrong in perception that is not just a matter of false belief. The man has sensations he ought not have.

Similarly, the conception of and belief in the present existence of a hard object may be caused in a deviant way by, say, hypnotic manipulation. In such situations, a sort of mismatch is possible even in original perceptions. One may have sensations whose natural office is not to suggest the perception of hard objects; yet, through some deviant causal chain, one may conceive of and belief in the present existence of hardness nonetheless.

Because the laws underwriting original perceptions encode sufficient conditions, the inverse mismatch is more difficult to imagine. It seems impossible that one might have sensations which ought to suggest the perception of hard objects, yet not conceive of and belief in the present existence of hardness. But this underestimates the power of acquired perception. After repeated phantom limb experiences, one may eventually get wise and successfully suppress or override the natural cognitive response to certain sensations.[11] (We have this sort of power over bodily reflexes as well: we may suppress or override the natural bodily response to frightening stimuli, for example.) This opens up the possibility of the second sort of mismatch in original perception. One may have sensations that ought to produce belief in a hard object, yet one may fail to believe in the present existence of hardness because one has acquired habits that suppress or override natural cognitive systems.

5.

Smith's third critique gets more traction. Indeed, it raises a staple issue in the literature on Reid. But Smith thinks the issue renders Reid's view 'a disastrous position' (2002, 77). I think Reid has more resources to respond to the concern than Smith recognizes. My aim in this section is to identify those resources. Judging their decisiveness is too big a project for any one paper.

The concern in this case is relatively simple, and fairly captured by this argument:

Premise 1: An adequate theory of perception is a version of direct realism.
Premise 2: Reidian DCT is not a version of direct realism.
Conclusion: Reidian DCT is not an adequate theory of perception.

Proponents of Reidian DCT should be slow to join the ranks of idealists and representative realists in rejecting premise 1. There are no doubt some versions of direct realism Reid would reject – versions that eliminate or reduce the sensory component entirely, for example. But Reid clearly intended his account of perception to make the mind's relation to external objects as immediate as idealists and representative realists make the mind's relation to sensations. If his theory fails in this regard, he would likely agree that it is inadequate.

Why does Smith think Reid fails to make the mind's relation to external objects sufficiently immediate to count as direct realism? The answer has to do with the role of sensations. 'Reid's contention that sensations are "signs" that "suggest" conceptions of physical objects to us does not serve to distinguish his position from Indirect Realism' (2002, 76).[12] The only difference Smith sees is not about the nature of perception but about epistemology. The move from sensation to perceptual cognition is not inferential for Reid, and therefore not justified by inference. But neither need it be inferential for Indirect Realists. They are also free to understand the role of sensations in causal rather than inferential or justificatory terms (Smith 2002, 77).

Smith's contention is that sensations cause trouble for direct realism simply by virtue of being a conscious mental state involved in the perceptual process.

Due to the causal laws, we cannot stand in the perceptual relation to external objects unless we also have sensations. But sensations are conscious mental states. Smith takes this to mean that sensations are in some sense objects of awareness. It follows that there is something other than external objects – indeed, something mental – that we must take as an object of awareness in order to perceive external objects. The claim that there is something internal to the mind that we must take as objects of awareness in order to perceive external objects seems sufficient to make a view indirect realist. For it implies that perception of external objects is in some sense mediated by awareness of mental intermediaries. Hence Reidian DCT is a version of indirect realism.

For these reasons Smith says, 'the suspicion that the dual component theory fails to amount to Direct Realism will fail to be justified only if its proponents can convince us that sensations do not function as objects of awareness' (2002, 77). Yet he does not see how 'sensations can be in consciousness and yet not be an object of awareness' (2002, 78). I agree with Smith that Reid's own views make it impossible for him to hold that sensations are not objects of awareness in perception. I am not convinced, however, that he must make this claim in order for his account of perception to count as direct realist.

One way to make sense of the claim that sensations are in consciousness yet not objects of awareness is an adverbialist analysis of sensations. According to adverbialism sensations are not objects of awareness but something like a manner of sensing. Reid certainly says things that invite an adverbialist reading, and is indeed taken by many to be an early adverbialist. But, as I have argued elsewhere, Reid is not an adverbialist: in the context of Reid's work, the claim that sensations have no objects distinct from themselves implies that they do take themselves as objects (Buras 2006; cf. Ganson 2008).[13]

Smith is also right to hold that the problem is not resolved by Reid's claim that sensations often pass through the mind unattended[14] – though here I must quibble. Reid's claim about attention is not, as Smith claims, 'plainly false' (2002, 79). For Reid does not claim, as Smith suggests, that our sensations are ever altogether overlooked. He claims instead that certain sensations (those associated with the perception of primary qualities) tend to be (1997, 55–57). Setting this aside, however, I agree that unattended objects of awareness are still objects of awareness. Thus inattention does nothing to address the issue that perceptual awareness of external objects is mediated by awareness of a mental intermediary.

Unlike Smith, however, I do not think Reid's remarks about inattention are meant to answer concerns about indirectness. I know of only one passage in which Reid confronts the issue directly. In discussing Locke, Reid protests against the very idea of a thought with two objects, one immediate and one mediate. Reid calls this doctrine of double objects a 'hard saying,' noting that 'Every man is conscious of his thoughts, and yet, upon attentive reflection, he perceives no such duplicity in the object he thinks about' (2002, 134). This tempts him to conclude that 'to think of any object by a medium, seems to be words without any meaning.' But he sees a subtle distinction between this hallmark of indirect realism and his own sign theory.

> There is a sense in which a thing may be said to be perceived by a medium. Thus any kind of sign may be said to be the medium by which I perceive or understand the thing signified. The sign, by custom, or compact, or perhaps by nature, introduces the thought of the thing signified. But here the thing signified, when it is introduced to the thought, is an object of thought no less immediate than the sign was before: And here there are two objects of thought, one succeeding another, which we have shown is not the case with respect to an idea, and the object it represents (2002, 134).

Though he does not say so here, elsewhere he affirms the phenomenological aptness of the sort of 'double objects' implied by the sign theory (e.g., 1997, 56). Upon attentive reflection, those who perceive by signs ought to be able to discern a thought about a sensation and a thought about a bodily quality – even though the former often passes unattended.[15] And so it is. Just as those who communicate by signs are able, upon reflection, to distinguish awareness of the words used and of the thoughts communicated – even though the former often pass unattended.

There certainly is a difference between, on the one hand, a single thought about both a bodily quality and a sensation (and about the bodily quality by virtue of being about the sensation), and, on the other hand, two thoughts, one about a bodily quality and one about a sensation. The distinction may seem too subtle by half, as the saying goes. Or it may be Reid's most valuable contribution to dual component theory. It certainly opens a new response to Smith's third critique.

When presenting Smith's case for Premise 2, we accepted the following condition as sufficient for making a view a version of indirect realism: If an account of perception implies that there is something mental that must be an object of awareness in order for us to perceive external objects, then that account is indirect realist. The passage above disputes the sufficiency of this condition. Reid's idea is that external objects may be the immediate objects of perception even though something mental must be an object of awareness in order for us to perceive external objects. Direct realism, he is suggesting, need not deny the presence of intermediate objects of awareness, but need only deny instead something about the function of intermediate objects in perception.

On my interpretation, then, Reid grants that a mental intermediary is present in perception.[16] He grants that the intermediary cannot be present without being an object of awareness. He grants that awareness of the intermediary is causally necessary for awareness of the external qualities; and, in this causal sense, he grants even that one must be aware of the intermediary in order to be aware of the external qualities. What distinguishes his view from indirect realism is this: on Reidian DCT our awareness of external objects is not constituted by our awareness of a mental intermediary. Indirect realists typically claim that our awareness of external objects is constituted by our awareness of mental intermediaries, i.e., that we are aware of externals by virtue of being aware of mental intermediaries, where the 'by virtue of' is metaphysical rather than merely causal. By this standard Reid is no indirect realist. He does not analyze our awareness of external objects in terms of awareness of something other than external objects. He does not hold that our awareness of externals just is awareness of sensations that bear certain relations (e.g., causal or similarity) to external objects.

Call the view I am attributing to Reid *no analysis direct realism* (to distinguish it from *no intermediary direct realism*). On no analysis direct realism I am aware of sensations and I am aware of external objects. My awareness of the later follows quickly from my awareness of the former by natural laws – so quickly, in fact, that the paired acts of awareness may seem simultaneous. Yet there are no mediate objects of thought here. There is instead just one immediate object of thought and then another; the second no less an immediate object because it comes after the first.

For present purposes the question is not whether no analysis direct realism is an acceptable theory of perception, but whether it is a version of direct realism. In this connection it is worth noting that the crucial claim of direct realism is that mind-independent things are immediate objects of awareness in perception. The claim that sensations are also immediate objects of awareness in perception is certainly consistent with that claim. The crucial claim of indirect realism is not simply that we are immediately aware of mind-dependent objects, but that we are not immediately aware of mind-independent objects. On Reidian DCT we are. On both views, it is true, we are aware of mind-independent objects by virtue of being aware of mind-dependent objects. But on the indirect realist view this 'by virtue of' claim has more than merely causal force. On Reid's view it does not. Thus, contra Smith, we have identified something about Reid's contention that sensations are signs of physical objects that distinguishes his position from Indirect Realism.

6.

Smith considers his last critique the most serious. This concern alone elicits the charge that Reid's view is not just 'unintelligible,' and 'disastrous,' but 'incoherent' (2002, 81). But this last criticism is simply a mirror image of the second, and, as I will argue, presents no issues beyond those raised by the third.

The second critique, recall, aimed to identify something DCT must say about perceptual sensation that it cannot consistently say. The final criticism does the same with respect to perceptual cognition. Unlike the second criticism, however, this last is not driven by discussion of cases. So it is more difficult to discern exactly what Smith thinks an adequate account must say.

The concern has to do with the content of perceptual cognition. The content of perceptual cognition is supposed to differ fundamentally from simply thinking about external objects while having sensation. But thinking and sensation is all DCT has at its disposal to account for the content of perceptual cognition. So the basic structure of argument is this:

Premise 1: On Reidian DCT perceptual cognition can have no features which cannot be accounted for in terms of thinking accompanied by sensation.
Premise 2: Perceptual cognition has some feature, F, which cannot be accounted for in terms of thinking accompanied by sensation.
Conclusion: Perceptual cognition has some feature DCT cannot explain.

The critique gets murkier when Smith tries to specify F. Within the space of a few pages he describes the issue in several different ways, not all of which are equally clear or clearly equal. He says DCT's account of perceptual cognition fails to do justice to the presence of individual objects (2002, 81), the 'distinctively demonstrative content' (81), the '*de re* relationship with the object' (83), the centrality of 'acquaintance' (84), and 'truly perceptual consciousness' (89). I will not try to sort through all these different ways of filling out Premise 2. For, as we will see, not even Smith settles on an interpretation that convinces him it is true. Smith's ultimate complaint is not that there is something about the content of perceptual cognition for which Reidian DCT cannot account; the complaint is instead that what Reidian DCT must say in order to account for the content of perceptual cognition makes it 'phenomenologically absurd' (90).

To give Premise 2 its due, consider the function of perception in our cognitive lives. Perception serves to put us in cognitive contact with particular physical things in a way that is unique. The point is not that, without perception, we could never think of particular physical things at all. Perhaps we could, for instance, by thinking of whatever satisfies certain general descriptions. The point is rather that perception seems to make particular physical things available to cognition in a fundamentally different way than merely thinking, remembering or imagining.

Suppose perception does ground cognitive access to particular physical things in a way that other forms of cognition do not. It is reasonable to expect this difference in function is to be explained by a difference in content; that is, we would expect the content of perceptual cognition to feature a sort of conscious awareness of particular physical things that is not a matter of merely thinking of those things, even while having sensations. I could, for example, think of breakers on a certain beach, and I could do this while having the aural sensations associated with hearing waves. I could do all this without perceiving the waves. Perceiving the waves is obviously distinguished partly by the causal connections between the waves, sensations, and perceptual cognition. The idea on offer is that there is also a difference in the content of perceptual cognition, a difference having to do with the character of our conscious awareness of particular physical things.

Take this uniquely perceptual mode of conscious awareness of particular physical things – whatever it is – to be feature F. By design, F cannot be accounted for in terms of thinking accompanied by sensation. The unique cognitive access could not be explained in terms of mere thinking. For this would not respect the function of perception in our cognitive lives as the source of a unique mode of conscious awareness of particular physical things. Nor can the unique feature be grounded in sensations – at least not on DCT. For on DCT sensations do not constitute cognitive access to anything distinct from themselves. But thinking accompanied by sensations is all there is to perception on DCT. If the feature cannot be explained in terms of thinking and sensations, then, on DCT, it cannot be explained at all. Thus, it seems, DCT fails to account for the content of perceptual cognition.

It is certainly fair to note that thinking accompanied by sensations is all there is to perception on DCT. On Reidian DCT, the relevant mode of thinking is conception and belief. But nothing about this framework limits the account Reid can give of the mode of awareness of particular physical objects involved in perception, i.e., the mode of perceptual conception. There is little need to consider cases. If Smith thinks perceptual cognition requires acquaintance, Reidian DCT can give him conception in the mode of acquaintance.[17] If someone else thinks some form of demonstrative or *de re* awareness is the hallmark of perceptual cognition, Reidian DCT can offer that as well. To be sure, there are questions about whether Reid himself actually thought of perceptual cognition in any of these terms.[18] Reid himself actually offered little by way of a theory of the definitively perceptual mode of conception. Still there is no real question about what *Reidian* DCT can accommodate. Reidian DCT can help itself to whatever primitive modes of cognition it must in order to account for the unique content of perceptual cognition.

It is true that, on Reidian DCT, it is only perceptual cognition, and not sensation, that makes any sort of contact (unique or otherwise) with particular physical objects. This give Smith pause. For it seems to suggest that on DCT

> there is really no such thing as truly perceptual consciousness. What we are offered, rather, is a conscious state that consists in the occurrence of 'meaningless' sensation, and which is not, therefore, of itself perceptual, followed by the supposedly truly perceptual stage that is not itself conscious (2002, 89).

But this concern gets no purchase on Reidian DCT, since Reid does not think sensations are the only conscious acts in perception. He treats perceptual cognition as a conscious act as well (2002, 58, 191). For reasons that need not detain us, Smith calls the idea of conscious acts of conception and belief 'fanciful' (2002, 89). He does not, however, question the coherence of the idea, and that is the issue.

Locating the unique mode of awareness of particular physical objects in the context of perceptual judgment, rather than sensation, concerns Smith for a second reason as well. He suggests that the mode of awareness must be established in some other way (for instance in sensation) before it can be instantiated in a judgment (2002, 88). If this were so, Reidian DCT would have the order of explanation backwards: we cannot get particulars in mind in a unique way by forming perceptual judgments about them, rather we must first get particulars in mind in the requisite way so that we can form perceptual judgments. But cases of non-sensory perception force him to rescind any strict requirement of this sort. The case he considers involves a non-conscious ant that nonetheless perceives the objects it pushes about. Instances of blindsight are equally serviceable. In these cases, there is nothing prior to perceptual cognition to establish the mode of awareness characteristic of perception. So if, as it seems, the characteristic mode of awareness is instantiated in these cases, a 'prior contact' requirement on instantiating the definitive mode in perceptual judgment is not defensible.

For these reasons, we can drop the charge of incoherence – at least until further considerations are adduced to show that Reidian DCT cannot accommodate whatever it must in order to account for the content of perceptual cognition. Smith himself seems to concur. He ends the discussion of the fourth criticism with only a complaint about the phenomenological adequacy of what Reidian DCT must say in order to account for the content of perceptual cognition (2002, 90). He notes correctly that 'perception now emerges as featuring two distinct episodes of awareness.' But he calls this 'phenomenologically absurd,' and 'a bizarre view of perceptual awareness ... involving a blind hunch accompanied by a sensation.' As we have already noted, the movement in thought from sensation to cognition of mind-independent external things is, as Reid sees things, in some sense unaccountable; but no more so than it should be. We have also seen that the hunch is not really blind, if by that he means entirely independent of and unrelated to sensation. The deeper issue is whether it is true that 'as an account of ordinary perceptual consciousness, this [i.e., DCT] is barely intelligible.' As we noted in discussion of the third critique, the phenomenology of perception is sufficiently rich to accommodate a sign-theoretic approach. On such an approach, perception systematically involves awareness of two sorts of things, signs and the things they signify. So far from a phenomenological absurdity, the fact that DCT preserves a sense in which there are always two objects of awareness involved in perception may be its greatest strength. If perception really is like communicating through signs – and we have yet to find fault with the suggestion – the phenomenological absurdity would be to deny that perception involves some mode of awareness of both sign and signified. The denial would inevitably produce a one-sided account, like a theory of spoken communication that denies any sort of awareness of words or of what they communicate.

7.

No doubt, there is more to say about the phenomenology of perception – as well as the content of perceptual cognition, the nature of perceptual sensation, the explanation of perceptual illusions, as well as the intelligibility of the mind-world connection in perception. My aim in this paper has been simply to say enough on these topics to demonstrate that, Smith's criticisms notwithstanding, Reid's variety of DCT remains a live option. If Reid's approach to perception ultimately proves untenable, it will not be on account of the concerns Smith raises.[19]

Notes

1. The association of Reid's works with the works of his fellow travelers Oswald and Beattie is often noted by Reid's critics. See Somerville (1995) for a discussion of the association in Hume's 'enigmatic parting shot;' also see (Kant 2004, 66) and (Priestley 1978).
2. Falkenstein (2002) and (2000) offers important criticisms of some of Reid's central ideas; for criticism in the mode of sympathetic reconstruction see Hamilton's notes and dissertations in (Reid 1895), and (Wolterstorff 2001).
3. See Pelser (2010) and Smith (2001) for discussion of the wisdom of this decision. As Smith notes (2002, 73), objections to the belief requirement constitute another line of critique of Reidian DCT not addressed here.
4. Buras (2006) thinks Reid's view is not only consistent with the claim that sensations take themselves as objects, but requires it. See Ganson (2008) for textual and philosophical arguments to the contrary.
5. The connection is only loosely causal because of Reid's understanding of the strict and proper sense of causation, which always implies agency. But the constant conjunction of distinct events in experience suffices for the attribution of causation in the loose and popular sense; see (1997, 59).
6. To my knowledge, Reid never considers the possibility that the connection is established by a sort of mistake. Smith reads Hume as offering this sort of explanation (2002, 77). The vulgar are taken simply to mistake their sensations for mind-independent external objects. But the consistency of the connection clearly favors explanation in terms of laws.
7. The main arguments I take Reid to be alluding to can be found in sections 18–20 of Berkeley's *Treatise* (1998, 109–110); and section 1.4.2 of Hume's *Treatise* (2000, 125–144).
8. The interpretation of Reid's sign theory sketched here agrees with Copenhaver (2004), who puts the point in terms of the lack of any intrinsic feature that makes sensations them signs of external objects.
9. See (Copenhaver 2010) and (van Cleve 2004) for further discussion of the differences between original and acquired perception.
10. It is not vital to my argument in this section to determine whether Smith's cases are in fact, as I suggest, instances of acquired perception. As explained below, mismatch cases are possible in original perception as well. Giovanni Grandi notes, however, that Smith's cases fundamentally involve the perception of the location (or change of location, i.e., movement) of colors, and that Reid may indeed believe that the perception of the location of colors is an original perception. Reid does say that sensations of color suggest not only the present existence of certain external qualities, but also suggest 'individual direction and position' of those qualities in relation to the eye (1997, 99).
11. The key point for my argument is that the suppression of natural cognitive responses is possible, and Reid explicitly allows that in some cases acquired perceptions 'efface' original perceptions in the way suggested here (2002, 236). But in other cases he suggests that our original perceptual response is impervious to change by custom (1997, 154). I am not sure on what basis Reid would distinguish the two.
12. The concern goes at least as far back as Hamilton (see Reid 1895). For a sample of the more recent literature, see Madden (1986), Chapell (1989), Pappas (1989), Buras (2002), van Cleve (2004) and Copenhaver (2004).
13. The same considerations weigh against the claim that sensations are not objects of awareness in perception because of their alleged transparency or diaphanous character, as in (Harman 1990).

14. Indeed, I made the same point in my own discussion of the problem (Buras 2002, 472–473).
15. It is hard to see how Smith could disagree with this, given his insistence on the claim that our sensations are never wholly overlooked (2002, 79).
16. Here, again, my approach agrees with Copenhaver (2004).
17. Some Reid scholars do just this, e.g., (van Cleve 2004, 111–121).
18. I have raised doubts about whether Reid actually thought of perceptual conception in terms of acquaintance, for instance (Buras 2008, 630–632).
19. Grateful acknowledgement is hereby offered to students in graduate seminars on Reid at Baylor University, and to contributors to this volume, especially Giovanni Grandi, for comments on early drafts of this work.

References

Armstrong, David. 1961. *Perception and the Physical World*. London: Routledge & Kegan Paul.

Berkeley, George. 1998. *A Treatise Concerning the Principles of Human Knowledge*, edited by Jonathan Dancy. New York: Oxford University Press.

Buras, Todd. 2002. "The Problem with Reid's Direct Realism." *The Philosophical Quarterly* 52: 457–477.

Buras, Todd. 2006. "The Nature of Sensations in Reid." *History of Philosophy Quarterly* 22 (3): 221–238.

Buras, Todd. 2008. "Three Grades of Immediate Perception: Thomas Reid's Distinctions." *Philosophy and Phenomenological Research* 76: 603–632.

Buras, Todd. 2009. "The Function of Sensations in Reid." *Journal of the History of Philosophy* 47 (3): 329–354.

Campbell, John. 2002. "Berkeley's Puzzle." In *Conceivability and Possibility*, edited by Tamar Szabo Gendler and John Hawthorne. New York: Oxford University Press.

Chapell. 1989. "The Theory of Sensations." In *The Philosophy of Thomas Reid*, edited by Melvin Dalgarno and Eric Matthews. Boston: Kluwer Academic Publishers.

Chisholm, Roderick M. 1957. *Perceiving: A Philosophical Study*. New York: Cornell University Press.

Copenhaver, Rebecca. 2010. "Thomas Reid on Acquired Perception." *Pacific Philosophical Quarterly* 91 (3): 285–312.

Copenhaver, Rebecca. 2004. "A Realism for Reid: Mediated but Direct." *British Journal for the History of Philosophy* 12 (1): 61–74.

Dretske, Fred. 1997. *Naturalizing the Mind*. Cambridge, MA: The MIT Press.

Falkenstein, Lorne. 2000. "Reid's Account of Localization." *Philosophy and Phenomenological Research* 61: 305–328.

Falkenstein, Lorne. 2002. "Hume and Reid on the Perception of Hardness." *Hume Studies* (28): 27–48.

Foster, John A. 2000. *The Nature of Perception*. New York: Oxford University Press.

Ganson, Todd. 2008. "Reid's Rejection of Intentionalism." *Oxford Studies in Early Modern Philosophy* 4: 245–263.

Grave, S. A. 1960. *The Scottish Philosophy of Common Sense*. Oxford: Oxford University Press.

Harman, Gilbert. 1990. "The Intrinsic Quality of Experience." *Philosophical Perspectives* 4: 31–52.

Hume, David. 2000. *A Treatise of Human Understanding*. Edited by David Fate Norton and Mary J. Norton. New York: Oxford University Press.

Jackson, Frank. 1977. *Perception: A Representative Theory*. Cambridge, MA: Cambridge University Press.

Kant, Immanuel. 2004. *Prolegomena to any Future Metaphysics that will be able to Present Itself as a Science*. Edited by Gunter Zoller. Translated by Peter G. Lucas and Gunter Zoller. New York: Oxford University Press.

Madden, E. H. 1986. "Was Reid a Natural Realist?" *Philosophy and Phenomenological Research* 47: 255–276.

Mackintosh, James. 1837. *Dissertation on the Progress of Ethical Philosophy*. 2nd ed. Edinburgh.

Pappas, George. 1989. "Sensation and Perception in Reid." *Nous* (23): 155–167.

Pelser, Adam. 2010. "Belief in Reid's Theory of Perception." *History of Philosophy Quarterly* 27 (4): 359–378.

Priestley, Joseph. 1978. *An Examination*. New York: Garland Publishing.

Reid, Thomas. 1895. *The Works of Thomas Reid*. 8th ed. Notes and Supplementary Dissertations by Sir William Hamilton Edinburgh: James Thin.

Reid, Thomas. 1997. *An Inquiry into the Human Mind on the Principles of Common Sense: A Critical Edition*. Edited by Derek R. Brookes. Edinburgh: University of Edinburgh Press.

Reid, Thomas. 2002. *Essays on the Intellectual Powers of Man: A Critical Edition*. Edited by Derek R. Brookes. University Park, PA: The Pennsylvania State University Press.

Robinson, Howard. 1994. *Perception*. New York: Routledge.

Schopenhauer, Arthur. 1969. *The World as Will and Representation*. Translated by E.F.J. Payne. New York: Dover.

Sellars, Wilfrid. 1975. "The Structure of Knowledge." In *Action, Knowledge, and Reality: Critical Studies in Honor of Wilfrid Sellars*, edited by H. -N. Castaneda. Indianapolis, IN: Bobbs-Merrill.

Smith, A. D. 2001. "Perception and Belief." *Philosophy and Phenomenological Research* 62: 283–309.

Smith, A. D. 2002. *The Problem of Perception*. Cambridge, MA: Harvard University Press.

Somerville, James. 1995. *The Enigmatic Parting Shot: What was Hume's 'Compleat Answer to Dr. Reid and to that Bigotted Silly Fellow, Beattie'?* Avebury.

van Cleve, James. 2004. "Reid's Theory of Perception." In *The Cambridge Companion to Thomas Reid*, edited by Terence Cuneo and Rene van Woudenberg, 101–133. Cambridge: Cambridge University Press.

Wolterstorff, Nicholas. 2001. *Thomas Reid and the Story of Epistemology*. New York: Cambridge University Press.

Wood, P. B. 1986. "David Hume on Thomas Reid's *An Inquiry into the Human Mind, On the Principles of Common Senses*: A New Letter to Hugh Blair from July 1762." *Mind* 95: 411–416.

PERCEPTION

Reid's response to Hume's perceptual relativity argument

Lorne Falkenstein

Philosophy Department, Western University, London, CANADA

Reid declared Hume's appeal to variation in the magnitude of a table with distance to be the best argument that had ever been offered for the 'ideal hypothesis' that we experience nothing but our own mental states. Reid's principal objection to this argument fails to apply to minimally visible points. He did establish that we have reason to take our perceptions to be caused by external objects. But his case that we directly perceive external objects is undermined by what Hume had to say about the role played by color in our perception of the primary qualities of bodies.

1. Introduction

In his *Essays on the Intellectual Powers*, Thomas Reid declared David Hume's appeal to variation in the magnitude of a table with our distance from it to be the best argument that had ever been offered for the 'ideal hypothesis' that we experience nothing but our own mental states or ideas.[1] Reid's principal objection to this argument has been widely endorsed.[2] Nicholas Wolterstorff (2001, 143–144) describes it as 'brisk and devastating' and repeats it with amplification. Philip de Bary (2002, 98–100) describes it as a 'knockdown' and 'simple and effective' refutation. Others who repeat and accept the objection include Keith Lehrer (1989, 100–101), René Van Woudenberg (2000, 69–79), and James Van Cleve (2004, 103).[3] But Reid's objection is not as devastating as has been maintained. The objection appeals to a distinction between real and apparent magnitude. That distinction misses how Hume understood magnitude, and so misses Hume's point. The real force of Reid's objection rests with a 'transcendental' consideration regarding spatial perception that is raised only at the close of his discussion. This consideration rivals Kant's transcendental arguments in ingenuity but even it does not suffice to refute representational realism. It does, however, pose a challenge for the skepticism about the existence of external objects that Hume considered to be a consequence of his argument.

2. Hume's Argument

Intellectual Powers II.14 quotes, with all necessary accuracy, an argument 'against our perceiving external objects immediately ... proposed by Mr. HUME.'

> But this universal and primary opinion of all men [that "the very images, presented by the senses" are external objects which do not depend "on our perception, but would exist, tho' we and every sensible creature were absent or annihilated"] is soon destroyed by the slightest philosophy, which teaches us, that nothing can ever be present to the mind but an image or perception; [perception,] and that the senses are only the inlets[,] through which these images are received [1777: conveyed], without being ever able [1777: being able] to produce any immediate intercourse between the mind and the object. The table, which we see, [table we see, 1777: table, which we see,] seems to diminish as we remove farther from it: But the real table, which exists[,] independent of us, suffers no alteration. [alteration:] It was[,] therefore[,] nothing but its image[,] which was present to the mind. These are the obvious dictates of reason; and no man[,] who reflects, ever doubted[,] that the existences[,] which we consider, when we say[,] *this house*, and *that tree*, are nothing but perceptions in the mind, and fleeting copies and [or] representations of other existences, which remain uniform and independent. [New paragraph.] So far [,] then, we are necessitated, by reasoning, to [are we necessitated by reasoning to] depart from [or contradict, 1777: to contradict or depart from] the primary instincts of nature, and to embrace [and embrace] a new system with regard to the evidence of our senses.[4]

Prior to offering this argument, Hume had drawn a distinction between 'the more trite Topics, employ'd by the Sceptics in all Ages, against the Evidence of *Sense*;' and 'other more profound Arguments against the senses, which admit not of so easy a Solution' (EHU 12.6). The argument just given is supposed to be an argument of the latter, 'more profound' sort. Included among the former 'topics' are a number of instances of 'the Imperfection and Fallaciousness of our Organs, on numberless Occasions' including the way they present 'various Aspects of Objects, according to their different Distances' – which is, oddly, just what the 'more profound' argument, quoted above, appeals to.

This does not signal any confusion on Hume's part. The difference between 'trite topic' and 'more profound argument,' does not arise from the specific illustration that is employed, but the use to which it is put. The 'trite topics' take variation in the appearance of the same object to teach us that the senses sometimes mislead us (they are 'fallacious' on 'numberless occasions'), and so are not 'implicitely to be depended on.' The 'more profound arguments,' in contrast, take this same variation to teach us that the senses at least sometimes present us with images or representations, rather than the very objects themselves. As Hume noted, and much as Reid was to do later in *Intellectual Powers* II.22, 'Of the Fallacy of the Senses,' the 'trite topics' can be readily answered by claiming that the information supplied by the senses can be made trustworthy by taking relevant circumstances into account, and correcting for the influence of those circumstances. The more profound arguments are not so easily dealt with.

According to the more profound version of the argument from variations in the size of a table, when we look at a table we see something, not nothing. The question is whether this thing that we see is an object that exists outside of us or independently of being perceived, or is instead an image or representation.

Hume did not say all that he might have to answer this question. He seems to have taken the answer to be simply obvious. But a fuller account might be given, based on things he can be presumed to have accepted. Background knowledge would tell us that a change in the size of an object requires that something happen to it that causes it to gain or lose parts, or be compressed or decompressed. This is nothing more than analysis of what it means for a thing to change in size. But it entails that acts like cutting, gluing, inflating, squeezing, or (in the case of decompression) opening or breaking a surrounding container would have to be performed on the thing that we see or its immediate surroundings. Background knowledge would further suggest that motion from one place to another does not change hard and solid objects like tables, and that the act of retreating from the thing that we see produces only a change in us and not in anything that exists outside of us at the spot we are retreating from. In this case, the background knowledge is based on our consciousness of our acts of volition, our visual experience of our own body parts, and our past experience of constant conjunctions. We will to move our legs, and we subsequently feel and see the motion of our legs. Moreover, we do not will to move our legs towards the table we see in ways that past experience tells us are likely to break parts off the table or compress it into a smaller area. We will a motion in the opposite direction, away from the place that the table we see appears to us to occupy.

But experience teaches us that this action nonetheless has an effect on 'the Table, which we see.' The number of minimally visible parts composing the thing that we see diminishes, and those parts may also change in color. This diminution in number of parts occurs without the sort of change in shape that normally occurs as a consequence of cutting or squeezing.

Since infancy, we have learned to distinguish changes in ourselves from changes in the things around us. The former are regularly preceded by acts of will. The latter are not, or if they are, they are preceded by acts of will that are followed by visual and tactile experiences of motions of our own bodies, involving contact with the bodies that change and accompanied by sensations of effort and resistance. In the case of hard and solid bodies like tables the sensations of effort and resistance are considerable. We find ourselves only able to effect a change in the arrangement of parts constitutive of the object through the use of tools and our efforts result in notable distortions in the shape of the object. Once produced, these distortions are permanent. The original constitution of the object cannot be restored simply by returning to a viewpoint we had occupied earlier.

The diminution in the size of the table we see resulting from moving to a more remote position is therefore naturally taken for a change in us rather than in anything that exists independently of us. Things that exist independently of us would hardly be 'independent of us' if they were regularly experienced to change consequent to an effortless act of will on our part, especially when they are disposed at some (increasingly great) distance from us and especially when the change, once effected, is not permanent but can be undone by as facile a means as

27

returning to the original viewpoint.[5] But if the diminution in the size of the table we see when moving to a more remote location is due to a change in us, what we see must be at least in part dependent on us. This forces us to question whether what we see would continue to exist were we not to perceive it.[6]

Hume went on to write that 'no Man, who reflects, ever doubted, that the Existences, which we consider, when we say, *this House*, and *that Tree*, are... fleeting Copies or Representations of other Existences, which remain uniform and independent.' But this was not said in his own voice (it is an opinion attributed to reflective people), and was quickly retracted.[7] While the argument leads to the conclusion that the things that we see are dependent on us, and that some of them are copies or representations of others, it does not lead to the further conclusion that any of them are copies or representations of independently existing objects. This is a conclusion that Hume immediately went on to declare to be unjustifiable (EHU 10). Though it is drawn by reflective people it turns out to be the effect of a compulsion to attempt to preserve a naturally induced belief in the reality of external objects. Hume considered it to be unjustified by argument, and liable to unanswerable skeptical objections.

3. Reid's objections

Reid had three principal objections to Hume's argument. First, he charged that the argument equivocates. It fails to take account of the distinction between two different and equally real qualities of the table: its 'real' magnitude and its 'apparent' magnitude ('apparent' being a misnomer for a quality that is equally real in its own right). Rather than recognize that the table we see varies in *apparent magnitude* under conditions where background knowledge would suggest that it is not changing in *real magnitude*, Hume had simply said that the table we see varies in *magnitude* under conditions where an independently existing table would not be expected to vary.

1. The table we see varies in magnitude with changes in distance. Ms[8]
2. The real table does not vary in magnitude with changes in distance. $\sim Mr$
   The table we see is not the real table. $\sim s = r$[9]

Reid charged that the evidence ought to lead us to draw a rather different distinction – not a distinction between different objects, each with its own magnitude, but a distinction between different sorts of magnitude. As a consequence Hume's apparently valid argument turns out to be invalid on the grounds of equivocation.

1. The table we see varies in *apparent* magnitude with changes in distance. PMs[10]
2. The real table does not vary in *real* magnitude with changes in distance. $\sim RMr$
   The table we see is not the real table. $\sim s = r$[11]

In further explaining this response, Reid noted that 'those who are conversant in the mathematical sciences' take real magnitude to be determined by juxtaposition with standard units ('measured by some known measure of length, as inches, feet, or miles'[12]) and apparent magnitude to be 'measured by the angle which an object subtends at the eye.'[13]

Real magnitude, Reid went on to note, is something that must remain the same while the object remains unchanged. Apparent magnitude, in contrast, is the sort of thing that must by its very definition vary depending only on real features of the external world: the size of the object and its distance from the observation point. Accordingly, there is no skeptical lesson to be drawn from the fact that apparent magnitude changes with changes in observation point while the real magnitude remains the same. Mounting a second objection to Hume's argument, Reid charged that even aside from any appeal to logic, common sense would tell us that this occurrence is consistent with realism.

> Let us suppose, for a moment, that it is the real table we see: Must not this real table seem to diminish as we remove farther from it? It is demonstrable that it must. How then can this apparent diminution be an argument that it is not the real table? When that which must happen to the real table, as we remove farther from it, does actually happen to the table we see, it is absurd to conclude from this, that it is not the real table we see. It is evident therefore, that this ingenious author has imposed upon himself by confounding real magnitude with apparent magnitude, and that his argument is a mere sophism. [*Intellectual Powers*: 182: 31–39]

Further developing this last point, that the change in apparent magnitude is not just a change in 'the table we see,' but in the real table, Reid offered a third objection, charging that,

> Mr HUME's argument not only has no strength to support his conclusion, but that it leads to the contrary conclusion; to wit, that it is the real table we see; for this plain reason, that the table we see has precisely that apparent magnitude which it is demonstrable the real table must have when placed at that distance.

Continuing with the symbolization used earlier, we might represent this contrary argument as follows:

1. The table we see varies in apparent magnitude with changes in distance. PMs
2. The real table varies in apparent magnitude with changes in distance. PMr
   The table we see is the real table. s=r

Unfortunately, identities are not so easily established. We might charitably interpret Reid to have only meant to say that Hume's argument *tends* to the opposite conclusion, or that it provides inductive support for the opposite conclusion. But then an equitable application of charity would also dictate considering whether the magnitude Hume attributed to the table we see is the apparent magnitude Reid described.

4. Hume's sense of 'Magnitude'

It is demonstrable that the angle subtended by an object must diminish as that angle is measured from increasingly remote vantage points. But it is not so obvious that this diminution in angular magnitude is the diminution in magnitude Hume took us to see when he claimed that the table we see diminishes with distance. When discussing the perception of visible distance, and hence of visible magnitude, in the *Treatise* Hume had written 'The angles, which the rays of light flowing from [visible points], form with each other; the motion that is requir'd in the eye, in its passage from one to the other; and the different parts of the organs, which are affected by them; these produce the only perceptions, from which we can judge of ... distance' (T 1.2.5.12).[14] But in the appendix to that work he had already retracted the claim about angles, writing, 'The first [error of less importance] may be found in [1.2.5.12], where I say, that the distance betwixt two bodies is known, among other things, by the angles, which the rays of light flowing from the bodies make with each other. 'Tis certain, that these angles are not known to the mind, and consequently can never discover the distance.'[15] In making this correction he was echoing Berkeley, who had pointed out that 'those *Lines* and *Angles*, by means whereof *Mathematicians* pretend to explain the Perception of Distance, are themselves not at all perceiv'd, nor are they in Truth, ever thought of by those unskilful in *Optics*' (1709, 7).[16] As a consequence, angles, or angles in conjunction with distance, cannot be 'the *Medium* whereby [the mind] apprehends the Apparent Magnitude of Objects' (NTV 52).

Elsewhere, Reid himself declared that though astronomers measure visible extension 'by the angle, which is made by two lines drawn from the eye to the two distant objects, yet it is immediately perceived by sight, even by those who never thought of that angle' (*Intellectual Powers* II.10: 140/8–10). But he did not go on to say what those who never thought of that angle immediately perceive by sight when they see visible extension.

In the eighteenth century, the standard answer to the question of what gives an object its extension was that it consists of parts set outside of parts. Ephraim Chambers began the article on extension in his *Cyclopedia: or an universal dictionary of the arts and sciences* by reporting that '*Extension* is usually described, as consisting in the situation of parts, beyond parts; which some authors cavil withal, as holding, that we can conceive absolute *extension*, without any relation to parts.'[17] Consistently with this, and in response to the 'cavil' Chambers mentioned, Berkeley had maintained that all magnitudes, visible as well as tangible 'are greater or lesser, according as they contain in them more or fewer Points; they being made up of Points or *Minimums*. For, whatever may be said of Extension in *Abstract*, it is certain sensible Extension is not infinitely divisible' (NTV 54). For Berkeley, the 'medium' whereby those people who have never thought of visible angles come to apprehend the apparent magnitude of objects is the number of minimally sensible points intervening between their extremities. The visible moon, for instance, is 'a round, luminous Plain of about thirty visible Points in Diameter' (NTV 44).

In the *Treatise*, Hume had mentioned that there are not just two, but three standards relative to which the magnitude of an object can be perceived. One is juxtaposition with standard units – Reid's 'real' or 'tangible' magnitude (1.2.4.21). The other is 'the whole united appearance and the comparison of particular objects' (1.2.4.22), which we can take to be something like Reid's apparent magnitude, though divested from the association with angles and cashed out instead in terms of our ability 'at one view to determine the proportions of bodies, and pronounce them equal to, or greater or less than each other, without comparing the number of their minute parts' (1.2.4.22). The third is the number of those minute parts (1.2.4.19), which accords with the standard definition of extensive magnitude as *partes extra partes*. Hume had considered this standard to be useless for practical purposes because the parts in question are too small and too densely packed to make an exact enumeration possible, but he also considered it to be 'just as well as obvious' that apparent magnitude is the product of the (necessarily finite) number of minimally visible or minimally tangible points into which the visible or tangible image can be divided (1.2.4.19, cf. 1.2.2.2, 1.2.4.6). For Hume, what makes one image – be that image visible or tangible – appear 'at one view' to be larger or smaller than another is that it is built up from a significantly greater or lesser number of minimally sensible points, even if we cannot say precisely how many more. Angles at best serve as one way of determining or estimating the number of those points, given that they are too small or confused to distinguish and count up individually.

Reid went some way towards accepting this himself. Though he rejected Hume's geometrical finitism, he granted Hume's perceptual finitism. He allowed that 'there is a limit beyond which we cannot perceive any division of a body,' and that 'The parts become too small to be perceived by our senses.' He only insisted that 'we cannot believe that it becomes then incapable of being further divided, or that such division would make it not to be a body' (*Intellectual Powers* II.19: 219/34–37).

But if magnitude is determined by number of parts, and angular measures serve as merely one way of determining or estimating the number of parts, then there is no equivocation in Hume's argument.

1. The table we see varies in apparent magnitude (= angular magnitude = number of parts) with changes in distance. Ns[18]
2. The real table does not vary in real magnitude (= number of parts) with changes in distance. $\sim$Nr

The table we see is not the real table. $\sim$ s = r

If there is any equivocation in this argument it would be on 'parts rather than 'magnitude – on minimally visible points as opposed to real, constituent parts. But invoking a distinction between the minimal points that we see and real parts would not be comfortable for someone like Reid, who wanted to maintain that we see the real object.

5. Reid's sense of magnitude

Though Reid accepted that there is a limit beyond which the parts of objects become too small to be perceived by our senses, we should not be too quick to assume that his case against Hume flounders just for this reason. Reid believed that visual space is finite. It corresponds to the inner surface of a sphere centered on the eye. This put him in a position to approach the question of the nature of apparent magnitude from the other end, as it were – from the appearance of the whole rather than the existence of the parts – and maintain that what people see when they see apparent magnitude is a greater or lesser portion of a finite visual space – the portion of visible space that the real object takes up at a given distance.[19] This portion is accurately measured by and corresponds to the angle subtended by the object at the eye.[20] But it can be estimated independently of such mensuration. Hume himself admitted as much when he allowed that the magnitude of objects can be perceived by 'the whole united appearance and the comparison of particular objects' (1.2.4.22). When understood in this sense, apparent magnitude is exclusively determined by two real features of the external world, the size of the object, which is taken to remain constant, and its distance from the observation point, which varies. This makes it an equally real, albeit position-relative, feature of objects.

> it is evident that the real magnitude of a body must continue unchanged, while the body is unchanged. This we grant. But is it likewise evident, that the apparent magnitude must continue the same while the body is unchanged? So far otherwise, that every man who knows any thing of mathematics can easily demonstrate, that the same individual object, remaining in the same place, and unchanged, must necessarily vary in its apparent magnitude, according as the point from which it is seen is more or less distant; and that its apparent length or breadth will be nearly in a reciprocal proportion to the distance of the spectator. This is as certain as the principles of geometry. [*Intellectual Powers* II.14: 181/21–31]

Understanding the portion of the visible field taken up by the object to be the apparent magnitude Reid was talking about does not by itself expose an equivocation in Hume's argument. Of course this argument is a *non sequitur*:

1. The real table varies in angular magnitude with changes in distance. GMr
2. The real table does not vary in real magnitude with changes in distance. ~RMr

The table we see is not the real table. ~s = r

But it is so far from what Hume said that it no longer engages Hume's point. Hume claimed that the table we see changes while the real table remains unchanged. It would be quibbling to object that the real table does change in some way that Hume did not think of. Hume could admit that he had been wrong to say that the real table suffers no alteration whatsoever, while pointing out that the table we see still diminishes with distance in some way in which the real table does not – if not in the portion of the visible field it takes up, then in its number of apparent parts, for example.

However, Reid did more to substantiate the charge of equivocation. He argued that what Hume would have described as a diminution in the table we see is nothing other than a diminution in the portion of the visual field the real table occupies, thereby identifying GMr with PMs and converting the GMr, ~ RMr argument just mentioned into the PMs, ~ RMr argument mentioned earlier. To do this, Reid cited Berkeley's authority to make a further identification of real magnitude with what he called tangible magnitude, and of angular or apparent magnitude with visible magnitude.

> [Real] magnitude is an object of touch only,[21] and not of sight; nor could we even have had any conception of it, without the sense of touch, and Bishop BERKELEY, on that account, calls it *tangible magnitude.*
>
> ... apparent magnitude is an object of sight, and not of touch. Bishop BERKELEY calls it *visible magnitude.* [*Intellectual Powers*: 181/3–6 and 11–12]

Here, it is not the mathematical sciences that are being invoked, but vision science. But, Berkeley's (questionable[22]) imprimatur notwithstanding, this science is not on Reid's side. When real magnitude is understood as magnitude determined by juxtaposition with standard units, it is not 'an object of touch only' (or of touch and mediate visual perception only). I may count paces, and so measure by touch, but I can just as well hold a yardstick up against the side of a table and see that the table top rises to the 30-inch mark on the yardstick. In this way, 'real' magnitude can be immediately[23] seen as well as touched – and can be seen to be invariant with changes in distance as well as felt to be so. Regardless of how far away I am from the yardstick leaning against the table, as long as I can see the marks on the yardstick at all, I can see the table top continue to rise to the 30-inch mark.

A similar point might be made about apparent magnitude. After a recent filling, my teeth would not close properly. The dentist commented that while the filling was high by only a small fraction of a millimeter, it must have felt to me 'like there was a boulder in there.' And, indeed, I would have judged that an object at least the size of a grape seed was caught in my tooth. The same object felt on different body parts, can be felt to be larger or smaller even though, when measured by juxtaposition with standard units, it is unchanged. More to the point, it can be immediately felt to be larger or smaller, because the feeling in question is the feeling of an aggregate number of adjacently disposed minimally tangible parts, which is sensed immediately and not an effect of judgment.

The remarks that have just been made only serve to establish a peripheral point: that what Reid described as real magnitude is not as tightly connected to tactile experience, and what he described as apparent magnitude not as tightly connected to visual experience as he thought. But they also show that tangible magnitude is not as robustly 'real' as he thought, and that vision can make us aware of the same measures as touch. Tangible points have as indeterminate a relation to really constituent parts as visible points, and the standard units relative to which length is described are themselves objects of vision.

But this is by the way. The crucial identification is that of visible magnitude with apparent magnitude, where apparent magnitude is understood as the portion of a finite visible field an object occupies, and so as something that can be further identified with the angular magnitude of the object. This identification would allow Reid to take minimally visible points to be small angular measures, and the aggregate pointal magnitude of the table that we see to be a feature of the real table – an angular magnitude determined in accord with mathematical laws by real features only: the real magnitude of the table and its real distance.

6. A Humean response to Reid

Hume need have been no more impressed with this way of understanding Reid's objection. He could have responded that angular measures serve only to impose a specious appearance of demonstrative connection on a phenomenon that, at its base, defies any such treatment. Just as it is demonstrable that the real table must subtend a smaller angle, and so come to occupy a smaller portion of the visual field as we retreat from it, so it is demonstrable that each of the smallest visible parts of the real table must subtend a smaller angle, and so come to occupy a smaller portion of the visual field as we retreat from it. But notwithstanding that this is what is demonstrable, it is not what we see. Unlike the table, the smallest visible parts of the table do not appear to diminish as we retreat from them. Instead, they become confused. The edges that define them blur. Their distinct colors mix. They amalgamate into a smaller number of differently shaped and differently colored parts. In effect, rather than shrink, they disappear, to be replaced by a lesser number of differently appearing parts. The table appears to shrink. But only because its minimally visible parts disappear, not because they, too, appear to shrink. The mathematics that would describe the rate at which these changes occur with increases in distance defies us, in part because it is not clear that there is any regularity in the sequence of changes for different objects or any continuity in the changes from one remove to a yet greater remove. External factors interfere as well. The strength of illumination enhances visual acuity, leading parts that would otherwise appear to amalgamate to appear to shrink. And, as Reid himself may have admitted when he added the qualification, 'nearly' to 'in reciprocal proportion to the distance' (*Intellectual Powers* II.14: 181/20–30), strongly luminescent objects, like stars, will continue to appear as minimally visible points regardless of distance.

For these reasons, what we see is not just a demonstrative consequence of the real magnitude of the object and its distance. The appearance of the object at different distances is dependent on contingent features of human nature responsible for distinct vision. That makes what we see dependent on us, and not just on the world around us. And that in turn suggests that what we see is an image and not the real object. If we want, we can consider the visual field to be a portion of the inner surface of a sphere centered on the eye and so take this portion to have an angular magnitude. But the angle is just a useful fiction for measuring the magnitude of a mental image, constituted from a number of minimally visible points set at no distance from us.

Hume could therefore have shrugged his shoulders over Reid's attempt to find a flaw in either the logic or the common sense of his perceptual relativity argument. In attacking the common sense of Hume's argument, Reid had written, 'Let us suppose, for a moment, that it is the real table we see: Must not this real table seem to diminish as we remove farther from it? It is demonstrable that it must' (*Intellectual Powers*: 182/31–33). But what is demonstrable in this case is that the angle subtended by the real table must diminish. It is not demonstrable that the real table must lose parts as we remove further from it. (If anything is demonstrable it is that the parts must continually diminish as the table does.) Since we do not think that the real object is losing parts, we are compelled to accept that, as the distance increases, increasingly fewer *visible* parts come to stand for or 'represent' increasingly large numbers of *real* parts. This does not happen in accord with the laws of mathematics, but in accord with the subjective conditions on visual acuity. And that does not demonstrate any inconsistency between 'common sense' and the conclusion Hume wanted us to draw, that we immediately perceive mental images.

Turn then to Reid's response to the logic of Hume's argument. Reid charged that Hume had equivocated between apparent and real magnitude (*Intellectual Powers*: 182/21–29). But Hume could have maintained that visible and tangible magnitudes can be equally apparent and that angular and linear magnitudes can each be an object of immediate visual perception. He could have allowed that the magnitude he was talking about is the whole united appearance of the thing (magnitude in the second sense of *Treatise* 1.2.4) but insisted that this magnitude is ultimately a function of the number of minimally sensible parts constitutive of the thing (magnitude in the third sense). Visible magnitude is the product of the number of minimally visible points, tangible magnitude the product of the number minimally tangible points, and real or objective magnitude is determined by visual or tangible juxtaposition with standard units. The standard units are themselves only known to us by means of visible and tangible images that lose or gain minimally sensible parts with such circumstances as distance from the observer or locus on different body parts, just like all the other objects of vision and touch (cf., Berkeley, NTV 61).

The best Reid could do to base a charge of equivocation on these claims would be to represent Hume's argument as follows:

1. The table we see varies in apparent magnitude ($=$ number minimally visible of parts) with changes in distance. NVs
2. The real table does not vary in real magnitude ($=$ number of juxtaposed standard units) with changes in distance. $\sim$ NRr

The table we see is not the real table. $\sim$ s $=$ r[24]

Hume could have granted that this argument is invalid – but only because it has not been properly reformulated in response to Reid's demand that we distinguish real from apparent magnitude.

1. The parts we see vary in number with changes in distance. $\forall x(Sx \rightarrow Vx)$
2. The real parts do not vary in number with changes in distance. $\forall x(Rx \rightarrow {\sim}Vx)$[25]

The parts we see are not the real parts. $\forall x(Sx \rightarrow {\sim}Rx)$

To contest the soundness (not the validity) of this argument Reid would have needed to make a case either for taking some minimally visible or tangible points to be real points or for some sort of demonstrative or regular connection between at least some sets of minimally sensible points and real magnitudes. Where angular magnitudes are concerned, making such a case is easy. But, as Berkeley had already pointed out (NTV 62) the prospects for doing the same with minimally sensible points are dim. In the *Treatise* Hume had maintained that our minimal perceptions must be adequate representations of the smallest possible parts of extension, for the plausible reason that they have no parts and that nothing could be smaller than a thing that has no parts (T 1.2.2.1). But he had also maintained that our minimal perceptions can often be (and so far as we know are always) revealed by experience to be inadequate representations of vastly more compound and complex objects (T 1.2.1.5). As we approach an object, parts that appeared as minimal points begin to appear as variously shaped compounds of a number of points. Often, these points are differently colored as well. As a consequence, the view of the same object from different distances can exhibit markedly different numbers, shapes, arrangements, and colors of parts. While the angular magnitude of the whole varies in accord with sine laws, the appearance of the thing that subtends the angle is dependent on us and its changes from distance to distance cannot be anticipated simply by applying sine laws. The angle is merely a useful fiction employed to measure the size of a mental image that is in fact at no distance from us.

7. A case for representational realism

There is nonetheless something about Reid's case that Hume ought to have found unsettling. Granting that the immediate objects of vision are mental images, it turns out that those images occupy just those portions of the visual field that they would if they were projections cast by three dimensional objects on the inner surface of a sphere centered on the eye. Even if this does not mean that we perceive external objects, it suggests that what we see might be determined by such objects.

It is undeniable that we learn to correlate visual images seen at one distance with visual images seen at another distance, and visual images with tangible experiences. In the *Treatise* Hume had himself appealed to these correlations when accounting for such things as why we see distance between luminous objects that are separated by complete and total darkness (T 1.2.5.15–19) or why the view from atop a mountain conveys a greater sensible impression of vastness than the view of the inside of a room, supposing that the visual field at all times contains the same number of minimally visible points (T 1.3.9.11). And he had gone some way towards recognizing that these correlations are foundational for our formation of concepts of objects (T 1.4.2.18–24). We do not consider every different visual image to be a different object, but instead associate large classes of distinct visual and tangible images under the name of the same object, considering them to be different ways the same object appears from different distances, from different angles, or in vision as opposed to touch.

Reid pointed out that we do not just learn these correlations after the fact, as a consequence of experience and association. They are mathematically demonstrable.

> In a word, the appearance of a visible object is infinitely diversified, according to its distance and position. The visible appearances are innumerable, when we confine ourselves to one object, and they are multiplied according to the variety of objects. Those appearances have been matter of speculation to ingenious men, at least since the time of EUCLID. They have accounted for all this variety, on the supposition, that the objects we see are external, and not in the mind itself. The rules they have demonstrated about the various projections of the sphere, about the appearances of the planets in their progressions, stations, and retrogradations, and all the rules of perspective, are built on the supposition that the objects of sight are external.
> [*Intellectual Powers*: 183/17–27]

The question here is not about the relation between visible appearances and real objects. It is about the relation between visible appearances and other visible appearances and what leads us to consider different appearances to be appearances of the same object (or, in the planetary case, of a particular sort of orbital path of an object). Reid noted that three-dimensional external objects, and an external space containing them, are hypothesized to explain the relations between visible appearances. To do this, we imagine ourselves to be placed at the center point of a large sphere. We imagine three-dimensional objects to be placed at various distances between us and the inner surface of this sphere. We draw lines of projection from our position at the center point through each point of the object to a point on the inner surface sphere. These lines define a concave projection of the object that varies in apparent magnitude with our distance from it and in shape with how it is turned relative to our position. The projections correspond, in figure and proportions, to the images we immediately see. Different visible images are considered to be images of the same object if they are projections of that object under any given distance or from any given angle.

This is just a theory. But it is a theory we are so deeply committed to that we anticipate or decide in advance of experience how an object would have to look from a given angle or from a given distance, and expect our anticipations or decisions to be confirmed. If they are not, we do not revise our theory, but our original assessment of what sort of object we were inspecting. The theory is immune to revision because it is too well confirmed by past experience to be abandoned by the occasional recalcitrant experience. And, as further experience in the recalcitrant cases shows, there always proves to have been some mistake in our original assessment of what sort of object we were inspecting.

[The] real table may be placed successively at a thousand different distances; and in every distance, in a thousand different positions; and it can be determined demonstratively, by the rules of geometry and perspective, what must be its apparent magnitude, and apparent figure, in each of those distances and positions. Let the table be placed successively in as many of those different distances, and different positions, as you will, or in them all; open your eyes and you shall see a table of precisely that apparent magnitude, and that apparent figure, which the real table must have in that distance, and in that position. [*Intellectual Powers*: 183/6–16]

Reid rhetorically concluded, 'Is this not a strong argument that it is the real table you see?'

It is not. But it is a strong argument for the conclusion that the things you see are *at least* images or projections of a real table, if not the real thing, which is not an option to be discounted. Even supposing the immediate objects of vision to be nothing more than mental images, distinct from external objects, we are able to account for the objective unity of those images by supposing that there is an external space, containing three-dimensional objects set at a distance from us, and affecting us in ways that correspond to the laws of mathematical projection.

'Shall we say that a false supposition, invented by the rude vulgar, has been so lucky in solving an infinite number of phænomena of nature?' Reid went on to ask (*Intellectual Powers*: 183/30–32), laying on the rhetoric more thickly. The question has become more belligerent, the suggestion that the reader would be stupid to answer in any other way more brazen. And the 'ingenious men' of the previous paragraph have been demoted to the 'rude vulgar,' who can now no longer be supposed to have been so 'ingenious' as to come up with any hypothesis that is likely to be true unless it is based on something obvious and certain.

Hume might have objected that we can learn to associate the various visible appearances of an object with the rather less varied tangible appearances of that same object (insisting, contrary to Reid, that tangible experiences are no more real than visual). The strong resemblance of various tangible appearances with one another would suffice to lead the 'rude vulgar' to consider them to all be appearances of the same object. Association of various visible appearances with this supposedly single tangible object would lead them to collect one group of visible appearances together, as appearances of the same object, under one name. No recourse to geometrical demonstration would be required.

But Reid could reply that, having once arrived at this 'rude vulgar' theory on the basis of experience and association alone, we can see how 'ingenious men' might have noticed that the visible appearances vary in regular ways with distance and viewing angle, and that their variety can be accounted for by supposing a three-dimensional object set outside us in ambient space and projecting images onto the inner surface of a sphere. This theory serves so well to explain why the various visible appearances are as they are that it is natural to infer that it must be something more than a mere device that fortuitously serves to enable us to calculate what sort of experiences we will have as we shift perspective.

Add to this, that upon the contrary hypothesis, to wit, that the objects of sight are internal, no account can be given of any one of those appearances, nor any physical cause assigned why a visible object should, in any one case, have one apparent figure and magnitude rather than another. [*Intellectual Powers*: 183/33–38]

Once again, there is some overstatement here. The contrary hypothesis would now have to be some form of anti-realism, which either denies that there is an external world, or claims that we have no good reason for believing there is any such thing. It could not just be the hypothesis that the immediate objects of vision are internal, since that hypothesis is compatible with taking the immediate objects of vision to be representations of the real objects that cause those representations. But Reid's observation does go at least part way in the direction that he wanted to go. It gives us some reason to think that Hume's skepticism about the existence of an external world is over-blown.

8. A case for direct realism?

Reid charged that Hume's perceptual relativity argument equivocates, that it does not point to any phenomenon that is inconsistent with direct perceptual realism, and that it does more to establish direct perceptual realism than to refute it. These charges flounder, but Reid had further points to make that establish that skepticism about the existence of external objects remains unwarranted. I close this paper by considering what he could do to defend the stronger claim that we directly perceive external objects.[26]

Reid attempted to reconcile his position on visible appearances with a realist account of visible appearance in a set of remarks on visible and tangible space made over the closing pages of *Intellectual Powers* 2.19, 'Of matter and space,' (222–225), a text that merits close consideration in connection with his remarks on Hume's perceptual relativity argument. He there noted that a direct perceptual realist is not committed to holding that our perceptions tell us everything there is to know about the objects around us. Our perceptions of space and the spatial properties of things can be partial and incomplete, as long as they are correct and consistent. One sense might tell us more than another or different senses might tell us different things. We might learn to read what one sense tells us as a sign for what another sense will tell us. As long as what the different senses tell us is compatible and what each of them tells us is independently true of external objects, we have no reason to suppose that any one of them acquaints us only with images. And no sense or combination of senses may tell us everything there is to know about the spatial properties of objects. 'Perhaps there may be intelligent beings of a higher order, whose conceptions of space are much more complete than those we have from both senses' (*Intellectual Powers* II.19: 223/17–19).

On Reid's account, touch tells us about the spatial relations holding between the parts of objects. But it only tells us about some of those parts: those lying on the surface. It tells us little about what lies beneath the surface of objects. Moreover, it only tells us about those bodies that are in contact with our skin. It tells us nothing about more remote objects.

Vision is more limited than touch in some ways, but less in others. Unlike touch, vision informs us of the existence of bodies that lie at some distance from us – something that the inhabitants of a world populated by blind people would consider to be unaccountable and prophetic (*Inquiry* 6.1: 77–78). But while vision has this extraordinary power, it does not tell us how far out objects lie (at least not immediately). It only tells us in what direction we would need to go in order to reach them. In virtue of an innate law of our constitution the objects of vision – or, more properly, the smallest visible parts of the objects of vision – are seen to lie in the direction indicated by a line passing through the center of the eye from the point on the retina where light from that part is focused (*Inquiry* 6.12: 122–23). This line directs us to what Reid called the 'visible position' of an object or a part of an object. Visible position is a point located to the left or the right, up or down, on a two dimensional visual field.

The visible positions of the parts of objects are distinct from the tangible positions of their parts. Touch tells us about the position of the parts of an object in relation to one another – excluding those parts lying beneath the surface of hard bodies, which are effectively 'occluded' from the sense of touch by those on the surface. Vision, in contrast, tells us about the position of the parts of an object in relation to the position of the eye – with more forward facing parts occluding the view of more rearward ones in opaque objects. Each sense tells us something different, but that does not mean they present us with different objects. The things they tell us are about mutually compatible features of one and the same object: where its parts are in relation to one another, and what direction each part lies in relative to the position of the eye.

Because visible figure and magnitude can vary even while the object remains the same, we think of them as appearances or images. But that is not the case with our experience of visible position. Objects really do lie in the directions in which they are immediately perceived to lie. In hunting, pointing, and shooting, in reaching and dodging, in a word, in some of the most essential activities of primitive survival, we rely implicitly on objects to lie exactly in the directions they are immediately seen to lie. Though visible position is a projection of tangible position, it is not an appearance of tangible position. Instead, it is a true, albeit position-relative feature of objects in its own right. An object simultaneously has all of its visible positions ('the appearance of a visible object is infinitely diversified'). Which of them is perceived depends on the position occupied by the perceiver.

Furthermore, our perceptions of visible position are almost as reliable, and as immune to error or distortion, as our perceptions of tangible position. There are very few instances of illusions of tangible localization (phantom limbs and the instance of grasping a little ball between crossed fingers being almost the only ones ever mentioned). There are a few more instances of illusion in visual localization: objects seen in mirrors, through lenses, fog or opaque air, or under circumstances responsible for double vision or other impediments to the normal functioning of the visual system. Beyond these cases, we need to turn to such things as dreams or hallucinations for examples of errors in tangible or visual localization.

Our experiences of visible position are therefore almost on all fours with our experiences of tangible position as far as accuracy and reliability are concerned. Each is considered to be a real property of objects. And there is no inconsistency in this because the properties are different and compatible. Our perceptions of both can deceive us on occasion, but the mistakes we make on these occasions fall under the heading of 'trite topic.' Admittedly, it is possible to appeal to perceptual errors and illusions to make the more 'profound point' that what we perceive when we misperceive must be something and not nothing, and since that thing does not actually exist outside of us it must be an image in us. And it is possible to go on from there to argue that this puts us in a position to doubt whether we ever experience anything other than private mental images. But this is an argument Reid could reply to in any of a number of ways, beginning with a claim that our senses were designed for use in normal circumstances. When they misinform us in occasional and abnormal cases, we still conceive an external object – just one that happens not to exist even though it is mistakenly believed to exist.

But this is by the way, because Hume's perceptual relativity argument is not an argument from instances of perceptual error or illusion. It is an argument from dependence of what is perceived on the perceiver. That argument will not work for visible position, because visible position varies with viewpoint rather than viewer. Even were there no perceivers, given a point outside of an object or group of objects, those objects and their parts would still lie in the directions that they lie in relative to that point. Putting a sighted perceiver at that point only adds a being who becomes visually aware of this fact.

Because a subjectivity argument will not work for visible position, a case can be made that it will not work for visible figure, either. We are inclined to consider visible figures to be images or appearances. Reid maintained to the contrary that they are partial perceptions of real figures. The figure of a body is a product of the relative positions of its parts. Vision does not immediately inform us of these positions but instead informs us of the directions in which parts lie relative to the position of the eye. Nonetheless, since the parts really do lie in the directions in which they are perceived to lie, we see how the parts really are positioned relative to one another over two dimensions, judging from the position of the eye. These positions describe a figure. Since the positions of the parts describing this figure are seen correctly, this figure is seen correctly in the sense that the parts of the object really do describe that figure when viewed from that position (*Inquiry* 6.7: 96/19–34). Visible figure is an 'appearance' of real figure only in the sense that it leaves something out (how close or far the parts are from the eye), not in the sense that puts something else in the place of what is really there. That makes the figure that we see a partial or incomplete perception of the real figure rather than the perception of a representation of the real figure.

However, there is a limit to the applicability of this 'apology' for visible figure. Given sufficient illumination and sufficient distance, all objects appear as minimally visible points, regardless of their figure. Reid might object that this is simply another way in which vision is limited. Direct perceptual realism does not entail perceptual omniscience. Our senses are limited in various ways and one way in which vision is limited is in terms of its acuity. Because of this limitation the parts of objects disappear with distance as they fall below the limits of visual acuity and the remaining parts can come to appear as but a single point. This is a case of limitation in the perception of what is really there rather than of perception of something other than what is really there. Nonetheless, there is something unsettling about this result. A point is a kind of figure, and it ends up being the case that real objects are represented in vision by luminous points, regardless of their figure.

When we turn to visible magnitude the strain increases. Unfortunately, though Reid explained in some detail what makes our perceptions of visible figure partial but correct, and described how they are grounded in the perception of visible position, he did not provide the same analysis for visible magnitude. One thing that might be said on his behalf is that the sense of vision was not designed to inform us of the magnitude of objects but only of their visible positions. It tells us something about the magnitudes of objects only when those objects are close enough that their parts can fall within the limit of visual acuity, and even then it tells us about the magnitude of objects only by telling us about the visible positions of their peripheral parts. Knowledge of the visible position of an object's peripheral parts gives us a sense of the extent of the interval between those parts, which can be estimated as a portion of a bounded visual field, or measured by comparison with other objects on the visual field, or measured by considering the objects of vision to be projections and measuring the angular magnitude between their extremities. But these visible magnitudes are not what we were principally designed to see and in fact mature perceivers seldom attend to them. Instead they are taken as signs of real or tangible magnitudes, which are almost always invariant as long as the objects remain the same, and which visible magnitudes reliably signify.

An uncomfortable consequence of this position is that it presents visible magnitudes as signs for tangible or objective magnitudes. This opens the door to Hume's objection, that our immediate perceptions of visible magnitudes are perceptions of variant, subjective mental states or images that at best serve to represent external objects, but that are distinct from those objects. But Reid could respond that our perceptions of visible magnitudes reduce to perceptions of the visible positions of their peripheral parts. As those parts really do lie in the directions in which they are perceived to lie, we perceive those visible positions correctly, and so we have every reason to think that we directly perceive a true quality of the external object rather than a mental image. So, even though visible magnitudes serve to represent objective magnitudes, this does not make them images distinct from the objects they represent. They are simply partial perceptions of those objects that we have learned to read as signs for other features that are not immediately perceived but have in the past been associated with them.

This is where the dispute between Hume and Reid comes to rest. More could be said, but neither Hume nor Reid said any more, at least not in this particular context. Whether we are working with a partial perception of the real object, or instead with a mental image is a difficult question, and neither Hume nor Reid did a very good job of addressing it. Hume was too quick to declare idealism to be a consequence of 'the slightest philosophy' and too quick to take the mere fact of variations in magnitude to alone make the point that we are working with images rather than partial perceptions. Reid was wrong to think that Hume's case could be dealt with by as facile a means as distinguishing between real and apparent magnitude.

It is not enough to claim that our perceptions change while the object remains the same, and it is not enough to respond that the change could simply be an effect of the limitations under which our sense organs work to deliver information about the object at different distances. We need to consider more carefully how what we perceive is related to what we take to be the real object. A map and the surface mapped are isomorphic with regard to the positions of their parts, and maps of different scales vary with respect to the fine features of the surface mapped in the same way that views of an object from different distances vary with respect to the fine features of the object. More detailed maps show more parts, just like closer views. But a person who navigates a vehicle by looking a GPS device screen, or a surgeon who performs an operation while looking at a computer monitor is for all that perceiving an image of the real object rather than having a partial perception of that object. This is proven by the fact that the GPS screen is only a small object located within the surrounding environment, and the computer monitor an object located at an entirely distinct place from the patient's body. The person who looks at these devices is not aiming to perceive them, as would be the case were they playing a video game, but aiming to move within a larger environment, or within a different environment by using them as representations of that larger or separate environment.

In the case I have just described the spatial distinction between the monitor and the object mapped by the image on the monitor suffice to establish that we are not dealing a partial perception of an object, but with two different objects, one of which is an image of the other. But of course the existence of any spatial distinction between the object that is perceived and the real object is contested in the case perception. While we cannot appeal to this particular way of distinguishing partial perceptions from images in the case of perception, there are further considerations that might be brought to bear. Maps do not just differ from the objects mapped in their scale and in their spatial location. They also differ in content. While maps exhibit some degree of isomorphism with the objects that they map, there comes a point at which they cease to become isomorphic and begin to contain iconic elements. A map will represent a city as a dot, a larger city as a dot with a circle around it, a church as a dot with a cross on top of it, roads of one sort using a line, of another sort using two lines, of a third sort using a color between lines, parkland, industrial land, commercial land, residential land, farmland, marshland, lakes, etc. using color patches, etc. Large parts of what a map contains are only iconically related to the objects being mapped.[27] The merely iconic status of much of its content establishes a map as an image distinct from its object as much as its physical separation from the things it represents and its smaller scale.

The role played by color in delimiting the constituent parts of visible objects does likewise. As distance from an object changes, colors change, and as colors change the numbers, figures, and arrangements of the shapes they define change. This variation in the structure of constituent parts with changes in distance gives the smaller parts of visible objects a kind of iconic status, like the qualities depicted on maps. They do not represent in virtue of isomorphism of their parts with the parts of the object they represent.

The appearance of color was a stumbling block for Reid. He maintained that all there is to immediately seeing an object is immediately conceiving the directions in which each of its peripheral parts lie. We do not perceive anything else. In particular, we do not perceive the interval between the peripheral parts to be filled in or painted over with anything that is seen. What we see is, in effect, a sort of empty frame. While looking at this empty frame, we might experience various sensations of color, and we are naturally inclined to believe that there is something (something we do not immediately perceive by vision) contained in the apparently empty frame that causes our sensations of color. But this invisible thing is nothing like our sensations, which, being ways of feeling enjoyed by minds, exist only in us and not in external objects. The closest Reid would have been willing go in the direction of ascribing content to the immediately perceived empty frame is allowing that we might immediately perceive it to be divided into further empty frames. But then, as he himself admitted, there is a limit to how far down this division can be visually perceived (*Intellectual Powers* II.19: 219/34–37).

This is a hard doctrine to square with common sense, and it is not one that was shared by Hume. Common sense maintains that we experience the manifest qualities that Reid called sensations of color to be spread out in space over the surfaces of external objects.[28] Hume maintained that we can only see frames in virtue of seeing a contrast between spatially disposed manifest color qualities (EHU 12.15). But he did not bring this consideration to bear when presenting his perceptual relativity argument. On the contrary, he represented it as playing a role in a distinct argument, credited to Berkeley.

That having been said, if we grant that we not only see a gap between the peripheral parts of an object, but see that gap filled with colored parts, and see the number, shape, arrangement, and color of those parts change with distance in ways that depend on such subjective factors as visual acuity, it remains plausible to maintain that what we see is a mental image that might appear to have a location outside of us in space, and a figure and an angular magnitude, but that would not exist were it not perceived and that is at best an effect of something located outside of us.

9. Conclusions

Like his treatment of Hume's views on other topics, Reid's reaction to Hume's perceptual relativity argument exhibits an almost schizophrenic quality, alternating between respect and contempt. Described on the one hand as containing more reasoning than is found in any other author (*Intellectual Powers* II.14: 179/13–14) the argument is nonetheless denounced as illogical, contrary to common sense, and adequate only to establish the opposite of its stated conclusion (*Intellectual Powers* II.14: 182/28–29; 182/29–34; 183/1–5). Perhaps Reid's point was just that even the very best argument to have ever been offered for the ideal theory is no better than this. But it may be that Reid's show of respect for an argument that appeals specifically to relativity in the perception of visual magnitude is indicative of his own sense of where the weakest point in his case for direct perceptual realism lies.[29]

Notes

1. Reid (1785) 2.14: 179/12–15. References to this work are to essay and chapter numbers, supplemented by references to the pagination and line numbers of Reid (2002). These works will hereafter be referred to as *Intellectual Powers*.
2. *Intellectual Powers* 2.14: 178–183. One commentator who does not endorse Reid's objection is John Wright (1983, 81 n.20).
3. James Somerville (2006) is more concerned to take Reid to task for not following his own line of criticism of Hume's argument than to identify any particular mistake in Reid's actual objection. Van Cleve does go so far as to mention, in a footnote (2004, n.4), that aspects of Reid's argument depend on a 'dyadic' analysis of the notion of appearance, but does not consider whether Reid was entitled to that analysis – a supposition that will be questioned in what follows.
4. *Intellectual Powers*: 178–179, citing Hume. The actual text of Hume, 1750, 239–240, is given in square brackets, where it deviates from Reid's citation, omitting variations in spelling, capitalization and the use of equivalents, e.g., 'betwixt' for 'between'. I compare Reid's citation to this edition (which is readily available in the ECCO database) rather than Beauchamp's modern critical edition because it is the one that was consulted by important contemporary critics such as Campbell and Price. In the absence of further indication I consider it likely to have been the one consulted by Reid as well. Principal differences from Hume 1777, the last edition to have been edited by Hume, are also noted. Text in the initial set of brackets is explanatory by reference to earlier passages. Hume (1750/1777) will hereafter be referred to as EHU and cited by section and paragraph numbers, following the numbering scheme in Hume (2000).
5. Compare Hume (1739, 367–368) on the crucial role of lack of independence in establishing sceptical doubts about the evidence of the senses. This work will hereafter be referred to as *Treatise* or T and cited by book, part, section, and paragraph numbers, following the numbering scheme established in Hume (2007). The passage just cited is from 1.4.2.44–45.
6. For a rather more fraught and less sympathetic take on Hume's argument see Somerville (2006). For textual justification for reading Hume's references to diminution as references to loss of parts, see section 4 below.
7. Not all would agree. For an opposed opinion, see Butler (2008).
8. Take M to be the property 'varies in magnitude with changes in distance,' s to be the table we see, and r to be the real table.

9. The argument would continue: We nonetheless see something: $\exists xs = x$. Call what we see an image of the table: $s = i$. / The thing we see is not the real table but an image of the table: $\exists xx = s \, \& \sim s \, = r \, \& \, s = i$.

10. Take P to be the second order property, 'apparent,' and R the second order property, 'real.' Of course Reid did not use the apparatus of second order predicate logic to diagnose the problem with Hume's argument. Using the terminology of the logic of the day, he declared it to be a syllogism that fails because it has two middle terms (*Intellectual Powers* II.14: 182/25–26). Either way, the problem being brought up is the same: the argument equivocates.

11. 'The argument is this, the table we see seems to diminish as we remove farther from it; that is, its apparent magnitude is diminished; but the real table suffers no alteration, to wit, in its real magnitude; therefore it is not the real table we see' *Intellectual Powers* II.14: 182/21–24.

12. *Intellectual Powers*: 180–181.

13. *Intellectual Powers*: 181/7–8. Since the object really does subtend a specific angle for each particular vantage point, 'apparent' is something of a misnomer for what is actually another among the real qualities of an object. See further *Intellectual Powers* II.19: 225/9–12.

14. I take it that apprehending magnitude or the distance between points on the periphery of an object is not something that can be readily distinguished from measuring this distance or magnitude, particularly in contexts where what is at issue are claims about a diminution in the magnitude of the table we see. Measurements may be made by more precise or more approximate means, but apart from some means of estimating the magnitude of an object it is hard to understand what it would mean to ascribe any magnitude to it, and particularly hard to understand what it would mean to say that the magnitude diminishes.

15. Hume 1740, 305–6. The appendix contained in this work will hereafter be referred to as Ax and cited by the paragraph numbers established in Hume 2007, 396–401. The passage just cited is Ax 22.

16. This work will hereafter be referred to as NTV and cited by the paragraph numbers published with the original edition. The passage just cited is from NTV 12.

17. For a raft of citations from other authors see George (2006, 147–148).

18. Take N to be the property 'varies in number of parts with changes in distance'

19. *Intellectual Powers* II.19: 224/30–31, cf. Reid, 1764, 219, 241. This work will hereafter be referred to as *Inquiry* and referenced by chapter and section number supplemented by the page and line numbers of Reid, 1997. The passage just referenced is *Inquiry* 6.7: 96/16–18 and 6.9: 104–105. Reid's antecedent tenet that visual space has the topology of the inner surface of a sphere, might be questioned by some, but the crucial claim is that any portion of visible space stands in a finite ratio to the whole of visible space, and this would have to be accepted by anyone who accepts that the momentary field of view is bounded and that immediate perceptions of magnitude are based on what is present on the momentary field of view. Though Hume did no declare himself on this matter anywhere that I am aware of, I assume that he would have agreed that both the visual and the imaginary fields are bounded. To suppose otherwise would be inconsistent with his declarations about the finite capacities of the mind at *Treatise* 1.2.2.

20. The connection is made by considering the center of the eye to be located at the center of a sphere and the objects of vision to be projections on the inner surface of this sphere made by lines passing from the center point through each point of the real object (*Inquiry* 6.7: 95/29–32). This construction is in turn justified by the claim that it is precisely by means of such a projection that retinal images are formed (*Inquiry*

6.7: 95/33–34), and the further claim that retinal images determine the immediate objects of vision (*Inquiry* 6.22: 120/18–25).

21. Though he spoke here of 'an object of touch only' it was important to Reid to establish that we do see real magnitude (*Intellectual Powers* II.14: 181–182). For Reid, we just don't see it immediately. However, in what follows it will be immediate visual (and tangible) perception that is at issue.

22. Reid considered tangible magnitude to be measured by lines and visible magnitude by angles (*Intellectual Powers* II.19: 224/27–30). But Berkeley measured the apparent visible magnitude of the moon by a line of minimally visible points (NTV 44) and maintained that both visible and tangible magnitude are a function of number of minimally sensible points (NTV 54, 112).

23. Reid identified real magnitude with juxtaposition with standard units, and if we can immediately see anything we can immediately see one thing standing alongside another thing and see that the one is as high or higher or shorter than the other, especially when all the objects lie in the focal plane (as is typically the case with measuring instruments visually aligned with their objects) so that depth perception is not an issue.

24. Take NV to be 'varies in number visible parts' and NR 'varies in number of real parts'.

25. This is a consequence of the second premise of the earlier argument. Given that the real table continues to equal the same number of juxtaposed standard units with changes in distance, we can infer that there has been no change in the number or distribution of its actually constituent parts.

26. For reasons to think Reid could not defend direct perceptual realism, independently of anything Hume said, see Van Cleve (2002). The account of Reid's views that I give here advances an interpretation originally proposed by Susan Weldon (1982), and further developed by Giovanni Grandi (2006).

27. Take an icon to be an object that bears no salient resemblance to another object but that is stipulated or conventionally recognized to serve as a sign for that object.

28. Like Hume, I believe that all of us become people of common sense when we leave the study and so are all qualified to say what common sense maintains. My common sense as a sighted person tells me nothing as clearly as that colors are not invisible qualities but manifest ones. It also tells me that these same manifest qualities are spread out in space. An indication that others share my common sense can be gleaned from how they use color terminology. They speak of the manifest qualities that Reid declared to be sensations of color as if they were external and located on the surface of bodies. Reid would have liked to deny this and maintain that our sensations of color are so insignificant to us that they have not been thought worthy of being given names in any language, so that all anyone ever means to do when speaking of color is to refer to the invisible causes of their color sensations, and all they ever say in consequence is that the invisible causes of their color sensations are external and located on the surfaces of bodies. The implausibility of this position is proven by the significant sums of money people of ordinary common sense are willing to spend on cosmetics, clothes, paint, interior decoration, gardens, etc. The members of a society of blind people would have no interest in spending money on such things, which are valued only for the sake of the visual sensations they produce in us. The members of a society that considers sensations of color to be so insignificant as not even to be worthy of being named should have attitudes that are no different from those of the blind. For more on this point, and a fascinating discussion of how it was anticipated by one of Reid's early critics, see Grandi's essay in this volume.

29.   Thanks to Patrick Rysiew and Todd Buras for astute and formative comments on an earlier draft of this paper, and to the other contributors to this volume for helpful reactions to a version presented at a joint symposium at the University of Vermont, November, 2013.

References

Berkeley, George. 1709. *An Essay Towards a New Theory of Vision*. Dublin: Aaron Rhames.

Butler, Annemarie. 2008. "Natural instincts, perceptual relativity, and belief in an external world in Hume's *Enquiry*." *Hume Studies* 34: 115–158.

Chambers, Ephriam. 1741. *Cyclopedia: or an universal dictionary of the arts and sciences*. 4th ed. London: D. Midwinter, et al.

De Bary, Philip. 2002. *Thomas Reid and Scepticism*. London: Routledge.

George, Rolf. 2006. "James Jurin Awakens Hume from his Dogmatic Slumber." *Hume Studies* 32: 141–166.

Grandi, Giovanni. 2006. "Reid's Direct Realism about Vision." *History of Philosophy Quarterly* 23: 225–238.

[Hume, David.]. 1739. *A Treatise of Human Nature*. Vol. 1. London: John Noon.

[Hume, David.]. 1740. *A Treatise of Human Nature*. Vol. 3. London: John Noon.

Hume, David. 1750. *Philosophical Essays concerning Human Understanding*. 2nd ed. London: A. Millar.

Hume, David. 1777. *An Enquiry concerning Human Understanding*. In David Hume, *Essays and Treatises on Several Subjects*. Vol. 2. London: T. Cadell.

Hume, David. 2000. *An Enquiry concerning Human Understanding: A critical edition*, edited by Tom L. Beauchamp. Oxford: Clarendon Press.

Hume, David. 2007. *A Treatise of Human Nature: A critical edition*, edited by David Fate Norton, and Mary J. Norton. Oxford: Clarendon Press.

Lehrer, Keith. 1989. *Thomas Reid*. London: Routledge.

Reid, Thomas. 1764. *An Inquiry into the Human Mind on the Principles of Common Sense*. Edinburgh: A. Millar.

Reid, Thomas. 1785. *Essays on the Intellectual Powers of Man*. Edinburgh: John Bell.

Reid, Thomas. 1997. *An Inquiry into the Human Mind on the Principles of Common Sense*, edited by Derek Brookes. Edinburgh: Edinburgh University Press.

Reid, Thomas. 2002. *Essays on the Intellectual Powers of Man*, edited by Derek Brookes. Edinburgh: Edinburgh University Press.

Somerville, James. 2006. "The Table, Which We See: An Irresolvable Ambiguity." *Philosophy* 81: 33–63.

Van Cleve, James. 2002. "Thomas Reid's Geometry of Visibles." *Philosophical Review* 111: 373–416.

Van Cleve, James. 2004. "Reid's Theory of Perception." In *The Cambridge Companion to Thomas Reid*, edited by Terence Cuneo and René Van Woudenberg, 101–133. Cambridge: Cambridge University Press.

Van Woudenberg, René. 2000. "Perceptual Relativism, Scepticism, and Thomas Reid." *Reid Studies* 3: 65–85.

Weldon, Susan. 1982. "Direct Realism and Visual Distortion: A Development of Arguments from Thomas Reid." *Journal of the History of Philosophy* 20: 355–368.

Wolterstorff, Nicholas. 2001. *Thomas Reid and the Story of Epistemology*. Cambridge: Cambridge University Press.

Wright, John. 1983. *The Sceptical Realism of David Hume*. Minneapolis: University of Minnesota Press.

PERCEPTION

The extension of color sensations: Reid, Stewart, and Fearn

Giovanni B. Grandi

Assistant Professor, Philosophy, University of British Columbia, Okanagan Campus, Irving K. Barber School of Arts and Sciences, Kelowna, BC, Canada

According to Reid, color sensations are not extended nor are they arranged in figured patterns. Reid further claimed that 'there is no sensation appropriated to visible figure.' Reid justified these controversial claims by appeal to Cheselden's report of the experiences of a young man affected by severe cataracts, and by appeal to cases of perception of visible figure without color. While holding fast to the principle that sensations are not extended, Dugald Stewart (1753–1828) tried to show that 'a variety of colour sensations is a necessary means for the perception of visible figure.' According to John Fearn (1768–1837), two motives appear to be central to Reid's views about color sensations and extension: his commitment to the Cartesian doctrine of the immateriality of the soul, and his attempt to evade 'Hume's dilemma' about the existence and immateriality of the soul.

If a painter were to be seen attempting to paint a name, or a sign, with the same color as that of the sign board; the very million would set him down for insane. But I ask; What avails this, provided Philosophers in their speculations have been altogether blind to the fact; which it is wholly undeniable they have been? (Fearn 1820, xxi)

1. Introduction

In *An Inquiry into the Human Mind on the Principles of Common Sense* (1764), Thomas Reid argues that what we know of colors at first is simply that they are hidden qualities in the objects that give rise to certain sensations in our mind. According to Reid, these sensations do not resemble the hidden qualities that occasion them. Departing from Reid's terminology, we can identify color sensations with the 'manifest color qualities' we immediately experience, or, in different terms, with color *qualia*.[1] Thus, to say that color sensations in the mind do not resemble hidden color qualities in the objects would be tantamount to saying that the manifest color qualities we immediately experience do not resemble hidden color qualities in the objects.

If it is plausible to agree with Reid that manifest color qualities, color as *qualia*, do not resemble colors as they are in themselves, it would nonetheless appear to be against common sense to hold the view that manifest color qualities are not spatially extended, or that they are not arranged in figured patterns. We can reject the view that the manifest qualities we immediately experience in vision are originally experienced as being located on the surface of objects at a distance from us, especially if we do not think that distance is an immediate object of sight. But it is difficult to dismiss the view that these manifest qualities are at least spatially extended and arranged in a two-dimensional field of vision. We can claim that these qualities are qualities of non-existent objects of perception (or non-existent qualities of such objects) and hence that vision is systematically deceptive in what it tells us about the external world, or we can claim that these manifest qualities are spatially located sensory states of an extended mind. But in whatever way we might seek to account for them while denying that they really are located outside of us on the surface of objects, one thing that is just too obvious to common sense to deny is that manifest color qualities are spatially located relative to one another and so compose color patches of various sizes and shapes.[2] Apparently, this is what Reid thought: manifest color qualities are sensations or ways of feeling that are not spread out in patches and their order of coexistence is not spatial. While we are allowed to say that a particular color is spread out on a canvas by a painter, we are not allowed to say that the sensations it occasions are spread out in a corresponding two-dimensional array existing in the mind of the painter. In a similar manner, while we are allowed to say that a red object we are looking at is located to the left of a green one, we are not allowed to say that a sensation of red is located to the left of a sensation of green. This view is just a consequence of Reid's general claim that sensations do not resemble the qualities of bodies – a thesis that he was willing to extend to the point of saying that the order of sensations does not resemble the spatial order of the qualities that occasion these sensations. To argue otherwise would be tantamount to falling back into what he called 'the way of ideas,' the copy-theory of perception that he saw as the harbinger of skepticism about the external world. Reid rather thought that we know the qualities of bodies directly through acts of perception. Acts of perception are different from sensations: while sensations are acts of mind that have only themselves as objects (if they have any object at all), acts of perceptions are acts of mind that are directed to objects distinct from themselves, the qualities of bodies. In the perception of a primary quality, a sensation is regularly followed by the conception and belief of an object whose qualities are manifest (qualities such as extension, figure, size, rest or motion, solidity, hardness or softness, roughness or smoothness). In the perception of a secondary quality, a sensation is merely followed by the conception of an unknown cause of the sensation itself. As Reid says, secondary qualities are in this sense 'occult.'

Reid also thought that he would manage to preserve the immateriality of the soul by denying that mental operations could ever be arranged in a spatial order. Indeed, a spatial order of mental operations could make the soul extended and therefore divisible into parts.

There is another element of complication in Reid's account of color sensations. In the *Inquiry*, Reid claimed that 'there seems to be no sensation that is appropriated to visible figure, or whose office it is to suggest it' (Reid 1997, VI.8: 101/15). Although sensations of color are usually presented along with the perception of visible figure, there is no connection between the two arising from the nature of things. We could have the sensation of color without the perception of visible figure, as is actually the case for people affected by severe cataracts. Reid also claimed that we could have had the perception of visible figure without the sensation of color, if God had so decided. The sensation of color only suggests the quality of color. Visible figure is suggested directly by the impression upon the retina.

Reid explicitly singled out the case of visible figure as an exception to his standard account of the relation among various events in the process of perception. According to this account, each particular sensation regularly precedes a particular act of perception that is distinct from the sensation itself. Although the sensation does not resemble the quality we get to know through this act of direct perception, the sensation never fails to occur before the perception of that particular quality. In this limited sense, the sensation may be said to be 'appropriated' to that quality. However, in the case of sight, no particular sensation regularly precedes our perception of visible figure.[3]

These difficulties did not escape the notice of Reid's student, Dugald Stewart (1753–1828), the most renowned apologist of what came to be known as the Scottish school of common sense. While not rejecting Reid's view that color sensations are not spatially extended, Stewart came to the conclusion that a variety of color sensations is the 'necessary means' for the perception of visible figure. Although Stewart saw an essential connection between color sensations and visible figure, as a self-professed disciple of Reid he stopped short of saying that color sensations themselves are arranged spatially. Contrary to Stewart, John Fearn (1768–1837) thought that Reid's views about the non-spatiality of color sensations fly in the face of common sense. He argued that Reid had made a mistake in accepting the commonly held view that the spatiality of sensations would imply that the soul is material and divisible. Fearn also offered the first systematic reconstruction of the arguments that led Reid to his views on color sensations and visible figure. Following Fearn, I will show how the claim that color sensations are not extended emerged from Reid's rejection of Hume's dilemma about the existence and immateriality of the soul.[4]

Before I come to these points, I will explain how the thesis that sensations are not extended is related to the question concerning color sensations and visible figure raised in the *Inquiry*.

2. The dissimilarity of sensations and extension, and Hume's dilemma

That color sensations are not spatially extended or arranged is a specification of the claim that sensations are not spatially extended or arranged. There are two contexts in Reid's *Inquiry* for the emergence of this thesis: his attack on the theory of ideas, with its primary focus on the theory's skeptical consequences concerning the belief in a material world, and his more explicit discussion of what the theory of ideas implies concerning the existence and immateriality of the mind.

In the context of his strictures on the theory of ideas in the chapters on touch and vision, Reid argues that sensations do not resemble the qualities of material objects. Material objects are spatially extended and arranged. Thus, if sensations do not resemble these objects' spatial features, sensations themselves are not spatially extended and arranged. There is admittedly a different way of reading Reid's claims about the dissimilarity of sensations and qualities: each sensation by itself does not resemble the quality that occasions it, but the order of coexisting sensations is spatial.[5] However, this reading appears to be excluded by what Reid says. Discussing the imaginary case of a blind man who has lost all notions of external objects he previously got by the sense of touch but has retained all his tactual sensations, Reid explicitly states that not even the order of sensations is spatial: 'no feelings, *nor any combination of feelings*, can ever resemble space or motion' (Reid 1997, V.6: 66/25–26, emphasis added).

A further consequence of the theory of ideas that worried Reid is discussed at the end of the *Inquiry* and has to do with the existence and immateriality of the soul. Reid refers to an argument developed by Hume in *A Treatise of Human Nature*.[6] The argument proceeds from the claim that there are both extended and unextended perceptions to the conclusion that neither an unextended immaterial substance nor an extended material substance could be 'locally conjoined' with all our perceptions. In Reid's estimation, two alternative consequences appear to follow from this argument: either (1) the mind is not a substance, or (2) the mind, where the ideas of bodies inhere, must be an extended and divisible substance, 'because the ideas of extension cannot be in a subject which is indivisible and unextended' (Reid 1997, VII: 217/8–9).[7] Both consequences are unacceptable, according to Reid. The first conclusion should be rejected, since we know that the mind is a substance: this is a principle of common sense whereby we conceive of a subject of inherence for all our mental operations. The second conclusion is unacceptable too: Reid thinks he can provide arguments to show that this substance is unextended and indivisible.[8]

The two contexts we have described above appear to be connected. Fearn noticed that the *Inquiry* was 'in reality *an inquiry concerning the extension or inextension of the mind*,' but that 'Dr. Reid had in a great measure contrived *to conceal from himself that it was so*. He indeed neither any where, I believe, *asserts* nor *denies* this truth, that this is the nature of his *Inquiry*' (Fearn 1820, I.2: 44). Reid rather chose to use the 'softening expression' that 'sensations have no resemblance to figure or extension,' probably motivated by a strong aversion to conceiving the possibility of the mind's extension (Fearn 1820, I.2: 44). According to Fearn, anything that resembles extension would have to be literally extended. Reid claimed that sensations do not resemble extension and that they are modifications of the mind. Thus, Reid meant to argue that the mind is unextended. A metaphysical investigation about the nature of mind and body lay behind the veneer of a mere concern about skepticism about the external world.

But even if sensations are not literally extended, it is still an open question whether there is something in the coexisting order of sensations that corresponds or is analogous to the spatial order of qualities that occasion them. According to Reid, there is indeed a covariance between the qualities in the external objects affecting the sense organs and the sensations they occasion. This covariance does not imply that sensations and qualities are literally similar to each other. For example, the sensation caused by hardness is different from the sensation caused by color, and both are different from the sensation caused by sound, and so on for different sensations and their causes. Moreover, as a quality varies in degree the sensation that ensues also varies in degree without the two ever being literally similar to each other.[9] It is then legitimate to ask whether there is something in each sensation that corresponds or stands in a one-to-one relation to the location in space of the quality (or perhaps only to the location in space of the part of the sense organ affected either directly or indirectly by the quality). In early nineteenth-century German psychology this aspect of an unextended sensation correspondent to the particular point of stimulation of our sense organs was called a 'local sign.'[10] A local sign does not make the sensation itself actually located in space or extended, but stands in a one-to-one sign-signifier relation to a particular location in our body. If we reject the existence of local signs, or, in Reid's terms, the existence of sensations appropriated to specific locations, we are then espousing a more radical reading of the thesis that sensations do not resemble the qualities of material objects. Without local signs it would not even be possible to construct an abstract topology of sensations that could be interpreted according to the model given by the space we ultimately end up perceiving.

If the notion of visible figure depends on the notion of visible position, as will be explained, then the question concerning the existence of a sensation appropriated to visible figure can be interpreted as a question concerning the existence of local signs in our color sensations.

3. Color and visible figure

Color poses particular problems for Reid's philosophy. First, it seems that color sensations, colors as *qualia*, if they ever exist, are spatially located and extended. Second, color is a case of a secondary quality that is innately perceived to be located in a precise direction from the eye. Reid also specifies the law that regulates our perception by sight of the position of objects with regard to the eye. It is a modification of a perceptual law first enunciated by the Scottish optic writer William Porterfield (ca. 1696–1771):

[I]t appears to be a fact, that every point of the object is seen in the direction of a right line passing from the picture of that point on the *retina* through the centre of the eye. As this is a fact that holds universally and invariably, it must either be a law of nature, or the necessary consequence of some more general law of nature (Reid 1997, VI.12: 122/39–123/4).[11]

By contrast, our perception of the position or location of other secondary qualities (such as smell, taste, and sound) depends on the past experience of the constant conjunction of the sensations they cause with certain objects we perceive at the same time.[12]

Reid holds that originally by sight we only perceive the position of objects with regard to the eye but not their distance from us. The perception by sight of distance is not original but acquired through experience (the experience of the constant conjunction of certain purely visual clues with distances as originally perceived by touch).[13] The position of an object with regard to the eye is determined by both the compass direction from the eye and the degree of elevation the object has with respect to the plane where the eye is located:

Objects that lie in the same right line drawn from the centre of the eye, have the same position, however different their distances from the eye may be: but objects which lie in different right lines drawn from the eye's centre, have different position; and this difference of position is greater or less in proportion to the angle made at the eye by the right lines mentioned (Reid 1997, VI.7: 96/20–25).

The visible figure of an object is defined as 'the position of its several parts with regard to the eye' (Reid 1997, VI.7: 96/28–29). If there are no defects in the refractive mechanisms of the eye, and if there are no intervening media reflecting or refracting light on the way to the eye, Porterfield's law guarantees that we do manage to perceive the position of the parts of an object, and thus visible figure, correctly.

Visible figure results from the conjunction of the several positions with regard to the eye of the parts of an object. We can thus try to reduce Reid's claim that there is no sensation appropriated to visible figure to the claim that there is no sensation appropriated to a particular direction from the eye. It seems that the very same non-spatial sensation of a particular color can precede the perception of two different directions from the eye: we can see an identically red object (an object that causes exactly the same sensation of red, in Reid's parlance) in two different directions at the same time. Moreover, the perception of the same direction from the eye can be preceded by two qualitatively different sensations of color. We can see two objects of different colors (two objects that cause different sensations of color) in the same direction from the eye, at different times. In short, Reid's denial of a sensation appropriated to visible figure is equivalent to a denial of local signs in our sensations of color.[14] However, the observation that the same color sensation can precede the perception of two distinct positions and that two different color sensations can precede the perception of the same position does not play a role in Reid's actual argument in the *Inquiry*. Reid rather insisted on two points: 1) the possibility of perceiving a color without perceiving any visible figure; 2) the possibility of perceiving a visible figure without perceiving any color.

4. Reid's argument in the *Inquiry*

Reid proposed to solve the question whether 'there be any sensation proper to visible figure, by which it is suggested in vision,' or 'by what means it is presented to the mind' by comparing the sense of sight with other senses (Reid 1997, VI.8: 99/5–7). His purpose was to 'distinguish things that are apt to be confounded,' as he said (Reid 1997, VI.8: 99/10–11).

He first compared the sense of sight with other senses 'that give us intelligence of things at a distance' (Reid 1997, VI.8: 99/12–13). In addition to sight, the other two senses that give us intelligence of things at a distance from our body are smell and hearing, both senses by which we perceive secondary qualities. It is in the context of this comparison with other senses that Reid remarked that while smell and hearing give us no knowledge previous to experience of the direction of the smelling or sounding body in relation to our sense organs, sight works differently. The sensation of color seems to suggest not only its cause, but also the position of this cause with regard to the eye. However, as Reid remarked at the end of the paragraph, thus anticipating his final position, the position of the colored thing is presented to the mind 'without any additional sensation' thanks to the peculiar laws of our constitution (Reid 1997, VI.8: 99/31).

After this comparison between sight on one hand and smell and hearing on the other hand, Reid proceeded by considering two thought experiments.

First, he asked us to imagine the sense of sight to work just like smell and hearing. He envisaged the possibility of an eye so constituted as to give us no intelligence of the figure or position of the body seen: 'The operation of such an eye would be precisely similar to that of hearing and smell; it would give no perception of figure or extension, but merely of colour' (Reid 1997, VI.8: 99/37–39). This thought experiment is not altogether imaginary:

> [I]t is nearly the case of most people who have cataracts, whose crystalline, as Mr Cheselden observes, does not altogether exclude the rays of light, but diffuses them over the *retina*, so that such persons see things as through a glass of broken gelly: they perceive the colour, but nothing of the figure or magnitude of the object (Reid 1997, VI.8: 100/1–6).

In the case of an eye affected by severe cataracts, the rays of light coming from any single point in the external object are not collected in one distinct point on the retina, but they are diffused over the whole of the retina's surface. As a result, all the rays coming from different points of the object meet in each point of the retina, mixing with each other and giving rise to a unique compound material impression. This impression is regularly followed by a sensation of color. Reid followed closely the text of Cheselden, but, as Fearn pointed out, it is debatable whether he correctly understood Cheselden's point.[15] According to Reid, persons affected by severe cataracts would be conscious of one sensation of color but not of any figure or extended magnitude. He seemed to imply not simply that such persons do not perceive the figure and magnitude of the object placed at a distance, but that the sensation of color of which they are aware does not have any figure or magnitude. Moreover, by describing the cataract case as the perception of a single color without any perception of figure and extension, Reid implicitly contrasted this special case with the normal case of perception: whenever we perceive visible figure and extension, we do also perceive a multiplicity of different colors at the same time. This can be taken as an implicit recognition that, as a brute matter of fact of our experience, a variety of color sensations is a necessary condition of our perceiving visible figure.

Second, Reid asked us to imagine the sense of hearing and smell to work like sight. We normally see a visible point of an object in the direction of a line passing through the centre of the eye from the point of the retina where the image of that point falls. Since the figure of an object is the conjunction of the positions of its parts, we see the figure of objects thanks to this law of our constitution. We could smell or hear the figure of objects, if a similar law applied in the operation of these two senses. In that case, 'every smell or sound would be associated with some figure in the imagination, as colour is in our present state' (Reid 1997, VI.8: 100/12–13).

The purpose of both these thought experiments is to make us conceive better the similarity of the sense of sight with the other two senses in one fundamental respect: the object to which the sensation, in each of these senses, is appropriated. The sensation of color in vision is appropriated to its unknown cause, color. We have no sufficient reason to say that visible figure and extension too are the proper objects of the sensation of color, just on the basis of the usual presentation of these spatial relations along with color. Visible figure and extension are rather presented along with color without any proper, specific, or additional sensation.[16]

Reid then presented a series of remarks preliminary to a final thought experiment. We know that the rays of light coming from the outward objects make some impressions on the retina, but we do not know the nature of such impressions, nor are we conscious of them. These material impressions do not resemble the sensations that follow them. We know that these material impressions suggest (either directly or indirectly through the medium of sensations) the perceptions of position and color. However, we do not perceive any 'necessary connection' between the various items involved in this process, that is, between the material impressions, the sensations, and the ensuing perceptions. By 'necessary connection,' Reid meant a connection arising from the nature of things, whereby the notion of one object necessarily involves the notion of the other. No man can give a reason why the same material impression could not suggest sound or smell, or either of these along with position, instead of color and position.

Reid not only stressed in this passage that there is no necessary connection between the material impression, the sensation, and the ensuing perception of a quality. He also admitted that there is no necessary connection between qualities such as color, smell, and sound, and the position of the objects that bear such qualities. Otherwise, how could the material impression conceivably suggest one of these qualities without position, if position were necessarily presupposed in their notion? That a particular material impression suggests both color and position, and nothing else, is ultimately due to 'our constitution or the will of our Maker' (Reid 1997, VI.8: 100/29).

Since there is no necessary connection between color and figure, we can consider a third thought experiment, where the eye is so framed as to perceive only visible figure without color. In his early manuscripts, Reid thought that this is more than a mere possibility. He conceived of a case where we perceive a black triangle against a colored background. Since no impression on the retina and no sensation of color are caused by the black triangle, the perception of this visible figure occurs without the perception of color.[17]

After considering an eye framed to perceive only visible figure, Reid supposed that this eye had the power of perceiving color restored to it. This supposition corresponds to the actual case.

The argument that leads to Reid's conclusion that there is no sensation appropriated to visible figure can thus be summed up in this manner:

1.1. The sensation of color is certainly appropriated to color (we cannot conceive of the quality of color unless we have a sensation of color, and to have a sensation of color is enough to make us conceive of a hidden quality, color, which gives rise to the sensation).

1.2. Color and visible position (and consequently visible figure and extension too, given the dependence of their notion from that of visible position) do not have a necessary connection between them. In different terms, color, understood simply as the hidden cause of a sensation, does not presuppose position in its notion: this is clearly shown, had there been any doubt about it, by the cataract case.

1.3. The sensation of color is not also appropriated to visible position (by 1.1 and 1.2.)

1.4. There are no other sensations of which we are conscious in vision in addition to that of color.

1.5. There is no sensation appropriated to visible position (and consequently to visible figure and extension).

1.6. Thus, visible figure 'seems to be suggested immediately by the material impression upon the organ, of which we are not conscious' (Reid 1997, VI.8: 101/16–17).

The main object of Stewart's criticism is Reid's remark that it would be possible to see visible figure without having any sensation of color. That Reid was drawn to such a position can be understood on the basis of two conflicting demands: on the one hand, his desire to preserve the secondary quality status of color; on the other hand, the recognition that by sight we perceive a primary quality, visible figure. But Stewart thought that Reid's position was untenable: by sight, we cannot perceive that different parts of an object have different position with regard to the eye, unless these parts reflect differently light to the eye, and thereby cause different sensations of color.

That a variety of color sensations is necessary for perceiving visible figure can be easily understood. As we have seen, visible figure is defined by Reid as the position of the several parts of an object with regard to the eye. The parts of an object that are visible are the parts that reflect light to the eye. Normally, these parts make up the object's external surface facing the eye. But if the light coming from the surface of the object facing the eye were not different from the light coming from adjacent or background objects, there would not be any perception of visible figure. We can think of a possible case that would replicate the cataract case, without any disturbance of the refractive mechanisms of the eye. Let's imagine different solid objects next to each other that reflect light of such wavelength as to cause the very same material impression on the eye. We can make the additional assumption that their background reflects light in such a way as to cause the very same impression on the retina. A case like this would not be different in its results from the cataract case as understood by Reid: the retina would be affected all over its surface by the same type of impression and as a result only one color sensation would arise.[18] So while it is true that there is no local sign in color sensations, a variety of color sensations is a necessary means for the perception of visible figure.

Reid appeared to be oblivious to the fact that visible figure is detectable by the eye only insofar as the boundaries of an object are perceived as having a different color from the color of adjacent or background objects. As Fearn wryly pointed out, every painter of signs knows that the letters he draws have to be in different color from the background in order to be visible.[19] Moreover, the two points Reid insisted on to make the case that there is no sensation appropriated to visible figure seem inadequate. The first point, made explicitly in the *Inquiry*, is the cataract case. As we have seen, the cataract case turns out to be an implicit admission, by way of contrast with the most usual case of perception, that whenever we do perceive visible figure we also do perceive a variety of colors. The second point, only alluded to in the *Inquiry* but presented in the manuscripts, is the perception of a black figure against a colored background. A black triangle against a colored background does not reflect light to the eye: in this case, no light affects the retina and therefore no sensation of color follows, and yet we do see a figure. This example, however, is defective for Reid's purposes, for two reasons. First, as Hamilton pointed out, even our awareness of black can be considered a sensation from a merely psychological point of view.[20] Second, and most importantly, we can perceive the black triangle precisely because of the contrast with the colored background. The triangular shape belongs as much to the black spot as it belongs to the colored background. As Fearn was to notice, Reid made a mistake when he considered visible figure simply as a property of a body with regard to the eye, without any consideration for the other bodies around it: visible figure is precisely the relation of contrast between one expanse of color and another in our visual field.[21] The challenge facing Stewart was then to reconcile the Reidian dogma of the non-spatiality of the mind and sensations with the common sense view according to which no object is visible if its color is not different from the color of the background or adjacent objects.

5. Stewart's *Dissertation* (1815)

In the *Elements of the Philosophy of the Human Mind* (1792), Stewart explicitly recognized that color sensations are not extended. He also spoke of a constant association between unextended color sensations and the extension or figure of external objects. This constant association leads us to conceive, albeit confusedly, the sensations themselves as spread over bodies.[22] This position is more advanced than that of Reid: Reid never explicitly admitted that we conceive, albeit confusedly, color sensations as extended.

In a later work, the *Dissertation: Exhibiting the Progress of Metaphysical, Ethical, and Political Philosophy, since the Revival of Letters in Europe* (1815), Stewart seems to establish an even stronger connection between sensations and extension.[23] The discussion of the relation between sensations of color and visible figure occurs in a passage where Stewart discusses the role of signs in sensory perception. Signs in sensory perception escape our attention because we immediately pass on to the things signified by them. We perceive distance by sight by comparing a variety of signs, but, just a moment later, we can hardly recollect any step of this process. In the same manner, we do not pay attention to color sensations. These modifications of our mind were intended by nature to be just signs 'indicating to us the figures and distances of things external' (Stewart 1854, 132). If we perceived just one color, without variety of light and shade, the organ of sight would be useless. Indeed 'it is by the *varieties* of colour alone that the outlines or visible figures of bodies are so defined, as to be distinguishable one from another' (Stewart 1854, 132). Moreover, the variety of colors is also essential for the perception of distance. The various signs by which we judge of distance by sight 'presuppose the antecedent recognition of the bodies around us, as separate objects of perception' (Stewart 1854, 132). Stewart probably thought that the various clues for distance have to be applied to an object distinguishable from others in our visual field. We can distinguish an object from others in our two-dimensional visual field, only if there is some variety of colors. This variety allows me to separate different patches of colors in my visual field and consider each one of them as representative of a distinct three-dimensional object at a distance.[24] But the identification, preliminary to distance perception, of two-dimensional shapes in our visual field is after all just the identification of the visible figures of objects. So the primary function of the variety of colors is really to signify the visible figure of an object. Speaking of the cataract case in his manuscripts, Reid seemed to imply that a variety of colors is a necessary condition for perceiving visible figure. In the *Inquiry*, however, the cataract case is not so much used to show that without variety of colors there is no perception of visible figure, but rather to make the point that the perception of color can be separated from the perception of visible figure, and, consequently, that the sensation of color only suggests color.

6. Stewart's letter to Reid

Like many commentators, Stewart had trouble making sense of what Reid had said concerning the relation between color and visible figure in the *Inquiry*. In a footnote, he recorded his longstanding reservations:

> In Dr. Reid's *Inquiry*, he has introduced a discussion concerning the perception of *visible figure*, which has puzzled me since the first time (more than forty years ago) that I read his work. The discussion related to this question, 'Whether there be any sensation proper to visible figure, by which it is suggested in vision?' (Stewart 1854, 132, note 1)

Stewart then recorded Reid's conclusions on the subject: the eye might have been so framed as to suggest visible figure without color; hence, there is no sensation proper to visible figure. Visible figure is suggested immediately by the impression upon the retina of which we are not conscious.

He then stated again his point: the variety of sensations of color is necessary in order for us to perceive visible figure.

> To my apprehension, nothing can appear more manifest than this, that, if there had been no *variety* in our sensations of colour, and still more, if we had no sensation of colour whatsoever, the organ of sight could have given us no information, either with respect to *figures* or to *distances*; and, of consequence, would have been as useless to us, as if we had been afflicted, from the moment of our birth, with a *gutta serena* (Stewart 1854, 132–33, note 1).

The editor of Stewart's works, William Hamilton, adds to these remarks a letter that Stewart sent to Reid. In his letter, Stewart refers to a letter he received from Reid.[25] Reid apparently conceded that the way we perceive visible figure is not different from the way we perceive tangible figure, a position that seems at odd with the text of the *Inquiry*.[26] Notwithstanding this concession, Stewart still thought Reid had not given a sufficient answer to his strictures:

> Although, however, I flatter myself we agreed in this general point, that our perception of visible figure is obtained in a way similar to that in which we obtain the perception of tangible figure, I cannot help being of opinion that the perception in neither case is obtained without the intervention of a sensation. You have said, indeed, that you allow it to be impossible for us in our present state, to perceive figure without colour, and consequently, without the sensation of colour; but I am inclined to suspect that you imagine the impossibility in the case to arise, not from any connexion or dependence between these perceptions established by nature, but merely from their happening to be received by the same organ of sense, so that they always enter the mind in company. To this opinion I cannot subscribe; because it appears to me to be evident, that our perceptions of colour and figure are not only received by the same organ of sense, but that the varieties in our perceptions of colour are the *means* of our perception of visible figure.

> I formerly observed, that our perception of visible figure appears to me to be a necessary consequence of that law of our nature, that every visible point is seen in

the direction of a straight line passing from the picture of that point on the retina through the centre of the eye. If a blind man was made acquainted with this law of our nature, he could himself infer the necessity of our perceiving visible figure. If it is allowed, then, that our perception of the visible figure of an object is the result of our perceiving the position of all the different points of its boundary, it is evident, that if visible figure can be perceived without any other quality, then position may likewise be perceived without any other quality (Stewart 1854, 133–134, note 1).

Although Reid said that, in the cataract case, we perceive one uniform color without visible figure and extension, he also implied that as a matter of fact of our experience every time we perceive visible figure and extension, we also perceive some color. He added that there is no connection between the two from the nature of things, that God could have framed our eyes in such a manner as to suggest visible figure without color, and that visible figure is suggested immediately by the impression on the retina. In the passage quoted above, Stewart recognized that Reid agreed with him in the opinion that we do not actually perceive either tangible or visible figure without some preceding sensation. However, he suspected that for Reid the impossibility of perceiving visible figure without color seems to arise 'not from any connexion or dependence between these perceptions established by nature, but merely from their happening to be received by the same organ of sense, so that they always enter the mind in company' (Stewart 1854, 134, note 1). According to Stewart, the connection between sensation and figure is established on a more fundamental basis: the variety of sensations is the means by which we perceive visible figure.

Out of this discussion, four points should be distinguished:

(1) We cannot perceive visible figure without perceiving color.
(2) We cannot perceive visible figure without perceiving a variety of colors.
(3) We cannot perceive color without perceiving visible figure.
(4) We cannot perceive a variety of colors, all at the same time, without perceiving visible figure.

Point (1) is implied by (2), and point (3) is implied by (4). It is clear that both Reid and Stewart agree on rejecting thesis (3): in the cataract case we perceive color without perceiving visible figure. Stewart was primarily interested in making point (2), that is, that the perception of a variety of colors is necessary for the perception of visible figure. It is not certain whether he also conceived of our perception of a variety of colors as a sufficient condition for our seeing visible figure (point [4]). We should also recall that when we speak of some perceptions as being necessary and sufficient conditions of others, we understand that they are so because there is 'a connexion or dependence between these perceptions established by nature,' and not simply because 'they always enter the mind in company' (Stewart 1854, 134, note 1).[27] This latter point would mark the difference between Stewart's and Reid's positions: as we have seen, Reid's discussion of the cataract case could be interpreted as implying that, as a matter of fact of our experience, whenever we perceive visible figure we also perceive a variety of colors. Thus, Stewart's 'connection or dependence established by nature' would have to be something stronger than the mere law-like regularity due to 'our constitution or the will of our Maker' Reid refers to. This connection or dependence established by nature would be more akin to the 'necessary connection' between color and visible figure that Reid explicitly rejects.

The argument that shows that we cannot perceive visible figure without variety of colors depends on Reid conceding certain points.

2.1. We see every point on the surface of an object that reflects light to the eye in the direction of a straight line passing through the centre of the eye from the point on the retina where the image of the point falls (Porterfield's law, as modified by Reid).

2.2. The direction of the straight line passing through the centre of the eye, from the point where the image of the point of an object falls, is the position of the point of the object with regard to the eye.

2.3. The visible figure of an object is equivalent to the conjunction of the positions of the points that make up the 'boundary' of the object.

2.4. If we see the visible figure of an object, we see the positions of the points of an object that make up its 'boundary'.

2.5. We see the visible figure of an object.

2.6. We see the positions of the points that make up the 'boundary' of an object.

Given the equivalence between seeing visible figure and seeing the position relative to the eye of points of an objects, one can move on to the following argument:

3.1. If we can see visible figure 'without any other quality,' then we can see position 'without any other quality.'

3.2. But we cannot see position without the quality of color.

3.3. Then, we cannot see visible figure without the quality of color.

It is not clear why Reid should grant premise 3.2. Of course, he would agree that a point of the retina has to be stimulated by some ray of light reflected from a point on the surface of the object, in order for us to see the position of the point on the object's surface. But why should he grant that we cannot possibly see this point as having that particular position, without at the same time conceiving it to be colored? On top of that, why should he grant the more fundamental point that there is a connection 'established by nature' between its being colored and its having that position? If we bear in mind that Stewart's objective is to show that the 'varieties in our perception of colour are the *means* of our perception of visible figure,' we can conjecture the following tentative reconstruction:

4.1. If we can see visible figure without variety of colors, then we can see the position of a point without the point itself appearing to the eye to have a color different from the color of at least some of the adjacent points.

4.2. But we cannot see the position of a point without the point itself appearing to have a color different from the color of at least some of the adjacent points.

4.3. Then we cannot see visible figure, without variety of colors.

Reid could not dispute premise 4.2, otherwise he would have to admit that we can see visible figure in the cataract case, where there is no distinction of colors among different points appearing to the eye. Thus, Stewart claims that Porterfield's law is not sufficient by itself to explain our perception of visible figure. We have to add to it as an additional requirement that there be a variety of colors. In fact, Porterfield's law is suspended in the cataract case.

The variety of sensations of color is what allows us to perceive different colors at the same time. Stewart does not seem to have thought that sensations themselves, when we carefully reflect upon them, appear to be ordered in space, although, as we have seen, he admitted that we have a confused notion of them as spread over bodies. Rather, his view seems to have been that the variety of sensations constitutes a pattern of resemblances and differences in these mental items that has some kind of isomorphism or one-to-one correspondence with visible figure itself. The analogy with language seems to have driven his thought on this score.[28] Although letters and their various combinations in words do not resemble the objects they stand for, the words that result from letters' combinations can be mapped, as in a dictionary, on to objects and events in the world. Perhaps this is the connection 'established by nature,' more fundamental than just a simple constant conjunction, that Stewart saw between the perception of visible figure and sensations of color.[29]

7.   John Fearn's critique of Reid and Stewart

In the previous section, I interpreted Stewart's remarks in the *Dissertation* on the basis of his letter to Reid. This reading tries to make Stewart's remarks compatible with the orthodox Reidian view that color sensations are not extended. However, the most obvious way to read Stewart's claim that a variety of color sensations is necessary for the perception of visible figure is to suppose that he took these sensations to be extended. John Fearn indeed took the incidental remarks in the *Dissertation* as a complete surrender by Stewart of Reid's position.[30] As Fearn said, if Stewart had given up the view that color sensations are extended, then he should have offered a more open reassessment of Reid's philosophy. Moreover, just before the publication of the *Dissertation*, Fearn had published essays in which he defended the view that visible figure is precisely the perception, due to an act of judgment, of a relation of contrast between extended color sensations. He therefore insisted on Stewart giving him some acknowledgement of his priority in the presentation of the view that a variety of color sensations is necessary for the perception of visible figure. I cannot enter the details of this controversy here. In his only letter to Fearn, Stewart disputed the originality of Fearn's 'discovery' and downplayed the importance of the issue of color and visible figure.[31] Stewart's declining health and the non-academic status of his critic may also have contributed to his reluctance to reply to Fearn.[32] But also as a result of Stewart's dismissal, Fearn was driven eventually to publish two books, *First Lines of the Human Mind* (1820) and *A Manual of the Physiology of Mind* (1829), where he attacked Reid and Stewart.

According to Fearn, the absurd views of the 'Scotch School' on color sensations were the inevitable result of the conjunction of two claims endorsed, either implicitly or explicitly, by Reid and his follower Stewart: (1) 'immaterialism,' or, in different terms, the Cartesian view that the mind is an unextended substance, and (2) the view that ideas, and consequently color sensations, are only modifications of the mind. This latter view, in its turn, was the outcome Reid's rejection of the theory that ideas are 'loose and detached beings' standing between the mind and the external objects.

In Fearn's terminology, 'immaterialism' does not refer to Berkeley's denial of the existence of a material world but to a view about the nature of the mind. Immaterialists conceive of the mind as a substance that has thought as its only attribute – a substance perfectly simple and thus completely devoid of extension and location in space. As Fearn explains, the origins of the immaterialist view of the soul can be found, among ancient philosophers, in the notion of an intellectual or spiritual soul separate from the body and its sense-organs. Both Plato and Aristotle subscribed to this view, but these philosophers also conceived of a sensitive soul that was literally extended and 'spread' in the body and its sense organs. Aristotle, in particular, explicitly stated that the sense-images apprehended by the sensitive soul are extended and spatially located. Ancient immaterialism was thus only a half-way house to immaterialism. Descartes eventually reduced both the intellectual and sensitive soul to 'one same essence,' but 'in order to accomplish this, he judged it requisite to deny the *extension* of the Sensitive Soul' (Fearn 1820, I.1: 19). According to Fearn, this is 'the most erroneous and most mischievous innovation that has ever been imagined' (Fearn 1820, I.1: 19). Descartes's innovation has given rise to 'a great and general schism between the whole race of Pneumatologists' (Fearn 1820, I.1: 20). Two factions have been at war since Descartes: the 'immaterialists,' who, following Descartes, hold the mind to be an unextended substance, and the 'materialists,' best represented by some eighteenth-century French philosophers who hold the mind to be a mere mode of an extended inanimate substance.

Both parties to this debate agree on the momentous consequences that would follow from the assumption that sensations, understood as being mere modifications of the mind, are extended: if (a) sensations are extended and if (b) sensations are modifications of the mind, then (c) the mind itself must be extended; and if (c) the mind is extended then (d) it must be a 'material essence;' but if (d) the mind is a 'material essence,' then (e) it is not immortal. As Fearn further explains, if the mind, in its essence, is a material being, then 'it cannot be a *simple principle*, but must be a *mere mode*, the result of an organization of material atoms, and, consequently, a thing generable and corruptible' (Fearn 1820, I.1: 20–21).

According to Fearn, the modern divide between immaterialism and materialism represented a false dichotomy. A 'third party' of philosophers, with Locke and Newton as their foremost representatives, considered the mind to be both immaterial and extended.[33] The elimination of the distinction between an intellectual and a sensitive soul should then have led Descartes to recognize that the mind is essentially extended, just like the sensitive soul, and yet indivisible and thus immortal like the intellectual soul. Once we recognize that sensations are nothing but states or modifications of the mind and that sensations are undeniably extended, we have to admit that the mind itself is extended. But the unity of our consciousness gives us immediate and incontrovertible evidence for the indivisibility of the mind, notwithstanding the mind's modifications over time and its spatial extension and location. Thus, contrary to what immaterialists stated, '[t]he *Supposed Simplicity of the Mind*' is not necessary for the unity of consciousness (Fearn 1829, I: 34).

According to Fearn, the attributes of thought and extension are inseparable, and so the view that there is any such thing as 'dead matter,' an inert and inanimate substance, has to be rejected. In the *First Lines* and the *Manual*, Fearn came to subscribe explicitly to a revised form of Berkeleian immaterialism, although he took pains to stress that while he shared with Berkeley the goal of denying the existence of matter, his own system was not a mere revival of the scheme of the Irish philosopher.[34]

Fearn entered into further details of the genealogy of Reid's views on color sensations. As we have seen, philosophers who subscribed to the Cartesian immaterialist view of the mind accepted the argument we sketched above: if (a) sensations are extended and if (b) sensations are modifications of the mind, then (c) the mind itself must be extended, and, therefore, (d) it must be material and (e) generable and corruptible. According to Fearn, these philosophers could not openly deny an obvious datum of consciousness – that is, that our color sensations are extended (thesis [a]). Thus, in order to avoid the consequences of the argument, they found themselves under the necessity of denying thesis (b) with regard to color sensations. They denied that all those sensations that are figured and extended, including color sensations, are modifications of the mind, and turned them all into a third kind of beings, 'loose and detached beings,' intermediary entities distinct from mind's modifications and the external objects. Fearn recognized that this 'ideal theory' did not originate with early modern philosophers and that it was present in ancient philosophers, for example in the theory attributed (wrongly) to Aristotle by Descartes and Malebranche of 'films' flying off the surface of things. He also recognized that the theory of ideas as loose and detached beings took different forms in various philosophers and that it was held inconsistently along with the view that the same ideas are modifications of the mind.

Fearn takes seriously an autobiographical remark made by Reid in the *Essays on the Intellectual Powers of Man* (1785), where he confesses to have subscribed to the whole of Berkeley's system in his youth as a consequence of his belief in the theory of ideas as immediate objects of knowledge:

> If I may presume to speak my own sentiments, I once believed this doctrine of ideas so firmly, as to embrace the whole of BERKELEY's system in consequence of it; till, finding other consequences to follow from it, which gave me more uneasiness than the want of a material world, it came into my mind, more than forty years ago, to put the question, What evidence have I for this doctrine, that all objects of my knowledge are ideas in my own mind? (Reid 2002a, II.10: 142/10–17)

The consequences Reid alludes to are not immediately spelled out in what follows this remark. Fearn, however, conjectures that Reid's main worry was Hume's skepticism concerning the existence of the mind as a subject of inherence for ideas:

> Upon this passage, I shall in the first place offer the collateral remark, that it fully proves Dr. Reid to have had, in the beginning, *no predilection in favour of a material world*; and it shows, therefore, that his whole anxiety was, (as he himself has expressly avowed) to oppose the skepticism of Hume with regard to the *existence of minds* (Fearn 1820, II.1: 152).

Berkeley, like most other philosophers, subscribed to the theory of ideas, which makes sensations loose and detached beings that can enter and exit the mind at will. Berkeley held this position, according to Fearn, inconsistently with the further claim that ideas cannot exist without the mind, a claim that Fearn interprets as an admission that ideas must ultimately be modifications of the mind. Whatever inconsistency may have been present in Berkeley's view of ideas, once sensations were conceived as loose and detached beings and were denied their status as modifications of the mind, the way was left open to Hume to deny that sensations and their copies in imagination and memory – 'impressions and ideas' in Hume's terms – must have a subject of inherence. Reid realized that this consequence was far worse than the denial of the existence of matter. He was thus led to reject the theory that makes sensations ideas, that is, loose and detached beings, and embraced the view that they are just modifications of the mind.[35] But in order to avoid the other horn of Hume's dilemma that makes the mind extended and divisible, Reid had to deny that our color sensations are extended:

> There cannot be a doubt, that it was AFTER *his dissatisfaction with the system of Berkeley* that he FIRST *began to suppose* our sensations of colors are *not spread out*.
>
> In the act of revolt, therefore, Dr. Reid had two great objects to accomplish, *vastly different in their natures*: The one was to put the question, *What evidence we have for the existence of loose detached ideas in the mind?* The other, *to deprive our sensations of colors of that outspread or extended nature* which, both as a Berkeleian and as an ordinary man, he must always, prior to that time have ascribed to them (Fearn 1820, II.1: 154–155).

Fearn's genealogy of Reid's thought appears to be borne out in its essentials by the text of the *Inquiry*.[36] As we have seen, Reid saw two alternative undesirable outcomes to Hume's argument about the mind in *Treatise* 1.4.5.

According to Reid's reconstruction of Hume's argument, it follows from the doctrine that ideas exist in the mind that 'the mind either is no substance, or that it is an extended and divisible substance; because the ideas of extension cannot be in a subject which is indivisible and unextended' (Reid 1997, VII: 217/7−9). First, we can deny the existence of a mind as a substance, that is, as a subject of inherence for ideas. This consequence is the one pointed out by Fearn as lying behind Reid's turn away from Berkeley's system. Second, Hume argued that if the ideas are extended, then the mind itself must be extended and therefore divisible and mortal. This is the consequence that follows from taking ideas, understood as modifications of the mind, as being extended. We can thus understand the necessity for Reid to deny that color sensations are extended, as Fearn pointed out in his extended discussion of materialism and immaterialism about the mind.

Fearn not only gave an account of the alleged motivations lying behind Reid's views on the non-spatiality of color sensations. He moved further into a dissection of what evidence Reid actually presented for his case.

What kind of evidence could be provided for the 'new doctrine' that denied the extension of color sensations? This appeared to Fearn to be a hopelessly indefensible position. The new doctrine indeed 'violated the universal apprehension of all ordinary men,' even more than the universal opinion of the learned (Fearn 1820, II.1: 140). As Stewart had to concede, 'it is a natural bias in us to conceive white, blue, and yellow, as something spread over the surfaces of bodies' (Stewart 1792, 73−74, quoted in Fearn 1820, II.1: 141).[37] This is a bias, according to Fearn's interpretation of Stewart's words, insofar as 'our *sensations of colors* are NOT IN REALITY *spread out*, although they *appear to us* to be so' (Fearn 1820, II.1: 141). But color sensations are phenomena of our consciousness. Consequently, as Fearn argues, if we say that 'our *sensations of color* are NOT IN REALITY *spread out* although they *appear to us* to be so,' we would have to conclude that 'we are grossly mistaken in the most confident judgments that we can form upon the phenomena of our own *consciousness*' (Fearn 1820, II.1: 141). By parity of reasoning, it would follow that we might as well be mistaken about the sensations themselves of color and not simply about their spatial arrangement:

> All parties, with regard to this subject, are perfectly agreed, that white, blue, and yellow, are purely *phenomena of consciousness*. But, since this is so; I confidently apprehend, it must be quite as easy for any man to be mistaken as to whether a sensation is *in reality white, blue, or yellow*, as for him to mistake whether it is in *reality spread out* (Fearn 1820, II.1: 141).

One can answer to this stricture by pointing out some replicable experiment that shows that we can be indeed mistaken about what we normally take to be immediate data of consciousness. Falkenstein has pointed out that Reid himself adopted this procedure. We are not normally aware of the existence of double appearances in our visual field, but we can become aware of these under suitable experimental circumstances, as Reid explains at length. We think we do not have a blind spot in our visual field but we can become aware of it, again with a proper experiment.[38] However, it is debatable how we should interpret these experiments. Do they really show that we are mistaken about what we think we are conscious of? Or do they simply present us with new phenomena of consciousness that were not present just a moment before?

For Fearn the question was easily decided by the case narrated by Cheselden concerning a young man who recovered vision after surgical removal of a severe cataract. The case confirmed Berkeley's view that we do not originally perceive objects at a distance from the eyes, but it also clearly showed that the young man originally perceived colors as extended in two-dimensions:

> It is known that this youth, first of all, conceived the very truth of nature that everything he saw *touched his eye*, or, more properly speaking, was *a phantom in his own mind*. AFTER this, *by degrees*, he fell into a BIAS and error, (common to the whole species,) under which he conceived all colors to be WITHOUT AND AT A DISTANCE FROM HIM. Now the question which concerns the present subject is this; Did the young man, in the *very first* instance of his being conscious of color, *believe that colors are not spread out*; in the same way that he, *at first*, believed they were NOT *at a distance*? (Fearn 1820, II.1: 142–143)

For Fearn, the answer to this question is negative: the terminology of colors 'touching' the eyes used by the young man clearly implies that the colors he saw were extended.

According to Fearn, Reid presented only two pieces of evidence to defend the thesis that colors are not extended. The first is the cataract case, which Reid derived from his reading of Cheselden's report. The second is a 'vague' hint, probably derived from Hutcheson, that space, extension, and figure are not, properly speaking, objects of the senses, but of judgment.

Fearn thought that Reid had completely misunderstood the import of Cheselden's description of the experience of color had by persons affected by severe cataracts. Cheselden compared this experience to seeing an object through a 'glass of broken jelly' (Fearn 1820, II.1: 146). According to Fearn, when we look through a glass of broken jelly at a man 'in a blue, a yellow, or a scarlet *coat*; we shall immediately become *conscious of a sensation of color* of blue, of yellow, or scarlet, of *some irregular* FIGURE' (Fearn 1820, II.1: 146). In different terms, we see an expanse of color with fuzzy boundaries, but we cannot see the distinct figure of the coat placed beyond the jelly. Thus, when Cheselden said that the 'persons laboring under cataract "*perceive the color but nothing of the figure or magnitude of* OBJECTS",' all he meant is that these persons do not see the figure and magnitude of the object placed at a distance (Fearn 1820, II.1: 146). But the color they are conscious of is certainly extended and somewhat figured. Reid, however, interpreted these remarks as meaning that the persons having cataracts are '*conscious of color* without being able to perceive that *this colour itself is figured or extended*' (Fearn 1820, II.1: 147). According to Fearn, the text of Cheselden presupposes the contrary:

So far is Cheselden from supposing, for a moment, that *the color we are conscious of*, when looking through a glass of broken jelly, is *not extended*; that, on the contrary, he expressly asserts, that the light is so *differently refracted by 'a great variety of surfaces,'* that the several distinct pencils of rays CANNOT BE COLLECTED. Thus, upon the evidence of Cheselden, it is *because of the* DIFFUSION OR EXTENSION *of color in the mind* that the shape of *any object* SEEN THROUGH *a cataract cannot be discerned*: for, to say that the rays of color *'cannot be collected,'* is manifestly but another mode of saying that they are *scattered or extended* (Fearn 1820, II.1: 147).

Moreover, this is the language used by Reid himself to describe the case of the person affected by cataract: 'the "*Chrystaline* [. . .] does not exclude the rays of light but DIFFUSES THEM OVER THE RETINA." Now what is DIFFUSION, but EXTENSION? And what, but some overwhelming bias, could have betrayed Dr. Reid into so glaring contradiction, as that of denying the extension of color in face of this concession?' (Fearn 1820, II.1: 147–148). The bias Fearn alludes to is the 'dogma of the inextension of the mind.' But a different bias might be at work in Fearn's critique: he presupposes that the extension of the physical impressions made by the rays of light on the retina necessarily implies that the color sensations in the mind are extended.[39]

Fearn identifies another element of evidence that may have justified to Reid's mind the claim that sensations are not extended. Following an observation made by Stewart on the ancestry of Reid's views, he refers to Hutcheson's occasional remark that figure and extension are not, properly speaking, sensations: '*Extension, Figure, Motion* or *Rest* seem [. . .] to be more properly called *Ideas accompanying* the Sensations of *Sight* and *Touch*, than the Sensations of either these Senses' (Hutcheson 2002, 16, note).[40] According to Stewart, this passage and other similar passages in other authors 'were either unknown to Dr. Reid, or had altogether escaped his recollection, when he wrote his *Inquiry*' (Stewart 1855, Note G, 420). Stewart was eager to defend the originality of Reid's arguments for the view that our notions of external qualities have no resemblance to sensations.[41] Thus he affirmed that these passages 'exhibit, in fact, nothing more than momentary glimpses of the truth [. . .]' (Stewart 1855, Note G, 420). Fearn agreed that Hutcheson's remark only added 'a vague suffrage' to the opinions of Reid and Stewart, and it conveyed 'no definite meaning whatever' (Fearn 1820, II.1: 144). It is clear that remarks such as that of Hutcheson were reflections in the empiricist camp of the claim that figure and extension are the objects of a judgment of the intellect and not simply copied from sensations. Early manuscripts by Reid show that he did not at first deny that color sensations are arranged spatially, but that he simply wanted to show that figure and extension are not copied from atomic sensations of color and that they are relations that can be discerned only by a faculty of judgment distinct from the power of sensation.[42]

8. Conclusion

The bizarre claim that color sensations, colors as *qualia*, are neither extended nor arranged in figured patterns exposes Reid's philosophy to ridicule. As Fearn noticed, Reid himself evaded a direct statement of the thesis by using a 'softening expression': he simply claimed that sensations do not resemble extension. Stewart understood this claim to mean that sensations are not extended, and then struggled to reconcile this thesis with common sense, addressing also the related question about the sensation that is appropriated to visible figure. Fearn finally tried to give an account of how this thesis came about. Faced with Hume's skepticism about the existence of the mind, Reid rejected the view of loose and detached ideas, flitting in and out of the mind like swallows, and turned them into modifications of the mind.[43] But his prior commitment to the immateriality of the mind led him to deny that color sensations are extended. This interpretation bears some similarity to the one proposed independently in recent times by Lorne Falkenstein, although Falkenstein does not take such a definite stance as Fearn does on the theory of ideas that Reid rejected.[44] If Fearn and Falkenstein are correct, Reid's commitment to a metaphysical dualism of mind and body is central to his philosophy. It follows that attempts to read his philosophy of mind in light of contemporary views are always in danger of being anachronistic if they underestimate or disregard his substance dualism. Fearn noticed how Stewart himself originated a modernizing reading by emphasizing the experimental aspect of Reid's project, aimed at finding regularities in the working of our cognitive powers or 'laws of thought.' As a result of this emphasis, the core of Reid's philosophy can be seen as non-committal when it comes to metaphysical questions such as the one concerning the extension of the mind.[45]

Acknowledgements

I would like to thank Lorne Falkenstein and Patrick Rysiew for comments on this paper. I would also like to thank the participants to the meeting 'New Essays on Reid,' held at the University of Vermont, 1–2 November 2013.

Notes

1. Reid also refers to color sensations as 'the appearances of colors.' Thus, to speak of 'manifest color qualities' is only a slight departure from Reid's own terminology.
2. Writing in this volume Lorne Falkenstein has observed that ordinary people speak of manifest color qualities 'as if they were external and located on the surface of bodies. Reid would have liked to deny this and maintain that our sensations of color are so insignificant to us that they have not been thought worthy of being given names in any language, so that all anyone ever means to do when speaking of color is to refer to the invisible causes of our color sensations, and all they ever say in consequence is that the causes of their color sensations are external and located on the surfaces of bodies. The implausibility of this position is proven by the significant sums of money people of ordinary common sense are willing to spend on cosmetics, clothes, paint, interior decoration, gardens, etc. The members of a society of blind people would have no interest in spending money on such things, which are valued only for the sake of the visual sensations they produce in us. The members of a society that considers sensations of color to be so insignificant as not even to be worthy of being named should have attitudes that are no different from those of the blind.'

3. On the question whether there is a sensation proper to visible figure, see Reid (1997), VI.8: 99/5–101/23 and VI.21: 176/30–37. This part of Reid's *Inquiry* has been object of debate: Yaffe (2003a); Falkenstein and Grandi (2003); Yaffe (2003b); Nichols (2007). Reid also claimed that the vulgar always ascribe the name 'color' to the unknown quality in the external object rather than to the appearance of which they are conscious: see Reid (1997), VI.4: 87/9–25.

4. Fearn's interpretation is similar to that presented independently in recent times by Lorne Falkenstein: see Falkenstein (2000) and (2005).

5. See Yaffe (2003a).

6. See Hume (2000), 1.4.5.7–16 and 33.

7. The alternative that the soul might be extended is not an option Hume recognized, though Reid claimed he did.

8. See Reid (1997), VII: 217/5–26. Reid does not discuss these arguments in the *Inquiry*. On the question of the immateriality of the soul, see also the *Three Lectures on the Nature and Duration of the Soul*, published in Reid (2002a), 617–631, and Paul Wood, Introduction, in Reid (1995).

9. See Reid (2002a), II.2: 76/17–25.

10. See Hatfield (1990), Ch. 4, especially 131–143.

11. Reid explains the reasons for his modification of Porterfield's original statement in Reid (1997), VI.12: 123/17–27.

12. Another case of innate mechanism of localization of a secondary quality is probably that of heat and cold, although Reid does not clearly say so. The localization of the causes of pain and pleasure also appears to be a case of perception of the location of a hidden cause of sensations in our body on the basis of an innate mechanism. However, in some cases, we do not simply perceive the causes of pain and pleasure to be situated in a particular location in our body. In some instances, we do also have a conception of what causes pain and pleasure (an object touching us with gradually increasing pressure, first giving rise to sensations that are neither painful nor pleasurable and then giving rise to a painful sensation is a case in point). On the localization of the causes of pain and pleasure, see Reid (2002a), II.18: 211–215. See also Falkenstein (2000), 314–317.

13. See Reid (1997), VI.22: 178–187.

14. An interpretation of Reid (1997), VI.8, based on this point is proposed by Falkenstein (2000), 318, note 39, and by Falkenstein and Grandi (2003). For an alternative interpretation, see Yaffe (2003a). According to Yaffe, color sensations have a dual function: they suggest both color and visible figure.

15. See below section 7, where I discuss extensively Fearn's critique. Reid first presented the cataract case in an Aberdeen University Library (AUL) manuscript from 1 December 1758: AUL MS 2131/6/III/8, fols. 1r-v, in Reid (1997), 319/15–320/4. The origin of Reid's interest in the visual abilities of patients affected by severe cataracts is certainly due to his reading of Cheselden's case in the *Philosophical Transactions of the Royal Society* (1728). William Cheselden, a surgeon at St. Thomas Hospital, London, removed the cataracts from the eyes of a young man. The experiences of the newly sighted young man could finally provide a solution to Molyneux's Question (Reid himself takes the report of the experiences of the young man after the removal of cataracts as confirmation that originally by sight we do not perceive distance). But Reid was also interested in the beginning of Cheselden's report which describes the visual experiences of the young man before surgery: 'Tho' we say of the gentleman that he was blind, as we do of all people who have ripe cataracts, yet they are never so blind from that cause, but that they can discern day from night; and for the most part in a strong light, distinguish black, white, and scarlet; but they cannot perceive the shape of any thing; for the light by which these

perceptions are made, being let in obliquely thro' the aqueous humour, or the anterior surface of the crystalline (by which the rays cannot be brought into *focus* upon the retina) they can discern in no other manner, than a sound eye can thro' a glass of broken jelly, where a great variety of surfaces so differently refract the light, that the several distinct pencils of rays cannot be collected by the eye into their proper *foci*; wherefore the shape of an object in such a case cannot be discern'd, though the colour may,' quoted by Morgan (1977), 19.

16. In the manuscripts, Reid also draws an analogy between the constant association of color with visible figure and the constant association of heat and cold with tangible figure: see AUL MS 2131/6/III/8, fol. 3r, in Reid (1997), 324/38–325/11. This analogy may be the background for the analogy drawn between sight and touch in Reid (1997), VI.8: 101/17–23.

17. See AUL MS 2131/6/III/8, fol. 3r, in Reid (1997), 324/23–37. See also AUL MS 2131/8/II/21, fol. 2v.

18. In comments to this paper, Lorne Falkenstein mentions cases of uniformly colored visual field caused by 'white-out' weather conditions (thick fog or a snow-storm), and by 'red-out' weather conditions (a dust-storm). But even in the absence of such conditions affecting the medium between the objects at a distance and the eyes, it is still conceivable to think of objects that reflect the same light to the eyes.

19. See Fearn (1820), xxi (the epigraph to this paper).

20. See William Hamilton, *Dissertations, Historical, Critical, and Supplementary, Note E*, in Reid (1880), vol. 2, 918a.

21. See Fearn (1820), viii. The analysis of visible lines and figure as relations of contrast between color sensations is carried out by Fearn in Fearn (1820), II.5: 197–212, and Fearn (1829), I: 25–27. He here gives four laws for the perception of visible lines and figures. According to Fearn, lines are external relations holding necessarily among color sensations and known through an act of judgment distinct from mere sensation. He distinguishes this act of judgment whereby borders between contrasting color sensations are seen (similar to 'ploughing') from the act of judgment whereby atomic color sensations of the same hue are seen as a continuous expanse (this is similar to 'harrowing'): see Fearn (1829), IV.2: 153–155. He also comments explicitly on Kant's views, known only second hand (Fearn 1829, IV.3: 161–169).

22. Stewart (1792), 73–74, and 561–562.

23. The *Dissertation* was prefixed to the supplemental volumes of the *Encyclopedia Britannica*. Stewart's speculations on color occurred in a part where he discusses what he considers to be one of the achievements of Descartes, the distinction between primary and secondary qualities.

24. For example, if I judge of the distance of a tree by interposition, I must be able to pick out a particular two-dimensional patch of colors, brown and green, distinct from other patches of color in my visual field that signify closer objects.

25. Stewart's (second) letter to Reid is not included in the critical edition of Reid's correspondence (Reid 2002b), but only in Hamilton's edition of Stewart's works. The first letter of Stewart to Reid is missing, as well as Reid's reply to it to which Stewart refers in the letter published by Hamilton. So we have to rely on Stewart's second letter to Reid to reconstruct Reid's reply to Stewart's criticism. Stewart criticized Reid's use of the term 'suggestion' in Chapter 6, Section 8 of the *Inquiry*. Reid had claimed that the impression on the retina immediately suggests the notion of visible figure. Stewart noticed that this is the only place in the *Inquiry* where Reid uses the word 'suggest' 'to express the communication of knowledge to the mind by means of something of which we are not conscious' (Stewart 1854, 133, note 1). Stewart evidently thought that if sensory perception works like a natural language,

we must be conscious of the signs at work in it, however little attention do we actually pay to them; in the same manner, we pay little attention to spoken or written words of our artificially constructed languages, and yet it is certain that we are conscious of them, if we have to attend to their meaning. In his second letter to Reid, Stewart proclaimed himself satisfied with Reid's answer on this issue, although it is not exactly clear from Stewart's remarks what Reid's answer was. Probably, Reid said that by the use of the term 'suggestion' he just meant a regular succession of events in the process of our perception. Some events in this process are conscious states (our sensations, for example), others are not conscious like the impressions on our sense organs: see Reid (1997), VI.21: 174–178.

26. Here is what Stewart says in his letter to Reid: 'I am happy to find, indeed, that our sentiments upon the subject are not so different as I first apprehended, but I do not imagine that they yet entirely coincide. You seem to acknowledge that the mode in which we obtain the perception of visible figure is precisely similar to the mode in which we obtain the perception of tangible figure. So far I perfectly agree with you. And I apprehend you will likewise acknowledge the reasonings which you have advanced upon the perception of visible figure are applicable to our perception of extension both by sight and touch. This observation had occurred to me before the first time I wrote to you. But as you have taken no notice of it in your *Inquiry*, and as, in another part of your book, ([Ch. 6, Sec. 8] p. 306 of the 3rd Edition) you have spoken of our perception of visible figure, as an exception from all our perceptions, I was led to conclude that you conceived some peculiarity about it which I did not fully comprehend. It was this which first turned my attention particularly to the subject, and gave rise to the observations which I sent you in my last letter' (Stewart 1854, 133, note 1). Stewart claims that Reid admitted in his reply that the mode by which we perceive visible figure is precisely similar to the mode by which we perceive tangible figure. This might seem strange, because while Reid thought that there are sensations regularly preceding and thus suggesting our perception of tangible figure, he clearly stated that visible figure is suggested immediately by the impression on the retina. It is true that it is not clear whether he thought there are sensations *exclusively* suggesting tangible figure, or if he thought there are sensations that suggest multiple items such as hardness and softness, roughness and softness, motion, and tangible figure at the same time. The second reading is justified by the passage in Reid (1997), V.5: 63/3–14. Reid also makes clear that the same sensation by suggesting hardness or softness also suggests extension since this notion is implied in that of hardness and softness: see Reid (1997), V.5: 62/33–63/2. In comments on this article, Lorne Falkenstein suggests that Reid's apparent concession to Stewart should be taken as recognizing that the perception of tangible figure is like that of visible figure: there is no sensation appropriated to tangible figure, and tangible figure is suggested immediately by the material impression. On Reid's account, pressure sensations are confined to suggesting just those primary qualities of a body having to do with the spatial relations among its own parts. They do not tell us where the body is located relative to other bodies causing other pressure sensations.

27. As we have seen, Reid could grant Stewart that we cannot perceive visible figure without color, that is, that the perception color is a necessary condition of our perceiving visible figure. This is a matter of fact of our experience, not yet disconfirmed by any contrary instance.

28. See Stewart (1854), 133–135.

29. Moreover, this isomorphism would not be as strict as the one demanded by the doctrine of local signs, since sensations can somehow change in their mutual order of coexistence without any change in the figure signified: a red triangle against a green background can be identical in visible figure to a green triangle against a red

background, but the corresponding color sensations would switch 'position' in their non-spatial order of coexistence.

30. William Hamilton, probably influenced by Fearn, claimed that Stewart's views on color and visible figure in the *Dissertation* are not compatible with his views in the *Elements* (Reid 1880, vol. 2, 919). Hamilton reviewed the whole question of color and visible figure in Note E of his edition of Reid's works: see Reid (1880), vol. 2, 917–923. Hamilton, although critical of Fearn's claims to originality, begrudgingly acknowledged his merits: '[. . .] I am far from doubting the personal originality of this perverse, but acute psychologist' (Reid 1880, vol. 2, 918b). Hamilton also described Fearn as 'a rare metaphysical talent though unendowed with even an ordinary faculty of expression' (Reid 1880, vol. 2, 923b). John Fearn was a retired officer of the Royal Navy and the merchant navy. As a captain of a whaling ship he discovered an island in the South Pacific, now the independent country of Nauru. In a sketch of autobiography in one of his late works, he writes that after his retirement from the 'maritime life,' he spent some years 'occupying a position in the Interior Regions of one of those Lands,' presumably somewhere in South-Asia or Southeast-Asia. In this 'lone and long seclusion,' he spent a considerable amount of time reading Locke's *Essay concerning Human Understanding* ('a fortunate accident, which gave to my mind its first cast towards Philosophy'). The only other diversion was that of hunting, or as he says 'riding, frequently, upon an elephant, or on horseback; and invading the repose, and disturbing the life, of the Wild Boar, and the Buffalo in their lairs: Together with a varied, and most unsparing, slaughter of the lesser animals which Providence had subjected to my truly savage propensity' (Fearn 1837, 7–9). After his return to London, he published a plethora of works during the course of almost thirty years of activity. Fearn's various contributions on the problem of color and visible figure are listed in the bibliography: in Fearn (1810/1812), (1813a) and (1813b), he still subscribes to a form of realism about matter. For his mature and complete views on the question, see in particular Fearn (1820) and (1829). Fearn's philosophy is briefly discussed by Atherton (2005).

31. See Stewart's letter, in Fearn (1820), xiii–xiv. Fearn did not accuse Stewart of plagiarism, and he only insisted on his priority in the discovery that a variety of sensations is necessary for the perception of visible figure. Most importantly, he insisted on his priority in the discovery of the principle of explanation lying behind this fact, that is, that visible figure is a relation of contrast between two color sensations. Hamilton, as editor of Stewart's works, defended Stewart in the priority controversy with Fearn. According to Hamilton, Stewart's letter to Reid, '"of forty years before" [. . .] completely vindicates' Stewart's statements (Stewart 1854, ix, note). Thus, Stewart was already stating that the 'varieties in our perceptions of colour are the *means* of our perception of visible figure' in his letter to Reid from 1775 (Stewart 1854, 134, note 1).

32. Fearn had submitted to Stewart his first work, *An Essay on Consciousness* (1st edition 1810, 2nd edition 1812) sometime before the publication of Stewart's *Dissertation* in 1815, thus justifying in his mind an unspoken suspicion that the view that color sensations are extended had been gleaned from that early work. In that work, Fearn had explicitly conceived the mind to have the shape of a 'spherule,' a small sphere located somewhere inside the brain. The work was later repudiated by Fearn not only because of the hypothesis of the spherule (revived later in his life by Fearn), but also because of its realism about matter. Stewart had quickly dismissed the work upon reading of the hypothesis of the spherule. This hypothesis may have irremediably tainted the reputation of Fearn in Stewart's mind.

33. See Fearn (1820), I.1: 21.

34. Fearn (1820), I.1: 24–25. Fearn compared his metaphysics to ancient 'Hindoo' philosophy. The external bodies we know through sensations are only activations of latent 'energies' of an infinite spirit – a spirit infinitely extended in three-dimensions and ultimately identical to space itself. Despite the radical aspects of his views about the nature of the external world, Fearn was aware that his ideas on the mind were not original. Fearn explicitly mentioned Newton's view of space as the sensorium of God and Newton's allusions to a seat of the soul somewhere in the brain as representatives of the more sensible view that, without giving up thought as an essential attribute of mind, makes the mind spatially extended. Oblivious to the possibility of a materialist interpretation of Locke, Fearn also enlisted the author of the *Essay concerning Human Understanding* in this tradition. However, he did not mention Henry More, who, in his polemic with Descartes, best represented the 'third party' on the nature of the soul. Ralph Cudworth and Samuel Clarke also held views similar to those of Fearn. The view itself had a long history: see Bréhier (1937). Fearn's main source for his knowledge of ancient Indian philosophy is William Jones, an author mentioned by Stewart in his *Philosophical Essays* (1810): see Stewart (1855), 107–108. Schopenhauer also relied on William Jones' works for his knowledge of Indian philosophy, but he drew from them different conclusions.

35. Thus Fearn took a definite stance on the vexed question of what was the 'ideal theory' that Either Reid rejected in his writings. Either Reid's arguments are only against ideas considered as special entities standing between the mind and external qualities, or his arguments also take into account a more nuanced view according to which ideas, which are in themselves modifications of the mind, can make us acquainted with external qualities by being somehow resemblant in their 'objective reality' to external qualities. Whatever view we adopt on Reid's critique of the theory of ideas, Fearn was among the originators of the more reductive interpretation, an interpretation towards which the first editor of Reid, William Hamilton, eventually inclined. The other source for the reductive interpretation was Thomas Brown, *Lectures on the Philosophy of the Human Mind* (1820).

36. The remarks about Hume's argument in the *Inquiry* do not allow us to draw a definitive conclusion about the origin of Reid's philosophy. However, we find that Reid worried about the origin of our idea of the self as early as 1749, as one of his early manuscripts show: see AUL MS 2131/6/I/18, in Reid (1997), 316–318.

37. The original passage in Stewart is slightly different from what Fearn gives as a quotation: '[O]ur natural bias is surely to connect colour with extension and figure, and to conceive *white, blue,* and *yellow,* as something spread over the surfaces of bodies' (Stewart 1792, 73–74).

38. See Falkenstein (2000), 322–323. Falkenstein notices that Reid fails to point out those experiments that make us see that color sensations are not extended. Reid describes an experiment revealing the existence of double appearances in our visual field in Reid (1997): VI.13: 133/36–134/10.

39. The hypothesis that what we immediately see is similar to the image on the retina has been called the 'constancy hypothesis': see Pastore (1971), 11–13.

40. Hutcheson's passage is quoted by Stewart (1855, Note G, 420) and Fearn (1820, II.9: 248, and 1829, IV.2: 149). The original passage occurs in a wider context in Hutcheson: 'Some *Ideas* are found accompanying the most different Sensations, which yet are not to be perceived separately from some *sensible Quality*; such are *Extension, Figure, Motion,* and *Rest,* which accompany the *Ideas* of Sight, or Colours, and yet may be perceived without them, as in the *Ideas* of Touch, at least if we move our Organs along the Parts of the Body touched. *Extension, Figure, Motion,* or *Rest* seem therefore to be more properly called *Ideas accompanying* the Sensations of *Sight* and *Touch,* than the Sensations of either these Senses. The

Perceptions that are purely sensible, received each by its proper sense are *Tastes, Smells, colours, Sound, Cold, Heat,* &c.' (Hutcheson 2002, 16, note).

41. Stewart had particularly in mind the *experimentum crucis* of Reid (1997), V.7: 70/16–27.
42. See AUL MSS 2131/8/II/21, fol. 2v; 2131/8/VI/3, fol. 1r-v; and the continuous manuscript constituted by MSS 2131/6/III/8 and 2131/6/III/5 (see Reid 1997, especially 327). I consider these manuscripts in Reid (2012), 6–7.
43. The image of loose and detached ideas 'flitting, like swallows, into and out of the mind' can be found in Fearn (1820), I.3: 93 and I.4: 121.
44. See Falkenstein (2000) and (2005).
45. See Fearn (1820), I.2: 30–57. The relation between Reid's substance dualism and Newtonian methodological principles is examined by Nichols (2007), 35–38.

References

Atherton, Margaret. 2005. "Reading Lady Mary Shepherd." *Harvard Review of Philosophy* 13 (2): 73–85.

Bréhier, Émile. 1937. "Matière cartesienne et creation." *Revue de Métaphysique et Morale* 44 (1): 21–34.

Brown, Thomas. 1820. *Lectures on the Philosophy of the Human Mind.* Edinburgh: Tait.

Falkenstein, Lorne. 2000. "Reid's Account of Localization." *Philosophy and Phenomenological Research* 61 (2): 305–328.

Falkenstein, Lorne. 2005. "Condillac's Paradox." *Journal of the History of Philosophy* 43 (4): 403–435.

Falkenstein, Lorne, and Giovanni Grandi. 2003. "The Role of Material Impressions in Reid's Theory of Vision: A Critique of Gideon Yaffe's 'Reid on the Perception of Visible Figure'." *Journal of Scottish Philosophy* 1 (2): 117–133.

Fearn, John. 1810/1812. *An Essay on Consciousness; or a Series of Evidences of a Distinct Mind.* 1st edition 1810, 2nd edition 1812. London: Printed by D. Cock; and Published by Longman, Hurst, Rees, Orme, and Brown; and by Black, Parry, and Kingbury.

Fearn, John. 1813a. *A Review of First Principles of Bishop Berkeley, Dr. Reid, and Professor Stewart. With an Indication of Other Principles.* London: Printed by D. Cock for Longman, Hurst, Rees, Orme, and Brown; and Black and Parry.

Fearn, John. 1813b. *Essay on External Perception.* Enlarged edition, appended to *A Review of First Principles of Bishop Berkeley, Dr. Reid, and Professor Stewart.* London: Printed by D. Cock for Longman, Hurst, Rees, Orme, and Brown; and Black and Parry.

Fearn, John. 1815a. *A Demonstration of the Principles of Primary Vision. With the Consequent State of Philosophy in Great Britain.* London: Printed by D. Cock for Longman, Hurst, Rees, Orme and Brown; and Black and Parry.

Fearn, John. 1815b. *A Demonstration of Necessary Connexion*. London: Printed by D. Cock for Longman, Hurst, Rees, Orme and Brown; and Black and Parry.

Fearn, John. 1818. "A Letter to Professor Stewart, on the Objects of General Terms and on the Axiomatical Laws of Vision. Second Edition. To which are here added some Remarks on the Monthly Review on this Subject." In *The Pamphleteer*. vol. 12. London: Printed by A.J. Valpy. Sold by Fenner; Lloyd; Black; Kingbury, Parbury, and Allen.

Fearn, John. 1820. *First Lines of the Human Mind*. London: Printed by A.J. Valpy; and Sold by Longman, Hurst, Rees, Orme, and Brown; Black, Kingbury, Parbury and Allen; and Roland Hunter. [References by chapter, section, and page numbers].

Fearn, John. 1829. *A Manual of the Physiology of Mind, Comprehending the First Principles of Physical Theology: with which are Laid Out the Crucial Objections to the Reidian Theory. To which is Suffixed a Paper on the Logic of Relations Considered as a Machine for Rationative Science.* London: Printed by A.J. Valpy; Sold by Longman, Rees, Orme, and Green; and Hunter. [References by section and page numbers].

Fearn, John. 1837. *An Appeal to Philosophers, by Name, on the Demonstration of Vision in the Brain, and Against the Attack by Sir David Brewster on the Rationale of Cerebral Vision*. London: Longman, Rees, Orme, Brown and Green.

Hatfield, Gary. 1990. *The Natural and the Normative: Theories of Spatial Perception from Kant to Helmholtz*. Cambridge, MA: MIT Press.

Hume, David. 2000. *A Treatise of Human Nature,* edited by David Fate Norton and Mary J. Norton. Oxford: Oxford University Press. [References by book, part, section, and paragraph numbers].

Hutcheson, Francis. 2002. *An Essay on the Nature and Conduct of Passions and Affections, with Illustrations on Moral Sense*, edited by Aaron Garrett. Indianapolis, IN: Liberty Fund.

Morgan, Michael J. 1977. *Molyneux's Question: Vision, Touch and the Philosophy of Perception*. Cambridge: Cambridge University Press.

Nichols, Ryan. 2007. *Thomas Reid's Theory of Perception*. Oxford: Oxford University Press.

Pastore, Nicholas. 1971. *Selective History of Theories of Visual Perception: 1650–1950*. New York: Oxford University Press.

Reid, Thomas. 1880. *The Works of Thomas Reid, D.D., with Notes and Supplementary Dissertations*, edited by William Hamilton. 2 vols, 8th edition. Edinburgh: MacLachlan and Stewart.

Reid, Thomas. 1995. *Thomas Reid on the Animate Creation: Papers Relating to the Life Sciences*, edited by Wood Paul. University Park, PA: The Pennsylvania State University Press.

Reid, Thomas. 1997. *An Inquiry into the Human Mind on the Principles of Common Sense: A Critical Edition*, edited by Derek R. Brookes. University Park, PA: The Pennsylvania State University Press. [References by chapter, section, page, and line numbers].

Reid, Thomas. 2002a. *Essays on the Intellectual Powers of Man: A Critical Edition*, edited by Derek R. Brookes. University Park, PA: The Pennsylvania State University Press. [References by essay, chapter, page, and line numbers].

Reid, Thomas. 2002b. *The Correspondence of Thomas Reid*, edited by Paul Wood. University Park, PA: The Pennsylvania State University Press.

Reid, Thomas. 2012. *Selected Philosophical Writings*, edited by Giovanni B. Grandi. Exeter: Imprint Academic.

Stewart, Dugald. 1792. *Elements of the Philosophy of the Human Mind*. London: A. Strahan and T. Cadell, and Edinburgh: W. Creech.

Stewart, Dugald. 1854. *Dissertation: Exhibiting the Progress of Metaphysical, Ethical and Political Philosophy since the Revival of Letters in Europe*. In *The Collected Works of Dugald Stewart*, edited by William Hamilton. Vol. 1. Edinburgh: T. Constable.

Stewart, Dugald. 1855. *Philosophical Essays*. In *The Collected Works of Dugald Stewart*, edited by William Hamilton. Vol. 5. Edinburgh: T. Constable.

Yaffe, Gideon. 2003a. "Reid on the Perception of Visible Figure." *Journal of Scottish Philosophy* 1 (2): 103–115.

Yaffe, Gideon. 2003b. "The Office of an Introspectible Sensation: A Reply to Falkenstein and Grandi." *Journal of Scottish Philosophy* 1 (2): 135–140.

MORAL THEORY
Reid on the moral sense

Rebecca Copenhaver

Department of Philosophy, Lewis & Clark College, Portland, OR, USA

Some interpret Reid's notion of a moral sense as merely analogical. Others understand it as a species of acquired perception. To understand Reid's account of the moral sense, we must draw from his theory of perception and his theory of aesthetic experience, each of which illuminate the nature and operation of the moral faculty. I argue that, on Reid's view, the moral faculty is neither affective nor rational, but representational. It is a discrete, basic, capacity for representing the real moral properties of humans and human conduct.

> ... *Men judge of the primary and secondary qualities of body by their external senses, of beauty and deformity by their taste, and of virtue and vice by their moral faculty.*
> -*Essays on the Active Powers of Man*, 352

1. Introduction

Although Thomas Reid depicts perceptual, aesthetic, and moral experience as unified by a common purpose and structure, his treatment of the moral faculty as a faculty of *sense* is far less committal than his treatment of, for example, aesthetic perception (Reid 2010, 352, 357).[1] Why does Reid hesitate in the case of the moral sense? In the *Essays on the Active Powers of Man*, he worries that identifying the moral faculty as a faculty of *sense* will lead readers to associate his theory with the views of his opponents: the sentimentalists (Reid 2010, 175–176, 300, 345). He fears that readers will saddle him with the view that moral properties depend on or consist in human feelings, emotions or other affective states and that moral judgment is justified and explained by appeal to affective states (Reid 2010, 175–176). But Reid faces a similar worry in dealing with aesthetic experience, and he confronts it more directly than he does in his discussion of the moral faculty. Should the moral faculty be called a faculty of *sense*? Reid is indecisive: 'It is of small consequence what name we give to this moral power of the human mind . . . I find no fault with the name *moral sense*, although I think this name has given occasion to some mistakes concerning the nature of our moral power' (Reid 2010, 300). So, does Reid mean 'perception' metaphorically or literally when he talks about the moral faculty?

Students of Reid are ambivalent too. Some think that his notion of moral perception is merely analogical. Others understand it as a species of acquired perception – but that settles the question only if we know whether acquired perception is to be taken literally or is merely a metaphor.[2] Reid's apparent ambivalence arises from not wanting to be misread: 'Modern Philosophers have conceived of the external senses as having no other office but to give us certain sensations . . . And this notion has been applied to the moral sense. But it seems to me a mistaken notion in both' (Reid 2010, 300). While Reid clearly sees the moral faculty as a faculty of sense, he knows that readers may try to understand him as if his version of perception were the usual version of his contemporaries, who promoted the sentimentalism that he opposes (Reid 2010, 345).

> The name of the *moral sense* . . . has got this name of *sense*, no doubt, from some analogy which it is conceived to bear to the external senses. And if we have just notions of the office of the external senses, the analogy is very evident, and I see no reason to take offence, as some have done, at the name of the *moral sense*.
>
> The offense taken at this name seems to be owing to this, That Philosophers have degraded the senses too much, and deprived them of the most important part of their office.
>
> This notion of the sense I take to be very lame . . . (Reid 2010, 175).
>
> When Mr. HUME derives moral distinctions from a moral sense, I agree with him in words, but we differ about the meaning of the word *sense*. Every power to which the name of sense has been given, is a power of judging of the objects of that sense, and has been accounted such in all ages; the moral sense therefore is the power of judging in morals. But Mr. HUME will have the moral sense to be only a power of feeling, without judging: This I take to be an abuse of a word (Reid 2010, 353).

Sentimentalism – like skepticism about the external world and subjectivism about aesthetic judgment – has its origin in a misguided view of perception, according to Reid. But to know whether Reid understands moral experience as a kind of perceptual experience, we need a clear account of his theory of perception. And we also need to consider his treatment of aesthetic experience for he also thinks that aesthetic sensitivity is perceptual rather than affective or intellectual (Reid 2002, 571, 603). Reid is unequivocal about aesthetic properties, calling them 'real excellences' of objects to which natural experience attunes us so that over time we become more sensitive to them (Reid 2002, 594–595). Accordingly, while Reid's account of the moral faculty is thin by contrast with his treatment of aesthetic experience, what he says about aesthetic experience can supplement his theory of perception to provide a more detailed account of the nature and operation of the moral faculty.

Deciding whether moral experience is perceptual is not just a matter of terminology, and Reid is clear about some of what needs to be settled: that there is a distinction between the outer sense and the inner senses, and that perception of external objects and their properties is via the outer sense (Reid 2002, 420–421, 573, 594; 2010, 351). Accordingly, aesthetic and moral experiences come by way of the inner senses (Reid 2002, 571, 594; 2010, 175). Then, if we stipulate that 'perception' refers only to the external sense, Reid's use of that term for aesthetic and moral experience will seem wrong. Nevertheless, Reid treats perceptual experience, aesthetic experience, and moral experience as faculties of *sense*. Each is a basic representational capacity, original to the human mind, attuned to features particular to that faculty of sense (Reid 2010, 175). Each is capable of development, whereby the faculty's sensitivity increases, enabling humans to become more sensitive to more features than those available in experience originally. Perceptual experience, aesthetic experience, and moral experience have distinct objects but not distinct functions: each is a basic capacity of the mind to represent the objects and features in its environment that figure most importantly in its proper and practical functioning.

If moral experience is a basic representational activity, alongside perceptual and aesthetic perception, the usual picture of Reid – standing with Clarke and Price as a moral rationalist, against Shaftesbury, Hutcheson, and Hume as sentimentalists – gets blurry.[3] If sentimentalists part with rationalists over the moral faculty's response to affect or reason, Reid has no stake in the fight. The moral faculty is neither affective nor rational, according to Reid, but representational: perceptual, moral, and aesthetic experiences are partly constituted by – but not reducible to – felt, affective elements, and none is a product of reasons or rationality, though each is reason-giving.

2. Perception

Central to Reid's theory of perceptual experience is his distinction between sensation and perception.[4] Sensations are the felt, qualitative, element in perceptual experience, while perceptions are the representational element. Sensations neither represent objects nor attribute qualities to them. Were a creature to sense but not perceive, the creature would have no objective experience – no experience as of objects or their qualities. By contrast, perception is a basic form of representational experience. Perceptions have a singular demonstrative element, which Reid calls a conception, and an attributive element, which he calls a belief (Reid 1997, 96). A perception consists in an apprehension of an object and an attribution of properties to the object apprehended. Perception represents apprehended objects as being thus-and-such.

Reid's use of 'conception,' and 'belief' can mislead. The conception by which objects are apprehended in perception does not involve concept-application: Reid's is a pre-Kantian notion of conception as 'simple apprehension' (Reid 2002, 295).[5] The belief or judgment – Reid uses the terms interchangeably – by which we attribute properties in perception is not a propositional attitude. Rather, belief or judgment represents the object apprehended by conception as being thus-and-such. In other words, the belief or judgment that partially composes perceptual experience is not independent of conception and is formed on the basis of it. Conception and belief together are the representational aspects of perceptual experience. A perceiver does not apprehend a blue sphere before acquiring a separate, propositional attitude to the effect that the object is blue and spherical (though she may do so). What Reid calls 'belief' or 'judgment' is what we might now call representational *content* of experience – the part of experience that presents the world as represented to the subject of experience.

While sensation and perception are distinct kinds of mental operation – the first purely phenomenal, the second representational – Reid holds that they are systematically related by laws that govern the human mind (Reid 1997, 58, 74, 122, 198). Laws of the human mind connect sensation-types with perception-types; typical humans form the same perception-types when they have the same sensation-types. Upon having a particular sensation type, for example, a properly functioning human will have a tactile experience as of hardness. According to Reid, the laws that systematically relate types of sensations to types of perceptions in humans are contingent on God's will: God could have willed (and could will) that we have some different sensation than the one we have upon touching solid objects. Because the laws that regulate the relations among sensations and perception are contingent, perceptions are metaphysically independent of sensations: the relations among sensations and perceptions are nomological rather than logical or metaphysical. As such, sensations leave perceptions underdetermined. If there were no laws governing their systematic relations to perceptions, sensations would lack the relations to perceptions that make one derivable from the other. Sensations do not represent objects or properties and do not provide an epistemic or otherwise cognitive basis for representing objects or properties.

Yet Reid claims that sensations *suggest* perceptions and are *signs* of features in the environment (Reid 1997, 177, 190–192). He takes the language of signs and suggestion from Berkeley in order to emphasize – like Berkeley – that the perceptual process should be studied in a Newtonian way through laws of nature rather than causes.[6] According to Reid, material objects and their properties *occasion* sensations while sensations *suggest* perceptions. But sensations are not of or about the objects or properties that occasion them – they have no representational content. Rather, a law of the human mind ensures that sensations suggest states with representational content: perceptions. Perceptions represent the objects and properties that occasion sensations. But because sensations suggest perceptions systematically, by a law of nature, they are about objects and their properties only in a derivative way. Absent such laws, sensations signify nothing.

According to Reid, laws of the human mind ensure that experience is attuned to basic, generic, ubiquitous features of ordinary objects – hardness, figure, color, extension, motion (Reid 1997, 57–58, 79, 105; 2002 181, 235–236). These *original* perceptions are modality-specific and stable for all properly functioning humans. For example, a normal human who has certain haptic sensations will immediately experience certain objects as having hardness, motion, and extension

(Reid 1997, 55–76). A normal human who has certain visual sensations will immediately experience certain objects as having color, illumination, and surface figure (Reid 1997, 77–87). Particular haptic sensations are original *signs* of hardness, while particular visual sensations are original *signs* of color. Original perceptions require no previous experience; they are 'judgments of nature,' grounded in the laws that establish common, basic cognitive functions attuned to basic features of objects (Reid 2002, 412).

Acquired perceptions – another notion borrowed from Berkeley – require previous experience (Reid 2002, 235). Like Berkeley, Reid holds that distance and three-dimensional figure are original only to touch; we do not see distance or depth originally. The spatial features original to visual experience are confined to two-dimensional surface figures (which Reid calls visible figure) and positions in two-dimensional space.[7] But early in their development humans notice systematic relationships between visual features and tactile features: between how things look and how things feel, thereby coming to have visual experience of spatial features previously experienced only by touch (Reid 1997, 50, 166, 191; 2002, 236, 238, 417). Visible features such as color, illumination, and surface figure acquire spatial significance – a significance to which we are not originally attuned. Once attuned, however, we experience visible features that are as much signs of hardness, motion, and extension as were the tactile sensations that originally signified those features.

> From the time that children begin to use their hands, nature directs them to handle every thing over and over, to look at it while they handle it, and to put it in various positions, and at various distances from the eye. We are apt to excuse this as a childish diversion ... but if we think more justly, we shall find, that they are engaged in the most serious and important study ... They are thereby every day acquiring the habits of perception, which are of greater importance than anything we can teach them. The original perceptions which Nature gave them are few, and insufficient for the purposes of life; and therefore she made them capable of acquiring many more perceptions by habit (Reid 1997, 201).

Though visual experience of depth and three-dimensional figure is Reid's central example of acquired perception, he extends his account of acquired perception to include experiences of higher-order properties for all sensory modalities. Though human perceptual capacities are originally attuned to a narrow range of basic features, the features to which mature humans may become perceptually sensitive in acquired perception are many and diverse (Reid 1997, 171–172, 191–192). Reid's examples highlight the miscellaneous contingency of the features to which perceivers become sensitive: the weight and quality of cattle, the weight of ships, the manner of an artistic work, kinds of jewels and whether they are counterfeits, the taste of cider and brandy, the smell of apples and oranges, the noise of thunder and ringing of bells, and the familiar example of a coach passing. The prospect of perceptual sensitivity to a cow's health seems odd to us, but Reid would feel the same about a car's speed on the street.

Is acquired perception a kind of perceptual belief – a belief formed on the basis of perception?[8] Though we often infer from perception to belief, Reid explains, what we achieve intellectually by inference is not an acquired perception. Acquired perception is uniquely *perceptual*. A person with no special knowledge of gems may *infer* that a jewel is a counterfeit from what she sees and feels. But an expert jeweler just sees the diamond for what it is, and likewise the cubic zirconia. Reid's idiosyncratic use of 'belief' and 'judgment' to describe the representational content of perceptual experience is not helpful here. Original and acquired perception, in his view, both consist in a *singular* element – a conception – and an *attributive* element – a belief or judgment. Acquired perception *attributes* features to which we are not originally attuned in perception, but it is no less perception for that. Indeed, Reid holds that original perception is impoverished and that perceptual experience of a rich, unified environment is a mature achievement based on acquired perception.

> From what has been said, I think it appears, that our original powers of perceiving objects by our senses receive great improvement by use and habit; and without this improvement, would be altogether insufficient for the purposes of life. The daily occurrences of life not only add to our stock of knowledge, but give additional perceptive powers to our senses... (Reid 2002, 239).

In *original* perception sensations – the felt, qualitative elements in perceptual experience – are the signs. The signs in *acquired* perception are the narrow range of features presented in original perception. The *objects* of original perception become the *signs* in acquired perception.[9] Vision is originally attuned to color, illumination, and surface figure, and visual sensations are original signs of those features. But humans soon develop visual sensitivity to the spatial significance of color, illumination, and surface figure, seeing cubes where they once saw two-dimensional surfaces, with color and illumination. In mature, acquired perception the original significance of sensations is screened off by – effaced by – the significance of the environmental features presented in original perception. The new role such environmental features play as signs in acquired perception dampens the significance of sensations. The sensations remain. They are partly constitutive of perceptual experience, but their significance decreases as the human perceptual system becomes increasingly sensitive to the significance of features in its environment. The development from original to acquired perception is a development towards greater objectivity; it is the normal development of the human perceptual capacity to experience a rich, detailed, fine-grained world of objects and properties.

	Faculties	Signs	Objects
External sense	Original Perception	sensations	hardness, softness, figure, motion, color, illumination, and other proper sensibles
	Acquired Perception	hardness, softness, figure, motion, color, illumination, and other proper sensibles	depth in vision, the size of bells by hearing, the weight of cattle by sight, and kind properties

One might expect that acquired perception is a kind of perceptual *belief* – not perception, strictly speaking. In addition, one might expect that aesthetic experience and moral experience are species of acquired perception. After all, an aesthetic property like beauty – and a moral property like wrongness – is a higher-order property, just the kind that may be experienced but surely cannot be *sensed*. Accordingly, James Van Cleve has argued that 'most cases of acquired perception probably do not count as perception,' an interpretation that I have contested (Van Cleve 2004; Copenhaver 2010). If acquired perception is not perception proper, and if aesthetic and moral experience belong to acquired perception, we can respond straightforwardly to Reid's frequent statements that perceiving beauty or perceiving goodness is merely analogical. Our response is at home with the taxonomy of the moral philosophers with whom Reid is customarily counted – alongside Clarke and Price – as a rationalist. If moral experience is an intellectual achievement rather than a kind of sensitivity, it is clear how he may be counted among those who hold that reason, not affect, is the ground of morality.

But acquired perception is perception properly so called, and aesthetic and moral experience mirror the external sense by each dividing into original and acquired kinds of experience. When we turn to Reid's account of aesthetic experience, we find that the inner sense of taste is structurally similar to the external sense of perception. Just as the human cognitive system is *originally* attuned to a sparse range of basic environmental features and *acquires* more developed perceptual powers through experience, so too, according to Reid, do we have both *original* and *acquired* aesthetic experience. This structural similarity between the external sense and the inner senses indicates that aesthetic experience is not confined to acquired perception. Aesthetic experience is an additional faculty of sense, with its own natural objects and its own range of features to which we become responsive through repeated experience.

Aesthetic experience, moral experience, and perceptual experience are originally attuned to, and develop sensitivities to, different features. Each is a basic representational capacity of the human mind, directed towards and increasingly responsive to objects and features in the environment.

3. Aesthetic perception

Reid's distinction between sensation and perception is central to his account of perceptual experience. Central to his account of aesthetic perception is a similar distinction between a felt, qualitative element and a representational element (Reid 2002, 592–594).[10] Aesthetic experience has two elements: an emotional or otherwise affective element, and an element by which we experience the world as being a certain way. Just as sensations are distinct from the objects and qualities that occasion them, so too the emotions that partially constitute aesthetic experience are distinct from the qualities in objects that occasion them (Reid 2002, 574, 578, 592). A law of the human mind ensures that emotions are connected to aesthetic qualities of objects such as beauty and grandeur: in this way, our emotions attuned to beauty and grandeur.

Because our emotions are systematically *connected* to basic aesthetic properties, they are *about* such properties in a derivative sense. The emotions are original signs of beauty and grandeur in the same way that our sensations are original signs of hardness, color, extension, etc. But as with sensations, the emotional element in aesthetic experience is itself non-representational. Rather, emotions suggest a state distinct from themselves, a state that represents objects as beautiful or grand. As with perception, Reid uses the terms 'belief' and 'judgment,' to describe this second element in perceptual experience (Reid 2002, 577, 578, 592). Emotions as signs of aesthetic properties suggest states that represent the world as beautiful or grand – judgments of taste. As in the case of perception, we should not be misled by Reid's description of such states as beliefs or judgments. The state is not a verdict on or attitude towards a proposition. Rather, it is a representation of an object in the environment as being a certain way. More precisely, it is like what we might now call the representational *content* of aesthetic experience.

Sensation underdetermines perception; emotions underdetermine judgments of taste (Reid 2002, 592–594). The relationship between the emotional and representational elements of aesthetic experience is nomological rather than logical or metaphysical. Emotions themselves do not represent objects as beautiful or grand, nor do they ground judgments of taste epistemically or cognitively. Absent the laws that connect emotions with experiences that represent objects as beautiful or grand, the agreeable emotions we enjoy in aesthetic experience signify nothing.

The structural similarities between Reid's account of perception and his account of aesthetic experience are not confined to his distinction between the phenomenal and representational elements of experience. He also reproduces the distinction between original and acquired perception (Reid 2002, 493). Recall that, according to Reid, the human mind is perceptually sensitive originally to a narrow range of very basic features such as hardness, color, motion, extension, and figure. The original signs of these features are sensations. This basic, original perceptual capacity is stable across humans: immediately upon having a particular haptic sensation, a normal human will experience an object as hard; immediately upon having a particular visual sensation, a normal human will experience an object as red. Likewise, according to Reid, immediately upon enjoying a particular emotion, a normal human will experience an object as beautiful.

> Some objects strike us at one, and appear beautiful at first sight, without any reflection, without our being able to say why we call them beautiful, or being able to specify any perfection which justifies our judgment. Something of this kind there seems to be in brute animals, and in children before the use of reason; nor does it end with infancy, but continues through life (Reid 2002, 596).

Such aesthetic experiences are original to our constitution; they are judgments of nature (Reid 1997, 169; 2002, 412). All properly functioning humans are disposed to form these *instinctive judgments of taste* regardless of previous experience, by laws that establish a common cognitive ability attuned to basic aesthetic features of the environment. This is why infants are drawn to shiny objects and regular forms. The emotions infants enjoy are attuned to such features. Upon having such emotions, we immediately experience objects as aesthetically valuable.

> In a heap of pebbles, one that is remarkable for brilliancy of color and regularity of figure, will be picked out of the heap by a child. He perceives a beauty in it, puts a value upon it, and is fond of the property of it. For this preference, no reason can be given, but that children are, by their constitution, fond of brilliant colors, and of regular figures (Reid 2002, 598).

Instinctive judgments of taste are like original perception. Upon having certain emotions, a normal human will experience an object as beautiful or grand. Accordingly, Reid's acquired perception finds its counterpart in aesthetic experience in what he calls *rational judgments of taste* (Reid 2002, 493, 595–596, 598–599, 602, 605, 607, 613). But moving from original to acquired perception shifts the significance – from the significance of sensations to the significance of the features presented in original perception, as when we respond to the spatial significance of color, illumination, and surface figure by seeing a cube, not just a two-dimensional figure variously colored and illuminated. Likewise, moving from instinctive judgments of taste to rational judgments of taste shifts the significance. According to Reid, humans develop increasingly sensitive aesthetic capacities as they mature, no longer merely sensing 'the beauties of the field, of the forest, and of the flower-garden' but also understanding their significance (Reid 2002, 493, 598, 607). Maturing humans no longer just enjoy big, shiny objects that they experience as beautiful or grand; they start to recognize what makes them beautiful or grand.

Rational judgments of taste are not rational in the sense of being products of reasoning, inference or any other discursive acts of mind. But they are reason-giving: by making the judgments, we respond to the aesthetic *significance* of the features presented in original aesthetic experience. Just as the infant playing with her blocks is learning the spatial significance of the visible features given her in original perception, so too, the infant drawn to big, shiny things is learning the aesthetic significance of the beautiful things to which she is instinctively drawn.

> To make an end of this subject, taste seems to be progressive as man is. Children ... are disposed to attend to the objects about them; they are pleased with brilliant colors, gaudy ornaments, regular forms, cheerful countenances, noisy mirth, and glee. Such is the taste of childhood, which we must conclude to be given for wise purposes ... It leads them to attend to objects which they may afterwards find worthy of their attention. It puts them upon exerting their infant faculties of body and mind, which, by such exertions, are daily strengthened and improved (Reid 2002, 613).

By rational judgments of taste we respond to the reasons that ground our experiences of objects as beautiful or grand. We begin to understand the significance of aesthetic properties in our environment – we understand *why* an object is beautiful or grand, we understand the beauty and grandeur of objects as expressions. But what is the significance of those properties? Behind a distinction that bears on the question, the distinction between original and acquired aesthetic experience – or between instinctive and rational judgments of taste – lies another of Reid's distinctions: between *original beauty* and *derived* beauty.

We are naturally attuned to beauty and grandeur in objects, but they are *derived* rather than *original* (Reid 2002, 599, 602). Beauty and grandeur are in objects only *derivatively*, as signs of *original* beauty. *Original* beauty and grandeur belong to minds, not to objects; they are excellences of the author, artist, or craftsman (Reid 2002, 587, 591, 599, 601–604). 'I apprehend, therefore, that it is in the moral and intellectual perfections of mind, and in its active powers, that beauty originally dwells; and that from this as the fountain, all the beauty which we perceive in the visible world is derived' (Reid 2002, 602). The derived beauty and grandeur of objects are signs of original properties of excellent minds.

Derived beauty is the proper object of *instinctive judgments of taste*, while *original beauty* is the proper object of *rational judgments of taste*. We make rational judgments of taste when the derived beauty of an object becomes legible as a sign of the original excellences of mind that created it – when, in aesthetic experience we 'begin to discern beauties of mind' (Reid 2002, 613). Where a child may instinctively recognize the beauty in a work of art, a mature human, having a developed aesthetic sense, understands how and why a work of art expresses and exemplifies the virtues of the craftsman.

> A work of art may appear beautiful to the most ignorant, even to a child. It pleases, but he knows not why. To one who understands it perfectly, and perceives how every part is fitted with exact judgment to its end, the beauty is not mysterious; it is perfectly comprehended; and he knows wherein it consists, as well as how it affects him (Reid 2002, 574).

The signs in instinctive aesthetic experience are emotions – the felt, qualitative elements in aesthetic experience. The signs in mature, rational, aesthetic experience are the derived beauties of objects presented in instinctive aesthetic experience. In other words, *the objects* of instinctive aesthetic experience – derived beauty and grandeur – become *the signs* in mature aesthetic experience. In mature aesthetic experience, the original significance of emotion is screened off by the significance of the derived beauties and grandeur of objects. The role derived beauty plays as a sign of an excellent mind dampens the significance of emotion. As with perceptual experience, the felt element of aesthetic experience remains. The emotions remain. They are partly constitutive of aesthetic experience. But their significance decreases as aesthetic experience becomes more and more sensitive to reasons that ground judgments of taste – more sensitive, that is, to the original beauty and grandeur of minds.

These are structural similarities between perceptual and aesthetic experience.

	Faculties		Signs	Objects
External sense	Original Perception		sensations	hardness, softness, figure, motion, color, illumination, and other proper sensibles
	Acquired Perception		hardness, softness, figure, motion, color, illumination, and other proper sensibles	depth in vision, the size of bells by hearing, the weight of cattle by sight, and kind properties
Internal sense	Aesthetic Perception	Instinctive Judgments of Taste	feelings/emotions	derived beauty: perfections in objects, e.g., shininess, symmetry, concordance, etc.
		Rational Judgments of Taste	derived beauty: perfections in objects, e.g., shininess, symmetry, concordance, etc.	original beauty: perfections of minds, e.g., moral virtues and intellectual virtues

Since Reid knew that he might be misread as a subjectivist about aesthetic qualities, he opens his essay *Of Taste* by distinguishing his account from those that make aesthetic qualities identical with or dependent on affective or emotional responses (Reid 2002, 574). He agrees that emotions are partly constitutive of aesthetic experience: normally functioning humans enjoy agreeable emotions upon perceiving beautiful and grand objects. Emotions are signs to which humans instinctively respond by representing objects as beautiful or grand. Moreover, the beauty and grandeur of objects derives from the original beauty and grandeur of minds, thus depending on qualities of mind. As mind-dependent, aesthetic qualities may be secondary: mere modes of mind, not of objects. Does Reid think that beauty and grandeur reside in feelings, emotions, or other affective mental states?[11]

Reid responds by insisting that the beauty and grandeur of objects, though derived, are real properties of objects, what he calls *real excellences* (Reid 2002, 595). An object is beautiful or grand if it expresses or exemplifies the virtues of the mind that created it (Reid 2002, 587). An object has beauty or grandeur independently of whether anyone experiences it as beautiful or grand (Reid 2002, 595). 'It depends no doubt upon our constitution, whether we do, or do not perceive excellence where it really is: But the object has its excellence from its own constitution and not from ours' (Reid 2002, 584). An object is excellent by expressing or exemplifying the original excellences of the mind of its craftsman or creator. An object may fail to excel – a painting may be badly painted, for example – but whether it fails or succeeds in expressing the excellences of its author turns on the object itself. It is the painting that is beautiful or crude because it fulfills or does not fulfill in greater or lesser degree its expressive function (Reid 2002, 574).

Beauty and grandeur are mind-dependent but not subjective; beauty and grandeur are mind-dependent but not response-dependent. They depend on the existence of subjects for their existence, but not upon the experiences of apprehending subjects. Were there no minds, there would be no beautiful or grand objects: the beauty and grandeur of objects resides in their ability to express or exemplify wisdom, magnanimity, innocence, gentleness, fortitude, self-command and so on (Reid 2002, 601). Though beauty and grandeur in objects depend on and are derived from the excellences of minds, the dependency or derivation makes them no less real or objective.

Discussing the emotions that instinctively signify beauty and grandeur, Reid insists that they are distinct from the real properties of objects that occasion them, just as sensations are distinct from the properties that occasion them. 'When a beautiful object is before us, we may distinguish the agreeable emotion it produces in us, from the quality of the objects which causes that emotion' (Reid 2002, 574). Beauty and grandeur are real properties of objects, neither identical with nor dependent on emotional responses: '... beauty belongs to this excellence of the object, and not to the feeling of the spectator' (Reid 2002, 595). Beauty and grandeur are metaphysically independent of feelings, emotions, or any other affective states of a subject. Although we respond to the beauty and grandeur of objects by enjoying agreeable emotions, the response is grounded in a law of the human mind. The relationship between emotions and beauty is merely nomological. Emotions, alone of themselves, are insufficient for aesthetic experience. They neither represent objects as beautiful nor provide a basis to form aesthetic judgments. We cannot explain or justify judgments of taste by appeal to emotions.

Yet Reid admits that 'some of the qualities that please good taste resemble the secondary qualities of body ... ' (Reid 2002, 574). The 'secondary qualities' that Reid has in mind, far from supporting any subjectivism, are his weapons against the theory of ideas, a theory that he regards as inevitably skeptical, idealist, sentimentalist and subjectivist. The theory of ideas proceeds upon a mistaken conception of secondary qualities. According to that theory, secondary qualities are identical with, or depend on, sensations. But this is just what Reid's theory of perception denies. He sees secondary properties as real properties of objects, distinct from the sensations that occasion them.

> This ought the rather to be observed, because it has become a fashion among modern Philosophers, to resolve all our perceptions into mere feelings or sensations in the person that perceives, without anything corresponding to those feelings in the external object. According to those Philosophers, there is no heat in the fire, no taste in a sapid body; the taste and the heat being only in the person that feels them. In like manner, there is no beauty in any object whatsoever; it is only a sensation or feeling in the person that perceives it.
>
> I had occasion to show, that there is no solid foundation for it when applied to the secondary qualities of body; and the same arguments show equally, that it has no solid foundation when applied to the beauty of objects, or to any of those qualities that are perceived by good taste (Reid 2002, 574).

In Reid's genealogy of skepticism, subjectivism, and sentimentalism, the trouble starts with Descartes, who taught that 'many things supposed to have an external existence, were only conceptions or feelings in the mind' (Reid 2002, 583–584). Locke then distinguished primary properties from secondary properties, locating the former in objects while transporting the latter to mind. Locke's disciples followed his habit of 'converting into feelings things that were believed to have an external existence,' by making 'extension, solidity, figure and all the primary qualities of body ... sensations or feelings in the mind' (Reid 2002, 583–584). Hutcheson was then 'carried away' by Locke's distinction and applied 'to beauty, what DES CARTES and LOCKE had taught concerning the secondary qualities' (Reid 2002, 594). Losing no momentum, modern philosophers recognized that it ...

> ... was then a very natural progress to conceive, that beauty, harmony, and grandeur, the objects of taste, as well as right and wrong, the objects of moral faculty, are nothing but feelings of the mind ... Mr HUME ... put the finishing stroke to it, by making truth and error to be feelings in the mind, and belief to be an operation of the sensitive part of our nature (Reid 2002, 584).

Reid's story shows that he does not treat secondary properties as modifications of mind or mind-dependent. Even though some aesthetic qualities are *like* secondary properties, secondary properties are real properties of objects. If some aesthetic qualities are like secondary properties, this is consistent with making aesthetic properties real excellences of objects.

> In objects that please the taste, we always judge that there is some real excellence, some superiority to those that do not please. In some cases, that superior excellence is distinctly perceived, and can be pointed out; in other cases, we have only a general notion of some excellence we cannot describe. Beauties of the former kind may be compared to the primary qualities perceived by the external senses; those of the latter kind, to the secondary (Reid 2002, 578).

Reid's rhetoric is a symptom of the bind he finds himself in when arguing that the aesthetic faculty is a faculty of sense. He wants the aesthetic faculty to take its place alongside the external sense of perception and the internal moral faculty as a capacity to represent real features in the environment. He claims that perceptual, aesthetic, and moral experiences are basic ways of representing a world of real objects and properties. However, those raised in the theory of ideas cannot help but construe sense-talk as the mere having of sensations, feelings, or emotions. Interpreting Reid's theory this way – as an appendix to the theory of ideas – saddles him with the very view that he rejects and attacks, whereby the mind is directed towards itself and its own subjective states rather than the world.

4. The moral faculty

On Reid's view, perceptual experience and aesthetic experience are distinct yet structurally similar representational capacities basic and original to the human mind. The range and responsiveness of these capacities is not static. Each faculty responds originally to a narrow range of features but eventually acquires greater sensitivity to many more through repeated experience. Each faculty is directed towards features in the environment rather than to the effects of such features on the mind. These features are real and independent of the responses of experiencing subjects. Perceptual experience represents objects as red, as round, as fruit, as tomatoes. Aesthetic experience represents objects as beautiful, as grand, as expressing gentleness, as exemplifying courage.

So too, what Reid calls the *moral faculty*, or *conscience*, or *the moral sense*, is directed towards and represents real properties in the environment: e.g., rightness and wrongness. 'We judge of colours by the eye; of sounds by the ear; of beauty and deformity by taste; of right and wrong in conduct by our moral sense or conscience' (Reid 2002, 424; Reid 2010, 170, 175, 180, 186–195, 185, 300). Moral experience represents behaviour as wrong, as right, as malicious, as just, as mean (Reid 2010, 195). As with perception and taste, the moral faculty is a representational capacity basic and original to the human mind. We do not first observe some behaviour and then judge that behaviour to be right. Rather, the moral faculty consists in a capacity to experience (for which Reid often uses the word 'perceive') conduct as right, wrong, just or unjust.

> [B]y an original power of the mind, which we call *conscience*, or the *moral faculty*, we have the conceptions of right and wrong in human conduct, of merit and demerit, of duty and moral obligation, and our other moral conceptions; and that, by the same faculty, we perceive some things in human conduct to be right and others to be wrong; that the first principles of morals are the dictates of this faculty; and that we have the same reason to rely upon those dictates, as upon the determinations of our senses, or of our other natural faculties (Reid 2010, 180).

Moral experience, like perceptual and aesthetic experience, consists in a felt element and a representational element. Aesthetic experience, according to Reid, consists in an emotion and a judgment of taste. Perceptual experience consists in a sensation and a perception. Perception itself, according to Reid, is composed of two elements: a singular demonstrative element, which he calls a conception, and an attributive element that represents the object conceived as thus-and-such: for example, as red or round. We find similar elements in Reid's account of moral experience, which – like aesthetic experience – consists in an emotion and a judgment: a felt element and a representational element (Reid 2010, 180, 350, 352). Like perceptual experience, moral judgment is also composed of two further elements: a conception of a behaviour that expresses or exemplifies rightness or wrongness, and an approval or disapproval of that behaviour *as* right or *as* wrong. Reid calls the former a *moral judgment* and the latter *approbation* or *disapprobation*. Just as the attributive element in perception depends on conceiving or apprehending the object to which properties are attributed, the evaluative element in moral experience depends on representing an action as right or wrong and thus worthy of approval or disapproval *as such*.

> Of this faculty the operations appear to me, the judging ultimately of what it right, what is wrong, and what is indifferent in the conduct of moral agents; the approbation of good conduct and disapprobation of bad in consequence of that

judgment, and the agreeable emotions which attend obedience, and disagreeable which attend disobedience to its dictates (Reid 2010, 185).

As we have seen, although sensations suggest perceptions by a law of nature, they are metaphysically distinct from perceptions. Sensation underdetermines perception and forms no cognitive or epistemic basis from which to infer to the objects and properties represented in experience. Emotions in aesthetic experience are connected to judgments of taste – again, merely nomologically. Emotions underdetermine aesthetic judgment and cannot justify or explain experiences of objects as beautiful or grand. So too, the emotions that partially constitute moral experience are distinct from and underdetermine the representational content of moral experience. 'I know, that what a man judges to be a very worthy action, he contemplates with pleasure; and what he contemplates with pleasure must, in his judgment, have worth. But the judgment and the feeling are different acts of his mind... ' (Reid 2010, 350; 180, 183, 348–349, 352). Humans respond emotionally to kindness, meanness, gentleness, and other morally significant behaviours we feel pleasure when we experience one person helping another person up after a fall; we feel displeasure when we experience one person rudely interrupting another. But our moral judgments do not consist in these responses, nor do they depend on them.

Indeed, the relationship between moral emotions and moral judgments is less salient in Reid's account than the relationships between sensations and perceptions and between aesthetic emotions and aesthetic judgments. Sensations suggest perceptions of extension, figure, color, illumination and so on, as original *signs* of these very basic properties. Aesthetic emotions, like a child's glee at seeing a shiny thing, suggest experiences of beauty as *signs* of excellences in objects. But moral emotions do not suggest states that represent behaviour as morally relevant and morally evaluable. The pleasure and displeasure felt in moral experience are the *result* of such apprehension and evaluation, not their antecedents (Reid 2010, 348–349). As such, moral emotions are not *signs* of moral features of human conduct. Sensations are signs because they suggest perceptions. Delight and glee are signs because they suggest our original experiences of beauty and grandeur. But because our agreeable and disagreeable feelings as we live with other persons do not suggest original experiences of rightness, wrongness, justice, injustice, etc., those feelings cannot be *signs* of basic moral features – at least not as sensations and aesthetic emotions are signs.

Given Reid's account of the role of emotion in moral experience, what is his etiology of our original conceptions of moral properties? Normal humans who have certain sensations immediately experience objects as hard, soft, extended and so on. Likewise for having certain emotions and experiencing objects as beautiful or grand. These original perceptions and instinctive judgments of taste have moral counterparts, according to Reid.

> As the eye not only gives us the conceptions of colors, but makes us perceive one
> body to have one color, and another body another... so our conscience, or moral

faculty, not only gives us the conception of honest and dishonest, but makes us perceive one kind of conduct to be honest, another to be dishonest...

That these sentiments are not the effect of education or of acquired habits, we have the same reason to conclude, as that our perception of what is true and what false, is not the effect of education or acquired habits (Reid 2010, 327).

The moral faculty, like the external senses and the internal sense of beauty and grandeur, is capable of *original* conceptions, and these are 'ideas of right and wrong in human conduct' (Reid 2010, 195; 176, 179, 180, 279, 327). But what occasions these original conceptions? What signs suggest the moral significance of human conduct immediately, prior to experience? Not the moral emotions. As noted above, the moral emotions are *effects* of our apprehending and evaluating the moral significance of features in our environment. They neither *suggest* such apprehension or evaluation, nor *signify* moral properties. Rather, according to Reid, *human conduct* suggests our original conceptions of rightness, wrongness, and other basic moral properties. Normal humans attending to human behaviour immediately experience it as honest, dishonest, right, wrong, magnanimous, mean and so on. The relevant human conduct is a *sign* of a moral property.

Our first moral conceptions are probably got by attending coolly to the conduct of others, and observing what moves our approbation, what our indignation. These sentiments spring from our moral faculty as naturally as the sensations of sweet and bitter from the faculty of taste. They have their natural objects (Reid, 2010, 279).

A man in company, without doing good or evil, without uttering an articulate sound, may behave himself gracefully, civilly, politely; or on the contrary, meanly, rudely, and impertinently. We see the dispositions of his mind, by their natural signs in his countenance and behavior, in the same manner as we perceive the figure and other qualities of bodies by the sensations which nature hath connected with them (Reid 1997, 191).

Human behaviour, in Reid's theory, does for moral experience what sensations do for perceptual experience and emotions do for aesthetic experience: as ensured by laws of the human mind, they suggest original conceptions of the most basic features to which those faculties are attuned. The laws governing the faculties give sensations, emotions, and behaviour a derivative significance. Absent such laws, sensation, emotion, and behavior signify nothing. There are laws of nature to assure that some sensations have an original spatial significance, some emotions have an original aesthetic significance, and some human behavior has an original moral significance.

Human behavior is a sign of moral properties, according to Reid. Yet he also holds that the moral significance of human behavior is the *object* of moral experience. The function of the moral faculty, he claims, is 'to shew us what is good, what bad, and what indifferent in human conduct' (Reid 2010, 191). Signs direct the mind to objects and features other than the sign itself. Sensations direct the mind toward such basic features of objects as hardness and color. Emotions direct the mind to the beauty and grandeur in the world. If human conduct is both sign and object, does it direct the mind to itself?

According to Reid, the object of *original* aesthetic experience is *derived* beauty: the beauty of objects, which he treats as a real excellence. Objects have real excellence inasmuch as they express or exemplify the artist's, craftsman's or creator's original beauty. Objects have beauty and grandeur as signs of an excellent mind. At first, a young mind is directed only or mainly to the derived beauty itself of objects. A mature mind, capable of acquired aesthetic experience, is directed to the significance of this derived beauty – directed by the *derived beauty of objects* to the *original beauty of minds*.

The moral significance of human behavior, according to Reid, is likewise derived from the original moral properties of mind. Human conduct is morally significant inasmuch as it expresses moral properties of the agent whose conduct it is: 'Their external behavior and conduct in life expresses the good and bad qualities of their mind' (Reid 2002, 603). Just as the beauty of an object is a real excellence of the object, the rightness of an action is a real property of the action.

> ...[E]steem and benevolent regard, not only accompany real worth by the constitution of our nature, but are perceived to be really and properly due to it; and...on the contrary, unworthy conduct really merits dislike and indignation.
>
> There is no judgment at the heart of man more clear, or more irresistible than this, That esteem and regard are really due to good conduct, and the contrary to base and unworthy conduct (Reid 2010, 181, 236).

An action is right insofar as it successfully expresses or exemplifies virtues of the agent who acts: '...all human actions, considered in a moral view, are either good, bad, or indifferent' (Reid 2010, 177; 180, 191). As an expression of agency, human behavior has moral significance, to which we are originally attuned. Detached from agency, human behavior lacks moral significance. Just as a purely accidental object could not be beautiful or grand, according to Reid, a mere event could not be mean or just. Human conduct is morally significant, but its significance derives from the original moral qualities of agents.

> ...[P]ower, wisdom, and goodness, are properly the attributes of mind only...
>
> Some figures of speech are so natural and common in all languages, that we are led to think them literal and proper expressions. Thus an action is called brave, virtuous, generous; but it is evident, that valour, virtue, generosity, are the attributes of persons only, and not of actions. In the action considered abstractly, there is neither valour, nor virtue, nor generosity... (Reid 2002, 587).

The goodness and fairness of an action is a sign of what a virtuous mind would do. In aesthetic experience, the human mind is directed originally to the derived beauty of objects. In moral experience, the human mind is directed originally to the derived moral value of human behavior. Human behavior is a sign in moral experience, and the moral value of human behavior derives from the original moral value of agents. Given this pattern of derivations from originals, will Reid extend his account of perceptual and aesthetic experience to understand moral experience developmentally? The moral faculty is originally attuned to basic moral features of behavior, he claims, and '...like all other powers, it comes to maturity by insensible degrees, and may be much aided in its strength and vigour by proper culture' (Reid 2010, 186; 186–195, 277–278). Something like the distinction between original and acquired perception, and like the distinction between instinctive and rational judgments of taste, underwrites Reid's account of the moral faculty.

Humans are instinctively attuned to the moral significance of facial expressions, tones of voice, gestures, and other body language: 'The features of the human face, the modulations of the voice, and the proportions, attitudes, and gesture of the body, are all natural expressions of good or bad qualities of the person, and derive a beauty or deformity from the qualities which they express' (Reid 1997, 60, 190–191; Reid 2002, 141, 185, 484–486, 493–494, 503, 603; Reid 2010, 141, 331–333). As with other signs, the relations between facial expressions, tones of voice, gestures, and the qualities of mind they signify is nomological, not metaphysical or logical. By themselves, a smile, a whisper, or a shrug signify nothing. But because they are systematically connected by a law of nature with friendliness, gentleness, and indifference, they are reliable (not infallible) signs of those mental qualities. Expressions, gestures, and tones are signs in an *original* way, claims Reid, not an acquired way because we respond to their significance immediately, prior to experience.

> The signs in natural language are features of the face, gestures of the body, and modulations of the voice; the variety of which is suited to the variety of things signified by them. Nature hath established a real connection between these signs, and the thoughts and dispositions of the mind which are signified by them; and nature hath taught us the interpretation of these signs; so that, previous to experience, the sign suggest the thing signified, and creates the belief of it (Reid 1997; Reid 2010, 331–332).

A keen observer of children, Reid notes their sensitivity to the moral import of an angry look, a soothing voice, or a melancholy tone. Infants play with blocks to learn the spatial significance of visible features (Reid 1997, 160; 2002, 484–485). Children pick shiny, symmetrical pebbles from a heap to learn the aesthetic significance of the beauty of objects. A father playing peek-a-boo with his daughter; a mother raising and lowering her voice in telling a story; a sibling play-pinching and sticking out his tongue at his little sister: each is teaching the child the moral significance of human behaviour.

The perceptual, aesthetic, and moral faculties are attuned to basic, ubiquitous features in the environment. Originally, the mind is directed in perception to such features as shape, extension, and color. In mature, acquired perceptual experience, the mind is directed to the significance of these features. Originally, the mind is directed in aesthetic experience to the beauty of objects. In mature, acquired aesthetic experience, the mind is directed by the derived beauty of objects to the original beauty of minds. Originally, the mind is directed to the moral value of human behaviour. In mature, acquired moral experience, the mind is directed to the *significance* of human behaviour. It is directed by the derived moral value of *behaviour* to the original moral value of *agents*. The mind attends not to the behaviour, but to what that behaviour expresses or exemplifies, to what it says about the person whose behaviour it is. The object of instinctive moral experience – human conduct – becomes *the sign* in mature moral experience. In mature moral experience, the original significance of facial expressions, vocal inflection, and gesture is screened off by the significance of moral qualities of the agent. The role of human conduct as a sign of a virtuous or vicious mind dampens the significance of behaviour itself.

Though Reid does not use the phrases 'instinctive moral judgment,' 'rational moral judgment,' 'derived moral value,' and 'original moral value,' these phrases help show how his theories of perception and aesthetic experience extend to his account of the moral faculty:

	Faculties		Signs	Objects
External sense	Original Perception		sensations	hardness, softness, figure, motion, color, illumination, and other proper sensibles
	Acquired Perception		hardness, softness, figure, motion, color, illumination, and other proper sensibles	depth in vision, the size of bells by hearing, the weight of cattle by sight, and kind properties
Internal sense	Aesthetic Perception	Instinctive Judgments of Taste	feelings/emotions	derived beauty: perfections in objects, e.g., shininess, symmetry, concordance, etc.
		Rational Judgments of Taste	derived beauty: perfections in objects, e.g., shininess, symmetry, concordance, etc.	original beauty: perfections of minds, e.g., moral virtues and intellectual virtues
	Moral Perception	Instinctive Moral Judgments	facial expressions, body language, vocal inflections	derived moral value: behaviour, conduct, actions
		Rational Moral Judgments	derived moral value: behaviour, conduct, actions	original moral value: moral virtues: valor, generosity, magnanimity, etc.

5. Conclusion

Is Reid's moral faculty a faculty of sense? Is moral experience perceptual? The best answer to these questions is that the moral faculty is a basic representational faculty, independent of – but on a par with – such other basic representational faculties as the external senses and the internal sense of taste. By the moral faculty, we experience the world as being a certain way, becoming sensitive to real features in the environment, becoming responsive to a larger range of morally relevant properties. At first we respond only or mainly to real moral properties of human conduct. But as we mature, we recognize the moral *significance* of human conduct, coming to understand how and why human behaviour expresses and exemplifies the equally real virtues and vices of agents. We become sensitive to the goodness, fairness, maliciousness, and meanness of other people. We see through the signs in human behaviour to what behaviours signify: the real moral qualities of persons.

> The involuntary signs of the passions and dispositions of the mind, in the voice, features, and action, are a part of the human constitution which deserves admiration. The signification of those signs is known to all men by nature, and previous to all experience.
>
> They are so many openings into the souls of our fellow-men, by which their sentiments become visible to the eye. They are a natural language common to mankind... (Reid 2010, 141).

Reid's reluctance to call the moral faculty a faculty of sense reflects his antagonism to sentimentalism and to the theory of mind that he sees as the source of sentimentalism, skepticism, idealism, and subjectivism. The moral faculty, a faculty of sense, is not reducible to or grounded in the having of sensations, feelings, emotions or any other affective state. Emotions are partially constitutive of moral experience. But moral emotions underdetermine moral experience. They are distinct from the real moral properties represented in experience and from the judgments by which we represent conduct and persons as good or bad. Appeal to the moral emotions neither justifies nor explains our apprehension and evaluation of the morally relevant features in the environment. Though we respond to such features with emotion, our apprehension and evaluation of morally relevant features does not depend on this response.

Reid wants to recognize the affective elements in aesthetic and moral experience without obligating himself to a theory of mind that reduces our capacities for objective representation to mere sensation or affect. In the final essay of the *Active Powers*, Reid reiterates his gloomy genealogy in order to explain his ambivalence about the phrase 'moral sense.' The passage is strikingly similar to his defense of aesthetic experience against the subjectivist interpretation.

> DES CARTES and Mr LOCKE went no farther than to maintain that the secondary qualities of body, heat and cold, sound, colour, taste and smell, which we perceive and judge to be in the external object, are mere feelings or sensations in our minds, there being nothing in bodies themselves to which these names can be applied; and that the office of the external senses is not to judge of external things, but only to give us ideas or sensations, from which we are by reasoning to deduce the existence of a material world without us, as well as we can.
>
> ARTHUR COLLIER and BISHOP BERKELEY discovered, from the same principles, that the primary, as well as the secondary, qualities of bodies, such as extension, figure, solidity, motion, are only sensations in our minds; and therefore, that there is no material world without us at all.
>
> The same philosophy, when it came to be applied to matters of taste, discovered that beauty and deformity are not any thing in the objects, to which men, from the beginning of the world, ascribed to them, but certain feelings in the mind of the spectator.

The next step was an easy consequence from all the preceding, that moral approbation and disapprobation are not judgments, which must be true or false, but barely, agreeable and uneasy feelings or sensations.

Mr HUME made the last step in this progress, and crowned the system by what he calls his *hypothesis*, to wit, That belief is more properly an act of the sensitive, than of the cogitative part of our nature (Reid 2010, 345).

Reid is no sentimentalist. Nor is he a moral rationalist who takes moral judgments to be products of reason. On Reid's view, the moral faculty is a faculty of moral judgment, but moral judgments are not products of reason, rationality or other discursive acts of mind. Humans do not first perceive human conduct and then proceed to moral judgments of the conduct or of the person whose conduct it is. Our relevant experience represents persons and conduct as having moral properties in the first instance. Mature moral experience is rational only in the sense that it is reason-giving. Mature humans do not merely sense a cold shoulder or a friendly voice; we understand what these behaviours express and how and why they express them. Reid's moral faculty is neither affective nor rational, but representational. It is a discrete, basic, capacity for representing the real moral properties of humans and human conduct.

Notes

1. I wish to thank the departments of philosophy at Williams College and Harvard University, at which earlier versions of this paper were presented. I thank Brian Copenhaver, Terence Cuneo, Esther Kroeker, Patrick Rysiew, and James Van Cleve for their comments. I thank my fellow participants at the New Essays on Reid workshop for their comments and conversation.
2. There is a significant and growing literature on Reid's account of the moral faculty. Roeser (2010) collects several contributions to this literature, including: Kroeker (2010) and Broadie (2010). See also Cuneo (2003, 2006).
3. For an extended treatment of the ways in which Reid ill-fits the rationalist-sentimentalist distinction, see Cuneo (2013).
4. For extended treatments of Reid's theory of perception, see Copenhaver, (2004), Nichols, (2007) and Van Cleve, (2004).
5. See Wolterstorff, (2004), and Van Cleve (2004).
6. For an extended treatment of Reid's indebtedness to Berkeley, see Copenhaver (2013).
7. On this point Reid begins to depart from Berkeley. Berkeley insists that original visual experience is in no way spatial – not even two-dimensional. Reid holds that visible figure and what he calls 'real figure,' are inter-derivable, while Berkeley holds that the features present in visual and haptic experience are heterogeneous and incommensurate.
8. For an extended treatment of Reid's theory of acquired perception, see Copenhaver (2010).
9. I intend this as a point concerning the *general* structure of original and acquired perception. Though there are cases of acquired perception in which sensations are signs, the general case is one in which the objects of original perception become signs in acquired perception.
10. For an extended treatment of Reid's theory of aesthetic perception, see Copenhaver, forthcoming.
11. Indeed, some current scholars read Reid as a subjectivist. See Manns (1998).

References

Broadie, Alexander. 2010. "Reid Making Sense of Moral Sense." In *Reid on Ethics*, edited by Sabine Roeser, 91–102. Basingstoke: Palgrave Macmillan.

Cuneo, Terence. 2003. "Reidian Moral Perception." *Canadian Journal of Philosophy* 33 (2): 229–258.

Cuneo, Terence. 2006. "Signs of Value: Reid on the Evidential Role of Feelings in Moral Judgment." *British Journal for the History of Philosophy* 14 (1): 69–91.

Cuneo, Terence. 2013. "Reason and the Passions." In *The Oxford Handbook of British Philosophy in the Eighteenth Century*, edited by James A. Harris, 226–247. Oxford: Oxford University Press.

Copenhaver, Rebecca. 2004. "A Realism for Reid: Mediated but Direct." *British Journal for the History of Philosophy* 12 (1): 61–74.

Copenhaver, Rebecca. 2010. "Thomas Reid on Acquired Perception." *Pacific Philosophical Quarterly* 91 (3): 285–312.

Copenhaver, Rebecca. 2013. "Perception and the Language of Nature." In *The Oxford Handbook of British Philosophy in the Eighteenth Century*, edited by James A. Harris, 107–127. Oxford: Oxford University Press.

Copenhaver, Rebecca. Forthcoming. "Thomas Reid on Aesthetic Perception." In *Mind, Knowledge and Action: Essays in Honor of Thomas Reid's Tercentenary*, edited by Todd Buras and Rebecca Copenhaver.

Kroeker, Esther R. 2010. "Reid on Natural Signs, Taste and Moral Perception." In *Reid on Ethics*, edited by Sabine Roeser, 46–66. Basingstoke: Palgrave Macmillan.

Manns, James. 1988. "Beauty and Objectivity in Thomas Reid." *British Journal of Aesthetics* 28 (2): 119–131.

Nichols, Ryan. 2007. *Thomas Reid's Theory of Perception*. Oxford: Oxford University Press.

Reid, Thomas. 1997. *Inquiry into the Human Mind on the Principles of Common Sense*, edited by Derek R. Brookes. Edinburgh: Edinburgh University Press.

Reid, Thomas. 2002. *Essays on the Intellectual Powers of Man*, edited by Derek R. Brookes. Edinburgh: Edinburgh University Press.

Reid, Thomas. 2010. *Essays on the Active Powers of Man*, edited by Knud Haakonssen, and James A. Harris. Edinburgh: Edinburgh University Press.

Roeser, Sabine. 2010. *Reid on Ethics Reid*, edited by Sabine Roeser. Basingstoke: Palgrave Macmillan.

Van Cleve, James. 2004. "Reid's Theory of Perception." In *The Cambridge Companion to Thomas Reid*, edited by Terence Cuneo and René van Woudenberg, 101–133. Cambridge: Cambridge University Press.

Wolterstorff, Nicholas. 2004. *Thomas Reid and the Story of Epistemology*. Cambridge: Cambridge University Press.

MORAL THEORY
Reid on the first principles of morals

Terence Cuneo

Department of Philosophy, University of Vermont, Burlington

What role do the first principles of morals play in Reid's moral theory? Reid has an official line regarding their role, which identifies these principles as foundational propositions that evidentially ground other moral propositions. I claim that, by Reid's own lights, this line of thought is mistaken. There is, however, another line of thought in Reid, one which identifies the first principles of morals as constitutive of moral thought. I explore this interpretation, arguing that it is a fruitful way of understanding much of what Reid wants to say about the role of moral first principles and drawing some connections between it and recent work on moral nonnaturalism.

Toward the end of *Essays on the Active Powers of Man*, Reid offers a list of propositions that he calls the first principles of morals, dividing this list into two sections. The first section, Reid says, includes propositions that pertain to 'virtue in general, or to the different particular branches of virtue, or to the comparison of virtues where they seem to interfere' (EAP V.i: 271). They are:

1$_G$. There are some things in human conduct, that merit approbation and praise, others that merit blame and punishment; and different degrees either of approbation or of blame, are due to different actions.

2$_G$. What is in no degree voluntary can neither deserve moral approbation nor blame.

3$_G$. What is done from unavoidable necessity may be agreeable or disagreeable, useful or hurtful, but cannot be the object either of blame or moral approbation.

4$_G$. Men may be highly culpable in omitting what they ought to have done, as well as in doing what they ought not.

5$_G$. We ought to use the best means we can to be well informed of our duty, by serious attention to moral instruction; by observing what we approve, and what we disapprove, in others and ourselves; by reflecting often on our own past conduct; and by deliberating coolly and impartially upon our future conduct.

102

6$_G$. It ought to be our most serious concern to do our duty as far as we know it, and to fortify our minds against every temptation to deviate from it; by maintaining a lively sense of the beauty of right conduct, and of its present and future reward, of the turpitude of vice, and of its bad consequences here and hereafter.

The second section of the list, Reid writes, contains those principles that are 'more particular.' They are:

1$_P$. We ought to prefer a greater good, though more distant, to a less; and a less evil to a greater.

2$_P$. As far as the intention of nature appears in the constitution of man, we ought to comply with that intention, and to act agreeable to it.

3$_P$. No man is born for himself only. Every man, therefore, ought to consider himself as a member of the common society of mankind, and of those subordinate societies to which he belongs, such as family, friends, neighborhood, country, and to do as much good as he can, and as little hurt to the societies of which he is a part.

4$_P$. In every case, we ought to act that part toward another, which we would judge to be right in him to act toward us, if we were in his circumstances and he in ours.

5$_P$. To every man who believes, the existence, the perfections, and the providence of God, the veneration and submission we owe to him is self-evident. (EAP V.i: 272–76)[1]

My project in this paper is to address the question of what role, according to Reid, these principles play in ethical thinking. Reid has an official line about their role, which I maintain cannot be correct by Reid's own lights. But there is an unofficial 'constitutivist' line of thought regarding the first principles of morals, also present in Reid's texts, which coheres with the overall pattern of Reid's thinking and is interesting in its own right. After explaining what the official line is and why it should be rejected, I lay out this alternative interpretation, drawing some connections between it and recent work on moral nonnaturalism.

I. Three issues of interpretation

To understand how Reid conceives of the role that the first principles of morals play in ethical thinking, I need first to address several issues of interpretation. The first issue concerns how narrowly Reid understands the domain of morality. In a chapter dedicated to Locke's claim that morality is demonstrable – demonstrable reasoning being 'applied only to truths that are necessary' (EIP VII.i: 545) – Reid raises the following concern about Locke's views:

The propositions which I think are properly called moral, are those that affirm some moral obligation to be, or not to be incumbent on one or more individual persons. To such propositions, Mr LOCKE'S reasoning does not apply, because the subjects of the proposition are not things whose real essence can be perfectly known. They are the creatures of God; their obligation results from the constitution which God has given them, and the circumstances in which he has placed them. That an individual has such a constitution and is placed in such circumstances, is not an abstract and necessary, but a contingent truth. It is a matter of fact, and therefore not capable of demonstrative evidence, which belongs only to necessary truths. (EIP VII.ii: 550–551; see also EIP VII.ii: 555).

In this passage, Reid works with a highly restrictive account of what counts as a moral principle. If it were correct, those propositions that tell us what moral reasons, moral rights, or moral virtues a person has would not necessarily count as moral, since they do not concern (and cannot be reductively analyzed in terms of) moral obligations. Moreover, this passage has the implication that some of the principles that Reid himself lists among the first principles of morals would not count as moral. Take, for example, the first three principles listed above. These principles concern not the conditions under which an agent is under a moral obligation, but those under which an agent can rightly be held morally accountable. Since both of these implications are, I believe, ones that Reid would wish to avoid, I am going to interpret Reid as working with a more capacious account of the moral domain than he states in the passage just quoted.

The second issue of interpretation concerns the modal status of the first principles of morals. In the passage just cited, Reid maintains against Locke that the principles of morality are not necessary but contingent. Just several chapters before his engagement with Locke, however, Reid identifies a domain of propositions that he calls the principles of common sense, dividing them into the contingent and the necessary. In the category of the necessary, he places the first principles of morals (EIP VI.vi: 494). It is because some moral principles are necessary, says Reid, that they could not be determined by the operations of the moral sense, which are contingent: 'if it be true that there is judgment in our determinations of taste and of morals, it must be granted, that what is true or false in morals, or in matters of taste, is necessarily so. For this reason, I have ranked the first principles of morals and of taste under the class of necessary truths' (EIP VI.vi: 495).

While it is not immediately apparent how to reconcile these rather different things that Reid says about the modal status of the principles of morals, there is, I believe, a way to harmonize them. The key is to understand Reid as operating with two different notions of necessity that he does not explicitly distinguish. The first is that of absolute necessity, which includes all and only those propositions that are true 'no matter what.' Candidates for the absolutely necessary would be propositions such as *that all bachelors are unmarried* and *that nothing is red and green all over at once*, since they are true but not relative to any set of conditions. Relative necessities, in contrast, are necessarily true but only relative to a set of specified conditions. Candidates for the relatively necessary would be propositions such as *that water freezes at 0 degrees Celsius* and (more controversially) *that Obama = Obama*, since both are necessarily true only relative to certain conditions.[2] As I understand him, in the passage on Locke, Reid rejects the claim that the first principles of morals are absolutely necessary. But in the passages on the necessary first principles, he accepts the claim that the first principles of morals enjoy relative necessity – the conditions to which they are relative being that of our existing and having the constitution that we in fact have. At any rate, in what follows, I will assume that Reid holds that the first principles of morals are necessary, albeit only in the relative sense.

The third issue of interpretation regarding Reid's position with respect to the first principles is more challenging, as there is something deeply puzzling about the list he offers us. The list is puzzling not because it is incomplete. Reid is careful to note that he does not pretend to offer a 'complete enumeration' of the first principles (EAP V.i: 270). Nor is the list puzzling because Reid seems to furnish an 'unconnected heap of duties' without providing any clues regarding how they should be weighted in ethical deliberation.[3] Rather, the list is puzzling because it is difficult to see how the first principles of morals could guide ethical deliberation and action at all. For unlike Ross's prima facie duties, the first principles of morals are not substantive moral principles; with perhaps the exception of principle 5_P, they do not identify descriptive features that make it the case that we have one or another obligation, the awareness of which could guide ethical deliberation and action.

Consider, for example, the last of the general principles that Reid lists:

4_G. Men may be highly culpable in omitting what they ought to have done, as well as in doing what they ought not.

5_G. We ought to use the best means we can to be well informed of our duty, by serious attention to moral instruction; by observing what we approve, and what we disapprove, in others and ourselves; by reflecting often on our own past conduct; by deliberating coolly and impartially upon our future conduct.

6_G. It ought to be our most serious concern to do our duty as far as we know it, and to fortify our minds against every temptation to deviate from it; by maintaining a lively sense of the beauty of right conduct, and of its present and future reward, of the turpitude of vice, and of its bad consequences here and hereafter.

Principle 4_G does not tell us what ought to be done. 5_G does not specify what the duties are about which we should be informed. Likewise, 6_G fails to specify what the right conduct is such that we should maintain a lively sense of its beauty. Or, to move to the particular principles, consider:

4_P. In every case, we ought to act that part toward another, which we would judge to be right in him to act toward us, if we were in his circumstances and he in ours.

Reid tells us that this principle is the 'most comprehensive,' as it 'comprehends every rule of justice without exception' (EAP V.i: 275). But unless one knows what the right actions are such that others should perform them toward us, this principle is of no help in determining how we should treat others. Since, taken by themselves, these principles could not offer practical ethical guidance, why would Reid offer them as especially vivid cases of moral principles?

The clue, I think, lies in Reid's gloss of principle 4_P. In this gloss, Reid says that this principle 'comprehends every rule of justice.' If this is right, while most of the principles on Reid's list express moral obligations, they are themselves second-order obligations that presuppose the existence of and concern the existence of other first-order moral obligations – among these first-order principles being the rules of justice. Properly understood, then, most of Reid's first principles are first principles *of* morals; they are *about* first-order moral principles that are not themselves first-order moral principles. Whether intentional or not, Reid's own way of speaking of the first principles as principles of morality reveals their character.

Does Reid elsewhere say what these other first-order moral principles, such as the rules of justice, might be? Yes, he does, although it must be admitted that connecting what Reid says about the first principles of morals with the rules of justice requires stitching together some texts that Reid himself does not explicitly link. That said, it is worth quoting at length what Reid writes in his discussion of justice:

> We may observe, that as justice is directly opposed to injury, and as there are various ways in which a man may be injured, so there must be various branches of justice opposed to the different kinds of injury.
>
> A man may be injured, *first*, in his person, by wounding, maiming, or killing him; *secondly*, in his family, by robbing him of his children, or any way injuring those he is bound to protect; *thirdly*, in his liberty, by confinement; *fourthly*, in his reputation; *fifthly*, in his goods or property; and, *lastly*, in the violation of contracts or engagements made with him. This enumeration, whether complete or not, is sufficient for the present purpose.
>
> The different branches of justice, opposed to these different kinds of injury, are commonly expressed by the saying, that an innocent man has a right to the safety of his person and family, a right to his liberty and reputation, a right to his goods, and to fidelity to engagements made with him. To say that he has a right to these things, has precisely the same meaning as to say, that justice requires that he should be permitted to enjoy them, or that it is unjust to violate them. For injustice is the violation of right, and justice is, to yield to every man what is his right. (EAP V.v: 312–313)

In this passage, Reid offers an enumeration of those first-order principles of justice to which he takes the first principles of morals to apply. Were we to list the correlative requirements to the rights that Reid mentions, the list would be something like this:

> We each have an obligation not to wound, maim, or kill others.
>
> We each have an obligation not to abduct others' loved ones or those under their guardianship.
>
> We each have an obligation not to confine others (over whom we do not have authority) against their will.
>
> We each have an obligation not to destroy the reputation of others.
>
> We each have an obligation to keep our promises and other commitments to others.

Call these the *principles of justice*.[4] In various places, Reid makes it evident that, when applied to particular cases, these principles can conflict with other first-order principles: 'between particular external actions, which different virtues would lead to, there may be an opposition .... it may happen, that an external action which generosity or gratitude solicits, justice may forbid' (EAP V.i: 276). The best way to interpret the principles of justice, then, is to see them as expressing defeasible or pro tanto moral obligations. Most importantly for our purposes, they are examples of the sorts of obligations to which most of the first principles of morals refer. It is the violation of these obligations for which an agent can be held accountable. It is these obligations about which we ought to be well-informed and keep before our mind's eye, and whose performance should be our 'most serious concern.'

Suppose, then, we distinguish *first-order moral principles* from the *first principles of morals*. When we do, we can better see the structure of Reid's thinking about moral obligation. Generally speaking, the latter are second-order moral principles that concern the former, enjoining us to bear various sorts of relations to them, such as keeping them before the mind's eye. But now puzzles loom. For when Reid offers his reasons for believing that there are first principles of morals, he voices familiar-sounding foundationalist doctrines similar to those which he presents when stating the principles of common sense. Regarding morality, Reid writes:

> Morals, like all other sciences, must have first principles, on which all moral reasoning is grounded.
>
> In every branch of knowledge where disputes have been raised, it is useful to distinguish the first principles from the superstructure. They are the foundation on which the whole fabric of the science leans; and whatever is not supported by this foundation can have no stability.
>
> In all rational belief, the thing believed is either itself a first principle, or it is by just reasoning deduced from first principles. When men differ about deductions of reasoning, the appeal must be made to the rules of reasoning, which have been very unanimously fixed from the days of ARISTOTLE. But when they differ about a first principle, the appeal is made to another tribunal; to that of common sense. (EAP V.i: 270; see also EAP III.iii.vi: 177)

Under a natural reading, this passage introduces chaos into Reid's thought. For one thing, in his discussion of moral judgment, Reid repeatedly stresses that the moral faculty yields not simply judgments about general moral principles but also particular judgments to the effect that 'this conduct is right, that is wrong; that this character has worth, that demerit' (EAP III.iii.vi: 176). But when one takes a closer look at Reid's account of particular moral judgments, it is clear that these judgments are by and large immediate or non-inferential; they are not the product of reasoning from general principles to particular cases. According to Reid, in 'the common occurrences of life, a man of integrity, who has exercised his moral faculty in judging what is right and wrong, sees his duty without reasoning, as he sees a highway. The cases that require reasoning are few' (EIP VII.ii: 553). And again: the person of integrity 'will rarely be at a loss to distinguish good from ill in his own conduct, without the labor of reasoning' (EAP V.ii: 280).

In fact, when Reid more fully develops his account of moral judgment, he draws explicit parallels with cases of perception in which agents are aware of external signs and move without reasoning from the awareness of those signs to particular judgments. Regarding our judgments of the character traits of others, Reid writes:

> Intelligence, design, and skill, are not objects of the external senses, nor can we be conscious of them in any person but ourselves....
>
> A man's wisdom is known to us only by the signs of it in his conduct; his eloquence by the signs of it in his speech. In the same manner we judge of his virtue, of his fortitude, and of all his talents and qualities of mind.
>
> Yet it is to be observed, that we judge of men's talents with as little doubt or hesitation as we judge of the immediate objects of sense.
>
> ... We perceive one man to be open, another cunning; one to be ignorant, another very knowing; one to be slow of understanding, another quick. Every man forms such judgments of those he converses with; and the common affairs of life depend upon such judgments. We can as little avoid them as we can avoid seeing what is before our eyes.
>
> From this it appears, that it is no less part of the human constitution, to judge of men's characters, and of their intellectual powers, from the signs of them in their actions and discourse, than to judge of corporeal objects by our senses. (EIP VI.vi: 503–504)

The claim that the formation of particular moral judgments is ordinarily immediate or non-inferential, then, is not incidental to but lies deep in Reid's thinking. But it is manifestly incompatible with what he says about the role of the first principles of morals, under a natural reading. For, to say it again, particular moral judgments are generally not inferred from the first principles of morals. Moreover, even if these particular judgments were inferred or based on other moral judgments, they would typically be inferred from or based on not the first principles of morals but first-order moral principles, such as the principles of justice. Reid, it seems, has identified the wrong sorts of principles to belong to the structure of well-formed moral belief.[5]

Which brings me to a second point: I have claimed that most of the first principles of morals are such that they concern or are about first-order moral principles, such as the principles of justice. But if they bear this relation to the first-order moral principles, then the first-order principles cannot (in any non-trivial way) be deduced from them, as Reid claims. Take a sample of the first principles of morals, such as:

3_G. What is done from unavoidable necessity may be agreeable or disagreeable, useful or hurtful, but cannot be the object either of blame or moral approbation.

4_G. Men may be highly culpable in omitting what they ought to have done, as well as in doing what they ought not.

5_G. We ought to use the best means we can to be well informed of our duty, by serious attention to moral instruction; by observing what we approve, and what we disapprove, in others and ourselves; by reflecting often on our own past conduct; by deliberating coolly and impartially upon our future conduct.

There is no way to derive any of the principles of justice from these propositions. They could not, then, function in a way similar to Kant's categorical imperative or Mill's principle of utility. For, under a standard interpretation, both the categorical imperative and the principle of utility play several distinct 'grounding' roles. In the first place, they are supposed to determine all our particular first-order moral obligations. According to Mill, for example, we have obligations not to harm others because acting in this way would maximize well-being on the whole. Second, were what Kant and Mill say true, the categorical imperative and the principle of utility would be the sorts of principles that could guide ethical deliberation and action. For by consulting them and engaging in some reasoning in which one appreciates their implications, one could in principle determine what one ought to do. And, third, if Kant and Mill are right, an agent's belief in either the categorical imperative or the principle of utility could epistemically justify her belief that she has some first-order obligation, as an agent can base her belief that she ought to act in some way on the further belief that it is implied by one of these principles.

Reid's first principles of morals, by contrast, do not and could not play any of these roles. Given Reid's description of them, in no interesting sense are they foundational.[6]

II. Realist constitutivism

The problems that afflict Reid's understanding of the first principles of morals are not, I believe, superficial. To make what he says about the first principles of morals cohere with other things he says, Reid would have to recast a good deal of his thought. Among other things, he would have to retract his claim that the first principles of morals ground or are the epistemic basis of other moral principles, such as the principles of justice – at least in the sense he specifies in the passage quoted above (i.e., EAP V.i: 270).[7] Rather than explore whether Reid's views could survive this alteration, I want in this section to head in a different direction, further mining Reid's thought. Specifically, I want to ask whether the first principles of morals and first-order moral principles might play some other important role in moral thinking to which Reid is, perhaps indirectly, drawing our attention.[8]

To that end, let me bring Reid into conversation with contemporary ethical theorists by drawing a comparison between Reid's thought and recent work by Kantians such as Christine Korsgaard (Korsgaard 2008). In her recent work, Korsgaard defends a position that I shall call *constitutivism*. The defining feature of constitutivism of the Kantian variety is that acting in accordance with normative principles of certain kinds is constitutive of practical agency. Specifically, Korsgaard argues, there are two master principles – the hypothetical and the categorical imperatives – the conformance to which is constitutive of practical agency. The hypothetical imperative commands us to take the necessary means towards our ends; this corresponds to what Korsgaard calls the 'norm of efficacy' because it is only by taking the necessary means that we can successfully bring about our ends.[9] The categorical imperative, by contrast, corresponds to what Korsgaard calls the 'norm of autonomy.' It governs the choice of actions by posing an admissibility test for acts being taken in pursuit of ends. Korsgaard makes additional claims about these principles that needn't concern us here. The important thing to see is that she holds that when agents fail to conform to these principles – as they often do – they do not thereby make practical mistakes. Rather, they fail to be practical agents. For example, failure to conform to the categorical imperative is, according to Kantian constitutivism, to fail to be a moral agent.

Korsgaard has her own reasons for defending a version of constitutivism. She maintains that moral principles would be authoritative, trumping any competing practical principles, only if it they are immune to skeptical doubts. And for this to be the case, Korsgaard holds, 'our substantive principles must be derivable from formal ones,' such as the categorical imperative, the conformance to which is constitutive of practical agency (Korsgaard 2008, 2.1.7 and 46).

One will search in vain for any similar line of thought in Reid. Although Reid believes that moral principles are authoritative, he does not hold that in order for them to be authoritative they must be derivable from purely formal principles such as the categorical imperative or the Golden Rule. This difference notwithstanding, I want to suggest that there is a plausible interpretation of Reid according to which Reid is also a constitutivist, albeit of a decidedly non-Kantian variety. Under this reading, Reid holds that assenting to a range of substantive moral propositions is constitutive of competent moral thinking; failure to do so is not to make a moral mistake in which one accepts false substantive moral views but marks a failure to be a moral agent. If this reading were correct, Reid's view would represent an interesting type of position that is often overlooked in contemporary discussions in metaethics, as his view would be a version of *realist constitutivism*. The reason why this would represent an oft-overlooked position is that constitutivism is almost always presented as a version of constructivist antirealism according to which the existence of moral principles depends on our practical activity. Korsgaard, for example, maintains that we 'create' these principles by engaging in practical activity. Reid's constitutivism, by contrast, is thoroughly realist in the sense that he rejects the claim that moral principles depend in any interesting sense on our practical reasoning.

Here is a pair of passages in which Reid's constitutivist commitments are evident:

> It is a first principle of morals, that we ought not to do to another, what we should think wrong to be done to us in like circumstances. If a man is not capable of perceiving this in his cool moments, when he reflects seriously, he is not a moral agent, nor is he capable of being convinced of it by reasoning.

> From what topic can you reason with such a man? You may possibly convince him by reasoning, that it is his interest to observe this rule; but this is not to convince him that it is his duty. To reason about justice with a man who sees nothing to be just or unjust; or about benevolence with a man who sees nothing in benevolence

preferable to malice, is like reasoning with a blind man about colour, or with a deaf man about sound. (EAP III.iii. vi: 177–178)

If any man could say with sincerity, that he is conscious of no obligation to consult his own present and future happiness; to be faithful to his engagements, to obey his Maker, to injure no man; I know not what reasoning, either probable or demonstrative, I could use to convince him of any moral duty. As you cannot reason in mathematics with a man who denies the axioms, as little can you reason with a man in morals who denies the first principles of morals. The man who does not, by the light of his own mind, perceive some things in conduct to be right, and others to be wrong, is as incapable of reasoning about morals, as a blind man is about colours. Such a man, if any such man ever was, would be no moral agent. (EIP VII. ii: 551–552)[10]

In these passages, Reid presents us with a pair of different scenarios that it might be helpful to more sharply distinguish. In the first scenario, Reid asks us to imagine a case in which we manage to persuade someone that it is in his interest to conform to principle 4$_P$, which is Reid's version of the Golden Rule. Call this person *the egoist*. While Reid concedes that we might convince the egoist to conform to this principle by persuading him that it is in his self-interest to do so, the egoist would nonetheless have a grasp of this principle that would be deeply defective, since he would see nothing that genuinely favors conforming to it beyond self-interest. The egoist fails to see that moral principles themselves favor acting in conformance to them.

In the second scenario, Reid asks us to envision a person whom we cannot persuade to accept moral principles, as he can 'see no obligation' whatsoever to act in certain ways, such as not harming others. Call this person *the amoralist*. The amoralist, Reid seems to suggest, would be like someone who fails to grasp moral concepts altogether, much like a blind person would fail to grasp color concepts.[11] In both cases, Reid suggests, the figures in question fail to be moral agents not simply in the sense that they would not be people with whom one could convince of certain ethical truths or engage in moral co-deliberation, but also in the sense of suffering from serious conceptual deficiencies. Under either scenario, these figures would either fail to grasp moral concepts, have a deeply confused grasp of them, or fail to see or acknowledge their manifest implications. (I hasten to add that this could be explained by any number of factors, such as having a moral sense that does not work well.) If we want a guiding metaphor for thinking about the role that moral principles play in these cases, they are not so much the *basis* for particular moral judgments so much as what set the *boundaries* of competent moral thought.

We can make progress with this interpretation of Reid by distinguishing two ways in which moral principles are constitutive of moral thought. Suppose, in the first place, that we mean by 'moral thought' the objects of moral thinking, namely, moral propositions. Moral principles are, in this first sense, constitutive of moral thought insofar as any reasonably comprehensive and consistent body of moral thoughts or propositions would have to include them. Suppose, by contrast, that we mean by 'moral thought' the activity of moral thinking.

Moral principles are, in this second sense, constitutive of moral thinking inasmuch as one could not competently engage in such thinking without affirming these principles.

Let's explore the first half of this distinction by introducing some terminology. Suppose we say that a *moral system* is a reasonably comprehensive and consistent body of moral propositions, which concerns beings like us in a world such as ours. Let's say, furthermore, that such a system is *minimally eccentric* just in case it does not incorporate eccentric empirical assumptions about us and the world. In Reid's terms, a minimally eccentric moral system would be one that is constrained by the principles of common sense, particularly those that he calls the 'first principles of contingent truths' – these truths specifying, among other things, that you are numerically identical with the person you were yesterday, that you are embodied, sentient, and have 'life and intelligence' (EIP VI.vi: 482). Now take any moral system that is minimally eccentric. Under the constitutivist interpretation, Reid's position is that, necessarily, any such system includes both the first principles of morals and certain first-order moral principles, such as the principles of justice. For ease of reference, call this constellation of propositions the *moral fixed points*.[12]

Nowhere, to my knowledge, does Reid present first-order moral principles as themselves self-evident or necessarily true. Still, in the central constitutivist passages just cited, it is telling that, when engaging with both the egoist and the amoralist, Reid himself refers to both the first principles of morals and the principles of justice. That he does, I take it, is good evidence that these propositions would be, in Reid's view, among the moral fixed points of any minimally eccentric moral system (at least for beings such as us). If so, any such system would include moral propositions such as:

> It is wrong to wound, maim, or kill others.
> It is wrong to abduct others' loved ones or those under their guardianship.
> It is wrong to confine others (over which one has no authority) against their will.
> It is wrong to destroy the reputation of others.
> It is wrong to break our promises and other commitments to others

–where, once again, the wrongness in question is pro tanto. Such a system would also include moral propositions that are first principles of morals such as:

> It is wrong to blame someone for doing something that is in no degree voluntary.
> It is wrong to fail to employ the best means we can to be well informed of our moral obligations.

And:

> It is wrong to treat others in such a way that we would judge to be wrong for him or her to act toward us, if we were in his or her circumstances and he or she in ours.

In calling a body of moral propositions that includes these principles a 'moral system,' I have been employing Reid's own terminology. In his chapter 'Of Systems of Morals,' Reid discusses various characteristics of moral systems, among which are the evidential role of the propositions that compose them:

112

a system of morals is not like a system of geometry, where the subsequent parts derive their evidence from the preceding, and one chain of reasoning is carried on from the beginning; so that, if the arrangement is changed, the chain is broken, and the evidence is lost. It resembles more a system of botany, or mineralogy, where the subsequent parts depend not for their evidence upon the preceding, and the arrangement is made to facilitate apprehension and memory, and not to give evidence. (EAP V.ii: 281)

This passage presents a striking reversal of the foundationalist imagery Reid uses when he presents the first principles of morals, as Reid here denies that the propositions that constitute a system of morals are like those that constitute a system of geometry in which some small set of foundational propositions are supposed to evidentially support the others. When understood against this passage, Reid's view begins to more closely resemble those defended by rational intuitionists, such as Ross. For these views maintain that there is no master principle or small set of principles from which all other moral principles, such as the principles of justice, can be derived.[13]

I have been suggesting that, in Reid's view, there are definite limits as to what could count as a moral system. For a moral system is necessarily constituted by an array of moral propositions – the moral fixed points – which include not only the first principles of morals but also various first-order moral principles, such as the principles of justice. The moral fixed points, in turn, are necessarily true, at least concerning agents such as us in world such as ours. Given what Reid says about their role in moral thinking, moreover, the sort of necessity in question seems to be in the vicinity of conceptual necessity – where conceptually necessary truths would be those that are true in virtue of the essences of their constituent concepts. Take, for example, the proposition (in a world such as ours) *that it is wrong to maim another human being*. If such a proposition were true of conceptual necessity, then it would belong to the essence of the concept 'being wrong' that (in a world such as ours) if any action taken with regard to a fellow human being falls under the concept 'being a case of maiming another human,' then it must also fall under the concept 'being wrong.'[14] The primary reason for thinking that the moral fixed points would have to be conceptually necessary truths is this: suppose, for argument's sake, that such propositions were true but only of metaphysical necessity. Suppose, for example, that the truth *necessarily, it is wrong to maim another human being* were like the truth *necessarily, the atomic number of gold is 79*. If it were, then someone who denied it would make a mistake. But this mistake would provide no reason to hold that the agent who made it fails to be a moral agent, as Reid elsewhere indicates. If, however, the moral first principles were conceptually necessary, then we could make sense of Reid's claim that someone who considered but failed to assent to them would suffer from such a lack of understanding that she failed to be a moral agent.

Here, however, we must tread lightly. Those of us who work in the shadow of Frege are accustomed to distinguishing concepts, on the one hand, from properties, on the other. Concepts, according to the broadly Fregean tradition are mind-independent, sharable, abstract ways of conceiving or thinking about objects or properties. Understood thus, they are not only abilities or devices for referring to objects and properties, since employing them allows us to refer to objects and properties, but also meanings, for they are the constituents of propositions. Reid was not, however, a proto-Fregean; he worked with no such distinction.[15] Rather, he posits entities of one kind – namely, universals – to play the role of both concepts and properties. Universals, as Reid thinks of them, are predicables, entities that are both predicated of and belong to objects. In Reid's view, however, universals are also meanings and, thus, the constituents of propositions.[16] This tendency of Reid's part to identify universals, meanings, and what he elsewhere calls conceptions is on display in the following passage:

> To conceive the meaning of a general word, and to conceive that which it signifies, is the same thing. We conceive distinctly the meaning of general terms; therefore we conceive distinctly that which they signify. But such terms do not signify an individual, but what is common to many individuals; therefore we have a distinct conception of things common to many individuals, that is, we have distinct general conceptions.
>
> We must here beware of the ambiguity of the word *conception*, which sometimes signifies the act of the mind in conceiving, sometimes the thing conceived, which is the object of that act. If the word be taken in the first sense, I acknowledge that every act of the mind is an individual act; the universality, therefore, is not in the act of the mind, but in the object, or thing conceived. The thing conceived is an attribute common to many subjects, or it is a genus or species common to many individuals. (EIP V.ii: 364; cf. EIP IV.i: 323, IV.ii: 311)[17]

Reid's tendency to not distinguish concepts from properties makes it much more difficult within his scheme to distinguish conceptually necessary truths from other sorts of necessary truths. But, to say it again, to vindicate the claim that a person who denies the moral fixed points suffers from something akin to a conceptual failure, it would appear that Reid needs to affirm the thesis that these truths hold of conceptual necessity (or something very much like it). Reid cannot, then, simply say that it belongs to the property *being wrong* that, necessarily, anything which is a case of maiming another is wrong. For its denial needn't imply a conceptual deficiency; there must be something about this property such that those who sincerely deny that cases of maiming are wrong (and do not hold eccentric empirical beliefs) suffer from the sort of deficiency in which we have excellent reason to doubt they are moral agents. However, short of making all necessary truths into conceptual ones – a position that Reid appears to reject – or introducing the idea that universals have modes of presentation, it is not evident whether Reid has available the resources to tell us what it might be.[18]

Be that as it may, let me now return to a distinction that I introduced a few paragraphs back. There I said that moral principles could be constitutive of moral thought in two senses. In one sense, moral principles are the objects of moral thought, as they are moral propositions; these principles are constitutive of moral thought inasmuch as they are the fixed points of anything that could be denominated a moral system. In another sense, however, 'moral thought' concerns not the objects of moral thinking but moral thinking itself. Along the way, we have had our eye on this sense of the phrase, too, noting that Reid appears committed to the thesis that, if a figure such as the egoist or the amoralist were to hold minimally eccentric beliefs about the world and also sincerely to reject the moral fixed points, he would not thereby make a moral mistake, drawing the wrong substantive moral conclusions about how to act. Rather, he would fail be a moral agent. He would not only be a person whom we could not convince to accept moral propositions or with whom we could engage in genuine common moral deliberation, but also someone who does not engage in competent moral thinking. For in denying the moral fixed points, this person would suffer from a serious conceptual deficiency, being such as either to fail to grasp moral concepts, have a deeply confused grasp of them, or not see or acknowledge their manifest implications.

To claim that accepting certain substantive moral claims is constitutive of competent moral thinking is controversial. Philosophers in the broadly expressivist tradition have long resisted it (see Hare 1952). On this occasion, my aim is not to defend this claim but to explore its implications. Suppose, then, for argument's sake, it is true that accepting certain substantive moral claims is constitutive of competent moral thinking. If it were, would Reid be committed to the thesis that denying the truth of the fixed points is a conceptual failure of such a kind that it renders an agent's thinking about morality unintelligible?

Given other things that Reid says, I believe that the answer is No. For example, in his discussion of first principles in general, Reid raises the question of whether people 'who really love truth, and are open to conviction, may differ about first principles' (EIP VI.iv: 460). Reid's answer is that such a disagreement 'is possible, and that it cannot, without great want of charity, be denied to be possible' (ibid.). Admittedly, when one holds that something is a first principle and one's interlocutor does not, one 'must be convinced that there is a defect, or a perversion of judgment on the one side or the other.' In the chapter 'Of Prejudices, the Causes of Error,' Reid elaborates at some length on what he takes to be the most common sources of error, identifying analogical reasoning, the love of simplicity, and the tendency to apply our cognitive faculties to matters to which they are not fit to be applied among them (see EIP VIII). What is especially interesting given our purposes is that Reid seems alive to the possibility not simply that a proposition may not in fact be a first principle but also that it may be confused or false (see Wolterstorff 2001, 97–98). In being alive to this possibility, Reid does not commit himself to the claim that, for any putative first principle, upon carefully reflecting on that principle, one can discern how it might be confused or false. It might be that, under favorable conditions, such principles would always seem necessarily true upon such reflection. The better way to interpret Reid is probably this: we are familiar with or can imagine cases of such a kind in which something that seemed to be a first principle turned out to be confused or false. Call such propositions *illusory*. Reid can agree that we cannot rule out that, given our evidence, the moral fixed points belong to the class of illusory propositions.

If this is right, the best way to understand Reid's view would be more nuanced than he himself states it in the central constitutivist passages cited earlier. Rather than say that a person, such as the amoralist, who denies that there are first principles of morals is similar to a blind person who had never seen colors, Reid could say that we have powerful pro tanto reason to believe that such a person suffers from a similarly serious conceptual deficiency. It is within the realm of imagination, however, that the amoralist has spotted confusions in our moral concepts that would render the moral fixed points confused or false. In that case, the principles might still seem to be true upon careful reflection but the seeming would be systematically misleading.

III. Realist constitutivism?

At various points in our discussion, I have described Reid's position as a version of realist constitutivism. I might have also described it as a version of *nonnaturalist* realist constructivist, since Reid holds that moral truths are not part of the natural order (see Cuneo 2011). This type of position, I also suggested, is unusual, since nearly all versions of constitutivism are presented as versions of not realism but constructivist antirealism. That said, by calling Reid's position a version of realist constitutivism, I am in danger of offering a rather misleading picture of Reid's view. For Reid's metaethical commitments are, in an important respect, highly idiosyncratic. Let me close by explaining why.

Reid tells us that the constituents of moral principles are universals or predicables, writing:

> If we examine the abstract notion of duty, or moral obligation, it appears to be neither any real quality of the action considered by itself, nor of the agent considered without respect to the action, but a certain relation between the one and the other ... So that, if we seek the place of moral obligation among the categories, it belongs to the category of *relation*. (EAP III.iii.v: 173)

If Reid is right, these abstract relations are the constituents of what I have called the moral fixed points, these being necessary moral truths of a certain range. And yet when Reid describes what it is for something to be a property or relation, he repeatedly makes claims of the following sort:

> Simple attributes, species and genera, lower or higher, are all things conceived, without regard to existence; they are universals, they are expressed by general words, and have an equal title to be called by the name of *ideas*. (EIP VI.iii: 442)

Ideas or universals, thus understood,

> are not things that exist, but things conceived, they neither have place nor time, nor are they liable to change.
>
> When we say that they are in the mind, this can mean no more but that they are conceived by the mind, or that they are objects of thought. The act of conceiving

them is no doubt in the mind; the things conceived have no place, because they have no existence. (EIP VI.iii: 440; cf. EIP V.iii: 367; V.iv: 373, 375; V.vi: 393)

These passages can be interpreted in such a way that Reid is using the term 'exist' narrowly to include all and only those things that exist in space/time. But it is clear that Reid is not simply using the term 'exist' in this way. Reid, for example, holds that God exists, although God is presumably neither spatially nor temporally located. Moreover, elsewhere Reid acknowledges that, as he thinks of them, universals are what Plato called Ideas if we 'take away the attribute of existence, and suppose them not be things that exist, but things that are barely conceived' (EIP V.v: 386).[19] It was, however, Plato's view that the Forms exist but are not temporally or spatially located. By denying that the Forms exist in the sense that Plato had in mind, which is a non-temporal/spatial sense, Reid seems to be denying that they exist simpliciter.

The resulting position is striking. On the one hand, we are told that there are necessary moral truths whose existence and nature does not depend on our being disposed to respond to non-moral reality in certain ways. On the other, we are told that the constituents of these truths do not exist; they are merely 'thinkables.' However striking this position may be, it is worth noting that it has contemporary analogues. In the section devoted to moral ontology in his recent *On What Matters*, Derek Parfit describes his own version of nonnaturalist 'Non-Metaphysical cognitivism' as committed to these two claims:

There are some claims that are, in the strongest sense, true, but these truths have no positive ontological implications.

When such claims assert that there are certain things, or that these things exist, these claims do not imply that these things exist in some ontological sense. (Parfit 2011, 479)

Parfit continues:

When we claim that there are some things that are merely possible, we must admit that, compared with things that are actual, such merely possible things have a lesser ontological status. That is why it matters, for example, whether good or bad possible events will also be actual and real. But when we consider certain abstract entities, such as prime numbers and logical truths, these distinctions do not apply. These numbers and truths are not less actual, or *real*, than stars, or human beings. These abstract entities have no ontological status. They are not in relevant senses, either actual or merely possible, or either real or unreal. When we are trying to form true beliefs about numbers or logical truths, we need not answer ontological questions. As one way to sum up these claims, we can say that, through there are these numbers and truths, these entities exist in a non-ontological sense. (Parfit 2011, 481)

Speaking now of normative features and truths, Parfit writes:

Like numbers and logical truths, these normative properties and truths have no ontological status. These properties and truths are not, in relevant senses, either actual or merely possible, or either real or unreal. In asking whether there are such normative truths, we need not answer ontological questions. There are, I believe, some such truths, which are as true as any truth could be. (Parfit 2011, 487)

I find these claims of Parfit's deeply puzzling mostly because it is difficult to see what Parfit means when he claims that there are things that exist 'in a non-ontological sense.' Puzzling or not, Parfit's views closely resemble Reid's position about the normative realm, as Reid also wants to speak of there being moral truths that fail to have any positive ontological implications in the sense that they are wholly composed of universals, which do not exist.[20]

Reid's reputation in the history of philosophy is that of being a staunch defender of common sense. When one begins to dig deeper into his views, however, it becomes apparent that this reputation is only partially deserved. Reid sometimes defends positions that could hardly be called commonsensical. His views about the ontological status of moral truths, like his quasi-occasionalism about causality, are among them.[21] Not only are his views about the ontological status of moral truths not commonsensical, they are also paradoxical. When discussing the modal status of moral truths, I briefly noted that Reid objects to response-dependent accounts of moral truths – which maintain that moral truths are determined by the operations of the moral sense – because these views fail to vindicate a sufficiently robust account of these truths. Defenders of the response-dependent view could, however, insist that Reid's objection does not come to much. They might rightly point out that their view, at least, is compatible with there being moral truths that exist in a very robust sense, having important positive ontological implications. Reid could not say the same about his position. For, in Reid's view, one would be speaking the literal truth when one says that moral truths do not exist.

Parfit, for his part, seems comfortable with the result that his metaethical views have no positive ontological implications and that there are antirealist views more ontologically committed than his. When pressed, I do not know whether Reid would be comfortable admitting the same. None of Reid's rivals, to my knowledge, challenged his metaethical views by drawing attention to this implication of his position.[22]

Notes

1. In my formulation of these principles, I stay close to Reid's own wording but in some cases phrase them slightly differently from Reid or abbreviate them. I use subscripts

to distinguish the general from the particular principles. I do not know why Reid designates the first set of principles as general and the latter particular. The members of both sets of principles seem equally general.

2. An identity sentence states a truth only if both terms flanking '=' refer to the same thing. In the example I use, they both refer to Obama. Had Obama not existed, however, they would not have so referred. So, the proposition is necessarily true only relative to Obama's actually existing. See Leftow (2012), 4.

3. The phrase comes from McNaughton (1996).

4. Reid offers a somewhat fuller list of the principles of justice in PE, 140.

5. There are two ways to address the concern raised above. First, one could deny that the first principles of morals are general principles. Van Cleve (1999) explores this 'particularist' reading with regard to the first principles of contingent truths. Wolterstorff (2004), 92–95 addresses this interpretation, noting that it is difficult to square with Reid's insistence that first principles are principles of common sense, propositions that agents believe in common. Second, one could maintain that Reid also wishes to include among the first principles of morals what I have called the principles of justice. While I cannot rule out this possibility, it is worth noting that in his presentation of the first principles, Reid does not include the principles of justice, which is surprising if Reid thought of them as first principles in the sense specified in the passage quoted above.

6. An exception might be principle 1P, which states (roughly) that we ought to prefer a greater good to a lesser one. In his gloss of this principle, however, Reid specifies that by 'good' he means one's *good on the whole* (EAP V.i: 272). Strictly speaking, then, this principle is one regarding prudential action: 'And though to act from this motive solely may be called *prudence* rather than *virtue*, yet this prudence deserves some regard upon its own account, and much more as it is the friend and ally of virtue, and the enemy of all vice ....'

7. Patrick Rysiew has suggested to me that there is a third option, which is to reinterpret the sort of epistemic basing or grounding relation that Reid intends to employ. Under this re-interpretation, the grounding relation on which Reid has his eye would be of the presuppositional variety – 'things we take for granted' (EIP I.ii) in the forming of various judgments and in whose absence of we could not form such judgments. While the details of this interpretation would have to be worked out, it strikes me as a promising approach that is compatible with the reading of Reid that I offer in this section.

8. Those familiar with Rysiew (2002) and Wolterstorff (2001), Ch. IX will notice that the interpretation of Reid that I am about to develop regarding the first principles of morals has affinities with their proposals concerning how to understand the role of the principles of common sense.

9. As it is typically understood, the hypothetical imperative is disjunctive, enjoining us either to take the necessary means toward our ends or to surrender those ends. Korsgaaard does not emphasize the second disjunct of this injunction. Perhaps this is because thus understood the hypothetical imperative is not clearly a norm of efficacy.

10. Reid's constitutivism is not limited to the moral domain, as he sounds similar themes with regard to some non-moral matters. Regarding reasoning, for example, Reid writes: 'A man who perfectly understood a just syllogism, without believing that the conclusion follows from the premises, would be a greater monster than a man born without hands or feet' (EIP VI.v: 481).

11. Reid elsewhere indicates that the blind do not conceive colors and the deaf do not conceive sounds: 'Thus a man cannot conceive colours, if he never saw, nor sounds, if he never heard' (EIP IV.i: 308–309).

12. This terminology is borrowed from Cuneo and Shafer-Landau (2014), which offers a defense of moral nonnaturalism that appeals to the fixed points.

13. Reid is careful to note that a system of morals is not to be equated with a *theory* of morals. For the latter, Reid writes, is simply 'a just account of the structure of our moral powers' (EAP VI.ii: 282). Thus understood, a theory of morals, Reid points out, has 'little connection with the knowledge of our duty; and those who differ most in the theory of our moral powers, agree in the practical rules of morals which they dictate' (ibid).

14. Cuneo and Shafer-Landau (2014) work out the details of this approach, distinguishing different types of conceptual necessity. Fundamental to the approach is the claim that conceptual truths needn't be empty of content or obviously true.

15. Reid, as I will note in a moment, does say that we have *conceptions*. What Reid means by a 'conception' is, however, a vexed issue. But it is clear that he does not have anything like Fregean concepts in mind. As Castagnetto (1992) points out, Reid seemed to think that when it comes to the nature of thinking, we have two options: either its immediate objects are Lockean ideas or worldly objects themselves. Reid opts for the latter.

16. 'In every other proposition,' Reid writes, 'the predicate at least must be a general notion; a predicable and an universal being one and the same' (EIP VI.i: 415; cf. EIP IV.i: 302 and VI.iii: 439).

17. Might Reid be using the term 'meanings' simply to talk of referents? Other passages suggest that he is not. Concerning the meaning of general terms, Reid writes: 'That such general words may answer their intention, all that is necessary is, that those who use them should affix the same meaning or notion, that is, the same conception to them. The common meaning is the standard by which such conceptions are formed, and they are said to be true or false, according as they agree or disagree with it. Thus, my conception of felony is true and just, when it agrees with the meaning of that word in the laws relating to it, and in authors who understand the law. The meaning of the word is the thing conceived; and that meaning is the conception affixed to it by those who best understand the language.' (EIP IV.i: 303) While this passage raises questions about Reid's views, it strikes me as good – albeit not decisive – evidence that meanings are not, for Reid, merely referents. Cf. EIP 408. For a different view, see Rysiew (forthcoming).

18. See, for example, what Reid says about real essences at EIP V.ii. One might propose, on Reid's behalf, that these moral principles are not conceptual truths but metaphysically necessary truths that are self-evident. This proposal would not, I believe, dissolve the puzzle facing Reid's view. Reid's understanding of self-evidence is, after all, the traditional one: self-evident propositions are 'no sooner understood than they are believed. The judgment follows the apprehension of them necessarily' (EIP VI.ii: 452). It might be that, according to this understanding of self-evidence, those who deny self-evident moral propositions are not competent moral agents. But now suppose that propositions are constituted by universals, as Reid believes. We still need to know what is it about those universals that constitute the self-evident moral propositions which guarantees that when someone considers and fails to believe these propositions, he thereby fails to engage in competent moral thought in the sense that Reid specifies.

19. 'The nature of every species, whether of substance, of quality, or of relation, and in general every thing which the ancients called an universal, answers to the description of a Platonic idea, if in that description you leave out the attribute of existence' (EIP IV.ii 319).

20. Reid does not always state his position so starkly. Elsewhere he writes: 'Ideas are said to have a real existence in the mind, at least, while we think of them; but universals have no real existence. When we ascribe existence to them, it is not an existence in time or place,

but existence in some individual subject; and this existence means no more that they are truly attributes of such a subject. Their existence is nothing but predicability or the capacity of being attributed to a subject. The name of predicables, which was given them in ancient philosophy, is that which most properly expresses their nature' (EIP V. vi: 393). In this passage, Reid's view sounds even closer to Parfit's, as Reid is willing to talk of more or less robust ways in which a thing exists. In EIP.iv: 373, Reid claims that only individuals exist. Universals, since they are not individuals, do not exist. This thesis would allow Reid to claim that God exists even though God is not temporally or spatially located. To my knowledge, Reid never offers an argument for thinking that only individuals exist, simply following Locke and Berkeley on this issue.

21. Tuggy (2000) explores Reid's quasi-occasionalism.

22. Thanks to Rebecca Copenhaver, Patrick Rysiew, and René van Woudenberg for their feedback on an earlier draft of this essay, as well as to the participants at the New Essays on Reid Conference at the University of Vermont in November 2013.

References

Castagnetto, Susan V. 1992. "Reid's Answer to Abstract Ideas." *Journal of Philosophical Research* XVII: 39–60.

Cuneo, Terence. 2011. "Thomas Reid's Ethics." In *The Stanford Encyclopedia of Philosophy*, edited by Edward Zalta. http://plato.stanford.edu/entries/reid-ethics/ (1/11).

Cuneo, Terence, and Russ Shafer-Landau. 2014. "The Moral Fixed Points: New Directions for Moral Nonnaturalism." *Philosophical Studies*. DOI: http://dx.doi.org/10.1007/s 11098-013-0277-5

Hare, R. M. 1952. *The Language of Morals*. Oxford: Oxford University Press.

Korsgaard, Christine. 2008. *Self-constitution*. Oxford: Oxford University Press.

Leftow, Brian. 2012. *God and Necessity*. Oxford: Oxford University Press.

McNaughton, David. 1996. "An Unconnected Heap of Duties?" *Philosophical Quarterly* 46: 443–447.

Parfit, Derek. 2011. *On What Matters, Vol. II*. Oxford: Oxford University Press.

Reid, Thomas. 1990. *Practical Ethics*. Edited by Knud Haakonssen. Princeton: Princeton University Press. (Abbreviated as PE).

Reid, Thomas. 2002. *Essays on the Intellectual Powers of Man*. Edited by Derek R. Brookes. Edinburgh: Edinburgh University Press. (Abbreviated as EIP).

Reid, Thomas. 2010. *Essays on the Active Powers of Man*. Edited by James Harris and Knud Haakonssen. Edinburgh: Edinburgh University Press. (Abbreviated as EAP).

Rysiew, Patrick. 2002. "Reid and Epistemic Naturalism." *The Philosophical Quarterly* 52: 437–456.

Rysiew, Patrick. forthcoming. "Thomas Reid on Language." In *Linguistic Meaning: New Essays on the History of the Philosophy of Language*, edited by Margaret Cameron, and Robert Stainton. Oxford: Oxford University Press.

Tuggy, Dale. 2000. "Thomas Reid on Causation." *Reid Studies* 3: 3–27.

Van Cleve, James. 1999. "Reid on the First Principles of Contingent Truths." *Reid Studies* 3: 3–30.

Wolterstorff, Nicholas. 2001. *Thomas Reid and the Story of Epistemology*. Cambridge: Cambridge University Press.

Wolterstorff, Nicholas. 2004. "Reid on Common sense." In *The Cambridge Companion to Thomas Reid*, edited by Terence Cuneo, and René van Woudenberg, 77–100. Cambridge: Cambridge University Press.

MORAL THEORY

Reid's moral psychology: animal motives as guides to virtue

Esther Kroeker

University of Antwerp, Center for Ethics, Stads campus, Antwerpen

My aim in this paper is to show that animal motives play an important role in guiding human agents to virtue, according to Reid. Animal motives, for Reid, are constituted of desires and of their objects. These desires are intrinsic desires for objects other than moral or prudential worth. However, from a rational and moral point of view, animal motives are good and useful parts of the human constitution that lead to happiness, teach self-government, create the habit of acting virtuously, and add force to rational motives. Understanding animal motives as guides to virtue provides Reid with the hybrid sentimentalist/rationalist account he seeks to offer.

It is ... a most important part of the philosophy of the human mind, to have a distinct and just view of the various principles of action, which the Author of our being has planted in our nature, to arrange them properly, and to assign to every one its rank.

By this it is, that we may discover the end of our being, and the part which is assigned us upon the theatre of life. In this part of the human constitution, the noblest work of God that falls within our notice, we may discern most clearly the character of him who made us, and how he would have us to employ that active power which he hath given us. (EAP 75)

Thomas Reid's account of the animal principles of action is rarely the main focus of any work on Reid. If they are discussed at all, it is usually as an introduction to the topic of Reid's rational principles of action, and of duty in particular, or as part of a discussion of moral liberty. The rational principles of action and moral liberty are undoubtedly central topics in Reid's *Essays on the Active Powers*. However, my aim in this paper is to show that the animal principles of action also play an important role in Reid's understanding of the virtuous life, and of how agents should order their lives.

Reid writes that he understands principles of action to be 'every thing that incites us to act' (EAP 74),[1] and he spends the longest essay of the *Essays on the Active Powers* writing about the different principles of action. And he devotes the largest part of this essay (Essay III) to his description and account of the animal motives. It is thus plausible to think that Reid considers that understanding the nature and role of animal motives is vital to his project. As the epigraph indicates, in fact, Reid thinks that understanding the principles of action will help us understand something about God's character, about how we are to use our human freedom, and about how we are to order our lives. Reid's account of animal motives is not easy to summarize, however, and it is difficult to understand their nature. Moreover, it might be that the important motives – those that guide us to what is good – are the rational motives and not the animal ones. The aim of this paper is therefore to consider whether Reid holds a theory of animal motives, and to consider their role in those actions that human beings find important. I will argue that animal motives are constituted of intrinsic desires for objects, and that their natural objects are not moral or prudential value. However, animal motives do, in reality, produce and lead to value, and they are, for Reid, guides to virtue.

1. Terminology and context

Reid contrasts animal principles of action with both rational principles and mechanical principles of action. He classifies animal motives into three groups: appetites (such as hunger, thirst, lust), desires (for knowledge, power and esteem), and affections (benevolent affections which imply a desire for the good of a person and malevolent affections which imply a desire for ill). Malevolent affections are motives such as emulation (ambition) and resentment (and Reid follows Butler here in distinguishing between sudden or instinctive resentment and deliberate resentment). Among the benevolent affections, Reid discusses affections such as the love of parents for their children, gratitude, compassion, esteem, friendship, love between the sexes, and public spirit.

Reid is not the only philosopher of his time to dedicate so much attention to the motives involved in human action. Passions, emotions, desires, and motives in general are topics that hold a central position in the accounts of most of Reid's predecessors and contemporaries. Reid recognizes this fact (EAP 55), but he writes that no consensus has been reached, and that, judging 'from the very different and contradictory systems of Philosophers on this subject, from the earliest ages to this day,' it is a matter of great difficulty to form a distinct notion of the various principles of action (EAP 77). Reid also notices that the names usually given to the different principles of action have very little precision, 'even in the best and purest writers in every language' (EAP 77):

> The words appetite, passion, affection, interest, reason, cannot be said to have one definite signification. They are taken sometimes in a larger, and sometimes in a more limited sense. The same principle is sometimes called by one of those names, sometimes by another; and principles of a very different nature are often called by the same name. (EAP 77–78)

In light of this lack of order and precision, Reid's aim is not to settle the question decisively, since he suggests in several passages that he might be mistaken in how he classifies the different principles (EAP 78; 117), but rather to contribute to an ongoing discussion. One of his objectives is to clean up and add precision to the debate as it stands in his day, and to help the science of the human mind progress.

In order to 'remedy this confusion of names' (EAP 78) and to offer a more 'distinct and just view of the various principles of action,' (EAP 75) Reid often finds himself correcting and commenting on what he considers to be misunderstandings among earlier philosophers. Among the views which Reid seeks to rectify we find explicit mention of the accounts of David Hume, Adam Smith, and those philosophers who tend to understand the ultimate end of human action to be pleasure (the *Epicureans*, as Reid calls them), and those who understand it as self-love (he calls their account the *Selfish* system). When it comes to the passions, Reid reproaches Hume of different shortcomings, such as attributing too much importance to the role of pleasure and displeasure as grounds of the passions, in thinking that all motives are passions, and in failing to recognize the existence of a different kind of motives: the rational motives. Reid thinks that a more careful observation of the motives that move many brute animals, infants, madmen, but also adult human beings, is in order. For Reid, the Epicureans, the Egoists, and other sentimentalist philosophers are wrong to stress the primary role of pleasure and displeasure in grounding moral evaluations. They are correct, however, to recognize that moral evaluation is not always a matter of deductive reasoning, and, as I will show in this paper, to acknowledge the importance of passions in human moral life.

Reid also disagrees with more rationalist approaches such as those of Samuel Clarke and Richard Price. Reid argues that characterizing moral motives as independent from animal motives, as pure judgments of reason, and sometimes as a priori, innate, or judgments about relations of fitness, is also to misunderstand the moral principles of action. The problem with views such as those of Price and Clarke is, first, that they seek the foundation of morality in reasoning, and, second, that they separate the moral realm from the realm of the passions (emotions, or animal motives). As many have noticed, moral judgments are closely associated to emotions for Reid (Roeser 2009 and Cuneo 2006). My claim in this paper is that animal motives also play a leading role in the moral theatre of adult human life for Reid, educating adults to know and practice virtue, and guiding and helping them to act virtuously. Reid's writings on the animal motives are central, on one hand, to his rejection of both the sentimentalist and rationalist accounts of motives and of the moral life, and, on the other, to his espousal of both sentimentalist and rationalist tenets. I will show here that Reid's account of animal motives as distinct from rational motives and yet as important actors in human moral life provides the hybrid sentimentalist/rationalist account that Reid seeks to offer.

2. Animal motives: conceptions or judgments?

As several philosophers have noticed, Reid often defines animal motives as principles of action which 'do not suppose any exercise of judgment or reason'

(EAP 92; see also EAP 52), and which 'we observe in brute-animals, and in men who have not the use of reason' (EAP 55). As Keith Lehrer observes, Reid writes that animal motives require conception, but not judgment (Lehrer 1989, 212; see EAP 78 and 92). Reid understands conception to be a mental state whereby a being holds an object in mind without predicating any quality to the object. The being who conceives an object need not necessarily form a belief or judgment about it, even though the object of conception could be a belief or judgment (one could hold it in mind without judging it to be so and so), or any other kind of object. Judgment and belief, by contrast, are mental states by which beings think of objects as having certain qualities. Hence, Reid writes that animal motives require conception but not judgment, and they are motives we share with brute animals.

To characterize animal motives in such a way, however, is vague and might give rise to puzzles. Indeed, once we examine Reid's description of each animal motive we realize that some of them require judgment. Affection, for instance, implies a desire for the good of a person who is the object of the affection. One ingredient of affection thus seems to be a belief or judgment about the good of a person (EAP 108). Other motives that seem to imply beliefs and judgments are, for instance, esteem, gratitude and resentment.

The fact that judgment is involved in many animal motives has perhaps lead William Rowe to be more nuanced in his interpretation of Reid's account. He writes that animal motives 'normally operate by influencing volitions but do not involve judgments concerning what is right or wrong, wise or foolish' (Rowe 1991, 92). According to Rowe's understanding, then, animal motives might require forming some judgment, but not about value or worth. This line of interpretation seems more promising, since Reid's animal motives are not typically a response to a value perceived. Still, some animal motives, for Reid, arise because of such a judgment. For instance, one of the benevolent affections that is classified as an animal motive is 'esteem of the wise and the good' (EAP 117). It is clear that being moved by an animal motive like esteem requires judging that a person performed some valuable action. Reid also writes, for instance, that gratitude is an animal motive, but among men, 'it is not every beneficial office that claims our gratitude, but such only as are not due to us in justice' (EAP 115). Gratitude moves human beings when they recognize that some actions performed in their favor go beyond what is required by justice. These motives therefore seem to require forming moral evaluations. Rowe's interpretation of Reid therefore faces problems as well, since judgments about value or worth might be involved in some animal motives for Reid. Nevertheless, I will show in the next section that Rowe is correct if we are more careful about the way judgments are involved in animal motives.

We are thus faced with some perplexity about the mental states involved in animal motives. Do animal motives require conception but no judgment at all, as Lehrer suggests, and as Reid himself often writes? Does Reid mean, rather, that they do not suppose judgments *necessarily*, but could? Does he mean that they only suppose some *kind* of judgment, as Rowe seems to think?

There is no clear answer to these questions. All animal motives require at least, and necessarily, some conception. Brute animals are all moved by instinctive kind of animal motives, according to Reid, and these do not require judgments. And the animal motives that influence the will of human beings sometimes require only conception. The desire for knowledge, for example, which is found in brutes in the form of curiosity, does not require forming any judgment at all (EAP 100), and yet it requires aiming at some object that one conceives. But many animal motives at work in the life of adult human beings might involve judgment, and sometimes could not exist without a judgment, even a judgment about worth, as I have pointed out above. Classifying animal motives in terms of conceptions and judgments is therefore not the best way to do so. A better way to understand them is to consider the mental state that is an ingredient of all animal motives, and to consider their objects. I will show in the next section that all of them imply a desire in the agent and an object of that desire.

3.   Animal motives: constituted of intrinsic desires and their objects

Animal motives are different from (but might include) general ideas, beliefs, or thoughts in that they are about something in virtue of being directed toward something. One must be careful not to call them feelings because Reid holds that feelings (or sensations) are not about anything at all (EAP 349); further, some animal motives, such as our permanent desires for superiority and for knowledge, have no feelings attached to them (EAP III.II.2). Contrarily to feelings, one element we find in Reid's description of every animal motive is desire. The first kind of animal motives are appetites (hunger, thirst, lust), and in these we find two ingredients, 'an uneasy sensation and a desire' (EAP 92). The second kind of animal motives are standing desires, like the desires of power, of esteem and of knowledge. These have no uneasy sensation proper to each, but seem to be constituted only of desires (EAP 99). Finally, benevolent and malevolent affections include a desire for the good or for the ill of the object of the desire, as well as associated feelings (and the object of affections, Reid holds, is always a person). Desires, therefore, are elements that appear in Reid's description of each animal motive.

What are desires for Reid? Strangely, Reid offers no definition of desires. In the *Active Powers*, Reid uses the term *desire* to designate only one class of animal motives: the desires for esteem, power and knowledge. However, he points out that he calls these *desires* 'for want of a better specific name' (EAP 99). Moreover, his use of this term is clearly not limited to this class of motives since, as I have just pointed out, desire is an ingredient of all animal motives, and since he repeatedly refers to animal motives, in general, as *natural desires*. Reid does seem to think of desires as mental states – or perhaps rather as mental acts – or as a conjunction of several states. It is a state in which beings are directed toward the external world, a state in which they are drawn to some object or moved toward some future state or object.

Reid warns his readers, in Essay II, not to confuse desire with will. Desire, in a general sense, characterizes what beings like us want, and what we want may be the object of any kind of motive, it may be some action of our own, or no action at all, or even something impossible. Desires might be conscious and occurrent, such as a present and temporary desire for food or to help a person in distress. But it might also be a standing or constant desire, such as a constant desire for knowledge. They are mental states that move or incite the will of human agents, even if they choose not to pursue the objects of their desires (EAP 48–50). Hence, desires and will should not be confused because desires are not acts of will or decisions to attain some state or pursue some object. They are not intentions to bring something about or to achieve something. Still, they are mental states that are directed to some object or state of affair and that expresses some need or concern for it, even if one does not decide or intend to pursue it. Whether Reid thought that the mental states involved in rational motives are also constituted of desires or not is a difficult and interesting question, but I will not try to answer it here. Animal motives, however, clearly include or are constituted by desire.

Moreover, the desires that are ingredients of animal motives are intrinsic desires: they are not directed toward an object in order to fulfill some further desire or end. In fact, all principles of action, for Reid, are about ultimate ends of actions. In the section on benevolent affections in general, Reid writes the following:

> A thing may be desired either on its own account, or as the means in order to something else. That only can properly be called an object of desire, which is desired upon its own account; and it is only such desires that I call principles of action. When any thing is desired as the means only, there must be an end for which it is desired; and the desire of the end is, in this case, the principle of action. (EAP 110)

Desires involved in animal motives are hence intrinsic desires for objects, and these objects are not desired in order to bring about some other end, object, or state of affairs.

So far, I have described animal motives mostly in terms of the mental states involved in them. But are animal motives, strictly speaking, desires, or are they the state of affairs one desires? We might wonder, that is, whether animal motives are the mental states themselves, or rather the objects of these mental states. The answer, in the case of animal motives, is 'both.' In most places, Reid seems to speak of them as mental states: they are appetites, affections, passions (EAP 55); they are natural desires (EAP 105) and impulses (EAP 57; 58). Terms like 'hunger,' 'thirst,' 'lust,' refer primarily to the agent's mental states. However, Reid also points out, for example, that when, by experience, we come to associate the uneasy sensation of hunger with the means of removing it, the desire and the object 'remain through life inseparable. And we give the name of hunger to the principle that is made up of both' (EAP 93).

For Reid, moreover, each animal motive has its own kind of object. Some objects simply satisfy our curiosity, and others do not, for example, whether we have thought about it or not, or experienced them or not. And some objects satisfy our appetites, whereas others do not. Water is not the object of hunger. The object of hunger is not the good of a person, and so on. Each animal motives has its own kind of object. Objects are also what distinguish one desire from another. One could not describe a desire without describing the aim of the desire. Desires for the good of certain persons, desires for knowledge, desire for power, etc. imply something in the agent who desires, and some object desired. Hence, the fact that animal motives are mental state/object pairs is implied by the fact that desires are essential ingredients of all animal motives.

In claiming that animal motives are best understood as mental state/object pairs I am not claiming that rational motives should be understood in such a way. In fact, I agree with Gideon Yaffe, for example, that rational motives are best understood as the non-existent states of affairs or objects aimed at rather than as the thought about that end in virtue of which the agent is committed to it (Yaffe 2004, 105–108). What gives us moral reason to help a sick person (provided it is in our power to do so) is that helping the sick person is a non-existent future state of affairs that is morally good. Our motive or reason to help is the moral value of the future action, or of the end we ought to bring about. Animal motives, however, are different in this respect. Describing the object of the motives is not sufficient to describe the motive. For instance, pointing out that I am staying home because a person is sick and that I ought to help the sick does not capture the animal motive at work. My motive for staying home is not only that a person is sick, but that this person is my son, and that I love him. I do not aim at love, in this case, but rather, I aim at something because I love. The fact that this book is interesting is an animal motive to continue reading it not only because it will give me knowledge (a non-existent end), but also because I care about knowledge, or, in Reid's terminology, because I desire knowledge. Therefore, rational motives are best understood as objects or states of affairs one should pursue, and animal motives are best understood as desire/object pairs. And a crucial element in Reid's account of the animal motives is that each animal motive, by nature, is directed toward its own kind of object.

Further, the ultimate end of animal motives is not pleasure or avoidance of uneasiness (except, perhaps, in the case of appetites), and it is not moral or prudential value. Let us first consider why pleasure is not the end of animal motives. Some philosophers, Reid writes, hold that what motivates us is the fact that certain objects alleviate our uneasiness, or provide satisfaction. Reid interprets Hume's account as an example of such a position: motivating passions, under Reid's interpretation of Hume, are directed toward pleasure and the avoidance of pain. But Reid enjoins us to pay closer attention to our experiences. He argues that observation shows that we are sometimes moved toward certain objects or ends like knowledge, the good of a benefactor, the happiness of our child, and so forth, for no further reason. True, knowledge gives us pleasure, but we would seek knowledge even if it gave us no pleasure. Reid also observes, for instance, that it is not because loving our children gives us pleasure that we are moved by parental affections. As a matter of fact, many actions we perform for our children (nursing them when they are infants every few hours of the day and night; encouraging them when they are teenagers despite their attitude, etc.)

are clearly not performed out of a desire for pleasure (EAP 101). He continues with further examples:

> Innumerable instances occur in life, of men who sacrifice ease, pleasure, and every thing else, to the lust of power, of fame, or even of knowledge. It is absurd to suppose, that men should sacrifice the end of what they desire only as the means of promoting that end. (EAP 101)

Hence, since agents often sacrifice pleasure to attain power, fame, and knowledge, it is absurd to think of pleasure as the natural object of such motives. Animal motives, therefore, are ultimate or intrinsic desires for certain objects as ends, and the objects or ends are not always sought in order to procure pleasure.

The objects or ends of animal motives are not prudential value or moral worth either. For Reid, prudential value is the value a future state of affairs possesses in virtue of the fact that this state of affairs will contribute to one's overall happiness. Human beings sometimes recognize that some action will lead to their overall happiness or good, and this fact constitutes a reason or motive for performing the action. Overall good or happiness is, according to Reid, the first rational motive. And moral worth is the object of the second rational motive. The object is a state of affairs that one ought to perform because it is what duty requires. Hence, when agents are moved by rational motives only, they aim to achieve some prudential or moral end. This is why Reid writes that 'it is the office of judgment to appreciate the value of an end, or the preference due to one end above another' (EAP 54). Human beings appreciate the value of ends by forming judgments about the value of such ends. And 'the ends of human actions' Reid has in view 'are two, to wit, What is good for us upon the whole, and what appears to be our duty' (EAP 154). Prudential and moral worth are the objects of rational motives. In fact, they *are* rational motives.

Now, couldn't prudential and moral worth, or value in general, also be the objects of animal motives? I have observed that animal motives involve a desire and an object of desires. The object of some animal motive could be some value, like the prudential good of our child, for instance. However, the crucial point, according to Reid, is that, even if the object of the desire is considered to be valuable, one pursues it not because of its value, but because of one's desires. Take away the desire, and the animal motive disappears. Moreover, objects of animal motives that are given to us from nature, and hence that are innate, are never moral or prudential ends. This fact is one that is observable in nature, according to Reid. Indeed, in the development and growth of human capacities animal motives appear before the rational capacities. Making long term judgments about issues of overall happiness require developed rational capacities. And forming judgments about moral worth requires a more developed rational faculty than what is required for animal motives. Hence, animal motives, by nature, are not directed toward ends such as what is required by prudence or duty. For example, the desire for knowledge is a desire that we find in the form of curiosity in the cat, or that is revealed by the number of questions small children pose. Animal motives are therefore not directed toward prudential or moral value. They have their own objects, and these objects are not pursued because of their moral or prudential worth.

Hence, this is how we should understand Reid's claim that animal motives do not suppose a judgment, or a judgment about worth, as Rowe claims. They might involve a moral judgment like, 'Alfred was so good (morally) in helping me with my work. He really shouldn't have.' This is the kind of judgment that is involved in gratitude, for example. However, gratitude is not directed toward morally or prudentially good ends, and hence need not suppose a judgment that the action I am moved to perform is one I perform because it is in my interest or is what duty require. The object of my gratitude is the good of Alfred. Hence, I might be moved to hug him, for instance, to wish him well, and to thank him, but not because I ought, morally (or prudentially), to do so.

However, it is possible that the object of some animal motive is some valuable object, and that one desires some valuable object. For instance, parental affection is constituted of a desire for the good of the child. The parent might thus recognize some state of affairs as good for their child, and even as morally or prudentially good. The reason, however, for which the parent acts, is the parent's affection. When parents wish to bring about something good, such as the good of their child, the value is sought because of the parent's natural desires for it. Still, parents who are moved by animal motives *only* do not act for the good of their child because *they* aim to achieve prudential and moral value. Animal motives are thus constituted of intrinsic desires for specific objects and these objects are not overall happiness and moral worth.

4. Animal motives: guides to virtue

Armed with Reid's understanding of animal motives, I will now try to show how animal motives play a role in our moral conduct, choices and actions, according to Reid. Several philosophers have (rightly) argued that *moral emotions* do not play a role in guiding us to virtue for Reid (Roeser 2009; Cuneo 2006).[2] They argue that moral emotions arise as a consequence of moral judgments, and hence do not help us perceive (existing) value. Terence Cuneo, for instance, writes that Reid rejects the model whereby feelings are signs of value, and hence Reid does not succeed in his attempt to offer a hybrid sentimentalist/rationalist account. He also argues that Reid should have offered such a model, and he attempts to reconstruct one that would follow from Reid's writings. Reid, it is true, does not think of (moral) feelings as signs of existing value. However, I think Reid presents another kind of hybrid account in which emotions play a role in moral judgments. Emotions do play a role in moral deliberation for Reid. However, the emotions that play this role are the animal ones, and although they might not typically help us perceive existing value, they do help us live a valuable life, one that leads to virtue and prudence. They teach and point the way, not to judgments about the moral quality of certain existing states of affairs, but to judgments about what one should do. They guide us toward as-of-yet non existing value.

I will argue in what follows that even though animal motives are not directed towards moral and prudential value, they do, in fact, from a rational point of view, lead to value. I have observed above that animal motives have their natural objects or aims, and that these aims are not moral or prudential ends. If one is moved by an animal motive alone, one will not perform the action for prudential or moral reasons. However, our judgment informs us that our animal motives are good and essential parts of our constitution, and our judgment also informs us that the objects of our animal motives are conducive to valuable states of affairs.

First, reason and observation will inform us that the consequences of acting on animal motives are conducive to valuable ends, like our overall happiness. It is in our best interest, Reid points out, to be moved and to act upon our animal motives. The person who is moved by animal motives is moved to perform actions that serve some objectively valuable end, even though the agent who acts according to some animal motive (only) does not aim at such ends. Reid writes, 'the impulse of passion is not always to what is bad, but very often to what is good, and what our reason approves' (EAP 139). Animal motives are instrumental to objective value:

> Reason, if it were perfect, would lead us to desire power, knowledge, and the esteem and affection of our fellow men, as a means of promoting our own happiness, and of being useful to others. Here again, nature, to supply the defects of reason, has given us a strong natural desire of those objects, which leads us to pursue them without regard to their utility. (EAP 107)

When we act out of a desire for knowledge, for example, we need not have any regard to our overall interest; we simply want to understand or to know. But, in reality, acting according to this motive will also lead to our overall happiness since it will help us understand the world we live in and how actions and events are related to each other. Other animal motives, like appetites, also serve our interest. Natural appetites, according to Reid, lead to 'the preservation of the individual, and... the continuance of the species' (EAP 93). These appetites therefore serve a valuable function. Reason, if perfect, might tell us when to eat and what, how much, and how often, but our reason is not perfect in this way (EAP 93). We could eat out of a sense of prudence, of course, but we would be moved to eat even if we had no regard to prudence. Reid writes: 'An appetite draws us to a certain object, without regard to its being good for us, or ill. There is no self-love implied in it any more than benevolence' (EAP 95). We need not aim at value when we are moved by appetites, but yet appetites contribute to our preservation and happiness.

The same could be said for affections. Affections will lead to the good of others and to harmonious life in society. Reid writes that benevolent affections are 'necessary for the preservation of society among men, without which man would become an easy prey to the beasts of the field' (EAP 110). He continues by pointing out that we do not love our children because we ought to, in any sense of ought. On the contrary, 'the peculiar sensibility of affection... is not the effect of reasoning or reflection, but the effect of that constitution which nature has given him' (EAP 113). Still, Reid points out, we judge that parental affection is absolutely necessary for the continuation of our species (EAP 114). And its utility is very great, he continues, since all of the benevolent affections promote good-will among men (EAP 115). Love between the sexes, together with parental affection, Reid writes, are the source of all domestic felicity or happiness, 'the greatest, next to a good conscience, which this world affords' (EAP 118). Animal motives thus have an instrumental value, in leading to valuable ends.

Second, our moral sense informs us of the moral value of animal principles of action – of the mental states as well as their object. Reid writes that when adult human beings perceive actions or think of actions (past, present or future) their conscience 'is altogether silent, or it pronounces the action to be good, or to be bad' (EP 291. Conscience meddles with every action and motive. We have a moral opinion about everything, and our moral opinion concerning animal motives is, in certain cases (which I will define in the next section) far from indifference or disapproval. On the contrary, it is a first principle of morals that we ought to act according to the intention of nature as it appears in the natural principles of action of the constitution of man (EAP 273). Reid, in his description of this moral principle, specifically mentions appetites, natural desires, affections and passions, in their natural degree. These motives have a natural function: preserving our species, producing happiness, and helping humans live harmoniously in society. And it is a self-evident moral principle, according to Reid, that we ought to act according to these motives. The actions and states of affairs that are produced by natural animal motives are objects of our moral approbation. We approve, morally, of those who live well with their neighbors and who act for the good of others. We also approve, morally, of ambition and knowledge, for example. And we approve of beings who are moved by such desires; their motives seem morally praiseworthy. Reid writes, for example, that affections move agents to act without any regard to duty, and yet love of our friends, neighbors, gratitude, and other affections are 'by the constitution of human nature... accompanied with a conviction of their being morally good' (EAP 294). Once the moral and rational faculties of a person have sufficiently matured, she is able to consider the different motives that influence her in her choices and actions, according to Reid, and she will approve, morally, of the objects desired and of the passions, appetites and desires of those objects.

Friendship, compassion, public spirit, benevolence, etc. are motives which human beings therefore find prudentially and morally good. Agents approve of beings who are moved by such affections. Reid writes of benevolence:

> The constitution of our nature very powerfully invites us to cherish and cultivate in our minds the benevolent affections...

> Benevolence, from its nature, composes the mind, warms the heart, enlivens the whole frame... It may justly be said to be medicinal both to soul and body. We are bound to it by duty; we are invited to it by interest; and because both these cords are often feeble, we have natural kind affections to aid them in their operation...
> (EAP 121)

We approve of the person who is moved by such motives, and we feel moral esteem for persons who are moved by affections like friendship and love.

Third, animal motives guide us to what is valuable. What I have shown above is that human beings may consider those animal motives that move them naturally, and the objects pursued, and recognize that they are valuable, in a backward looking kind of perception. But animal motives also guide in a forward looking way. They have a pedagogical role, teaching us about virtue, making it easier to acquire virtue, and producing virtuous action. Reid repeatedly points out that our rational faculties need help in influencing our choices and actions. If our reason were perfect, Reid writes, we would recognize the value to which animal motives lead. But since our reason is not perfect, we need the help of animal motives. Reid writes that we need their help to be virtuous persons:

> Without the natural appetites, reason, as was before observed, would be insufficient, either for the preservation of the individual, or the continuation of the species; and without the natural desires we have mentioned, human virtue would be insufficient to influence mankind to a tolerable conduct in society . . .

> It is true, indeed, that perfect virtue, joined with perfect knowledge, would make both our appetites and desires unnecessary encumbrances of our nature; but as human knowledge and human virtue are both very imperfect, these appetites and desires are necessary supplements to our imperfections. (EAP 102)

Animal motives guide us to virtue because our intellectual powers are not perfect, according to Reid. Given their imperfect capacities, human beings need help to live the kind of life that is good and virtuous, and animal motives provide this needed help.

They teach us how to be virtuous by moving us, as children, to objects or ends which we later come to recognize as prudentially and morally valuable. For instance, curiosity in children moves them, naturally, to gain knowledge. They later come to recognize the value of knowledge, but they are already used to pursuing it without any regard to its value. Even adults learn to act virtuously because of their animal motives. We are moved, naturally, to feel compassion and pity for those who are close to us. This affection is found in children early on, even before they may recognize its moral worth. And even adult human beings are more concerned with the pain and happiness of their close relations. These natural desires and affections such as love for their children, friends, and neighbors, will then help them acquire the habit of doing good to others. We may be at first partial in our love and in our attention, Reid points out, but this will teach us to have the concerns of others in mind. To add weight to his observation, Reid quotes Alexander Pope: 'Friend, parent, neighbor, first it will embrace – His country next, and then all human race' (EAP 119). Animal motives therefore help create the habit of doing good to others.

Animal motives also train children and adults to self-government. For example, the person who feels emulation, a natural sense of competition, will learn to restrain some appetites and passions in order to prepare for a race or a competition. This will help her order her passions and desires in light of the prescriptions of morality, for example. Reid writes:

> The pursuits of power, of fame, and of knowledge, require a self-command no less than virtue does. In our behavior towards our fellow-creatures, they generally lead to that very conduct which virtue requires. I say generally, for this, no doubt, admits of exceptions, especially in the case of ambition, or the desire of power. (EAP 102)

Animal motives often lead to what virtue requires, and they teach us to control ourselves in in order to reach some end. Attaining the object of some animal motives requires silencing the influence of other animal motives. This does not mean that one animal motive is better than another, but only that one cannot act on all of one's desires at the same time. Acting for the good of our child will require putting aside, in some cases, certain appetites, and even some desire for knowledge or fame (when one is led to spend considerable time with an infant, for example).

Animal motives lead us to virtuous ends (to bring about morally good states of affairs), they teach us self-government, and they help us become virtuous persons. Since they are friendly to virtue, Reid writes, and are given to us naturally, 'they make it more easily to be acquired' (EAP 103). The agreeable feeling, Reid suggests, that always attends to benevolent affections, is a present reward to cultivate and cherish benevolent affections (EAP 121). Hence, animal motives, and affections especially, are 'the most proper engines that can be used in the education and discipline of men' (EAO 103).

Furthermore, animal motives and rational motives may also work together, reinforcing each other. According to Reid, one can be moved to one action by several motives. For instance, one can be moved by love and also conceive of the action as virtuous. This does not mean that one loves because it is our duty to do so. One simply loves because one loves, but in loving one also sees that one is acting virtuously (as I argue in Kroeker 2013). One might be moved by parental affection (a natural desire) and also by the (most likely dispositional) moral judgment that one ought, morally, to act for the good of one's child. In some cases, the animal motive adds strength to the rational motive, and in some cases the opinion adds strength to the passion:

> Although natural affection to parents, children, and near relations, is not grounded on the opinion of their merit, it is much increased by that consideration. So is every benevolent affection. (EAP 147)

Animal and rational motives therefore work together and reinforce each other, when they lead to the same actions.

The beneficial role of the passions in leading to virtue and in adding strength to our rational motives is especially clear in Reid's chapter dedicated to the topic of passions in general. Passions are any kind of animal motive present in a strong or vehement degree. Those who tend to characterize Reid as one who recognizes the existence of emotions but who accords them no leading role will find it difficult to account for this chapter, given the positive manner in which Reid paints the value and beauty of human passions here. Reid spends several pages praising passions: 'All our natural desires and affections are good and necessary parts of our constitution,' he writes, 'and passion, being only a certain degree of vehemence in these, its natural tendency is to good, and it is by accident that it leads us wrong' (EAP 140). Passions, he continues, draw us to objects, interest us in it, and this is necessary in order to form correct judgments about the object. Passion aids reason, he observes, and gives additional force to its dictates (EAP 140). He writes:

> There is no bad action which some passion may not prevent; nor is there any external good action, of which some passion may not be the main spring; and, it is very probably, that even the passions of men, upon the whole, do more good to society than hurt. (EAP 140)

The representative content of animal motives, therefore, is not virtue or happiness, but they are directed toward virtue and happiness because of the intention of nature, and hence they play a vital role in teaching us about virtue, in guiding us to virtue, and in adding force to the dictates of reason.

5. Objections

If my interpretation is correct, and if animal motives lead us to what is valuable, and if animal motives show us what is virtuous and help us do what is virtuous, then how should we explain the fact that Reid constantly points out that the animal and the rational motives are often in conflict? Why does Reid write so often that reason must guide and restrain our passions? Reid often writes, the objection continues, that animal motives are in opposition to our rational motives (EAP 98), and that the role of conscience is in many cases to move us to act contrarily to what our animal motives move us to do (EAP 138–139). True, appetites lead to survival and happiness. However, Reid continues in the same passage that 'we see, that, in many cases, appetite may lead a man to what he knows will be to his hurt' (EAP 95). Moreover, although Reid praises the merits of passions, he also spends a considerable part of the chapter dealing with them arguing that passions are not easily kept within reasonable bounds, and that all folly and vice consists 'in the prevalence of passion over reason' (EAP 139). If animal motives lead us to what is good, as I have pointed out above, then we must explain why they often fail to lead us to what is prudentially or morally good.

Two considerations will remove this apparent inconsistency in Reid's account. The first is that animal motives lead to virtue and to valuable ends when they move us in their natural degree and kind. When Reid writes that animal motives are 'good and necessary parts of our constitution,' he is thinking of them in their natural state (EAP 140). Animal motives are natural principles which may easily become corrupted, but *natural* desires are awe-inspiring parts of our constitution *when they function according to nature*. Corrupted animal motives are not principles that are part of our constitution or given to us by nature, and they do not lead to virtue.

It is difficult, however, to understand how we may recognize the natural animal motives from the non-natural ones. By natural principles, Reid sometimes means that human beings are moved by them regardless of whether or not they think they should have these natural desires. This is why Reid writes about the affections that

> Our affections are not immediately in our power, as our outward actions are. Nature has directed them to certain objects. We may do kind offices without affection; but we cannot create an affection which nature has not given. (EAP 113)

Affections, as well as animal motives in general, are given to us by nature. They appear in children as soon as they can form a conception of an object, and hence are natural in the sense of being part of the human constitution and of moving humans prior to observation and reasoning. However, some animal motives that move adult human beings, like gratitude, esteem and resentment, do require reasoning capacities, as we have noticed earlier. Reid would point out that one way to know whether they are natural animal motives is to notice that both the vicious and the virtuous are moved by them. Another way is to notice that they are found in a more instinctive form in infants and the most sagacious brutes. Reid describes the way in which animals are moved to react to those who care for them (a pre-rational kind of gratitude) or how animals treat the leader of a herd or of a pack (a kind of esteem) or how they retaliate when faced with hurt and danger (sudden resentment). Hence animal motives that move adults and that require forming some judgment also move brute animals, but in a way that does not require judgment. Therefore, looking at the animal kingdom offers clues to what is natural in our animal nature. And only natural animal motives are useful and good.

Moreover, animal motives that are good and useful are those that move us in their natural degree. Hence when discussing the appetites, he writes, for example that

> Our natural appetites may be made more violent by excessive indulgence, and . . . they may be weakened by starving. The first is often called the effect of a pernicious luxury, the last may sometimes be the effect of want, sometimes of superstition. I apprehend that nature has given to our appetites the degree of strength which is most proper for us; and that whatever alters their natural tone, either in excess or in defect, does not mend the work of nature, but may mar and pervert it. (EAP 94)

Reid seems to think that one must take care of one's animal motives, by avoiding excess (eating when there's no hunger, for instance), but also by keeping them alive and being careful not to extinguish them. We may encourage our children to learn, to read, to know more things, but not to try to know all the (intimate) details of the lives of other human beings, for example. On the other hand, cutting children off from every source of knowledge and education is dangerous and contrary, according to Reid, to the very intention of their nature. Reid thus thinks of good animal motives as those which nature has given us in a certain degree. He also recognizes that some desires and passions were not given by nature, and these should also be avoided. It is possible to develop desires which nature has not given us. Hence, by 'frequent use of things which stimulate the nervous system,' it is possible to acquire a taste for things like 'the use of tobacco, for opiates, and for intoxicating liquors' (EAP 96–97). Reid's conclusion is often that

> As it is best to preserve our natural appetites, in that tone and degree of strength which nature gives them, so we ought to beware of acquiring appetites which nature never gave. They are always useless, and very often hurtful. (EAP 97)

> Although our natural desires are highly beneficial to society, and even aiding to virtue, yet acquired desires are not only useless, but hurtful and even disgraceful. (EAP 105)

In many cases, therefore, conscience and reason are contrary to passions because the latter are not natural, or because they are present in a degree that is unnatural, and we must avoid acquiring appetites and desires which we do not have by nature. Only natural, uncorrupted, animal motives are those that are trustworthy guides and teachers of virtue.

A second consideration which will remove the apparent inconsistency between, on one hand, the good and useful role of animal motives, and, on the other, their opposition to virtue, is that animal motives offer a limited perspective. Natural, uncorrupted, animal motives might be in opposition to the dictates of conscience. In a certain situation, doing one's duty might require silencing one's desire for superiority, for instance. And several natural animal motives, all of them good and useful to human life, might be in opposition with each other. Our desire for knowledge might sometimes be opposed to some affection; appetites might be opposed to desires for power, affection for a friend might sometimes require acting contrary to the good of one's community, etc. And agents might have to determine which animal motive to act upon according to some moral or prudential consideration. Hence even natural, uncorrupted, animal motives might conflict with our moral and prudential sense and might be considered to be wrong or bad.

Why should conscience be the referee in such cases? And why should we follow the dictates of conscience when they are opposed by some passion? Simply because animal motives do not provide human beings with the whole truth of the matter concerning what is best for them. When thinking about how one should act, and when there is a conflict between motives, one sometimes needs to weigh motives, to deliberate, to understand them and the possible actions they lead to in their particular context, to understand their relation to more general moral axioms, and so on. If there is a conflict between an animal motive and a rational motive, like duty, the outcome of this process, Reid holds, is a moral judgment. Animal motives simply cannot fill this role, since the desires involved in animal motives are not directed toward ends such as our overall good or what is our duty. If they are directed toward such ends, it is because of the intention of nature, and not because of their intentional content. They have, Reid writes, a more present gratification in view. A man, therefore, who has no other leader than these, would be like a ship in the ocean without hands, which cannot be said to be destined to any port. (EAP 150)

It is the role of conscience to regulate our animal affections and passions (EAP 304), and to determine the destination to reach. To know how we should live, we need a point of view that goes beyond the view provided by our many natural animal desires. Reid seeks to offer a hybrid position that embraces important aspects of sentimentalist and rationalist accounts. Hence, the important role of the passions does not eliminate the important role of the rational motives. Although reason is often defective and in need of help, our passions are also often limited and in need of reflection and of a more inclusive view point. On the other hand, attributing a more inclusive and leading role to conscience should not have the effect of eradicated animal motives. On the contrary, our deliberation and judgment about what we are to do should include thoughts about which animal motives are at work and in what degree.

Still, one might object, some animal motives might seem to be natural in some sense, and yet contrary to virtue or prudence. One might remark that anger, envy, jealousy and malice, for example, are vicious traits that seem to spring naturally from our animal motives, or that seem to be as natural as compassion and parental affection. Reid's answer is that such passions are not natural, they are corruptions of malevolent affections, and Reid is critical of malevolent affections because, he argues, these almost always go wrong, and there are many ways in which they get corrupted. Malevolent affections are emulation and resentment. These are natural tendencies which are found in some degree in brutes. And if they were found in the same degree in human beings, they would be useful and good. However, they are rarely found in the same way they are found in brutes. Emulation, when exercised according to the intention of nature, is 'a desire for superiority to our rivals in any pursuit, accompanied with an uneasiness at being surpassed' (EAP 124). We see it in brutes, in dogs, in horses, in many animals who 'contend for superiority in their flock or herd' (EAP 124). Resentment is also observed in animals who instinctively retaliate when hurt is done to them. Even a mouse, Reid writes, 'will bite when it cannot run away' (EAP 128). Hence, there is a degree of emulation and resentment, the animal degree, which is what Reid understands as the natural degree of animal motives. There is nothing wrong with 'fair and honest emulation' or with 'sudden resentment.' On the contrary, these passions help us create and achieve great projects and they protect us from hurt and destruction. In brutes, these motives contain no aim to do what is contrary to duty. But humans often use these motives for vicious ends.

Malevolent affections may lead to ill because human beings have wrong opinions, or because human beings tend to distort their effects, or because humans may aim at vice rather than virtue. Natural emulation incites a person 'to make more vigorous exertions, and to strain every nerve to get before his rival' (EAP 126). However, the evil dispositions of the human heart, Reid writes, often lead us to look at our competitors with an evil eye, and to endeavor to prevent their success. 'This,' he writes, 'is pure envy, the most malignant passion that can lodge in the human breast; which devours, as its natural food, the fame and the happiness of those who are most deserving of our esteem' (EAP 126). Emulation, in those who have a vicious character, might also lead them to form biased opinions of others, and to think wrongly of themselves as better than anyone else. It would be endless, he points out, to enumerate all the evils which 'passion and folly beget upon emulation' (EAP 127). The same could be said about resentment. There is a kind of resentment that is found in humans only because it supposes the opinion of injury intended. This resentment arises when one has been unjustly and intentionally wronged or injured. Again, the hurt felt often leads us to make a wrong estimation of the injury intended, and this passion is often blown out of proportion. The injured person, in fact, might react in a way that is also beyond the measure prescribed by justice. Therefore, malevolent affections are so easily corrupted in normal human beings that one should be cautious of them. Reid concludes that

> Malevolent affection, not only in its faulty excesses, but in its moderate degrees, is vexation and disquiet to the mind, and even gives deformity to the countenance . . . [Hence] it is evident that, by these signals, nature loudly admonishes us to use [benevolent affections] as our daily bread, both for health and pleasure, but to consider [malevolent affections] as a nauseous medicine, which is never to be taken without necessity; and even then in no greater quantity than the necessity requires. (EAP 133)

Motives such as envy and jealousy may therefore seem to be natural, but they are not. They are corruptions of good, useful and natural motives such as a good and healthy sense of competition and a natural desire to protect ourselves from hurt.

Animal motives, in their natural degree, teach us to care for others and to pursue some worthy ends. And reason, on the other hand, evaluates the animal motives, considering their consequences, their role in the animal kingdom and in the development of small children, and recognizes which ones should be trusted and cultivated. Reason also observes that natural animal motives tend to contribute to a good and happy disposition and to a sense of harmony. Animal motives therefore play an important role in the well rounded human life when there is a constant interplay between emotions and reason.

6. Conclusion

The hybrid sentimentalist/rationalist account that Reid offers is therefore a model in which our animal motives, in their natural degree and kind, move us toward objects that are valuable. They are guides to value. In deliberating about how a person is to order her life or about the course of action she should adopt, the wise and virtuous person will give due consideration to her animal motives. This person will seek to live a life in which rational motives and animal motives reinforce each other and concur in the course of action to which they aim. Moreover, if natural animal motives are such important teachers and guides, then the education of young children should not only foster intellectual and moral knowledge, but should also involve creating an environment that fosters the flourishing of animal motives in their natural degree and kind. Friendship, competition, bodily and mental health, community, curiosity, wonder, are elements that cannot be excluded from a child's *moral* education.

Reid therefore understands the moral domain to be larger than a set of rules and principles. It also involves other areas that human beings find as important. Discovering these areas requires turning our attention to our natural desires. To know what is best for us, Reid would claim, requires trying to understand which motives are natural and good parts of our constitution and which are not, and living according to what is best requires cultivating these motives.

We are now in a position to understand why having a just view of the different principles of action is a most important part of the philosophy of the human mind for Reid, as Reid writes in the quotation at the beginning of this paper (EAP 75). This study leads us to understand more about what it means to be a well-rounded virtuous person, for Reid. It helps us understand that the person who employs her active powers well is the person who is guided by conscience, by prudence, but also by natural appetites, desires and affections.[3]

Notes

1. All references to Reid's *Essays on the Active Powers* (EAP) are taken from the Edinburgh edition.
2. Moral emotions or affections are ingredients of Reid's moral sentiments. Moral sentiments are constituted, first, of a moral judgment, and this judgment gives rise to affections (a desire for the good of the object and pleasurable feelings). Moral approbation refers to the judgment–moral emotion combination.
3. I am grateful to Patrick Rysiew and Terence Cuneo for their detailed comments and suggestions, as well as to the participants of a workshop dedicated to this volume for their valuable questions and suggestions. This work was supported by the Fund for Scientific Research Flanders (FWO) [grant number GOB4812N. 5520]

References

Cuneo, Terence. 2006. "Signs of Value: Reid on the Evidential Role of Feelings in Moral Judgment." *British Journal for the History of Philosophy* 14 (1): 69–91.

Kroeker, Esther. 2013. "Acting from a Good Conscience: Reid, Love, and Moral Worth." *History of Philosophy Quarterly* 30 (4): 333–348.

Lehrer, Keith. 1989. *Thomas Reid*. London: Routledge.

Reid, Thomas. 2010. *Essays on the Active Powers of Man*, edited by Knud Haakonssen, and James Harris. Edinburgh: Edinburgh University Press.

Roeser, Sabine. 2009. "Reid and Moral Emotions." *Journal of Scottish Philosophy* 7 (2): 177–192.

Rowe, William. 1991. *Thomas Reid on Freedom and Morality*. Ithaca, NY: Cornell University Press.

Yaffe, Gideon. 2004. *Manifest Activity. Thomas Reid's Theory of Action*. Oxford: Oxford University Press.

EPISTEMOLOGY

Common sense in Thomas Reid

John Greco

Department of Philosophy, Saint Louis University, Saint Louis, MO

This paper explains the nature and role of common sense in Reid and uses the exposition to answer some of Reid's critics. The key to defending Reid is to distinguish between two kinds of priority that common sense beliefs are supposed to enjoy. Common sense beliefs enjoy epistemological priority in that they constitute a foundation for knowledge; i.e. they have evidential status without being grounded in further evidence themselves. Common sense beliefs enjoy methodological priority in that they constrain philosophical theory: they serve as pre-theoretical commitments that philosophical theories ought to respect in the absence of good reasons for rejecting them.

Thomas Reid's views on common sense have been criticized by friends and foes alike. For example, in a famous passage from the *Prolegomena*, Kant equates Reid's references to common sense with 'an appeal to the opinion of the multitude, of whose applause the philosopher is ashamed.' Wolterstorff (2001) is sympathetic toward Reid in general, but nevertheless finds fault with Reid's views on common sense, arguing that on this particular issue Reid was confused.[1]

In this paper I explain the nature and role of common sense in Reid and use the exposition to answer Reid's critics. The key to defending Reid is to distinguish between two kinds of priority that common sense is supposed to enjoy in Reid's philosophy: epistemological and methodological. In brief, common sense beliefs enjoy an epistemological priority in that they constitute a foundation for knowledge: such beliefs enjoy the kind of evidential status required for knowledge, even without being grounded in further evidence themselves. Common sense beliefs enjoy a methodological priority in that they constrain philosophical theory: such beliefs serve as pre-theoretical commitments that philosophical theories ought to respect, at least in the absence of good reasons for rejecting them.

With this distinction in hand, it is easy to show that Kant's complaint against Reid is misdirected. We can also show that Reid is not, as Wolterstorff has it, 'confused between two understandings' of first principles. Finally, a number of Reid's commentators take him to defend an 'innocent until proven guilty' approach to justified belief. That is, they attribute to Reid the position that all beliefs enjoy a kind of default epistemic justification; we are justified in believing unless we have good reasons to doubt. Our distinction between epistemological and methodological priority allows us to see that this is a misinterpretation.

Section 1 explains what Reid means by 'common sense' and 'the principles of common sense.' Section 2 distinguishes between two kinds of priority that Reid supposes the principles of common sense to have. Section 3 considers Reid's views regarding the sources of epistemological and methodological priority; i.e. why Reid thinks that first principles have the kinds of priority that they do. Section 4 uses the results of previous sections to answer Reid's critics. Section 5 addresses a more general issue. Davidson (1992) and Rorty (1979) (among others) have leveled a now familiar objection to foundationalism; that we are trapped in 'the circle of belief,' and therefore cannot hope to ground knowledge or justification elsewhere. I argue that a distinction between epistemological and methodological priority allows us to dissolve this objection as well.

1. What does Reid mean by 'common sense'?

The first task for interpreting what Reid means by 'common sense' is to resolve an ambiguity. Namely, Reid sometimes writes as if common sense is a faculty for making judgments. But sometimes he writes as if common sense is made up of the judgments themselves, or perhaps the contents of those judgments. Here are some representative passages.

a.   ... in common language, sense always implies judgment. A man of sense is a man of judgment. Good sense is good judgment. Nonsense is what is evidently contrary to right judgment. Common sense is that degree of judgment which is common to men with whom we can converse and transact business. (*Essays* VI, II, 421)

b.   We ascribe to reason two offices, or two degrees. The first is to judge of things self-evident; the second to draw conclusions that are not self-evident from those that are. The first of these is the province, and the sole province, of common sense; and, therefore, it coincides with reason in its whole extent, and is only another name for one branch or one degree of reason. (*Essays* VI, II, 425)

c.   Such original and natural judgments are, therefore, a part of that furniture which nature hath given to the human understanding ... They serve to direct us in the common affairs of life, where our reasoning faculty would leave us in the dark. They are a part of our constitution; and all the discoveries of our reason are grounded upon them. They make up what is called *the common sense of mankind*; and, what is manifestly contrary to any of those first principles, is what we call *absurd*. The strength of them is *good sense*, which is often found in those who are not acute in reasoning. A remarkable deviation from them, arising from a disorder in the constitution, is what we call *lunacy*; as when a man believes that he is made of glass. (*Inquiry*, 209, Reid's emphases)

d. If there are certain principles, as I think there are, which the constitution of our nature leads us to believe, and which we are under a necessity to take for granted in the common concerns of life, without being able to give a reason for them; these are what we call the principles of common sense; and what is manifestly contrary to them, is what we call absurd. (*Inquiry*, 108)

In these passages, 'common sense' is identified with 'common judgment' and 'common principles.' But here we have a three-way ambiguity among:

'judgment' as *faculty of judgment*; a disposition to judge (a, b);

'judgment' as *act of judgment*; the products of the faculty; the manifestation of the disposition (c);

'judgment' as *content of judgment*; the content expressed; the proposition affirmed (d).

The last notion is more naturally expressed with the word 'principle,' as in 'first principle' and 'principle of common sense.' But a principle can also be a disposition, and in passage c. Reid uses 'principle' as synonymous with 'judgment.'

So is common sense to be understood as a common faculty, a set of common judgments, or a set of common contents (or propositions)? I suggest that the ambiguity is to be resolved this way: 'common sense' proper is a faculty of judgment (or perhaps a collection of faculties of judgment). 'The principles of common sense' and 'first principles' refer both to the judgments that issue from the faculty and the contents of these.[2] As we will see, these judgments and their contents are not in fact 'common,' in the sense of 'shared' or 'held in common.'[3] What makes them principles of common sense, rather, is that they issue from common sense *qua* faculty, a faculty (or set of faculties) that is held in common by all normally functioning human beings. For example, some first principles issue from memory and perception. But, of course, not everyone shares the same memories or perceptions.[4]

More exactly, the principles of common sense come in two varieties: particular and general. It is true that the general principles are commonly shared. For example, 'that, in the phenomena of nature, what is to be, will probably be like to what has been in similar circumstances.' But there are also particular principles, i.e. judgments that are the product of an individual subject's perspective in time and space: 'I see the sun when he shines;' 'I remember the battle of Culloden.' In other words, there are the particular judgments of perception, memory, and 'consciousness' (or introspection).

The following passages confirm that the principles of common sense come in both the particular and general variety.

The first principles of mathematical reasoning are mathematical axioms and definitions; and the first principles of all our reasoning about existences, are our perceptions. (*Inquiry*, 185)

It is another property ... of many first principles, that they force assent in particular instances, more powerfully than when they are turned into a general proposition ... Many have in general maintained that the senses are not fallacious, yet there never was found a man so skeptical as not to trust his senses in particular instances when his safety required it; and it may be observed of those who have professed skepticism, that their skepticism lies in generals, while in particulars they are no less dogmatical than others. (*Essays* VI, V, 448)

Another point that we can make about first principles is that their instances are not always clear. In other words, it is not always clear what is or is not a first principle.

What the precise limits are which divide common judgment from what is beyond it on the one hand, and from what falls short of it on the other, may be difficult to determine; and men may agree in the meaning of the word who have different opinions about those limits, or who even never thought of fixing them. This is as intelligible as, that all Englishmen should mean the same thing by the county of York, though perhaps not a hundredth part of them can point to its precise limits. (*Essays* VI, II, 423)

Moreover, apparent instances can be challenged.

Upon the whole, I acknowledge that we ought to be cautious that we do not adopt opinions as first principles which are not entitled to that character ... We do not pretend that those things that are laid down as first principles may not be examined, and that we ought not to have our ears open to what may be pleaded against their being admitted as such. (*Essays* I, II, 234)

In sum, the principles of common sense do not have their status by virtue of being common. Neither do they have it by virtue of their content. Rather, the notion of 'common faculty' is prior to the notion of 'common principles.' The first principles of common sense have their status by virtue of their source in the faculty (or faculties) of common sense. Such principles can be general or particular, and apparent instances can be challenged.

2. Two kinds of priority for the first principles of commons sense: epistemic and methodological

In this section we distinguish two kinds of priority that Reid supposes the principles of common sense to enjoy.[5] The two kinds of priority are often confused by Reid scholars, resulting in misinterpretations of Reid's epistemology of common sense.

First, there is epistemic priority:

Epistemic priority: First principles have the status of non-inferential knowledge. That is, first principles are known, but not on the basis of reasoning, or inference, or argument from other things that are known.

Second, there is methodological priority:

Methodological priority: First principles have *prima facie* plausibility as pre-theoretical starting points. They can be rejected by philosophical theory, but only on the basis of very strong considerations. Put differently, first principles constrain theory: they act as (defeasible) pre-theoretical commitments that philosophical theories ought to respect.

In the following passage Reid emphasizes the epistemic priority of first principles, i.e. their status as non-inferential knowledge, or knowledge not inferred from other things that are already known.

> ... there are ... propositions which are no sooner understood than they are believed ... There is no searching for evidence, no weighing of arguments; the proposition is not deduced or inferred from another; it has the light of truth in itself, and as no occasion to borrow it from another. Propositions of this last kind, when they are used in matters of science, have commonly been called *axioms*; and on whatever occasion they are used, are called *first principles, principles of common sense, common notions, self-evident truths*. (*Essays* VI, IV, 434)

In the next passage, Reid echoes a familiar Aristotelian argument for the existence of first principles: they are necessary to stop a regress of reasons, or evidence.

> ... I hold it to be certain, and even demonstrable, that all knowledge got by reasoning must be built upon first principles. This is as certain as that every house must have a foundation ... When we examine, in the way of analysis, the evidence of any proposition, either we find it self-evident, or it rests upon one or more propositions that support it. The same thing may be said of the propositions that support it, and of those that support them, as far back as we can go. But we cannot go back in this track to infinity. Where then must this analysis stop? It is evident that it must stop only when we come to propositions which support all that are built upon them, but are themselves supported by none—that is, to self-evident propositions ... So that it appears to be demonstrable that, without first principles, analytical reasoning could have no end, and synthetical reasoning could have no beginning; and that every conclusion got by reasoning must rest with its whole weight upon first principles, as the building does upon its foundation. (*Essays* VI, IV, 435)

The epistemological priority of common sense in Reid's philosophy is universally acknowledged by his commentators. It is less often made explicit that the principles of common sense also have a methodological priority for Reid. That is, they have *prima facie* plausibility as pre-theoretical starting points. The priority is 'methodological' in the usual sense: it concerns *the method by which we ought to proceed* in our theorizing.

Here we may quote Reid at length:

> It is a bold philosophy that rejects, without ceremony, principles which irresistibly govern the belief and conduct of all mankind in the common concerns of life; and to which the philosopher himself must yield, after he imagines he hath confuted them. Such principles are older, and of more authority, than Philosophy; she resets upon them as her basis, not they upon her. If she could overturn them, she must be buried in their ruins ...

> Zeno endeavored to demonstrate the impossibility of motion; Hobbes, that there is no difference between right and wrong; and this author [Hume], that no credit is to be given to our senses, to our memory, or even to demonstration. Such philosophy is justly ridiculous, even to those who cannot detect the fallacy of it. It can have no

other tendency, than to shew the acuteness of the sophist, at the expense of disgracing reason and human nature, and making mankind Yahoos. (*Inquiries*, 102)

A philosopher is, no doubt, entitled to examine even those distinctions that are to be found in the structure of all languages [for example, the distinction between a thought and the object of thought]; and, if he is able to shew that there is no foundation for them in the nature of the things distinguished—if he can point out some prejudice common to mankind which has led them to distinguish things not really different—in that case, such a distinction may be imputed to a vulgar error, which ought to be corrected in philosophy. But when, in his first setting out, he takes it for granted, without proof, that distinctions found in the structure of all languages, have no foundation in nature, this, surely, is too fastidious a way of treating the common sense of mankind. When we come to be instructed by philosophers, we must bring the old light of common sense along with us, and by it judge the new light which the philosopher communicates to us. But when we are required to put out the old light altogether, that we may follow the new, we have reason to be on our guard. (*Essays* I, I, 224).

... I beg leave to dissent from philosophy till she gives me reason for what she teaches. For, though common sense and external senses demand my assent to their dictates upon their own authority, yet philosophy is not entitled to this privilege. (*Essays* II, XIV, 302–303)

In sum, the principles of common sense serve to constrain philosophical theory: any theory that violates them incurs a cost as a result. Reid insists that the priority is indeed *prima facie* – there is no absolute bar to violating common sense. The point, rather, is that the philosopher must have *good reason* to violate common sense. One's theory might end by violating common sense, but it should not *start off* that way.

3. Why do the principles of common sense have priority?

Why do the principles of common sense have both epistemic and methodological priority? It turns out that Reid's answer is different in the two cases, and so we have to consider one kind of priority at a time.

a. Epistemic priority

From what does the epistemic priority of common sense derive? Why do the first principles of common sense have epistemic authority? We may first consider two mistaken interpretations of Reid on this question, leading to two misinterpretations of Reid's epistemology of common sense.

The first misinterpretation is that Reid holds an 'innocent until proven guilty' view of epistemic justification. According to this view, Reid thinks that beliefs enjoy a kind of default justification; they are epistemically innocent 'by nature' or 'in themselves,' so long as we have no reason for doubting them.

Thomas Reid ... held that we may trust the common sense. For instance, he argued that our beliefs that we are acting freely and that the persons with whom we converse are thinking, intelligent beings are justified. They have, he said, 'what

> lawyers call a *jus* quaesitum, or a right of ancient possession, which ought to stand good till it be overturned' ... Reid held that many beliefs, including perceptual beliefs and beliefs of common sense, are 'innocent until proven guilty'. (Rot 2001, 25)

> Reid's general approach to rational belief is this: trust the beliefs produced by your cognitive faculties in the appropriate circumstances, unless you have good reason to reject them. (Clark 2004)

> I agree with Thomas Reid that we are rational in believing what we are told unless there is good reason to think that the source is untrustworthy. Beliefs are innocent until proven guilty. (Vanhoozer 2005, 197)

The position here ascribed to Reid is a version of 'epistemic conservatism,' the view that a belief has some degree of positive epistemic status simply in virtue of being believed (Foley 1983).[6] Although there is some textual evidence for this interpretation of Reid, we will see below that there is good reason for rejecting it. On the contrary, the 'innocent until proven guilty' character of first principles involves their methodological priority as pre-theoretical commitments, rather than their epistemological priority as first knowledge. As we shall see, however, Reid does not think that first principles, or anything else, are innocent until proven guilty in an epistemic sense. That is, no beliefs are epistemically innocent 'by nature' or 'in themselves,' so long as we have no reason for doubting them.

A second interpretation of Reid regarding the source of epistemic priority is the 'no view' view.[7] On this account, the authority of first principles is a kind of theoretical primitive: it is used to explain other things, but goes unexplained itself. Here is an oft-cited passage that lends support to the 'no view' interpretation.

> Philosophers have endeavored, by analysing the different sorts of evidence, to find out some common nature wherein they all agree, and thereby to reduce them all to one ... I confess that, although I have, as I think, a distinct notion of the different kinds of evidence above-mentioned, and, perhaps, of some others, which it is unnecessary here to enumerate, yet I am not able to find any common nature to which they all may be reduced. (*Essays* II, XX, 328)

That passage continues, however, in this way:

> They seem to me to agree only in this, that they are all fitted by Nature to produce belief in the human mind, some of them in the highest degree, which we call certainty, others in various degrees according to circumstances. (ibid.)

Throughout his writings, Reid notes that all sources of knowledge, including common sense, are 'fitted by Nature' to operate in us as they do, that they are 'given us by Nature' and 'the result of our constitution.' Reid also notes that the various sources of knowledge are equally trustworthy in their normal and healthy state:

> There is no more reason to account our senses fallacious, than our reason, our memory, or any other faculty of judging which nature hath given us. They are all limited and imperfect... We are liable to error and wrong judgment in the use of them all; but as little in the informations of sense as in the deductions of reasoning. (*Essays* II, XXII, 339)

These points taken together imply a kind of 'proper function' faculty reliabilism. According to Reid, our cognitive faculties give us knowledge so long as they are part of our natural constitution and 'not fallacious.' Put another way, knowledge arises from the proper functioning of our natural, non-fallacious (i.e. reliable) cognitive faculties.[8]

We are now in a position to answer our present question: From what does the epistemic priority of common sense derive? In general, positive epistemic status derives from the proper functioning of our natural, non-fallacious cognitive faculties. The faculties that make up common sense (for example, perception, memory, consciousness) are faculties of that sort. As such, they are of equal authority with reason, and with all other natural, non-fallacious cognitive faculties. Since they are non-inferential (non-reasoning) faculties, they are sources of non-inferential knowledge.

In sum, Reid's account of epistemic justification in general is that it arises from the proper functioning of our natural, non-fallacious cognitive faculties. This is true for the epistemic justification enjoyed by first principles as well. But since first principles enjoy this status without grounding in further evidence, they enjoy a kind of epistemological priority that is special to them; they are a kind of foundational knowledge, a kind of basic evidence. They are regress stoppers.

b. Methodological priority

From what does the methodological priority of common sense derive? Why do the first principles of common sense have methodological pride of place? Reid gives several reasons here.

First, it is inconsistent to begin our inquiry by trusting some of our faculties but not others. Reid notes that there are three options available in epistemology, and in philosophy in general: (a) we may begin by trusting none of our faculties until we have reason for believing them trustworthy, (b) we may begin by trusting some of our faculties but not others, or (c) we may begin by trusting all of our faculties until we have reason for believing them untrustworthy.

The first option, Reid argues, is a non-starter:

> If a sceptic should build his scepticism upon this foundation, that all our reasoning and judging powers are fallacious in their nature, or should resolve at least to withhold assent until it be proved that they are not, it would be impossible by argument to beat him out of his stronghold; and he must even be left to enjoy his scepticism .... For if our faculties be fallacious, why may they not deceive us in this reasoning as well as in others? (*Essays* VI, V, 447)

The second option, Reid argues, is inconsistent:

> Reason, says the sceptic, is the only judge of truth, and you ought to throw off every opinion and every belief that is not grounded on reason. Why, sir, should I believe the faculty of reason more than that of perception?—they came both out of the same shop, and were made by the same artist; and if he puts one piece of false ware into my hands, what should hinder him from putting another? (*Inquiry*, 183)

... the faculties of consciousness, of memory, of external sense, and of reason, are all equally the gifts of nature. No good reason can be assigned for receiving the testimony of one of them, which is not of equal force with regard to the others. The greatest sceptics admit the testimony of consciousness, and allow that what it testifies is to be held as a first principle. If, therefore, they reject the immediate testimony of sense or of memory, they are guilty of an inconsistency. (*Essays* VI, IV, 439)

That leaves the third option: begin by trusting all of one's faculties, until we have reason to doubt them. In sum, the only option that is both available and consistent is to begin by trusting all of one's faculties. But those include the faculties of common sense, and so our theorizing is constrained by the judgments that issue from common sense, i.e. by first principles. Again, this kind of constraint is *prima facie* and can be overridden – we should trust our faculties, including those of common sense, *until we have reason for doubting them*. But that is just the sort of methodological priority that Reid thinks first principles have.

A second reason that first principles have methodological priority is that what we ought to do is constrained by what we can do.

Even those philosophers who have disowned the authority of our notions of an external material world, confess, that they find themselves under a necessity of submitting to their power. Methinks, therefore, it were better to make a virtue of necessity; and since we cannot get rid of the vulgar notion and belief of an external world, to reconcile our reason to it as well as we can. (*Inquiry*, 127)

This, indeed, has always been the fate of the few that have professed skepticism, that, when they have done what they can to discredit their senses, they find themselves, after all, under a necessity of trusting to them. Mr. Hume has been so candid as to acknowledge this; and it is no less true of those who have not shewn the same candour; for I never heard that any sceptic run his head against a post, or stepped into a kennel, because he did not believe his eyes. (*Essays* I, II, 233–234)

A third reason for giving first principles methodological priority is that common sense has a better track record than philosophical theory. In other words, experience shows us that theorizing often goes wrong, and so it is reasonable to use common sense as a check.

Of all the discoveries that have been made concerning the inward structure of the human body, never one was made by conjecture... What we have said of the internal structure of the human body, may be said, with justice, of very other part of the works of God, wherein any real discovery has been made. Such discoveries have always been made by patient observation, by accurate experiments, or by conclusions drawn by strict reasoning from observations and experiments; and such discoveries have always tended to refute, but not to confirm, the theories and hypotheses which ingenious men have invented. As this is a fact confirmed by the history of philosophy in all past ages, it ought to have taught men, long ago, to treat with just contempt hypotheses in every branch of philosophy, and to despair of ever advancing real knowledge in that way. (*Essays* I, III, 235)

Finally, a methodology ought to be judged by its fruits. Results, results, results.

It may be observed, that the defects and blemishes in the received philosophy concerning the mind, which have most exposed it to contempt and ridicule of sensible men, have chiefly been owing to this—that the votaries of this Philosophy, from a natural prejudice in her favour, have endeavored to extend her jurisdiction beyond its just limits, and to call to her bar the dictates of Common Sense. (*Inquiry*, 101)

In this unequal contest betwixt Common Sense and Philosophy, the latter will always come off both with dishonour and loss . . . Philosophy (if I may be permitted to change the metaphor) has no other root but the principles of Common Sense; it grows out of them, and draws its nourishment from them. Severed from this root, its honours wither, its sap is dried up, it dies and rots. (Ibid.)

When a man suffers himself to be reasoned out of the principles of common sense, by metaphysical arguments, we may call this *metaphysical lunacy*; which differs from the other species of the distemper in this, that it is not continued, but intermittent; is apt to seize the patient in solitary and speculative moments; but, when he enters into society, Common Sense recovers her authority. (*Inquiry*, 209, Reid's emphases)

In other words, philosophical theorizing that is not constrained by common sense ends in dishonor and lunacy. That is not speculation – it is history. Better, then, to adopt the alternative methodology.

4. Reid and his critics

We have seen that Reid assigns two kinds of priority to the principles of common sense: a) epistemological priority as non-inferential knowledge, and b) methodological priority as a constraint on theorizing. Each kind of priority is defeasible in its own way. Thus the evidence of first principles can be overridden by other evidence, as when, for example, perception proves to be illusory. And philosophical theorizing can, in principle, discover good reasons for overriding common sense judgment. Moreover, the privileged status of common sense is not a theoretical primitive, something that is itself left unexplained. On the contrary, the epistemological priority of first principles is due to their source in natural, non-fallacious, non-inferential faculties of belief. Their methodological priority is due to several considerations regarding method, or how philosophical inquiry ought to proceed.

With these points in mind, we can see that Kant's complaints about Reid are off the mark. Here is what Kant writes:

To appeal to common sense, when insight and science fail, and no sooner – this is one of the subtle discoveries of modern times, by means of which the most superficial ranter can safely enter the lists with the most thorough thinker, and hold his own. But as long as a particle of insight remains, no one would think of having recourse to this subterfuge. For what is it but an appeal to the opinion of the multitude, of whose applause the philosopher is ashamed, while the popular charlatan glories and confides in it? (Kant 1902, 7)

First, it is clear that Reid's appeal to common sense is not an appeal to the multitude. In fact, we have seen that, for Reid, the authority of common sense, whether epistemological or methodological, is not owed to its being *common*, or something shared by the multitude, at all.

The passage from Kant continues as follows:

> Chisels and hammers may suffice to work a piece of wood, but for steel-engraving we require an engraver's needle. Thus common sense and speculative understanding are each useful in their own way, the former in judgments which apply immediately to experience, the latter when we judge universally from mere concepts, as in metaphysics, where sound common sense, so called in spite of the inapplicability of the word, has no right to judge at all. (Kant 1902, 7–8)

Regarding the epistemic priority of common sense, Kant and Reid are in agreement: common sense has authority 'in judgments which apply immediately to experience.' Regarding methodological priority, however, Reid would insist that Kant has it wrong. In metaphysics, Kant thinks, common sense 'has no right to judge at all.' On the contrary, Reid thinks, common sense has an important role to play in metaphysics and in philosophy more generally: methodologically, common sense should serve as a check on 'speculative understanding,' on pains of falling into dishonor and metaphysical lunacy.

We are now in a position to answer Wolterstorff's criticism of Reid as well. According to Wolterstorff, Reid was confused between two understandings of 'the principles of Commons Sense': first principles of reasoning vs. things taken for granted. 'My conclusion will be that two quite different lines of thought were in conflict in his mind: He thinks of the principles of Common Sense both as *shared first principles*, and as *things we all take for granted.*' (Wolterstorff 2001, 220) But, 'Obviously the concept of something taken for granted in one's activities is different from the concept of a justifiedly held immediate belief.' (Wolterstorff 2001, 224)

We may now see that, contra Wolterstorff, Reid was not confused between two understandings of the principles of common sense. Rather, Reid gives the same principles two kinds of privileged status, epistemic and methodological. The first principles have epistemic priority as 'first principles of reasoning.' That is, such principles serve as evidential starting points, as evidential grounds from which further reasoning can extend.

> ...all knowledge got by reasoning must be built upon first principles. This is as certain as that every house must have a foundation.

The same first principles have methodological priority as 'things taken for granted.' They are 'taken for granted' in the sense that they are pre-theoretical commitments for constraining further theory.

> It is a bold philosophy that rejects, without ceremony, principles which irresistibly govern the belief and conduct of all mankind... Such principles are older, and of more authority, than Philosophy; she resets upon them as her basis, not they upon her.

5. The circle of belief

There is a long-standing objection to foundationalism that goes roughly like this: A foundation of knowledge is impossible, because it is impossible to go outside our beliefs for the justification that knowledge requires. In more colorful terms, we are 'trapped' in a circle of belief, and the foundationalist's attempt to escape this circle is futile.

Here is a statement of the objection from Keith Lehrer:

> In whatever way a man might attempt to justify his beliefs . . . he must always appeal to some belief. There is nothing other than one's beliefs to which one can appeal in the justification of belief. There is no exit from the circle of one's beliefs. (Lehrer 1974)

Here is Richard Rorty:

> . . . nothing counts as justification unless by reference to what we already accept, and there is no way to get outside our beliefs and our language so as to find some test other than coherence. (Rorty 1979)

Here is Donald Davidson:

> What distinguishes a coherence theory is simply the claim that nothing can count as a reason for holding a belief except another belief. Its partisan rejects as unintelligible the request for a ground or source of justification of another ilk. (Davidson 1992)

There is a way of taking the 'circle of belief idea' as a platitude. We should all agree that, in some relevant sense, 'there is no way to get outside our beliefs and our language,' and 'nothing can count as a reason for holding a belief except another belief.' On the other hand, coherentism is a substantive epistemological position, and one with substantial reasons against it. (Cf. Sosa 1980) This suggests that the 'circle of belief' idea involves an ambiguity between two meanings, one platitudinous and one substantive.

Our distinction helps to resolve the ambiguity. In terms of methodology, we have no choice except to start from where we are. That is, we must begin with our pre-theoretical commitments, and then theorize from there. In fact, that idea is quite weak. It *is* a platitude. Reid's view regarding the methodological role of common sense is much stronger. Specifically, he thinks that the principles of common sense have a methodological *priority* – that a) they provide a defeasible *constraint* on theory, and b) the constraint is stronger than that provided by beliefs in general.

But we can also take the 'circle of belief' idea as an epistemological point. In that case, the idea is that all knowledge (or justified belief) depends for its status on evidential grounding in further knowledge (justified belief). If we add that evidential grounding can go in both directions, as talk of a 'circle' implies, then the idea expresses epistemological coherentism, and constitutes an alternative answer to the regress problem that we saw above. The issues involved in this dispute are, as we noted, substantive, and there is no hope in resolving them here. Suffice it to say that Reid gives good reasons for adopting the foundationalist alternative.

Taken as a methodological point, then, the 'circle of belief' idea is much weaker than what we find in Reid. It is in fact platitudinous. Taken as an epistemological point, the idea is substantive, and unsupported by the platitude.[9]

Notes

1. 'It has to be conceded that Reid's discussion of Common Sense is confusing. And not just confusing but confused... I judge it to be, in fact, the most confused part of Reid's thought.' (Wolterstorff 2001, 218)
2. Patrick Rysiew makes a similar suggestion in Rysiew (2002, 442).
3. This is contra Wolterstorff: 'Reid usually means, by principles of Common Sense, shared beliefs or judgments – that is, propositions believed or judged in common...' (Wolterstorff 2001, 219)
4. Thanks to John Stolt for useful conversation on this point.
5. The two kinds of priority are nicely distinguished and elaborated in Depaul (1986).
6. 'The view implies that regardless of what a person happens to believe there is something favorable to be said on behalf of the belief, namely that the person has that particular belief. This is not to say that any belief whatsoever is rational. It is to say, however, that any belief whatsoever as least has some presumption of rationality.' (Foley 1983, 165) Foley attributes the position to Chisholm, among others.
7. This seems to be Lehrer's view of Reid on the nature of evidence: 'Evidence, Reid says, is something that... can be felt more easily than described. It seems, however, to have no common nature... Evidence is what makes us justified in our beliefs. In some cases, those in which our beliefs arise immediately from first principles, we cannot explain the nature of this justification to ourselves or to another... ' (Lehrer 1989, 114)
8. Cf. Plantinga (1993), especially p. 50. For a more detailed discussion of Reid on the nature of evidence, see Rysiew (2005).
9. Thanks to Patrick Rysiew for valuable comments on an earlier draft.

References

Clark, Kelly James. 2004. "Religious Epistemology." In *Internet Encyclopedia of Philosophy*: http://www.iep.utm.edu/relig-ep/.

Davidson, Donald. 1992. "A Coherence Theory of Truth and Knowledge." In *Truth and Interpretation: Perspectives on the Philosophy of Donald Davidson*, edited by Ernest LePore. Oxford: Basil Blackwell.

Depaul, Michael. 1986. "Reflective Equilibrium and Foundationalism." *American Philosophical Quarterly* 23: 59–69.

Foley, Richard. 1983. "Epistemic Conservativism." *Philosophical Studies* 43: 165–182.

Kant, Immanuel. 1902. *Prolegomena to any Future Metaphysics*. Translated by Paul Carus. New York: Open Court.

Lehrer, Keith. 1974. *Knowledge*. Oxford: Oxford University Press.

Lehrer, Keith. 1989. *Thomas Reid*. London and New York: Routledge.

Plantinga, Alvin. 1993. *Warrant and Proper Function*. Oxford: Oxford University Press.

Reid, Thomas. 1983. *An Inquiry into the Human Mind on the Principles of Common Sense* and *Essays on the Intellectual Powers of Man*, both in *Thomas Reid, Philosophical Works*, edited by H. M. Bracken. Hildesheim: Georg Olms.

Rorty, Richard. 1979. *Philosophy and the Mirror of Nature*. Princeton: Princeton University Press.

Rot, Hans. 2001. *Change, Choice and Inference: A Study of Belief Revision and Nonmonotonic Reasoning*. Oxford: Oxford University Press.

Rysiew, Patrick. 2002. "Reid and Epistemic Naturalism." *The Philosophical Quarterly* 52: 437–456.

Rysiew, Patrick. 2005. "Reidian Evidence." *Journal of Scottish Philosophy* 3: 107–121.

Sosa, Ernest. 1980. "The Raft and the Pyramid: Coherence Versus Foundations in the Theory of Knowledge." *Midwest Studies in Philosophy* 5: 3–26. Reprinted in Ernest Sosa, *Knowledge in Perspective*. Cambridge: Cambridge University Press, 1991.

Vanhoozer, Kevin J. 2005. "Disputing about Words? Of Fallible Foundations and Modest Metanarratives." In *Christianity and the Postmodern Turn: Six Views*, edited by Myron B. Penner. Grand Rapids: Brazos Press.

Wolterstorff, Nicholas. 2001. *Thomas Reid and the Story of Epistemology*. Cambridge: Cambridge University Press.

EPISTEMOLOGY

Thomas Reid on truth, evidence and first principles

Keith Lehrer

*Regents Professor Emeritus, University of Arizona; Research Professor,
University of Miami*

Reid had a theory of the human mind containing a theory of truth, both of our
evidence of truth and the conditions of truth, fully consistent with
empiricism. The justification and evidence of first principles is something felt
in consciousness rather than some external relation. This is the result of our
faculties, original and natural powers of our constitution. Original
convictions and conceptions arise from our faculties in response to
experience as a result of our natural development. Reid combines elements of
foundationalism, coherentism, falliblism and nominalism. I distinguish and
compare Reid to Hume, Moore, Quine, James and Wittgenstein.

My object in this paper is to show that Reid had a theory of the human mind
containing a theory of truth, both of our evidence of truth and the conditions of
truth, fully consistent with empiricism. His project was to articulate a theory of the
human mind that was a better empirical theory than the ideal theory, advanced
most notably by Hume (1739). To say that the theory was empirical is to say that
the first principles of his theory, those that support the common sense claims to
knowledge, evidence and truth of the judgments of consciousness, perception,
memory, testimony, among others, are empirical and not *a priori* principles. The
first principles are confirmed by the truth of the particular judgments of experience
under those principles. The evidence of the first principles and evidence of the
particular judgments of experience are both immediate and do not depend on
reasoning. The justification and evidence of both is the result of our faculties,
which are original and natural powers of our constitution manifested in first
principles. These conceptions are not innate any more than the first principles are *a
priori*. The conceptions and convictions arise from our faculties in response to
experience as a result of our natural development. Reid's views on evidence, truth
and knowledge are scattered in his works, but there is a system of these topics
contained therein. My purpose here is to show that the subtle complexity of his

system, somewhat concealed, is a form of empiricism that combines elements of foundationalism, coherentism, falliblism and nominalism. Finally, I distinguish and compare Reid to Hume, Moore, Goldman, Quine, James and Wittgenstein.

Let us first consider the role of common sense, which Reid insists is important. He says,

> 'Common sense is that degree of judgment which is common to men with whom we converse and transact business.' (421)

> 'There is a certain degree of it which is necessary to our being subjects of law and government, capable of managing our own affairs, and answerable for our conduct toward others; this is called common sense, because it is common to all men with whom we can transact business, or called to account for their conduct.' (422)

Moreover,

> 'The same degree of understanding which makes a man capable of acting with common prudence in the conduct of life, makes him capable of discovering what is true and what is false in matters that are self-evident, and which he distinctly apprehends.' (422)

This leads him to appeal to common sense concerning perceptual claims of the existence of the external world. That may suggest that Reid's reply to skepticism is *only* a *modus tollens* style of argument against the skepticism of Hume (1739) that G. E. Moore (1925) employed in his defense of common sense against skepticism. However, this interpretation of Reid is a mistake, a natural but serious mistake. Reid regarded the skepticism resulting from the ideal theory to be a fault, but that fault could only be remedied in philosophy by presenting and articulating an empirical theory of the human mind that did not have the skeptical consequences of the ideal theory. Reid says that he would side with common sense against philosophy if the latter led to the skeptical conclusion, but Reid argues that philosophy, the philosophy of empiricism advocated by Newton, did not lead to skepticism. The critical point, however, is that he considered it essential to show that there was a philosophical theory of truth, evidence and conception that was consistent with common sense and empiricism. Reasoning as Moore (1925) did against skepticism is a *petitio* and proves nothing. For such an argument – as, indeed, *any* argument at all – assumes that our faculties lead us to truth.

Reid remarks, replying to the skeptical arguments of Hume,

> 'He [Hume] is, therefore, at liberty to retract them, and to rest his scepticism upon the sole foundation, That no reasoning can prove the truth and fidelity of our faculties. Here he stands upon firm ground, for it is evident that every argument offered to prove the truth and fidelity of our faculties takes for granted the thing in question, and is, therefore, that kind of sophism which logicians call a *petitio principii*.' (489)

The *modus tollens* argument against skepticism fails as a proof of the falsity of skepticism. A *petitio* is no proof.

However, the fact that we have no proof that skepticism is false should not lead us to conclude that we lack evidence for the truth of first principles or for the truth and fidelity of the first principles of our faculties. He says, concerning our apprehension of the propositions formulating first principles of our faculties,

'The judgment follows the apprehension of them necessarily, and both are equally the work of nature, and the results of our original powers. There is no searching for evidence, no weighing of arguments; the proposition is not deduced or inferred from another; it has the light of truth in itself, and has no occasion to borrow it from another. Propositions of the last kind, when they are used in matters of science, have commonly been called *axioms*; and on whatever occasion they are used, are called *first principles, principles of common sense, common notions, self-evident truths.*' (434)

It suffices to attend to the content of a first principle to discern the truth of it.

This argument for the evidence and truth of first principles rests on a further principle that is prior to the others in the order of evidence concerning our faculties. I have called it the First First Principle (Lehrer 1998), though it does not occur first in Reid's list of first principles. This principle affirms the truth and fidelity of our faculties. Reid formulates it as follows:

'Another first principle is–that the natural faculties, by which we distinguish truth from error, are not fallacious . . . . If any truth can be said to be prior to all the others in the order of nature, this seems to have the best claim; because, in every instance of assent, whether upon intuitive, demonstrative, or probable evidence, the truth of our faculties is taken for granted, and is, as it were, one of the premises on which our assent is grounded.

How then come we to be assured of this fundamental truth on which all others rest? Perhaps evidence, as in many other respects it resembles light, so in this also–that, as light, which is the discoverer of all visible objects, discovers itself at the same time, so evidence, which is the voucher for all truth, vouches for itself at the same time.' (448)

Given this principle, it is clear how Reid would reply to a philosopher who says that we cannot know of the existence of the external world or of anything else because we cannot prove it. His reply is that not all evidence, justification and knowledge depends on reasoning or proof. Some evidence of truth is immediate and does not require or admit of proof because it has all the evidence of truth the matter allows as it arises from our faculties. It is essential that the First First Principle be true, for otherwise we would lack evidence of the truth and fidelity of our faculties, but it is not required as a premise in reasoning to supply the evidence of the first principles. They have evidence in themselves like an axiom does.

'If the word axiom be put to signify every truth which is known immediately, without being deduced from any antecedent truth, then the existence of the objects of sense may be called an axiom; for my senses give me an immediate conviction of what they testified, as my understanding gives of what is commonly called an axiom.' (113)

Is the claim that the First First Principle has evidence, like that of an axiom, an *a priori* assumption? Reid would consider it empirical for two reasons. The first is that first principles are connected to each other like links in a chain. He says concerning a first principle,

'There is hardly any proposition, especially of those that may claim the character of first principles, that stands alone and unconnected. It draws many others along with it in a chain that cannot be broken. He that takes it up must bear the burden of all its consequences; and if that is too heavy for him to bear, he must not pretend to take it up.' (437)

The way in which a first principle draws others along with it amounts to the empirical claim that the principles confirm each other. For example, the principle of sense perception

'That those things do really exist which we distinctly perceive by our senses, and are what we perceive them to be.' (445)

supports the First First Principle, because it tells us that perception yields truth about the existence and character of the objects of perception, which supports the claim of the First First Principle that the first principles, such as this one of sense perception, are not fallacious. The character of linkage becomes manifest when Reid argues against Hume that Hume is inconsistent to trust one faculty, reason, and refuse to trust another, perception. There is no strict inconsistency, but rather a kind of incoherence in accepting the principle of one faculty and rejecting another, given the First First Principle.

The second reason for the claim that the First First Principle is empirical is based on the character of evidence itself. Reid insists that evidence is something we feel; we feel the evidence of a ground of belief. Here is what he says about evidence,

'We give the name of evidence to whatever is a ground of belief. To believe without evidence is a weakness, which every man is concerned to avoid, and which every man wishes to avoid. Nor is it in a man's power to believe anything longer than he thinks he has evidence.' (328)

'The common occasions of life lead us to distinguish evidence into different kinds, to which we give names that are well understood; such as the evidence of sense, the evidence of memory, the evidence of consciousness, the evidence of testimony, the evidence of axioms, the evidence of reasonings.' (328)

'What this evidence is, is more easily felt than described. Those who never reflected upon its nature, feel its influence in governing their belief.' (328)

We can feel the influence of evidence, which is an empirical sign of it, and therefore, we are aware of the evidence of belief, as we are conscious of what we feel. Evidence is something we feel, even the evidence of a necessary truth. This account of evidence separates Reid from contemporary reliablist theories of evidence that reduce evidence and justification by definition to some external relation, such as Alvin Goldman (1986) – which, if it can be known, cannot be felt. John Greco (2002) and Philip De Bary (2002) have argued in support of a reliablist interpretation of Reid, but they have been answered correctly by Patrick Rysiew (2005, 2002) in a way that supports the present interpretation of Reid's account of evidence. We may come to know that evidence is reliable from observation and induction, and some form of reliability seems to be itself evident from the First First Principle. But evidence is immediate and intuitive in a way that an external relation is not.

The evidence of first principles or their instances, for example particular perceptual beliefs, does not depend on reasoning about external relations or, for that matter, on reasoning from any first principle. The evidence of the particular beliefs that falls under a first principle is intuitive and immediate, as is the evidence for the principle itself. Those who feel and recognize the evidence they have for their perceptual beliefs may not have considered the question of whether the evidence of their beliefs satisfies an external relation. Moreover, evidence of different kinds is, Reid avers, not reducible to a single nature.

'There are different kinds of evidence, that of the senses, memory, testimony, consciousness, and axioms, but there appears to be no common nature to which they may all be reduced.' (328)

The evidence of each kind is felt to be evidence of truth. The evidence of first principles is intuitive and immediate, and it does not depend on reasoning from any other principles, not even the First First Principle. Consciousness, memory and perception testify to the truth of convictions and judgments involved in a way that is intuitive, immediate and felt. The evidence of the first principles, including the first principles of necessary truths, is empirical, however, because it is grounded in the First First Principle, even if that is not used as a premise in reasoning. It is an empirical matter and not something known *a priori* that our faculties, the grounds of evidence, are not fallacious.

This leaves us with a question about the relationship between evidence and truth. Evidence does not make us infallible. Examining Hume's reasoning about the manner in which fallibility reduces certainty, which Reid seeks to refute, Reid concedes something to Hume, when he says,

'Upon the whole, I see only two conclusions that can be fairly drawn from this profound and intricate reasoning against reason. The first is, That we are fallible in all our judgments and all our reasonings. The second, That the truth and fidelity of our faculties can never be proved by reasoning; and, therefore, our belief of it cannot be founded on reasoning. If the last be what the author calls his hypothesis, I subscribe to it, and think it not a hypothesis, but a manifest truth . . . ' (489)

Indeed, going beyond Hume, Reid affirms that we cannot even prove that consciousness is infallible and beyond the possibility of deception.

'Can any man prove that his consciousness may not deceive him? No man can; nor can we give a better reason for trusting to it, then that every man, while his mind is sound, is determined, by the constitution of his nature, to give implicit belief to it.' (487)

We are fallible, Reid acknowledges,

'That man, and probably every created being, is fallible; and that a fallible being cannot have perfect comprehension and assurance of truth which an infallible being has-I think ought to be granted . . . . If this be called a degree of scepticism, I cannot help approving of it.' (485)

But he insists that it is compatible with believing we are fallible that we should be certain of some truths,

'One who believes himself to be fallible may still hold it to be certain that 2 and 2 make 4, and that contradictory propositions cannot both be true. He may believe something to be probable only, and other things to be demonstrable, without making any pretense to infallibility.' (485)

We respond to the highest degree of evidence with certainty of truth. He affirms that the forms of evidence

'... are all fitted by Nature to produce belief in the human mind, some of them in the highest degree, which we call certainty...' (328)

Moreover, it is worth noting, such evidence and certainty are not restricted to propositions of mathematics and perception, but extend beyond them to morals.

'That I ought not to steal, or to kill or to bear false witness, are propositions, of the truth of which I am as well convinced as any proposition in Euclid. I am conscious that I judge them to be true propositions, and my consciousness makes all other arguments unnecessary with regard to the operations of my own mind.' (673)

The First First Principle tells us that our faculties are attuned to truth. A philosopher of contemporary bent will ask for a theory of truth. According to Reid, it is patient observation that brings truth to light, not speculative explanation of ingenious men. Observation is what brought to light the structure of the human body, for example.

'Such discoveries have always been made by patient observation, by accurate experiments, or by conclusions drawn by strict reasoning from observations and experiments; and such discoveries have always tended to refute, but not to confirm, the theories and hypotheses which ingenious men have invented.' (235)

These are reflections on how we attain truth, but a modern philosopher will ask what makes a proposition true. Here the answer is hard to discern in Reid, but it is important to his philosophy not to assume some simple correspondence between what is affirmed in a proposition and what exists in the world.

Such a simple correspondence with what exists is precluded by the fact that propositions affirm general conceptions, general attributes or properties, to subjects, but all that exists are individual subjects and individual qualities. Reid says,

'... every creature God has made ... is an individual.' (389)

'... the whiteness of this sheet is one thing, whiteness is another; the conceptions signified by these two forms of speech are as different as the expressions. The first signifies an individual quality really existing, and is not a general conception, though it be an abstract one; the second signifies a general conception, which implies no existence, but may be predicated of everything that is white, and in the same sense.' (395)

Though we form general conceptions of kinds and sorts of things, these kinds and sorts do not exist in nature but are our inventions. He says,

'Things are parceled into kinds and sorts, not by nature, but by men.' (364)

I shall not enter into a detailed account of Reid's theory of general conceptions, which is given by Susan Castagnetto (1992). I note, however, three things about his theory of them in passing. Firstly, abstraction and generalization are central to the formation of general conceptions. Second, they become the meaning of words that name them. Third, they are not innate. The conceptions of the young child are at first obscure and indistinct. But with experience some of our conceptions, those of primary qualities and moral qualities, for example, develop into clear and distinct conceptions governed by general principles.

To resolve the paradox that judgment presupposes conception, which requires judgment to abstract and generalize, Reid remarks concerning sense,

> 'It is acknowledged, on all hands, that the first notions we have of sensible objects are got by the external senses only, and probably before judgment is brought forth; but these first notions are neither simple, nor are they accurate and distinct: they are gross and indistinct, like the *chaos*, a *rudis indigestaque moles*. Before we can have any distinct notion of this mass, it must be analyzed; the heterogeneous parts must be separated in our conception, and the simple elements, which before lay hid in the common mass, must first be distinguished, and then put together into one whole.' (418)

This is a summary of his views on conception, which I have elaborated elsewhere (Lehrer 1989, 1991). Here my concern is with general conceptions affirmed of a subject in some proposition that is true. What accounts for the truth of propositions affirming a general conception of an individual? The individual must have some individual quality that is collected under the general conceptions. One might think Reid is committed to saying that if all that exists are individual subjects and their individual qualities, then it is such individuals that must account for truth; indeed, it must be individuals that make all true propositions true.

However, the matter of truth for Reid is not as simple as that, even if propositions about things that exist may be made true in this way. The reason is that we can conceive of things, of subjects, that do not exist, and there are truths about such things. It is true of a centaur that it is half man and half horse, for example, and false that it is half angel and half elephant. So, general properties, which do not exist, are true of some subjects that do not exist. I have argued (Lehrer 2013) that this is important in the case of contemplated future actions in morals. Those actions do not exist, but we judge the truth about the morality of such actions, nonetheless. Moreover, in science there are true propositions about properties, for example, there is the general property of motion, which may have the property of being rectilinear. In the example from physics a property that does not exist is affirmed of another property that does not exist, and the proposition affirming this is true. Finally, there are First Principles of Necessary Truth, which concern what *must* be the case. The property of necessity, like other properties, does not exist in nature, but that does not make the property any more problematic for the epistemology and empiricism of Reid. For Reid, some of the most important evident truths of morals and physics concern things that do not exist. Our conception and immediate knowledge of such necessary truth is the consequence of our faculties and the way they are tuned to truth expressed by the First First Principle.

Truth is not constrained to things that exist according to Reid. We might render his view of truth by saying that a proposition affirms an attribute of a subject, and the proposition is true just in case the subject has the attribute. But we cannot say the proposition is true just in case the subject *exists* with the attribute. There are truths about subjects that do not exist. What then is the empirical constraint on the truth of propositions about things that do not exist? We cannot observe them after all. There is nothing beyond the first principles of the mind, most notably, the First First Principle, and the way in which they cohere together as they confront experience that gives us an account of truth according to Reid. Our knowledge of the first principles, whether contingent or necessary, is grounded in the testimony of the First First Principle. That such testimony is trustworthy and not fallacious is a contingent first principle immediately apprehended, but one that may be confirmed or disconfirmed by experience. We can ask how we discern truth from error, but what truth is in itself is a question that takes us beyond empiricism.

Reid (418) says that 'judgment' and 'belief' are indefinable, and appears to have the same view of 'truth'. What matters is how we can discern truth from error. Observation can show us how to discern truth from error, but the question of what truth is in itself, beyond how we may determine it, would take us beyond empiricism into the arena of ingenious speculation. There, I propose, Reid drew the line. His theory extended to the limits of what observation of the human mind could reveal, and beyond that he chose to remain silent. He found the foundations of human knowledge in the first principles of our faculties, the coherence among those principles showing us how they connect with and confirm one another, and he insisted that the immediate evidence of the principles is revealed by the felt quality of them. He calls his list of first principles, First Principles of Contingent *Truth* and First Principles of Necessary *Truth*. (Italics mine.) Such principles tells what there is to say about truth

Reid might have said what Quine (1969) affirmed later, namely, that a theory of how we determine truth is part and parcel of the overall system of a scientific theory, and in the case of Reid's theory of the human mind, of how the human mind judges what is true and what is false. As Reid articulates his theory of the mind, the priority of the First First Principle in a theory of evidence of what is true or false, joined to the other first principles is Reid's theory of truth. Moreover, the theory of truth takes us back to common sense, which remains our power to judge according to first principles. This theory of truth, summarized in the First First Principle of contingent truth, may be the grandest insight of Reid's theory of truth as part and parcel of his theory of the constitution of the human mind.

> 'I conclude further, that it is no less a part of the human constitution, to believe the present existence of our sensations, and to believe the past existence of what we remember, than it is to believe that twice 2 makes 4.The evidence of sense, the evidence of memory, and the evidence of the necessary relations of things, are all

distinct and original kinds of evidence, equally grounded on our constitution; none of them depends upon, or can be resolved into another. To reason against any of these kinds of evidence, is absurd; nay, to reason for them, is absurd. They are first principles, and such fall not within the province of reason, but of common sense.' (108)

The principles of common sense may be discerned, as we have noted, by the absurdity of denying them, as well as by other marks of first principles mentioned above. We may determine these marks by observation. We may also identify first principles by the role they play in the conduct of life. To quote Reid and reiterate how we began,

'Common sense is that degree of judgment which is common to men with whom we can converse and transect business.' (421)

'There is a certain degree of that which is necessary to our being subjects of law and government, capable of managing our own affairs, and answerable for our conduct toward others: this is called common sense, because it is common to all men with whom we transect business, or call to account for their conduct.' (422)

'The same degree of understanding which makes a man capable of acting with common prudence in the conduct of life, makes him capable of discovering what is true and what is false in matters that are self-evident, and which he distinctly apprehends.'

'All knowledge, and all science, must be built upon principles that are self-evident; and of such principles every man who has common sense is a competent judge, when he conceives them distinctly.' (422)

It is notable that the appeal to common sense, which is a power of judging what is true and false, is necessary to the conduct of life, according to Reid. This claim, as well as his theory of conception, influenced both George. E. Moore (1925) and William James (1909). But unlike Moore, he did not conclude that an appeal to common sense could be offered as a proof of the existence of the external world, and unlike James, he did not conclude that truth could be defined in terms of usefulness. We may know the truth of the existence of the external world, Reid would affirm, and the usefulness of truth in the affairs of life. He gave as complete a theory of the powers of the human mind as observation allowed. Concerning his inquiry into 'the fabric of the human mind,' in nature he insisted,

'...there is but one way to knowledge of nature's works – the way of observation and experiment.'

Then

'...we have a strong propensity to trace particular facts and observations to general rules, ...'

and these methods like those of Newton, are

'maxims of common sense and are practiced every day in common life...' (97)

'A just interpretation of nature is the only sound and orthodox philosophy: whatever we add of our own is apocryphal, and of no authority.' (98)

This interpretation requires an analysis of what we observe into simple and original operations of the human mind. We seek an

'...*analysis* of the human faculties; and, till this is performed, it is vain to expect any just system of the mind-that is, an enumeration of the original powers and laws of our constitution, and an explication from them of the various phaenomena of human nature.'

'Success in an inquiry of this kind, it is not in human power to command; but, perhaps, it is possible, by caution and humility, to avoid error and delusion. The labyrinth may be too intricate, and the thread too fine, to be traced through all its windings; but if, we stop where we can trace it no further, and secure the ground we have gained, there is no harm done; a quicker eye may in time trace it further.' (99)

That is how Reid began his inquiry, and he remained faithful to it when he came to the account of truth formulated in terms of the powers of the faculties of our mind to discern truth from error. Where he could trace the matter no further, he stopped.

I conclude by noting the similarity of Reid to Wittgenstein in his later work, *On Certainty*, (1969–1975) shown by Henning Jensen (1979), later noted by Wolterstorff (2001), where Wittgenstein, like Reid, insists on the importance of practice to affirming what is true. This is probably not to be explained by Wittgenstein having read Reid, though discussion with Moore, who was a diligent reader of Reid, may have provided a link. There is a similarity between Reid and Wittgenstein on the importance of what could be observed or shown and on the connection between truth and practice that is worthy of further investigation for the illumination of the work of both authors. Of course, Reid differs from Wittgenstein on the importance Reid attaches to a theory of the faculties by which we discern truth from error, in contrast to the importance Wittgenstein attaches to language games. But both insist on the importance of the connection between a form of life and truth.

In summary, Reid's theory of truth, evidence and conception is based on an empirical argument for our original and natural faculties. Without those faculties, conception and judgment would be impossible. But we are endowed with them at birth, and they are powers to conceive and know. Our conceptions are not innate but arise from the development of our powers in experience. Our knowledge of self-evident first principles is not a *priori* but arises from the perfection of the use of our faculties in experience. Reid's theory of truth, evidence and conception is a system of principles. They are connected like links in chain. It is the way they fit together, the coherence of the system of rules that interpret observation, which gives us the epistemology of Thomas Reid. This is encapsulated in the First First Principle as a principle of the trustworthiness of our powers of judgment, including, of course, the use of those powers to arrive at the principles of Reid's empiricist system of the human mind.

References

Castagnetto, S. V. 1992. "Reid's Answer to Abstract Ideas." *Journal of Philosophical Research* xvii.

De Bary, Philip. 2002. *Thomas Reid and Scepticism: His Reliabilist Response*. London: Routledge.

Goldman, A. 1986. *Epistemology and Cognition*. Cambridge: Harvard University Press.

Greco, John. 2002. "How to Reid Moore." *The Philosophical Quarterly* 52 (209): 544–563.

Hume, D. 1739. *A Treatise of Human Nature*. London: John Noon.

James, William. 1909. *Pragmatism: A New Name for Some Old Ways of Thinking*. LLC: Wildside Press.

Jensen, J. 1979. "Reid and Wittgenstein on Philosophy and Language." *Philosophical Studies* 36 (4): 359–376.

Lehrer, K. 1998. "Reid, Hume and Common Sense." *Reid Studies* 2 (1): 15–26.

Lehrer, K. 1989, 1991pb. *Thomas Reid*. London and New York: Routledge.

Lehrer, K. 2013. "Thomas Reid on Common Sense and Morals." *The Journal of Scottish Philosophy* 11 (2): 109–130.

Moore, G. E. 1925. "A Defence of Common Sense." In *Contemporary British Philosophy (2nd series)*, edited by J. H. Muirhead. London: Allen and Unwin.

Quine, W. V. O. 1969. "Epistemology Naturalized." In *Ontology Relativity and other essays*. New York: Columbia University Press.

Reid, T. 1863. *The Philosophical Works of Thomas Reid, D.D.* edited by Sir W. Hamilton. 6th edition, Edinburgh: James Thin, *This is the source for all page references to Reid in the text.

Rysiew, P. 2002. "Reid and Epistemic Naturalism." *The Philosophical Quarterly* 52 (209): 437–456.

Rysiew, P. 2005. "Reidian Evidence." *The Journal of Scottish Philosophy* 3 (2): 107–121.

Wittgenstein, L. 1969–1975. *On Certainty (Uber Gewissheit)*, edited by G. E. M. Anscombe, and G. H. von Wright. translated by Denis Paul. Oxford: Basil Blackwell.

Wolterstorff, N. 2001. *Thomas Reid and the Story of Epistemology*. Cambridge: Cambridge University Press.

EPISTEMOLOGY

Reid's First Principle #7

Patrick Rysiew

Department of Philosophy, The University of Victoria, Victoria, BC, Canada

By Reid's own account, 'That the natural faculties, by which we distinguish truth from error, are not fallacious' (FP#7), has a special place among the First Principles of Contingent Truths. Some have found that claim puzzling, but it is not. Contrary to what's usually assumed, certain FPs preceding FP#7 do not already assert the better part of what FP#7 explicitly states. FP#7 is needed because there is nothing epistemological in the FPs that precede it; and its special place among the FPs is a straightforward consequence of its being both perfectly general and distinctively epistemological.

1. Introduction

Central to Reid's philosophy is common sense and its defense; central to the latter are the First Principles he articulates. But Reid's presentation gives rise to various problems of interpretation – for instance, whether first principles are general or particular, whether they are principles of truth or of evidence, in what sense they can really be said to be 'self-evident', in what sense they are things 'we all believe', and so on.[1] Another such concern, and the one to be addressed here, is just how to understand one of the First Principles of Contingent Truths (hereinafter, 'First Principles') and its relation to the rest. This is First Principle #7, which speaks to the 'non-fallaciousness' of 'the natural faculties, by which we distinguish truth from error'.

Reid himself says that there is something special about this principle: 'if any truth can be said to be prior to all others in the order of nature', he writes, it is FP#7 (EIP 447b, 481)[2]. According to one influential interpretation (Keith Lehrer's) FP#7 is special in that it is a 'meta-principle', a 'first first principle'; it serves to close 'the truth gap', providing assurance that our faculties are trustworthy, and our common sense beliefs true. According to Philip de Bary, however, FP#7 is really not special at all: while other FPs speak to the reliability of the senses, memory, and consciousness, FP#7 in fact speaks only to the trustworthiness of our judging and reasoning powers – it is simply one reliability principle among others.

Each of these interpretations faces *prima facie* difficulties: According to de Bary, Lehrer's interpretation invites a dilemma – first horn: FP#7 is redundant, because other FPs already speak to the reliability of our faculties; second horn: if such reliability principles leave a truth gap yet to be bridged, then *FP#7* does too, and so a *further* such principle (a meta-meta-principle) is required. On the other hand, de Bary's interpretation faces clear textual barriers, not least (but not only – see below) because, as just noted, Reid himself *says*, as Lehrer has it, that FP #7 enjoys a kind of priority over the others; in the end, de Bary's reading, as he admits, appears to force us to put down such claims as just 'bad Reid'.

But while each faces *prima facie* difficulties, both Lehrer and de Bary are each surely on to something: Lehrer is surely correct that there's something special about FP#7 – that it plays a special role in Reid's system and that there is *some* good sense in which Reid regards it as a 'first first principle'. On the other hand, it seems that de Bary is right: if other FPs already speak to the reliability of our faculties, and if we think that this still leaves some real question as to their veracity, then the addition of some further, *general* reliability principle shouldn't make that (supposed or perceived) problem go away. The trick is to retain these insights simultaneously. The key to doing so, I'll be suggesting, is to reject a widely-held belief about Reid's FPs – namely, that by the time we get to FP#7 in the Reid's enumeration, he has *already* claimed that various of our faculties are reliable. Other FPs that are typically taken to be reliability (or otherwise epistemological) principles are, I want to suggest, not epistemological[3] at all, but metaphysical. Once we see that, just why and wherein FP #7 is special becomes clear: *it is* properly epistemological, and perfectly general; and its priority consists in the epistemic fact that it, and it alone, is taken for granted whenever we form any beliefs (arrive at any truths) at all. So too: once we see that FP#7 is (almost! – see footnote 21) the uniquely epistemological FP, any concern that its introduction invites a vicious regress goes away.

That, in outline, is the view I'll be offering here. Now for a slower, more careful approach, beginning with a clearer statement of just why FP#7 poses an interpretive puzzle to begin with.

2. The puzzle of First Principle #7

Because we're concerned here with what exactly Reid's Principles say, and how they relate to each other, it will be handy to have them before us. Here, then, are Reid's twelve "First Principles of Contingent Truths"[4] (EIP 441a–452a, 470–490):

> 1. *First*, then, I hold, as a first principle, the existence of everything of which I am conscious.

2. Another first principle, I think, is, *That the thoughts of which I am conscious, are the thoughts of a being which I call myself, my mind, my person.*

3. Another first principle I take to be — *That those things did really happen which I distinctly remember.*

4. Another first principle is, *Our own personal identity and continued existence, as far back as we remember anything distinctly.*

5. Another first principle is, *That those things do really exist which we distinctly perceive by our senses, and are what we perceive them to be.*

6. Another first principle, I think, is, *That we have some degree of power over our actions, and the determinations of our will.*

7. Another first principle is — *That the natural faculties, by which we distinguish truth from error, are not fallacious.*

8. Another first principle relating to existence, is, *That there is life and intelligence in our fellow-men with whom we converse.*

9. Another first principle I take to be, *That certain features of the countenance, sounds of the voice, and gestures of the body, indicate certain thoughts and dispositions of mind.*

10. Another first principle appears to me to be — *That there is a certain regard due to human testimony in matters of fact, and even to human authority in matters of opinion.*

11. *There are many events depending upon the will of man, in which there is a self-evident probability, greater or less, according to circumstances.*

12. The last principle of contingent truths I mention is, *That, in the phænomena of nature, what is to be, will probably be like to what has been in similar circumstances.*

Those are the principles. What is the puzzle? It begins with a certain understanding of the various FPs' content – just what it is they're telling us. Here is a standard reading, from James Van Cleve:

> Some of these principles are purely or primarily metaphysical; for example, Principle 2 tells us that thoughts require a thinker and Principle 6 tells us that we have some degree of power over our actions. But others are plainly intended to have epistemological significance, proclaiming the trustworthiness of consciousness (Principle 1), memory (Principle 3), perception (Principle 5), our faculties in general (Principle 7), our beliefs concerning the minds of others (Principles 8 and 9), testimony (Principle 10), and induction (Principle 12) (1999, 3; cf. 2009, 297).

But wait! For consciousness, memory, and perception, for example, we *already have* principles 'proclaiming' their trustworthiness.[5] We have other natural faculties, to be sure, but conception and abstraction, for instance, while of fundamental importance, are not means by which we distinguish truth from error – they're not *themselves* aimed at the production of true beliefs. Perhaps we need a separate reliability principle for testimony, say.[6] But clearly there's *some* kind of superfluity here. Given FPs 1, 3, and 5, it's not clear what FP#7 is adding, and *vice versa*. So why *is* 7 there at all? Just as puzzling as FP#7's inclusion itself is that fact that, while 7 seems simply to generalize over what other FPs already say, *Reid* says that it is, in fact, quite *special*. He writes:

> If any truth can be said to be prior to all others in the order of nature, this seems to have the best claim; because, in every instance of assent, whether upon intuitive, demonstrative, or probable evidence, the truth of our faculties is taken for granted, and is, as it were, one of the premises on which our assent is grounded (EIP 447b, 481).

Well, perhaps so. But then, in any instance of memory-based assent, the reliability of memory is taken for granted; in any instance of perception-based assent, *its* reliability is taken for granted; and so too for consciousness. In short, the use of *any* faculty presumes its reliability;[7] and we already have reliability principles for the chief individual (truth-directed) faculties; so it seems that the only thing FP#7 is adding is generality. Which is just to say that, strictly speaking, FP#7 isn't really *so* special. And, after all, *how could* it be, really, if the FPs are *all* '*first* principles' and all, as such, self-evident?

That, then, is the puzzle: why do we need FP#7, and why think it's special, given what the rest of the FPs already say?

3. Lehrer's reading, and De Bary's response

Keith Lehrer (1989, 1990) has provided one influential answer to this question; de Bary refers to it as 't[he] new orthodoxy' (2002, 65). On this view, FP#7 is a 'meta-principle', a 'first first principle'. Other FPs already 'tell us that perception, consciousness, memory are not fallacious' (Lehrer 1998, 23). *FP #7*, however, serves to close 'the truth gap': *it* provides assurance that our natural principles of belief are trustworthy:

> The principle tells us that first principles, in addition to producing conviction, provide us with information vouching for the truth of the conviction. We assent to the convictions produced by our faculties because we take the truthfulness of our faculties for granted (1989, 162).

And that presumption – that the deliverance of our faculties are truthful – extends to FP#7 itself: besides vouching for the other FPs, FP#7 vouches for itself. 'It loops around and supports itself. We might [call] it the looping principle' (1990, 3–4).

Philip de Bary (2000, 2002[8]) has both criticized Lehrer's account, and proposed an alternative interpretation of FP#7. On the negative side, De Bary argues that Lehrer's interpretation invites a dilemma. Either

> (i) FP#7 is not necessary – #1, #3, #5 already speak to the reliability of the faculties; '....we have already been assured by principle 5 [for example] that the power of perception is not fallacious. What extra assurance do we get of the truth of this or any other faculty by being told, in a metaprinciple, that the faculties en bloc are not fallacious? If principles 1, 3, and 5 are good enough severally as foundations for knowledge, then some joint metaprinciple to back them up is redundant' (2000, 377);

or

(ii), there *is* 'some backing-up work for a metaprinciple to do' (2000, 377). Why would that be? Perhaps because we read FPs 1, 3, and 5, as psychological generalizations of common sense beliefs – they tell us that 'all healthy people form beliefs (early, irresistibly, immediately, etc.) in conformity with principles 1, 3, and 5.' That is, we all *believe* ('early, irresistibly, immediately, etc.') that memory, consciousness, and perception are reliable. FP#7 is then seen as affording us the information that such common sense (reliability-)beliefs *are true*. But, by parity of reasoning, a *further* such principle, *beyond* #7, is required. For why not read *FP#7 itself* as just another psychological generalization? 'It says, perhaps, that all healthy people have faculties which, taken together, lead them to *believe* (irresistibly, immediately etc.) that the truth gap is closed. But now we need a metametaprinciple to "inform" us that the (universal, irresistible) belief that the truth gap is closed is a true belief, and so on, and on' (377; emphasis added). What this regress argument shows, De Bary says, is that 'the truth gap cannot be bridged unless we import at some stage an externalist assumption that it is in fact bridged. Faced with having to bite the externalist bullet sooner or later, it is surely more philosophically hygienic to do it sooner-which in Reid's case will be at the level of the "first principles of contingent truths" themselves' (2000, 377–378).

How then *should* we understand FP#7? Enter de Bary's positive proposal: Contrary to appearances, and in spite of what Reid himself says, FP#7 is really not special at all. While other FPs speak to the reliability of the senses, memory, and consciousness, FP#7 in fact speaks only to the trustworthiness of 'our judging and reasoning powers'. Aside, however, from the (supposed) fact that the contrary interpretation runs into the problems just sketched, why think that's true?

Key to de Bary's interpretation is the observation that 'judging' and 'reasoning' are, like memory, perception, and consciousness, natural powers of the mind – 'intellectual powers'. And, like memory (Essay III) and perception (Essay II), say, both judging (Essay VI) and reasoning (Essay VII) have separate essays devoted to them in *EIP*. (Consciousness does not, de Bary notes, but it is 'plainly an *Intellectual Power*, or "faculty", in its own right' (2000, 375).) But while the faculties of memory, consciousness, and perception 'have individual [FPs] which apply to them; numbers 1, 3, and 5, respectively' (2000, 375), on *Lehrer's* reading, judgment and reasoning do not. According to de Bary, however, *that* is precisely the function of FP#7 – to give these faculties their own individual (though shared) principle.

In addition to avoiding the problems he thinks go along with interpreting FP#7 as not being merely the judging-and-reasoning counterpart of principles 1, 3, and 5, de Bary thinks, his interpretation is supported by the fact that, in a manuscript, the first comma in FP#7 is not there. That is, in an earlier version, FP#7 reads: '*the natural faculties [no pause] by which we distinguish truth from error, are not fallacious*' (see 2000, 380, n. 22). *Sans* comma, it's harder to take it as obvious that 'the natural faculties' in FP#7 is meant to refer to *all* such faculties together.

Finally, de Bary points out that, in the 13 paragraphs of comments following the statement of FP#7, there are four spots at which Reid clearly refers, not to *all* the faculties, but to *judging* and *reasoning* specifically (see 2000, 380–381). And each of these, de Bary writes, 'puts beyond question the claim that Reid intends the principle to apply only to the faculties of judgment and reasoning' (2000, 380).

What, then, of passages where Reid makes it sound like FP#7 is special – most notably, that beginning 'If any truth can be said to be prior to all others in the order of nature, this seems to have the best claim . . . '? On any reading, de Bary says, this passage is 'embarrassing' and 'simply "bad Reid".'[9] For, if FP#7 is a not a Metaprinciple, then what Reid says here 'is flatly inconsistent with Reid's implicit commitment to the parity of first principles. All first principles are equal in being, by definition, innate and unprovable; and they can all be identified only by certain "marks" – self-evidence, irresistibility, etc.' (2000, 382). Whereas, if FP#7 *is* a metaprinciple, that's problematic as well:

> Dr. Reid should surely not, by his own lights, be claiming that the truth of the set of human faculties is 'prior to all others in the order of nature.' We should expect whatever truth occupies that cosmic 'pole position' to include a reference to God, nature's Wise and Bountiful Author. And in any case, we can find a candidate with *at least* as good a claim to priority from among Reid's purely secular list of twelve first principles, namely principle 12: '*That in the phaenomena of nature. What is to be, will probably be like to what has been in similar circumstances.*' (2000, 382).

So, on either reading, de Bary thinks, this passage is problematic, indeed 'embarrassing' (*ibid*). So everyone has reason to disregard it. And we have, in any case, independent reason to think that FP#7 *isn't* special – that it's just a 'run-off-the-mill "first principle of contingent truths"' (2000, 382–383).

4.   Against De Bary's reading

While de Bary's reading is meant to avoid the dilemma facing (he thinks) anyone who takes FP#7 to be 'special', attributing significant – not to mention, unexplained – error is something to be avoided wherever possible. Quite apart from general considerations of charity, however, de Bary's interpretation of FP#7 is problematic.

For instance, while 'judging' and 'reasoning get mentioned numerous times in Reid's comments of FP#7, perception, consciousness, and memory do so as well. In showing how FP#7 *is* something to which we normally, and automatically, give our implicit assent, Reid refers, for instance, to the credit a person ordinarily gives to 'the testimony of his senses, his memory, or his reason' (EIP 448a, 482); and, in discussing Descartes' treatment of the possibility that all of our judging and reasoning powers are fallacious, Reid refers to the skeptical possibility that 'whatever evidence [a man] has from his consciousness, his senses, his memory, or his reason, yet possibly some malignant being had given him those faculties on purpose to impose upon him' (EIP 447b, 480–481). In short, while 'judging' and 'reasoning' are often referred to by Reid here, those references are intermingled with specific references to the faculties that it is supposed to be the business of FP's 1, 3, and 5 to address.

And there is a straightforward explanation of why that might be, an explanation that raises a more fundamental problem for de Bary's interpretation: namely, that while judgment and reason are *distinguishable* types of mental operation, while they can be analytically *isolated* in carrying out an anatomy of the mind, they are not *separate* from our other truth-oriented faculties. 'Judgment', Reid says, refers to 'every determination of the mind concerning what is true or what is false' (EIP 415b, 411) – any kind of 'mental affirmation or negation' (EIP 414b, 409). And such judgments are the normal attendants of various acts of consciousness, memory, and perception.[10] Such judgments are, to be sure, quick and automatic, but they are judgments nonetheless. Reid variously refers to them as 'natural judgments' and 'judgments of nature' (e.g., IHM 209a, 215), and he is explicit in wishing to regard consciousness, memory and the senses as 'judging faculties' (EIP 415a, 410).[11] And so too, it seems, must anyone: for it is only because they involve judgment that these faculties are in the business of helping us to 'distinguish truth from error'.[12]

In addition to raising a problem for his interpretation of FP#7 *per* se, the fact that other truth-directed faculties already include judgment makes de Bary vulnerable to the same style of argument he uses against Lehrer: Given that the faculties de Bary sees as being targeted by FPs 1, 3, and 5 already involve judgment, if de Bary wishes to see *it* (judgment) as among the real subjects of FP#7, his interpretation will face a dilemma: the reference to judgment in FP#7 is either redundant, or it's doing some real work; if the former, it should be dropped; if the latter, we need to know just what extra work it's doing, and why the explicit mention of judgment in FP#7 doesn't leave something wanting as well.

As to reason, Reid writes:

> We ascribe to reason two offices, or two degrees. The first is to judge of things self-evident; the second to draw conclusions that are not self-evident from those that are. The first of these is the province, and the sole province, of common sense.... (EIP 425b, 433).

So, it is reason, in the form of common sense, that *issues in* the natural judgments attending normal exercise of memory, consciousness, and perception. To be sure, unlike judging, reason*ing* – the other 'office' of reason, and the other faculty that de Bary thinks FP#7 singles out – is no part of the exercise of perception, consciousness, and memory; it couldn't be, since Reid is adamant that they produce judgments *immediately*. And reason*ing* does not already have a FP of its own. So, on anyone's view, FP#7 will have *some* element of non-superfluity to it – it at least gives reason*ing* the place it surely deserves among the FPs. The evidence before us, however, makes it hard to take seriously the idea that FP#7 is meant to refer *merely* to ratiocination.

Summing up this brief discussion: the textual case for reading FP#7 as referring *only* to judging and reason is difficult to make – quite apart from any weight being placed on the first comma in Reid's statement of the principle, and quite apart from any problems (e.g., a regress) to which such an interpretation might give rise.

What about de Bary's argument that, *just considered all on its own*, the passage in which Reid makes it sound like FP#7 is special is problematic? As we saw just above, de Bary claims that if FP#7 *is* supposed to be a metaprinciple, it's an incongruous choice for Reid to make. Again he writes:

> Dr. Reid should surely not, by his own lights, be claiming that the truth of the set of human faculties is 'prior to all others in the order of nature.' We should expect whatever truth occupies that cosmic 'pole position' to include a reference to God, nature's Wise and Bountiful Author. And in any case, we can find a candidate with *at least* as good a claim to priority from among Reid's purely secular list of twelve first principles, namely principle 12: *'That in the phaenomena of nature. What is to be, will probably be like to what has been in similar circumstances.'* (2000, 382).

However, the case for FP#7 over anything specifically theistic is clearly stated by Reid: '[T]he unjust *live by faith*, as well as the *just*' (IHM 95b, 4). As Wolterstorff says, 'accepting God's goodness as a reason for trusting in one's faculties presupposes, if nothing else, one's faculty of reason' (2001, 212).[13] So too: any reference to God as nature's wise and bountiful author would take for granted what's stated in FP#7 as well. And the same goes for de Bary's claim that, among purely secular principles, the inductive principle has *at least* as good a claim to occupying the 'cosmic "pole position"': our implicit commitment to *that* principle, indeed to *anything*, appears also to presume FP#7.

In this way, we're naturally led back to the thought that FP#7 *is* special, and in much the way that Reid (and, following him, Lehrer) appears to think. But that, as we saw, is supposed to be problematic. What to do?

5. Why FP#7 is special after all

The key at this point is to back up and examine a widely-held assumption about the FPs that precede FP#7 – namely, that by the time we get to FP#7 in the Reid's enumeration, he has *already* claimed that various of our faculties are reliable; specifically, that he has already claimed (with principles 1, 3, and 5) that consciousness, memory, and perception are reliable. It is only because this has been assumed that we've been led to grapple with the interpretive puzzle we've been considering. Thus: since these other faculties already have first principles asserting their reliability, there appears to be no further epistemological work for FP#7 to do,[14] so FP#7 is superfluous; or, there *is* extra work it's supposed to be doing, but we must then ask why the motivation for FP#7 doesn't lead to a regress; or, finally, in spite of appearances, and the problems facing such an interpretation, we limit the scope of FP#7 – it is just another reliability principle, alongside 1, 3, and 5, applying only to judging and reasoning.

But what else might FPs 1, 3, and 5 be asserting, if not the reliability of consciousness, memory, and perception? They are, I suggest, merely metaphysical; more specifically, these other FPs 'relat[e] to existence'; they tell me that the various acts of the mind of which I am conscious (FP#1), the past events I distinctly remember (FP#3), and the things that I distinctly perceive (FP#5) around me, *do really exist* or *did really happen*. Or, insofar as we're taking them to (at least) state our most deeply held commitments,[15] these principles are meant to capture the fact that the reality of these things is something that all normal humans (irresistibly, naturally, etc.) believe or take for granted.

Of course, in the statement of these principles, mention is made of the faculties (consciousness, memory, perception) that acquaint us with the relevant sorts of objects and events. But it does not follow that the principles are intended to be *about* those faculties. On the present interpretation, with 1, 3, and 5, Reid is expressing our natural (irresistible, etc.) belief in, or commitment to, the existence of various sorts of things. Which things?[16] Reid answers with (plural) definite descriptions – 'the sorts of things we are conscious of', 'the sorts of things we distinctly perceive and remember'. In this way, the mentioning of the faculties in question is merely a referential device, directing our attention to the relevant classes of things, the firm (etc.) belief in the existence of which is really what's at issue.

Further, *qua* definite descriptions, 'the things we distinctly perceive', 'the things we distinctly remember', and 'the things of which we are conscious' are being used referentially, rather than attributively (Donnellan 1966). To explain: *if* we take FP#5, e.g., as an epistemological principle asserting the reliability of perception, it is important not to give 'perception' a 'success' reading, since that would trivialize the principle (Sosa and Van Cleve 2001, 188; cf. Lehrer 1998, 22 and Wolterstorff 2001, 224). In the same way, on the present interpretation, FP#5 (e.g.) should not be read as stating, *There are things that we distinctly perceive, and they exist* – that would be trivial too. Rather, on the present view, the content of the descriptive phrases is inessential to what's being expressed; the relevant FPs have the force of, 'Such things as *those* ['pointing', to some ostensible object of perception, memory, or consciousness] exist'. What's important to Reid is to assert, or express the belief in, the existence of certain types of object. That we distinctly perceive them, for instance, is inessential to that claim. Again, the reference to the relevant faculty merely points our attention in the right direction.[17]

One source of support for reading 1, 3, and 5 in the manner I've been recommending is provided by FP#8 – more specifically, by how Reid prefaces its statement:

8. Another first principle **relating to existence**, is, *That there is life and intelligence in our fellow-men with whom we converse.* (Bold added.)

Obviously, Reid is not referring to FP#7 here – *it* doesn't 'relate to existence'; it's clearly epistemological; no one denies that. *Perhaps* Reid means to be referring merely to FP#6,

6. Another first principle, I think, is, *That we have some degree of power over our actions, and the determinations of our will.*

But why stop there? Strictly speaking, while clearly metaphysical, FP#6 doesn't mention existence. But, if we look at FPs 1–5, most of them do.[18] In fact, if we are not already assuming that 1, 3, and 5 are intended as epistemological, rather than metaphysical, it's not difficult to see them as being concerned *merely* with existence:

1. *First*, then, I hold, as a first principle, the existence of everything of which I am conscious.
2. Another first principle, I think, is, *That the thoughts of which I am conscious, are the thoughts of a being which I call myself, my mind, my person.*
3. Another first principle I take to be — *That those things did really happen which I distinctly remember.*
4. Another first principle is, *Our own personal identity and continued existence, as far back as we remember anything distinctly.*
5. Another first principle is, *That those things do really exist which we distinctly perceive by our senses, and are what we perceive them to be.*

Granted, if they're true, 1, 3, and 5, certainly have epistemological *implications*: if *those things do really exist which we distinctly perceive by our senses, and are what we perceive them to be,* then perception is reliable, for instance. In the same way, if it's true that, *in the phænomena of nature, what is to be, will probably be like to what has been in similar circumstances,* then induction is reliable. But FP#12 doesn't *assert* that, or indeed anything about any of our faculties or inferential practices. FP#12, rather, serves to mark the fact that *the uniformity of nature* – that metaphysical proposition – is among our natural, immediate, and fundamental commitments. So too: FP#8, if true, has the consequence that our beliefs about other minds are reliable; FPs 2 and 4, that my beliefs about my existence and continued identity are; and so on. But it doesn't follow that FPs 8, 2, and 4 are *themselves* epistemological.

So too, I want to suggest, with respect to FPs 1, 3, and 5: they may well have epistemological implications, but those implications are external to the principles themselves.[19] Nor do I think this interpretation is any kind of a stretch. After all: that the various things I (distinctly) see really exist, for example, and that perception is reliable, are clearly different beliefs – one concerns the world, the other concerns me and my faculties.[20] And, if we look at what Reid says in elaborating and commenting upon each of 1, 3, and 5, it becomes clear that it is really the former type of beliefs – beliefs about what *exists* – that he is concerned with there.

For instance, in connection with FP#1, Reid writes:

> When a man is conscious of pain, he is certain of its existence; when he is conscious that he doubts or believes, he is certain of the existence of those operations.

But the irresistible conviction he has of the reality of those operations is not the effect of reasoning; it is immediate and intuitive. The existence therefore of those passions and operations of our minds, of which we are conscious, is a first principle, which nature requires us to believe upon her authority. (EIP 442b, 470)

Having stated FP#3, Reid refers back to what he has just said about consciousness: 'the testimony of memory, like that of consciousness, is immediate; it claims our assent upon its own authority' (EIP 445b, 474). What is it that memory testifies to? The reality of various past things and events. It's *that* belief, Reid goes on to say, that Hume labors unsuccessfully to account for in terms of the vivacity of certain perceptions – as Hume shows, 'this vivacity gives no ground to believe the existence of external objects. And it is obvious that it can give as little ground to believe the past existence of the objects of memory' (EIP 445a, 475).

And so too for FP#5, *That those things do really exist which we distinctly perceive by our senses, and are what we perceive them to be*: what 'all men are led to give implicit faith to' is 'the testimony of their senses' – viz., the existence of 'certain [objects and] beings about us' (EIP 445b, 476–477). Here too, there is no reason to take the principle itself as epistemological.

Of course, in his comments following the statements of FPs 1, 3, and 5, the discussion does sometimes turn epistemological, with Reid mentioning some arguments for thinking various faculties might be fallacious, and so on. But this is no problem for the present view. In general, *any* kind of critical consideration of *any* claim or belief is bound to quickly turn epistemological, even where the claim/belief in question is clearly non-epistemological. Second, and relatedly: insofar as issues concerning the fallaciousness or not of various faculties do creep into the discussion of other FPs is to be expected, given the unique status that FP#7 has among the FPs. (On which, more below.)

Aside from being perfectly consonant with what Reid himself says, taking FPs 1, 3, and 5 to 'relat[e] to existence', rather than to matters epistemological, has the consequence that the *role* of FP#7, the *need* for it, now becomes perfectly clear: *it* is epistemological; *it* concerns, not the existence of various types of things and events, or other metaphysical matters, but the faculties – all of them – by which we gain knowledge of these and any other facts about the world.[21] FP#7, then, is not meant to plug an apparent gap in the epistemological assurance provided by principles 1, 3, and 5; for, on the present reading, these principles are not meant to provide any such assurance at all. Thus, the question of whether *FP#7* fills the gap that these other epistemological principles leave open, or whether some *still further* epistemological principle is required, does not arise.

So too, there is now a straightforward explanation of the *specialness* of FP#7: its 'priority' or 'specialness' consists in the fact that, just as Reid says, unique among the FPs, *it* is taken for granted whenever one forms any beliefs at all, including any beliefs in any of the other FPs. It is in this sense that FP#7 is a 'first first principle', as Lehrer puts it: it is, so to speak, the implicit commitment behind all others.[22]

Is FP#7 a 'looping principle', to use another of Lehrer's phrases? That FP#7 is true is itself a deliverance of our faculties, and if the latter are not fallacious, as FP#7 says they are not, then FP#7 itself is trustworthy as well. In this way, in vouching for the deliverances of our faculties generally, FP#7 'vouches for itself' (Lehrer 1990, 42–43).

However, while FP#7 in this way reflexively 'vouches for itself', it does not follow that *that* (FP#7's reflexive character) is what justifies the principle. In a well-known passage, Reid addresses the question of the grounds[23] we have for FP#7:

> How then come we to be assured of this fundamental truth on which all others rest [viz., FP#7; see my footnote 22]? Perhaps evidence, as in many other respects it resembles light, so in this also – that, as light, which is the discoverer of all visible objects, discovers itself at the same time, so evidence, which is the voucher for all truth, vouches for itself at the same time' (EIP 448a, 481).

This evocative and crucial claim about evidence is quite general, and it bears upon the other FPs, which of course have evidence attending them too. Thus, for example, it is not *merely* that I find myself naturally, irresistibly, automatically, believing that those things which I distinctly perceive exist, as I might find myself simply 'stuck with' some other belief (e.g., that I'm going to win the lottery). Rather, the relevant principle (here, FP#5) is (Reid thinks) *evident*, and its evidentness is itself evident. Moreover, its evidentness is not owing to anything else. If it were, the principle would not be self-evident. And while, for the reasons given above, there is a perfectly good sense in which FP#7 is the 'first first' principle, each of the FPs is of course self-evident, according to Reid.[24, 25]

A final point brings us back to the question of FP#7's specialness. As we've just seen, the evidentness of evidence – the fact that, like light, evidence discloses itself as it discloses other things – is involved in our consideration of and assent to each of the FPs, and not just FP#7. But if it is the reflexive character *of evidence* that assures us of FP#7, then it is not the looping (reflexive) character *of FP#7* – the quasi-formal fact that, *qua* deliverance of our intellectual faculties, it implies its own non-fallaciousness – which does so. In the same way, on the present account it is not the distinctive looping (reflexive) character of FP#7 *per se* that accounts for its specialness. FP#7's specialness, rather, derives from its perfectly general and distinctively epistemological character, because of which it has the kind of 'priority' that Reid describes.

6.   Conclusion

The First Principles are central to Reid's epistemological views; and, by Reid's own account, FP#7 occupies a special place among them. The discussion here has been meant to show how that can be so, given the rest of the FPs, and given the problems that de Bary has argued face any attempt to regard FP#7 as having some kind of priority. The key, I've suggested, is to let go of the idea that certain FPs preceding FP#7 already assert the better part of what FP#7 explicitly states. Once that's done, the need for FP#7 is clear: it is needed because there is nothing epistemological in the FPs that precede it. So too, far from being 'embarrassing' or 'simply "bad Reid"' (de Bary 2000, 382), that FP#7 has a special place among the FPs is a straightforward consequence of its being both perfectly general and distinctively epistemological.[26]

Notes

1. Discussions of these matters include Alston (1985), Lehrer (1989), Rysiew (2005), Sosa and Van Cleve (2001), Van Cleve (1999), and Wolterstorff (2001).
2. References to Reid will be followed by indication of the relevant work – *An Inquiry into the Human Mind* (IHM), or *Essays on the Intellectual Powers of Man* (EIP) – followed by as well page numbers in both the Hamilton and the Brookes editions. (For the former, 'a' refers to the left-hand column, 'b' to the right-hand side.)
3. Following Van Cleve, we can distinguish between *epistemic* principles and *epistemological* ones: the former 'specify[...] the conditions under which beliefs of various types are justified, rational, evident, or the like' (1999, 5); the latter have more broadly to do with matters epistemic. Cf. Alston, 437.
4. Note that these are first principles *of contingent truths* – i.e., they function as axioms upon which our thinking is based when inquire about contingent matters. While I myself think, and think Reid thinks, that the principles themselves are contingent (see especially, perhaps, EIP 442a, 469), as Van Cleve observes (1999, 21), that is a distinct issue.
5. '...consciousness, memory, and perception...[already] have individual "first principles of continent truths" which apply to them, numbers 1, 3, and 5 respectively' (de Bary 2002, 375). In the same vein, Alston refers to several of the FPs as 'epistemological principles hav[ing] to do exclusively with reliability' (1985, 437), and says that FP #5, e.g., is 'the thesis that sense-perception is reliable' (443). So too, Lehrer refers to FPs 1, 3, and 5 as 'tell[ing] us that perception, consciousness, memory are not fallacious' (Lehrer 1998, 23).
6. A propensity to rely on testimony is certainly natural ('the principle of credulity'; IHM 196b, 194), though it's not clear that it makes good sense to say that *testimony* is a natural faculty.
7. At least, insofar as such use involves assent to the faculty's deliverances, as it does in normal cases. (One can imagine, for instance, cases in which a faculty is known to be unreliable, but in a systematic enough way that one can nonetheless make good use of its deliverances without taking them at face value or forming the relevant beliefs.) Thanks to Todd Buras for this point.
8. De Bary's 2000 article appears, with very slight changes, as Section 5.3 in his 2002 book. Here, I cite de Bary's work using the pagination of the original paper.
9. De Bary is not the only recent commentator who has found this particular passage difficult to reconcile with his/her own preferred reading of Reid's epistemology – both van Cleve (2008, 301–302) and Lemos (2004, Chapter 4) think that this passage marks a significant, and unexplained, mistake on Reid's part. It's clear that, in van Cleve's case anyway, the interpretative problem stems from his wanting, like de Bary (and Greco 2002, 2010), to read Reid as an externalist – something that, I think, we have independent reason not to do (see Rysiew 2005, 2011, and footnote 23, below).
10. 'In persons come to years of understanding, judgment necessarily accompanies all sensation, perception by the senses, consciousness, and memory' (EIP 414a–b, 409). 'The man who perceives an object, believes that it exists, and is what he distinctly

perceives it to be; nor is it in his power to avoid such judgment. And the like may be said of memory, and of consciousness. Whether judgment ought to be called a necessary concomitant of these operations, or rather a part or ingredient of them, I do not dispute; but it is certain that all of them are accompanied with a determination that something is true or false' (EIP 414b, 409).

11. This passage is hardly idiosyncratic. At (EIP 329a–b, 231–232), e.g., Reid speaks of 'seeing' as itself doing the judging, producing various convictions, and so on; and he says similar things about consciousness and memory as well – they produce immediate belief, etc.

12. Given, then, that he wants to see FPs 1, 3, and 5 as already asserting the *reliability* of consciousness, memory and perception, de Bary cannot claim that, while judgment typically *follows* instances of these acts of mind, it should not be considered a *part* of them. For it is only insofar as consciousness, memory and perception incorporate judgment that they *can* be fallacious/non-fallacious, reliable or not.

13. Cf. Lehrer and Warner (2000, 367–372). And: '*Every* kind of reasoning for the veracity of our faculties, amounts to no more than taking their own testimony for their veracity' (EIP 447b, 481; emphasis added).

14. Apart, perhaps, from giving some place to reasoning among the FPs – see above. But, as discussed, it's implausible that that's *all* FP#7 is mean to do.

15. There is controversy over how best to characterize such commitments – whether it is appropriate to describe them (as Reid sometimes does) as beliefs, as opposed to saying (as Reid also does) that they are things all normal humans commonly take for granted. (For discussion of this issue, see Wolterstorff 2001, 215–227, and Sosa and Van Cleve 2001, 190–193.) Here, I move between these two ways of putting the relevant point; the present discussion is meant to be neutral on the question of which, if either, is to be preferred.

16. Here, I'm indebted to Todd Buras.

17. As does 'The man drinking the martini' in its referential use. In terms of that well-known example, if it turns out that the person to whom the speaker is referring has some other colorless liquid in their glass, the use of the phrase need not be defective, since the referential use doesn't presuppose the existence of a unique object satisfying the description – it's just serving to pick out the person about whom the speaker has something to say. (Donnellan's paper has of course spawned much debate as to whether the distinction in question is semantic or pragmatic, and so on, but there is broad agreement that the general phenomenon is real. Needless to say, nothing in the present paper hangs on such questions; the reference to Donnellan is meant merely to help clarify what's being claimed about the relevant FPs. Thanks to Mike Raven for discussion on these matters.)

18. FPs 1, 4, and 5 do so explicitly; the *pastness* of the *events* in FP#3 mandates 'did really happen' (vs. *do* really *exist*); and, as Reid's discussion of Hume's views in connection with FP #2 (EIP 444a–b, 473–474) makes clear, it is as much concerned with the reality (hence, the existence) of the self (mind, person) as with its being the subject of one's thoughts.

19. Todd Buras has suggested to me that there may be a relevant and important difference between FP#12, say, and FPs 1, 3, and 5: while the former might have epistemological implications, those can be derived only by addition of some further premise (that the assumption nature's uniformity is essential to inductive reasoning, say); whereas, it seems that the connection is much tighter in the case of the latter. E. g., if the things we distinctly remember did really happen, then the beliefs formed as a result of distinct memories are reliable. Essentially, it's just a rewording of the principle that's required to generate the epistemological moral. To reply: I am not sure that the example just given is merely a case of rewording what's already been

stated. (See below. See too what was suggested above about the function of such phrases as 'the things we distinctly remember', etc., in 1, 3, and 5.) But even it if were, rewordings can of course make for significant semantic differences.

20. Of course, when I assent to the former proposition, I thereby presume the latter. But this doesn't show that the two are not really distinct. What it illustrates, as Reid sees it, is the special role of FP#7 among the FPs. – See below.

21. FP#10 – *That there is a certain regard due to human testimony in matters of fact, and even to human authority in matters of opinion* – is like this as well; it is the interpersonal, social-epistemological counterpart of FP#7.

22. Reid says: the 'fundamental truth on which all others rest' (EIP 448a, 481). This is an unfortunate way of putting the point: it not that all *truths* rest upon the nonfallaciousness of our faculties. Nor is it that Reid thinks that FP#7 serves as a *premise* for other beliefs, except in some figurative sense – '[it] is, *as it were*, one of the premises on which our assent is grounded' (EIP 447b, 481; emphasis added; see Lehrer 1989, esp. 163). The better, non-figurative way of putting the point, again, is to say that FP#7 is, inevitably, taken for granted whenever one assents to anything at all.

23. Here, as elsewhere, 'ground' might be intended as either a descriptive-psychological or a normative-epistemic term. Reid tends to mean both of these, when speaking of evidence as 'the ground of belief' (EIP 328a, 228), and I think it's both of these questions that he's meaning to address in the passage at (EIP 448a, 481). In my 2005 and 2011, I explore this and other ideas central to Reid's thinking about evidence. As the present discussion suggests, among the consequences of that thinking is that Reid's epistemological views are not purely externalist.

24. Nothing in the present interpretation is 'inconsistent with Reid's implicit commitment to the parity of first principles. All first principles are equal in being, by definition, innate and unprovable; and they can all be identified only by certain "marks" – self-evidence, irresistibility, etc.' (de Bary 2000, 382).

25. Some commentators have found it hard to take seriously the idea that the first principles are really self-evident. Elsewhere (see footnote 23), I address such concerns. The more general question as to the nature and normative status of the FPs is a large and difficult one; I set out my own views on this in (Rysiew 2002).

26. For helpful comments and discussion, I'm indebted to Todd Buras, Alastair Crosby, Laurent Jaffro, Mike Raven, and the other attendants at the Vermont Reid conference.

References

Alston, William. 1985. "Thomas Reid on Epistemic Principles." *History of Philosophy Quarterly* 2: 435–452.

De Bary, Thomas. 2000. "Thomas Reid's Metaprinciple." *American Catholic Philosophical Quarterly* LXXIV (3): 373–383.

De Bary, Thomas. 2002. *Thomas Reid and Scepticism: His Reliabilist Response*. New York: Routledge.

Donnellan, Keith S. 1966. "Reference and Definite Descriptions." *The Philosophical Review* 75 (3): 281–304.

Greco, John. 2002. "How to Reid Moore." *The Philosophical Quarterly* 52 (209): 544–563. Reprinted in Haldane and Read eds., 131–150.

Greco, John. 2010. *Achieving Knowledge: A Virtue-Theoretic Account of Epistemic Normativity*. Cambridge and New York: Cambridge University Press.

Haldane, John, and Stephen Read, eds. 2003. *The Philosophy of Thomas Reid: A Collection of Essays*. Oxford: Blackwell.

Lehrer, Keith. 1989. *Thomas Reid*. London: Routledge.

Lehrer, Keith. 1990. "Chisholm, Reid, and the Problem of the Epistemic Surd." *Philosophical Studies* 60 (1–2): 39–45.

Lehrer, Keith. 1998. "Reid, Hume and Common Sense." *Reid Studies* 2 (1): 15–25.

Lehrer, Keith, and Bradley Warner. 2000. "Reid, God and Epistemology." *American Catholic Philosophical Quarterly* LXXIV (3): 357–372.

Lemos, Noah. 2004. *Common Sense: A Contemporary Defense*. Cambridge and New York: Cambridge University Press.

Reid, Thomas. 1885. *Philosophical Works*, edited by William Hamilton. 8th edition Georg Olms Verlag.

Reid, Thomas. (1764) 1997. *An Inquiry into the Human Mind on the Principles of Common Sense*, edited by Derek R. Brookes. Edinburgh: Edinburgh University Press.

Reid, Thomas. (1785) 1997. *Essays on the Intellectual Powers of Man*, edited by Derek R. Brookes. Edinburgh: Edinburgh University Press.

Rysiew, Patrick. 2002. "Reid and Epistemic Naturalism." *The Philosophical Quarterly* 52 (209): 437–456. Reprinted in Haldane and Read, eds., 24–43.

Rysiew, Patrick. 2005. "Reidian Evidence." *Journal of Scottish Philosophy* 3 (2): 107–121.

Rysiew, Patrick. 2011. "Making it Evident: Evidence and Evidentness, Justification and Belief." In *Evidentialism and its Discontents*, edited by Trent Dougherty, 207–225. Oxford University Press.

Sosa, Ernest, and James Van Cleve. 2001. "Thomas Reid." In *The Blackwell Guide to the Modern Philosophers: From Descartes to Nietzsche*, edited by S. Emmanuel, 179–200. Malden, Ma & Oxford: Blackwell.

Van Cleve, James. 1999. "Reid on the First Principles of Contingent Truths." *Reid Studies* 3 (1): 3–30.

Van Cleve, James. 2008. "Reid's Response to the Skeptic." In *The Oxford Handbook of Skepticism*, edited by John Greco, 286–309. Oxford and New York: Oxford University Press.

Wolterstorff, Nicholas. 2001. *Thomas Reid and the Story of Epistemology*. Cambridge and New York: Cambridge University Press.

EPISTEMOLOGY

Reason and trust in Reid

Nicholas Wolterstorff

Yale Divinity School, Yale University, USA; Institute for Advanced Studies in Culture, University of Virginia, USA

My theme in this essay is the anti-rationalism in Reid's thought. I explore three areas of Reid's thought in which anti-rationalism is a prominent feature: Reid's attack on the Way of Ideas and his own account of how beliefs are formed, in particular, perceptual beliefs, his response to the skeptic, and his understanding of the task of the philosopher.

When an American intellectual historian, a few years back, described to me the reception of Reid in nineteenth century America, I responded, half-jokingly, that it sounded to me as if Reid's American readers interpreted him as giving them permission to forget about Hume and return to Locke. Locke was for them the default position.

To interpret Reid thus is to miss his genius completely. And not only is it to miss his genius: it is to misinterpret him as badly as he can be misinterpreted. Reid's epistemology was a devastating attack on the line of thought that he called 'The Way of Ideas.' Nobody better exemplified that line of thought than John Locke. Astounding, then, that Reid's American readers would interpret him as having refuted Hume and thereby authorized them to return to Locke.

I cannot myself vouch for the accuracy of the impression I was given of how Reid's nineteenth century North America readers interpreted him. To the best of my knowledge there is no comprehensive account of Reid's reception in North America, or of his reception in any other country. [1] We know that Reid was enormously popular in Britain, France, Germany, and North America in the latter part of the eighteenth century and for much of the nineteenth; we also know that he was better understood by many in Germany in the late eighteenth century than he was by Kant, whose dismissive comments about common sense philosophy in his *Prolegomena to any Future Metaphysics* are almost painful to read. [2] But how many of his readers understood Reid? How many discerned the truly radical and innovative character of his thought? My impression is that the number was few.

If that impression is accurate, part of the fault has to be laid at Reid's own door. Reid spoke a good deal about common sense; his philosophy came to be known as 'common sense philosophy.' It was an unfortunate choice of terminology on Reid's part. Reid did not mean by 'common sense' what is ordinarily meant thereby. My grandfather used to say that common sense tells one not to fish in a lake after a heavy rain; the rain stirs up the bottom, and the fish have so much food floating around in front of them that they have no interest in bait. If one assumes that that's what Reid had in mind by 'common sense,' serious misinterpretation is bound to follow. Had that been what Reid had in mind, Kant's put-down of common sense philosophy would be well-deserved.

In this essay I want to identify and discuss Reid's genius. What was the heart of Reid's contribution to the history of modern Western philosophy? Or to speak more modestly: I want to present what I *take* to have been Reid's genius. Given my impression that most of his readers missed what I take to be Reid's genius, it behooves me to be humble and open to the possibility that his genius was not what I take it to have been.

When I speak here of Reid's genius, what I have in mind is the line of thought in his two books, *An Inquiry into the Human Mind* and *Essays on The Intellectual Powers*; I will not have anything to say, on this occasion, about his other major book, *Essays on The Active Powers.*[3]

I hold that Reid was the first great thinker in the modern Western tradition to combine ontological realism with anti-rationalism – not with *ir*-rationalism but with *anti*-rationalism. Reid was an ontological realist in the sense that he held that there is 'a ready-made world,' to borrow a nice turn of phrase from Hilary Putnam;[4] the world as we know it is not of our making in the way that Kant thought it was nor in the way that Nelson Goodman thought it was.[5] Reid does not argue for this position; he takes it for granted. It was with that sort of ontological realism that Reid combined his anti-rationalism. Let me develop this theme, of Reid's realist anti-rationalism, by looking at three major components of his thought in which anti-rationalism is a dominant feature.

First, anti-rationalism is a dominant feature of Reid's account of belief-formation, in particular, of his account of perceptual-belief formation.

What fascinated Reid, to the extent that it is the topic of almost all his published work, was the workings of the human mind; almost all of Reid's published writing is what we would now call *philosophical psychology*. When it came to what he called *the intellectual powers*, what especially fascinated him was how and why we form beliefs

Contemporary analytic epistemology has been almost obsessively preoccupied with developing theories of one and another merit in beliefs: theories of knowledge, theories of warrant, theories of justification, theories of entitlement, theories of rationality. Reid's analyses of various sorts of belief-formation are by no means irrelevant to this preoccupation; but the overarching topic of Reid's discussion is different. It's the principles governing the formation of beliefs that Reid wants to identify; his comments about merits in beliefs occur along the way.

It was especially *de re* beliefs that drew Reid's attention, that is, beliefs *about* things, in particular, beliefs about things other than one's presently occurring states of mind – about physical objects, about past events, about future events, and so forth. And of these, it was especially perceptual beliefs that drew Reid's attention. How do we get a cognitive grip, by means of perception, on items in our physical environment? And once we have such a grip, what accounts for our forming beliefs about those things?

Reid's presentation of his account of perceptual-belief formation was polemical through and through, intertwined with his attack on the Way of Ideas. So let me begin with a brief presentation of the analysis of perception offered by the Way of Ideas. To make things easier, let me focus exclusively on *visual* perception. The analysis goes like this. The object perceived – a tree, let us say – sends off light rays. These light rays from the tree strike the eye of the perceiver, causing neural impulses which travel to the brain. The resultant brain activity causes a sensation, sensations being a species of what Locke called 'ideas.' The sensation is a mental image of the tree; it resembles the tree in roughly the way that a mirror image of the tree resembles the tree. This tree-like sensation evokes awareness of itself and of various of the mental facts pertaining to the sensation. This awareness, in turn, immediately evokes beliefs about those mental facts, the propositional content of those beliefs corresponding directly to the mental facts of which one is aware. That done, the perceiver then infers that her sensation has been caused by some external, spatially located, object. That puts her in the position of being able to form beliefs about that external entity; she infers, about the external entity that caused her sensation, that it has properties resembling those of the sensation. She reasons from the beliefs she forms about her sensation, to conclusions about the existence and character of the external object. The formation of perceptual beliefs involves an exercise of inferential reasoning.

Reid found this theory preposterous; his attack on it is relentless and multi-facetted. For our purposes here it will be sufficient to mention just one of his many lines of attack. Reid challenged the assumption that the sensory images caused by the impact on us of items in our environment are images of those items; on this he thought Berkeley was right. He was especially fond of an example from the domain of touch. Touching a hard object evokes in one a pressure sensation. It's far from evident what a mental tactile image would be; but in any case, there's nothing at all about that pressure sensation which resembles the hardness of the object.

Let me now move on to Reid's alternative analysis of the workings of perception. Reid agrees with the first part of the analysis offered by the Way of Ideas theorist. In visual perception, the object perceived sends off light rays, the effect of the impact of these on the perceiver being a sensation. Reid describes the sensation as a *sign* of the perceived object – not an *image* but a *sign* – by which he means, essentially, that the sensation carries information about the external object that caused it. What then happens, Reid argues, is that the sensation evokes a cognitive grip on the external object that caused the sensation and an immediately formed belief about that object – to the effect, say, that it is a red ball with yellow stripes. Perception, on Reid's view, consists of the cognitive grip on the external object that the sensation evokes plus the immediately formed belief about the object that it evokes. Reid's theory of perception is, thus, a *doxastic* theory. 'The external senses,' says Reid, 'furnish us with a variety of sensations;... at the same time they give us a conception, and an invincible belief of the existence of external objects... This conception and belief which nature produces by means of the senses, we call *perception*.'[6]

Let me highlight a few aspects of this account. On Reid's account, we do not first form beliefs about our sensations and then employ our reason to draw inferences about the object that caused them. Reid thinks that usually we form no beliefs whatsoever about our sensations; so of course we don't employ our reason to draw inferences from those beliefs. He notes that it is in fact difficult to isolate the sensation and focus just on it; sensations do their work of evoking beliefs about the external world without calling attention to themselves. We are so created that we non-inferentially read off the information that the sensation carries about the object that caused it, usually without being aware of the sensation and without forming beliefs about it; we non-inferentially interpret our sensations. [7] Our perceptual beliefs are the products of the activation of dispositions, not the conclusions of inferences. Some of our dispositions for the formation of perceptual beliefs belong to our hard-wiring – obviously not a metaphor that Reid himself used. Some are dispositions that we acquire as the result of regularities in our experience.

When I walk into a room, I do not employ my reason to infer, from beliefs about my sensory experience, that there are chairs in the room; my sensory experience non-inferentially evokes in me the belief that these are chairs in the room. No inference. Perception is not an exercise of reason. Here, in Reid's own words, is a good summary of his analysis:

> The external senses have a double province; to make us feel, and to make us perceive. They furnish us with a variety of sensations, some pleasant, others painful, and others indifferent; at the same time they give us a conception, and an invincible belief of the existence of external objects. This conception of external objects is the work of nature. The belief of their existence, which our senses give, is [also] the work of nature; so likewise is the sensation that accompanies it. This conception and belief which nature produces by means of the senses, we call *perception*. The feeling which goes along with the perception, we call *sensation*. The perception and its corresponding sensation are produced at the same time. In our experience we never find them disjoined. (EIP II. xvii [318b])

I have highlighted the anti-rationalist dimension of Reid's analysis of perceptual-belief formation: perceptual beliefs are not the conclusions of inferences but the outputs of our dispositions to interpret our sensory experience in certain ways. Reid's analysis of the formation of inductive beliefs has a similar anti-rational dimension, as do his analysis of the formation of memory beliefs and his analysis of testimonial beliefs.

Before moving on, let me point to what I regard as a flaw in Reid's analysis of perception. When I wrote my book on Reid I had some intimation of this flaw; now, in retrospect, I believe that I did not give it the credence that I should have.[8] As I mentioned earlier, a question that fascinated Reid was how we manage to get a cognitive grip on things other than our states of mind that is sufficient for us to be able to form beliefs about those things, and what then accounts for our actually forming such *de re* beliefs. Reid used the term 'conception' for what I have called *a cognitive grip*.

One way in which we get a cognitive grip on something – in Reid's terminology, a conception – is by being aware of it. When I am dizzy, I am at the same time aware of being dizzy; that awareness is a cognitive grip on my dizziness that is sufficient for my forming beliefs that are about it, rather than about some other thing. Another way of getting a cognitive grip on something that is sufficient for forming a belief that is about it, rather than about some other thing, is by using a definite description that the entity in question satisfies, or by the use of a proper name.

So when Reid says that, in perception, the sensation evokes a conception of the external entity that is the object of the perception, what sort of conception (cognitive grip) does he think this is? Is it direct awareness of the external object? Is it a definite description of the external object? Or is it possibly some other form of cognitive grip?

I know of no passage in which Reid directly answers this question; indeed, I know of none in which he even recognizes that there is a question here. So we have to ask how he should have answered the question, given the other things he says. The view that I defended in my book on Reid is that, given the other things he says, what he should have held is that our cognitive grip on the external object does not take the form of direct awareness of the object but the form of a definite description of the object: 'that object which is the cause of this sensation.'

That interpretation has proved controversial.[9] Though I continue to think that it is the correct interpretation, it does have the following strange consequence. On Reid's doxastic account of perception, perception consists of a sensation, which is the effect and sign of some external object, along with what is evoked by the sensation, namely, a conception of that object and some immediate belief about it. Reid holds that of the sensation itself we normally take no notice; we do not attend to it. But this implies that in perception there's nothing of which we are aware other than the conception of the external object and the belief about it. But if the conception of the object is a definite description that the object satisfies, then there is clearly something not right about this analysis. On this analysis, there is no room for feeling something *as* hard, or feeling it *to be* hard; there is only the pressure sensation, of which one is usually not aware, plus a definite description of the object and the immediately formed belief, about the object, that it is hard.

In my book I took note of what its advocates have called 'The New Theory of Representation'; but I then dismissed it, for what I now regard as a confused reason.[10] Here's what the New Theory proposes: in visual perception, a part of my environment is visually presented to me as being a certain way – for example, presented as the sun rising above the trees. A part of my environment visually appears to me a certain way. This visual presenting or appearing is obviously not a definite description of the sun coupled with a belief about it; but neither is it a sensation. I now think that what we are aware of in perception is how our environment presents itself to us, how it appears to us, and that this is what evokes beliefs about external objects. The beliefs are evoked immediately. I think Reid was right about that; we don't employ our reason to make inferences from beliefs about how our environment presents itself to beliefs about how it is.

We have all had the experience, I'm sure, of finding oneself in the situation of having a visual experience that is not a case of the environment presenting itself a certain way. The situation is visually ambiguous; our normal interpretive dispositions don't know what to make of the situation. It's just a blur of colors. For adults, this experience is usually short-lived. Perhaps that sort of experience is rightly called a visual sensation; I don't know. But if so, it is not that sort of visual sensation that evokes perceptual beliefs; what evokes perceptual beliefs is how our environment presents itself. If I were to construct an improvement on Reid, this is the idea that I would try to work out.

Let me move to a second component of Reid's thought in which anti-rationalism is a prominent feature, namely, his answer to the skeptic. The Way of Ideas invites the skeptical question: what good reason is there for holding that our sensations are images of the objects that caused them and for inferring that those objects resemble the sensations in various ways? Our sensations do not, after all, advertise themselves as images. May it be that they don't resemble the objects at all? Surely that's possible. Indeed, it seems possible that they're not even caused by external physical objects.

Though Reid's theory is not susceptible to this particular skeptical question, it is obviously susceptible to a close cousin thereof. The theory holds that sensations non-inferentially evoke in us beliefs about the external world. May it be that those beliefs are mostly or entirely false? Surely that's possible. The fact that our sensations immediately – and on Reid's view, ineluctably – evoke beliefs in us is entirely compatible with the falsehood of those beliefs.

What are we supposed to do with these questions about possibility? I described them as 'skeptical' questions, meaning thereby that they are questions asked by skeptics. What response to his questions does the skeptic want? Clearly he wants some response. He's not content to raise his questions about possibility and let it go at that.

Different skeptics want different responses. Two stock figures pop up again and again in Reid's writing: the skeptic and the madman. Our concern here is the skeptic. What sort of response is the Reidian skeptic looking for?

'The skeptic' asks me, says Reid, 'Why do you believe the existence of the external object which you perceive?' adding that 'There is nothing so shameful in a philosopher as to be deceived and deluded; and therefore you ought to resolve firmly to withhold assent, and to throw off all this belief of external objects, which may be all delusion' (IHM VI.xx [183b; B 169]). Reid's skeptic is someone who enjoins the philosopher to 'throw off all this belief of external objects' until he, the philosopher, has established that there is an external world and that perception is a reliable mode of access thereto.

Why does the skeptic enjoin the philosopher to do that? Presumably because the skeptic has in mind a certain understanding of the philosopher's role in culture – a certain understanding of the high calling of the philosopher. He is simply applying that understanding to the case at hand.

And what is that high calling of the philosopher that the skeptic has in mind? Speaking of the skeptic, Reid says this: 'That our thoughts, our sensations, and every thing of which we are conscious, hath a real existence, is admitted in this system as a first principle, but everything else must be made evident by the light of reason. Reason must rear the whole fabric of knowledge upon this single principle of consciousness' (IHM VII [206b; B210]). All the necessary clues are there in that passage. Reid's skeptic is someone who insists that philosophers should be *foundationalists of the classically modern sort*. Let me explain.

'Foundationalism' is the name of a family of positions, not of some one position; if we were speaking strictly we would speak of *foundationalisms*, in the plural. I mentioned earlier that beliefs have a variety of truth-relevant merits: warrant, justification, entitlement, rationality, being reliably formed, and so forth. Every foundationalism is a theory as to the conditions under which one or another of these merits is present in beliefs.

What unites the various foundationalisms, and makes of them a family, is a certain structure that they all share. All foundationalisms operate with the distinction between beliefs formed on the basis of other beliefs, and beliefs not so formed – call the latter, *immediately* formed beliefs. Having made that distinction, every foundationalism first specifies the conditions under which immediately formed beliefs possess the merit in question, and then specifies the relation that non-immediately formed beliefs must bear to immediately formed beliefs which possess the merit if they are themselves to possess the merit. The idea is that when non-immediately formed beliefs are related in the right way to immediately formed beliefs that possess the merit, the merit is then transferred over to the non-immediately formed beliefs.

What distinguishes *classically modern* foundationalisms as a species of foundationalisms in general is the claim they make concerning the features that an immediately held belief must have if it is to possess the merit in question. The claim is that to possess the merit in question, an immediately formed belief must be *certain* for the person who holds the belief. The standard view is that there are just two sorts of beliefs that can be certain for a person: beliefs whose propositional content is some necessary truth that is self-evident to the believer, and beliefs about states of mind of which the believer is directly aware.[11] Every other belief, if it is to possess the merit in question, must be based in the requisite way on immediately held beliefs that are certain for the believer.

The description of the skeptic's demand that I quoted from Reid says that reason must rear the whole fabric of knowledge on those states of mind of which we are conscious; it says nothing about necessary truths that are self-evident. But Reid held that it is our reason that makes certain truths self-evident to us. So Reid's skeptic, to repeat, is one who enjoins on philosophers that they be classically modern foundationalists.

Reid's attack on the skeptic's injunction to the philosopher is devastating. But before I get to that, let me note that Reid has a certain sympathy with the skeptic's demand. The skeptic has put his finger on a feature of our human constitution which shows that we human beings fall short of a certain ideal. We don't just happen to fall short; we are so constituted as to fall short of that ideal. 'When I see a proposition to be self-evident and necessary,' says Reid,

> and that the subject is plainly included in the predicate, there seems to be nothing more that I can desire, in order to understand why I believe it. And when I see a consequence that necessarily follows from one or more self-evident propositions, I want nothing more with regard to my belief of that consequence. The light of truth so fills my mind in these cases, that I can neither conceive, nor desire any thing more satisfying. (EIP II. xx [330a])

With this thought in mind, Reid finds that when he turns to perceptual beliefs, he has a sense of dissatisfaction. He finds himself no less compelled to believe than when he has the experience of finding some proposition self-evidently true. But when he traces his perceptual beliefs to their origins, he is not able to 'resolve' the process 'into necessary and self-evident axioms, or conclusions that are necessarily consequent upon them.' He is forced to conclude that in perception he, along with human beings in general, lacks 'the evidence which [he] can best comprehend, and which gives perfect satisfaction to an inquisitive mind ... ' (ibid.) Yet it would be 'ridiculous to doubt, and I find it is not in my power' (ibid.).

To a philosopher, this is humbling. 'By his reason, he can discover certain abstract and necessary relations of things ....' But 'his knowledge of what really exists, or did exist, comes by another channel, which is open to those who cannot reason. He is led to it in the dark, and knows not how he came by it' (ibid.).[12]

> It is no doubt the perfection of a rational being to have no belief but what is grounded on intuitive [i.e., introspective] evidence, or on just reasoning; but man, I apprehend, is not such a being, nor is it the intention of nature that he should be such a being, in every [i.e., any] period of his existence .... [Our belief] is regulated by certain principles which are parts of our constitution .... [W]hat name we give to them is of small moment; but they are certainly different from the faculty of reason. (EIP II. xxi [332b–333a])

So much for Reid's sympathy with the demand of the skeptic; let me now take up the main lines of his attack on the skeptic's injunction. The skeptic insists that the philosopher must 'throw off all this belief of external objects' until he has established, along classically modern foundationalist lines, that perception is reliable. Reid's response is that 'it is not in my power' to throw off this 'belief of external objects.'

> Why then should I make a vain attempt?... My belief is carried along by perception, as irresistibly as my body by the earth. And the greatest sceptic will find himself to be in the same condition. He may struggle hard to disbelieve the information of his senses, as a man does to swim against a torrent; but, ah! It is in vain. It is in vain that he strains every nerve, and wrestles with nature, and with every object that strikes upon his senses. For after all, when his strength is spent in the fruitless attempt, he will be carried down the torrent with the common herd of believers. (IHM VI. xx [183b–184a; B 168])

As an extra fillip, Reid adds that even if it were possible to restrain the formation of beliefs while reliability is being determined, it would be most imprudent to do so. Consider the consequences.

> I resolve not to believe my senses. I break my nose against a post that comes in my way; I step into a kennel; and, after twenty such wise and rational actions, I am taken up and clapped into a mad-house.... If a man pretends to be a skeptic with regard to the informations of sense, and yet prudently keeps out of harm's way as other men do, he must excuse my suspicion, that he either acts the hypocrite, or imposes upon himself. (IHM VI. xx [184a; B 170])

Suppose that the skeptic concedes this point, that it is impossible to give up our perceptual beliefs; but then, rather than leaving the field, issues a revised, somewhat weaker, injunction to the philosopher. Be it conceded that since no one can throw off his perceptual beliefs, no one is obligated to do so or even try to do so. However, it does remain the obligation of the philosopher to go beyond offering an analysis of perception to determine whether there is an external world and whether perception gives us reliable access to that world – using arguments that satisfy the criteria of classical modern foundationalist.

Let's be clear, says Reid, on what is now being asked of the philosopher and what is being presupposed by that. The philosopher is being asked to run a credit check on perception as a producer of beliefs. He is being asked to do this because it seems possible that perceptual beliefs would be formed in the way indicated and yet be mostly or entirely false. And what is the philosopher allowed to use as evidence in running the credit check? He is allowed to use the deliverances of consciousness and of reason – only those.

This endeavor might or might not turn up results that are interesting in one way or another. But notice, says Reid to the skeptic, that you are allowing the philosopher to use the deliverances of consciousness and of reason without requiring that he first run a credit check on those. This implies that you are assuming the reliability of consciousness and of reason. But why do that? Isn't it possible that their deliverances are also false? After all, our various modes of belief-formation all came from the same shop.

> The skeptic asks me, Why do you believe the existence of the external object which you perceive? This belief, sir, is none of my manufacture; it came from the mint of

nature; it bears her image and superscription; and, if it is not right, the fault is not mine: I even took it upon trust, and without suspicion. Reason, says the skeptic, is the only judge of truth, and you ought to throw off every opinion and every belief that is not grounded on reason. Why, sir, should I believe the faculty of reason more than that of perception; they came both out of the same shop, and were made by the same artist and if he puts one piece of false ware into my hands, what should hinder him from putting another? (IHM VI. xx [183b; B 168–169])

In short, in the difference of treatment it accords to perception, on the one hand, and to reason and introspection, on the other, the skeptic's injunction is arbitrarily discriminatory.

Suppose that the skeptic recognizes the force of Reid's charge of arbitrary discrimination and that, in response, he once again revises his injunction to the philosopher. This time what he says is that it is the high calling of the philosopher to determine the reliability of *all* our fundamental modes of belief-formation. Since reason and introspection might also go wrong, it is the high calling of the philosopher to check out their overall reliability as well. If his results prove positive, he should then display to the rest of us the evidence he has discovered for their reliability. If, on the contrary, his results prove negative – reason and introspection either prove not to be reliable or there is no evidence that they are – well, then we'll just have to live with what Hume called our 'whimsical' condition.

If this is the skeptic's response, he will have avoided arbitrary discrimination at the cost of plunging himself into mindless absurdity. For now we are left with neither evidence nor inference – with neither premises nor arguments. You can't run a credit check on anybody if you are running a credit check on everybody. Let me quote Reid:

If a skeptic should build his scepticism upon this foundation, that all our reasoning and judging powers are fallacious in their nature, or should resolve at least to withhold assent until it be proved that they are not, it would be impossible by argument to beat him out of this stronghold; and he must even be left to enjoy his scepticism. (EIP VI. v [447b])

We have looked at two components of Reid's thought in which anti-rationalism is a prominent feature: his analysis of belief-formation, and his reply to the skeptic. Let us now look at a third component in which anti-rationalism is prominent, namely, his understanding of the task of the philosopher.

Reid's skeptic, I said, is someone who insists that it is the high calling of the philosopher to satisfy the demands of classically modern foundationalism with respect to his own beliefs – or if it is impossible actually to form one's perceptual beliefs, memory beliefs, inductive beliefs, and so forth in accord with these demands, then to determine by arguments of the classically modern foundationalist sort whether or not perception, memory, induction and so forth are reliable forms of belief-formation. Reid's arguments against the skeptic amount to rejecting this highly rationalist picture of the philosopher's task; Reid is, as it were putting reasoning 'in its place.'[13] So it comes as no surprise to learn that Reid's understanding of the philosopher's task proves to be a very anti-rationalist picture.

It is when presenting his own view of the task of the philosopher that Reid introduces his doctrine of common sense. So what is Reidian common sense?

I think it has to be conceded that Reid's explanation of what he means by 'common sense' is both confused and confusing; in his discussion one can see different lines of thought pulling in different directions. In such a case, the interpreter has to go beyond trying to discern what the author had in mind and be so bold as to suggest what it was that he was trying to get at. So that's what I will now do, without, on this occasion, identifying the various lines of thought that were conflated in Reid's mind. I do that in my book on Reid, where I also discuss alternative interpretations. It is, of course, ironic that that part of Reid's thought for which he became most famous is also one of the most confused and confusing parts of his thought.

A theme that emerges repeatedly in Reid's rejection of the skeptic's injunction is the theme of *taking for granted*, or *taking on trust*. We all take for granted, and in the nature of the case must take for granted, the fundamental reliability of our basic belief-forming dispositions. 'Who is voucher for consciousness?' Reid asks. 'Can any man prove that his consciousness may not deceive him? No man can; nor can we give a better reason for trusting to it, than that every man, while his mind is sound, is determined by the constitution of his nature, to give implicit belief to it, and to laugh at, or pity, the man who doubts its testimony. And is not every man, in his wits, as much determined to take his existence upon trust as his consciousness' (IHM I. iii [100a; B 17]). One can think of Reid's doctrine of common sense as taking this theme of *taking on trust* or *taking for granted* and running with it.

What Reid was pointing to, with his references to what he called 'principles of common sense,' was those things that we all do and must take for granted in our life in the everyday. Here is what he says in one passage:

> If there are certain principles, as I think there are, which the constitution of our nature leads us to believe, and which we are under a necessity to take for granted in the common concerns of life, without being able to give a reason for them; these are what we call the principles of common sense; and what is manifestly contrary to them, is what we call absurd. (IHM II. vi [108b; B 33])

And here are a few examples that Reid gives of principles of common sense:

> That everything of which one is conscious exists.
> That those things did really happen which one distinctly remembers.
> That those things do really exist which one distinctly perceives by one's senses, and are what one perceives them to be.

In the passage that I quoted from Reid just above, he says both that we *believe* principles of common sense and that we *take them for granted*. I think that, if pressed, Reid would agree that the right thing to say is the latter; we take them for granted. Speaking of one of the principles of common sense, this is what he says in one place:

> In most men [the principle] produces its effect without ever being attended to, or made an object of thought. No man ever thinks of this principle, unless when he considers the grounds of skepticism; yet it invariably governs his opinions. When a man in the common course of life gives credit to the testimony of his senses, his memory, or his reason, he does not put the question to himself, whether these faculties may deceive him; yet the trust he reposes in them supposes an inward conviction that, in that instance at least, they do not deceive him. (EIP VI. v [448a–b]).

In short, Reid's principles of common sense are the same as what Ludwig Wittgenstein would later call, in his little book *On Certainty*, 'our shared world picture.'

I mentioned earlier that two stock figures pop up over and over in Reid: the skeptic and the madman. The madman pops up when Reid is talking about common sense. If someone really does doubt some principle of common sense – does not just say that he doubts it but really does doubt it – we judge him to be deranged and don't reason with him but get treatment. To quote Reid: if 'any man were found of so strange a turn as not to believe his own eyes; to put no trust in his senses, nor have the least regard to their testimony; would any man think it worth while to reason gravely with such a person, and, by argument, to convince him of his error? Surely no wise man would' (EIP I. ii [230b]). He would instead be 'clapped into a mad-house' (IHM VI. xx [184a; B 170]).

Now for Reid's understanding of the role of the philosopher. The philosopher is related to the principles of common sense in the same way that everyone else is – and in the same way that he is when not doing philosophy. He does and must take these principles for granted in his posing of questions, in his raising of doubts, in his offering of reasons. They are and must be the background of his reflections – not the premises from which he draws his conclusions, but the ever-present background of his philosophical activity.

Philosophy is like all other human endeavors in that it 'has no other root but the principles of common sense; it grows out of them, and draws its nourishment from them: severed from this root, its honours wither, its sap is dried up, it dies and rots' (IHM I. iv [101b; B 19]). Rather often philosophers profess to reject the 'principles which irresistibly govern the belief and conduct of all mankind in the common concerns of life' (IHM I.v [102b; B 21]). But it turns out that to these principles 'the philosopher himself must yield, after he imagines he hath confuted them.' For 'such principles are older, and of more authority, than philosophy; she rests upon them as her basis, not they upon her. If she could overturn them, she must be buried in their ruins; but all the engines of philosophical subtilty are too weak for this purpose; and the attempt is no less ridiculous, that if a mechanic should contrive an *axis in peritrochio* to remove the earth out of its place' (ibid.).

Much of philosophy has the semblance of madness. The ordinary person, hearing the opinions of certain philosophers, 'can conceive no otherwise of [such opinions], than as a kind of metaphysical lunacy; and concludes, that too much learning is apt to make men mad; and that the man who seriously entertains [these beliefs], though in other respects he may be a very good man, as a man may be who believes that he is made of glass; yet surely he hath a soft place in his understanding, and hath been hurt by much thinking' (IHM V. vii [127a; B 68]).

But it's only appearance. Philosophers are not mad; they do not really doubt our world picture. In 'all the history of philosophy, we never read of any skeptic that ever stepped into fire or water because he did not believe his senses . . . ' (EIP II. v [259b]). The calling of the philosopher is to proceed in philosophy as he does in everyday life, namely, to take for granted the principles of common sense as he goes about his work of discussing philosophical issues. Included within philosophy so understood will be a careful anatomy of the principles of common sense and of how they work, along with a defense of those principles against misguided attacks. But philosophy done in a Reidian spirit is not confined to such topics; Reid's own philosophical endeavors were not so confined.

We have looked at three major components of Reid's thought in which anti-rationalism is a prominent feature: Reid's analysis of belief formation, his reply to the skeptic, and his own understanding of the task of the philosopher. At the bottom of the doxastic life of all of us lies not reason but trust. Trust likewise lies at the bottom of the philosophical enterprise.

Notes

1. Benjamin W. Redekop, in 'Reid's Influence in Britain, Germany, France, and America,' discusses who was influenced by Reid in these countries; but he does not discuss how Reid was understood. The essay is to be found in Cuneo and van Woudenberg (2004, 313–339).
2. The comments are to be found in the 'Introduction' to the *Prologemena*. Here are two sentences from the two paragraphs that Kant devotes to the topic: 'It is positively painful to see how utterly [Hume's] opponents, Reid, Oswald, Beattie, and lastly Priestley, missed the point of the problem [that Hume had raised].' 'Seen clearly, [an appeal to common sense] is but an appeal to the opinion of the multitude, of whose applause the philosopher is ashamed, while the popular charlatan glories and boasts in it.' I am quoting from the translation of Lewis White Beck (1950). For Reid's reception in Germany, see Kuehn (1987).
3. The standard edition of Reid's works is that by William Hamilton. I will employ the fifth edition, published in Edinburgh in 1858 by Maclachlan and Stewart. Recently Derek R. Brookes has published a critical edition of the *Inquiry*, published in Edinburgh in 1997 by Edinburgh University Press. I will employ the following system of references: References to Reid's *An Inquiry into the Human Mind* (1764) will be cited by the abbreviation IHM, followed by chapter and section number, followed by page and column in the Hamilton edition, and by page in the Brookes edition, thus: IHM V.ii [121a; B58]. *Essays on the Intellectual Powers of Man* (1785) will be cited by the abbreviation EIP, followed by essay and chapter, followed by page and column in the Hamilton edition, thus: EIP IV.iii [375b].
4. Putnam uses the phrase a number of times in (1992).
5. See Goodman (1978).
6. *Essays on the Intellectual Powers* II.xvii (Hamilton edition, 318b).

7. Reid makes the point often. One of the most vivid passages in which he makes the point is the following: 'Nature intended them [the sensations that evoke perceptions] only for signs; and in the whole course of life they are put to no other use. The mind has acquired a confirmed and inveterate habit of inattention to them; for they no sooner appear than quick as lightning the thing signified succeeds, and engrosses all our regard.' *Inquiry into the Human Mind* VI.iii (Brookes edition, 82).
8. Wolterstorff (2001).
9. See, for example, Van Cleve (2004).
10. Wolterstorff (2001, 96).
11. One could include the standard view, as to which beliefs are certain for one, in the definition of 'classically modern foundationalism.' I have included certainty in the definition but not the standard view as to which beliefs are certain.
12. To understand this passage, one must realize that Reid thought of what he calls 'reason' as having two distinct capacities: the capacity to discern self-evident necessary truths, and the capacity to draw inferences, that is, to reason, to engage in reasoning.
13. He is not putting reason understood as the apprehension of self-evident necessary truths 'in its place.' Reid never doubts the importance of reason so understood.

References

Cuneo, T., and R. van Woudenberg, eds. 2004. *The Cambridge Companion to Thomas Reid*. Cambridge: Cambridge University Press.

Goodman, Nelson. 1978. *Ways of Worldmaking*. New York: Hackett Publishing Co.

Kant, I. 1950. *Prologemena*, Translated by Lewis White Beck. New York: The Liberal Arts Press.

Kuehn, Manfred. 1987. *Scottish Common Sense Philosophy in Germany*. Kingston and Montreal: McGill-Queen's University Press.

Putnam, Hilary. 1992. *Renewing Philosophy*. Cambridge: Harvard University Press.

Van Cleve, James. 2004. "Reid's Theory of Perception." In *The Cambridge Companion to Thomas Reid*, edited by T. Cuneo and R. van Woudenberg, 101–133. Cambridge: Cambridge University Press.

Wolterstorff, Nicholas. 2001. *Thomas Reid and the Story of Epistemology*. Cambridge: Cambridge University Press.

MIND, LANGUAGE, METAPHYSICS

Reid on powers of the mind and the person behind the curtain

Laurent Jaffro

Philosophy Department, Panthéon-Sorbonne University, Paris, France

According to Thomas Reid, powers of will and powers of understanding are distinguishable in thought, but conjoined in practice. This paper examines the claim that there is no inert intelligence, the operations of the understanding involving some degree of activity. The question is: whose activity? For it is clear that a great deal of our mental activity is not in our power. We need to distinguish between a weak and a strong sense of 'power', and consider our dependence 'upon God and the laws of nature' in our mental exertions.

According to Reid, who is not original in this claim, the human mind has two kinds of powers, intellectual – powers of understanding –, and active – powers of will. The first are powers to conceive, perceive, remember, believe, judge, reason, etc. The second are powers to produce changes in the world, to move our body, to direct our thought. They differ only as their effects differ: We can align the distinction between active and 'speculative' or intellectual powers with the distinction between action and 'speculation' (Reid 2010 [hereafter EAP] 12). This is *the distinction thesis*. The way we categorise an act of the mind as being an operation of the will or of the understanding depends on the degree to which the mind is active in this operation, rather than on a sharp type distinction: 'We range the operation under that faculty which hath the largest share in it.' (Reid 2002 [hereafter EIP] 65)

This division is at least, and perhaps at most, a distinction of reason: 'The faculties of understanding and will are easily distinguished in thought, but very rarely, if ever, disjoined in operation.' (EAP 59) This thesis nicely fits in with the view that what is real is the individual human mind as a whole, powers not being agents in their own right. Reid interestingly complements the distinction thesis with what we may call *the reciprocal guidance thesis*: one of these powers cannot operate without being guided by the other; or, to put it in other terms, for the operation of one power, a necessary – in a sense to be determined – condition is the activation of the other.

Let us document the reciprocal guidance thesis, which considerably limits the scope of the distinction thesis:

> Although this general division may be of use in order to our proceeding more methodically in our subject, we are not to understand it as if, in those operations which are ascribed to the understanding, there were no exertion of will or activity, or as if the understanding were not employed in the operations ascribed to the will; for I conceive there is no operation of the understanding wherein the mind is not active in some degree. (EIP 64)

Intellectual powers and active powers are distinguishable in theory, but seldom separable in practice. Reid draws on the distinction mainly as a method of exposition. Also, let us pay attention to the fact that Reid does not assign activity to the operations of the understanding without any qualification; he says that in these operations the mind is active 'in some degree'. A few lines below, he reiterates:

> As the mind exerts some degree of activity even in the operations of the understanding, so it is certain, that there can be no act of will which is not accompanied with some act of understanding. (EIP 65)

This may indicate an asymmetry between the way activity is involved in the operations of the understanding and the way understanding is involved in the operations of the will: on one side, 'some degree of activity', on the other side, 'some act'. In *Essays on the Active Powers of Man*, at the beginning of the chapter 'Of operations of mind which may be called voluntary', we find the same contrast between 'some degree of activity in those operations which we refer to the understanding', and 'some operation of the understanding', which accompanies 'every act of will' (EAP 60). In other words, activity admits of gradation, whereas acts of understanding are mentioned without this qualification. However, Reid sometimes speaks of 'degrees of understanding'.[1] So all we can conclude from this is that, when discussing the reciprocal guidance thesis, Reid stresses degrees of activity rather than degrees of understanding.

Let us explore both directions of the reciprocal guidance thesis. First, active power presupposes understanding as well as will, or more precisely, it directly presupposes will and thus indirectly presupposes understanding:

> According to Mr Locke, therefore, the only clear notion or idea we have of active power, is taken from the power which we find in ourselves to give certain motions to our bodies, or a certain direction to our thoughts; and this power in ourselves can be brought into action only by willing or volition.

> From this, I think, it follows, that, if we had not will, and that degree of understanding which will necessarily implies, we could exert no active power, and consequently could have none: For power that cannot be exerted is no power. It follows also, that the active power, of which only we can have any distinct conception, can be only in beings that have understanding and will. (EAP 29)

Why does Reid claim that will necessarily implies a certain degree of understanding? Because we cannot will to φ if we do not think about φing.[2] Thus the part of the reciprocal guidance thesis that relates to the manner in which the understanding is instrumental to the will rests upon a *no blind agency* clause, which Reid formulates thus:

> As a man cannot think without thinking of something, nor remember without remembering something, so neither can he will without willing something. Every act of will, therefore, must have an object; and the person who wills must have some conception, more or less distinct, of what he wills. (EAP 48)

Symmetrically, intellectual power presupposes will as well as understanding, or more precisely, it directly presupposes understanding and thus indirectly presupposes will. We have yet to consider why Reid thinks this holds true. But before considering that, we should note a prima facie difficulty: Infinite regress threatens from the conjunction of premises (1) and (2) if the various operations of the minds are construed as many different voluntary, and thus intentional, actions of the agent:

(1) Every operation of the will involves an operation of the understanding.
(2) Every operation of the understanding involves activity.

Either this latter activity consists in an act of the will, or not. If it consists in an act of the will distinct from the operation of the will mentioned in (1), then (1) applies and we need another operation of the understanding, to which (2) applies, etc.

One option to block the regress is to claim that the activity involved in operations of the understanding is not an act of the will. But this would go against Reid's insistent – indeed Berkeleyan – affirmation that all activity amounts to volition.

Another option is to allow that activity involved in operations of the understanding is an act of the will, but that this second-order act of the will is blind. The *no blind agency* clause rules out this option.

A third option is to consider the mind as exhaustively active. Action involves both will and understanding. The primacy of action over speculation does not mean that the operations of the understanding are subordinate to the operations of the will, but that both kinds of operations are just different aspects of one basic intelligent activity. The infinite regress looms only if we wrongly construe will and understanding as two really distinct mini agents. The third option is plausible.

A fourth option, which may be combined with the third, is to suppose that the activity involved in operations of the understanding is either an act of the will of the agent involved, or a different kind of activity, or rather a lower degree activity, which does not depend on the will of the agent involved, since it consists in, or depends on, an act of the will of *another* agent. This paper defends this disjunctive interpretation.

In Section 1, I dwell on another problem with the reciprocal guidance claim: why should operations of the understanding be considered as involving some degree of activity? The answer is far from being obvious.

In Section 2, I claim that Reid uses 'active' or 'action' as a summary for operations of various kinds and degrees: there are mental operations that are not actions in the strong sense, and other mental operations to which the concept of action and all its normative implications fully apply. We have a philosophical bias towards the latter, of which Reid is aware.

In Section 3, I sketch out the metaphysical background of Reid's understanding of all mental operations as actions. I show that, whereas he considers some mental operations – notably attention – as actions of the human agent in the strong sense, he construes other mental operations, which are actions in the weak sense, as dependent on the actions in the strong sense of another agent, God. He also envisages that all mental operations of the human mind, including attention, are actions in the weak sense.

1. No inert intelligence

Whereas the *no blind agency* clause furnishes us with an unequivocal explanation of why active power indirectly presupposes understanding, we do not as clearly see why intellectual power presupposes will. We would need a symmetrical counterpart of the no *blind agency clause*: let us say, a *no inert intelligence* clause.

How should we construe such a clause? A minimal, simple, answer draws on the concept of power: an intellectual power is a power; a power is by definition a power to do something; therefore an intellectual power is a power to do and as such is active. This fits in with Reid's claim that impotence is a privation of power, not a contrary to power (EAP 12) and that there are no passive powers (37). We should thus distinguish between two senses of the expression 'active powers':

(1) In a specific sense, active powers are contrasted with speculative powers. In this sense, only certain powers are active.
(2) In a general sense, all powers are active – here 'active' is opposed to 'passive' –, because every power is a power to do something.[3]

A different answer would draw on the concept of exertion of power: an intellectual power is a power; a power is exerted by an agent, and this exertion obviously is an action of the agent; therefore an intellectual power cannot be exerted without an agent who is active in this exertion.

Both the first and second answers seek to ground the *no inert intelligence* clause in conceptual considerations. The difference between them is one of focus: the first one focuses on the action enabled by the power; the second one on the action of the agent, which consists in exerting the power. However, we might consider that they come to the same thing: to exert the power of walking consists in walking.[4]

I am not happy with either of these answers. I do not think that, for Reid, the *no inert intelligence* claim is a conceptual truth derived either from the notion of power or from the notion of the exertion of power. If it was just implied by either of these notions, we would grasp it without difficulty. Now Reid explicitly denies this:

> Whether it be possible that intelligence may exist without some degree of activity, or impossible, is perhaps beyond the reach of our faculties to determine; but, I apprehend, that, in fact, they are always conjoined in the operation of our minds. (EAP 60)

The *no inert intelligence* claim explicitly is a *de facto*, not *de jure*, truth. There might be exceptions, whereas the *no blind agency* claim admits of no exception. When Reid writes 'I conceive there is no operation of the understanding wherein the mind is not active in some degree' (EIP 64, quoted above), his formulation misleadingly suggests that the *no inert intelligence* clause has the status of an *a priori* truth. But we should remember that here, 'I conceive' just means 'I apprehend' (cf. EAP 60, quoted above).

The first answer downplays the *no inert intelligence* clause. If the reason for holding that intellectual powers involve some degree of activity is that any power is by definition a power to do, then the *no inert intelligence* claim would be formal and uncontroversial. Moreover this claim would be true of all operations of the understanding regardless of their degrees and types. I rather think that this principle is empirical and thus that we would need to examine each particular operation of the understanding in order to check which degree of activity it involves, and more specifically which degree of exertion of the will.

For it is quite significant that Reid does not rule out the possibility that there are operations of the mind drawing on only one faculty:

> It is therefore to be remembered, that *in most, if not all* the operations of the mind, both faculties concur; and we range the operation under that faculty which hath the largest share in it. (EIP 65, my emphasis)[5]

Which cases may Reid have in mind, when he hints at a situation in which only one faculty would be at work? Since the *no blind agency* clause is a conceptual truth, or at least an inescapable psychological necessity – we cannot will to φ without thinking of φing –, it cannot be the case of the will. It must be the case of the understanding, which accords with my proposal that the *no inert intelligence* clause is not a conceptual truth, but a contingent empirical principle, which is true of most operations of the mind.

There is a particular problem with the second answer, which considers the exertion of a power as an action of the agent: it does not take into account Reid's distinction between action and exertion. Action is not the exertion of any power, but of *active* power. Action and exertion are not synonymous: 'The exertion of active power we call action.' (EAP 13)

In the interpretation of Reid, we could go in two opposite directions: stressing either the univocality or the equivocality of action. If exertions of power are actions in the *same* sense as those actions that are the objects of active powers, then we should consider that voluntariness, command, responsibility, apply to the exertions of all intellectual powers as they apply to the deeds of an agent. If exertions of powers are actions in a weaker sense, then we are not accountable for the exertions of intellectual powers in the same manner and to the same extent as we are for our actions proper. For we are accountable for the actions that depend on our will:

> Every man knows infallibly that what is done by his conscious will and intention, is to be imputed to him, as the agent or cause; and that whatever is done without his will and intention, cannot be imputed to him with truth. (EAP 31)

Will-dependence is not only a necessary condition for responsibility; it is also a sufficient condition, insofar as the agent is aware of the action – which, according to the *no blind agency* claim, is always the case. For to will to φ, I must have the knowledge that, were my volition successful, then what I would be doing would be φing. Thus awareness of the action is already built in the will to act.

Therefore if all my thoughts and mental attitudes were voluntary, then I would be responsible for all of them. I could be blamed for my memories or my beliefs. Indeed, I can be blamed for indulging myself in certain sad memories, or for not taking into account available reasons for revising my belief. But then the focus is on my epistemic conduct. This suggests that only a part of the life of the mind is voluntary. Specifically, it suggests that it is only those mental operations that are actions, in a strong sense, of the agent – for instance, attention – which are voluntary.

2.   Exertions without power and the variety of mental activities

In this section, I show that Reid's concept of activity is not monolithic. Although the paradigm of activity is voluntary action, there are lesser degrees of activity, which play a major role in the life of the mind. Ferec Huoranszki thus formulates Reid's standard understanding of the connection between power, whether intellectual or active, and activity: 'Power is "active" and activity precludes the possibility of not having control over the exertion.' (Huoranszki 2003, 116) Now, if we apply this understanding of power to all intellectual operations, we face a difficulty: there are intellectual powers the operations of which we do not control.

It is commonly acknowledged that only some acts of the mind are voluntary. One of Reid's contemporaries, a disciple of Condillac, Destutt de Tracy, in his *Projet d'éléments d'idéologie* (1801), lists intellectual faculties the operations of which are not dependent on the will: sensation; feeling; judgement. As to the operations of attention, they are intrinsically voluntary. There are also mixed cases, such as that of memory, which is sometimes voluntary, sometimes involuntary (Destutt de Tracy 2012, 200–201).

Does Reid's concept of power lead him in a different direction? In his 1792 manuscript 'Of Power', Reid claims that 'volitions and what follows upon our volitions is all that we can conceive to be in our power' (Reid 2003, 21). He adds: 'In this sense, which I take to be the only proper sense of the word, it is evident that a being which has no will can have no power.' So, in Reid's conception of power, an agent has the power to φ if and only if φing is in the agent's power in the sense that it directly depends on or follows upon the agent's volitions.

So there is a strict sense of 'power', in which having power necessarily entails having control over what is thus in our power: we have the power to φ if and only if whenever we will to φ, provided that there are not external obstacles, we φ, and whenever we will not to φ, we do not φ:

> Power to produce any effect implies power not to produce it. We can conceive no way in which power may be determined to one of these rather than the other, in a being that has no will. (EAP 29)

If this is the 'only proper sense of the word', do I have, say, the power to believe that it is raining? No, although I have the power to check whether it is raining. Do I have the power to see the spider crawling up the wall? No, although I have the power to be attentive to it or to look away. Do I have the power to remember last summer's vacation? It depends.

However, the fact is that Reid does not claim that all exertions are voluntary. Exertion and volition are usually conjoined, but are distinct. As Reid insists in 'Of Power', we can have the one without the other:

> During my walk, my thought is wholly occupied, on some other subjects than the walk, so there is not a thought of it or will concerning it at present in my mind; yet the exertion of walking continues. (Reid 2003, 15)

We should pay attention to the fact that, although exertions and volitions are conceptually distinct, having – in the strict sense – a *power* of exertion is not only conjoined with, but conceptually linked to volition. As he puts it in 'Of Power', 'will is necessarily implied in the notion of power' (Reid 2003, 21). There is no contradiction between this and Reid's claim that 'our first exertions are instinctive, without any distinct conception of the event that is to follow, consequently without will to produce that event' (14), provided that we do not refer these instinctive exertions to powers in the strict sense.

But this seems to contradict Reid's claim that 'there can be no exertion without power' (EAP 11); in fact, there is no contradiction, since in this latter context it is clear that it is a specific claim about exertions *of active power*, not exertions in general.

To get back to the case of exertions without volitions, it is important to understand why they do not depend on powers, at least as far as we know: we know of no other kind of powers than the intellectual and active powers we exert; now, our instinctive exertions do not consist in acts of our understanding, and thus cannot depend upon acts of our will; therefore they cannot be exertions of our powers. Moreover, what is instinctively done is not in the agent's power, although it may afterwards pass under the jurisdiction of the agent's will: 'Finding by experience that such exertions are followed by such events, we learn to make the exertion voluntarily and deliberately, as often as we desire to produce the event.' (Reid 2003, 14) The same agent may start φing without having the power to φ in the strict sense, and afterwards gain the power, that is, learn to control the φing. In this situation it is clear that the acquired power is more properly a power than the natural capacity, because it involves a greater control. We can also think of situations in which the agent has lost the power of φing, and still continues to φ – for instance, the φing addict has become unable to stop φing. Therefore an exertion is dependent on a *power* of exertion in the full sense only when acts of understanding and acts of will collaborate in it. We might say, perhaps, that the power in the proper sense of φing does not supervene on the agent's φing or capacity to φ, but on the collaboration of the agent's will and understanding in the φing or activation of the capacity to φ.

Paul Hoffman doubts Reid really admits 'exertions of active power that are independent of the will' and he resists conceding that 'instinct can be the source of exertion' (Hoffman 2006, 439). Of course, by definition, an exertion *of active power* cannot be independent of the will, in so far as in the case of active powers the exertion consists in a voluntary action. The discussion is rather about the possibility of exertions that would be independent of the will because they are instinctive. There are exertions of the agent, or in the agent, which are not exertions of the agent's active power: the fact is that there are many things children and adults are able to do without willing them – *a fortiori*, without doing them 'deliberately'. Moreover the same exertions may at one time directly depend on the agent's will, and at another time be involuntary because they are instinctive or customary. In his comments on 'Of Power', Hoffman does not distinguish between having the power in the weak sense – the capacity to φ – and having it in the strong sense – the control over φing.

There is a problem with Reid's use of the notion of power: he does not always draw on the 'only proper sense'. For instance, when discussing intellectual powers, he writes: 'If all men had been blind, we should have had no conception of the power of seeing, nor any name for it in language' (EAP 30). But it is clear that people who have the natural power of seeing in this sense have not the power of seeing in the proper sense, since seeing does not depend on volition (on this, see Wolterstorff [2001, 74–76]). Being able to see does not require the kind of control over seeing that the application of power in the proper sense requires. Therefore, in this context, Reid draws on a weaker conception of 'power'.

So we need to distinguish between intellectual powers in Reid's 'proper sense', which concern voluntary operations of the mind, and intellectual powers in a weaker sense of power, even though this seems controversial, if not absurd, to expert Reidians.

Attention and reflection, by which we intentionally focus on our mental operations, are good instances of the former: since they are, at least in part[6], voluntary operations, the intellectual power of attention, and its species (EIP 42), reflection, 'by which alone we can have any distinct notion of the powers of our own, or of other minds' (58), obviously are powers in the strict sense. As the operations involved are voluntary, these powers may be seen as active as well as speculative. They play a major role in our knowledge of powers, which is relative: 'Our conception of power is relative to its exertions or effects' (EAP 11).

Thanks to the power of reflection, we can have a direct conception of subtle and discreet operations of the mind, and have thus a relative conception of the corresponding power.

We should note that Reid's discussion of reflection implicitly provides an answer to the question about the primacy of one kind of powers, speculative or active, over the other. On the surface, reflection is fundamental as an *intellectual* power in so far as it contributes to the knowledge of our powers, which is a necessary condition for the improvement of all kinds of powers. As Reid puts it:

> A just knowledge of our powers, whether intellectual or active, is so far of real importance to us, as it aids us in the exercise of them. And every man must acknowledge, that to act properly is much more valuable than to think justly or reason acutely. (EAP 6)

The power of reflection, without which the knowledge of our powers would be limited to what is given through consciousness, supposes 'some ripeness of understanding' and is 'greatly improved by exercise': 'Of all the powers of the human mind, it seems to be the last that unfolds itself' (EIP 59). Reflection thus exercised is a habit or acquired power (59–60). There is no contradiction in the late appearance of so crucial a power. The role of knowledge is to 'enlarge' our powers (EAP 5), and this is what reflection does.

Therefore, on a deeper level, reflection is fundamental as an *active* power. Were we not able – and trained – to voluntarily turn our attention to our own operations or to operations of other agents, we would be incapable of any progress in the exploration of the human mind. As a habit, reflection is not only a speculative power, but also a principle of action. This reflects what I have called the reciprocal guidance thesis. The power that conditions the knowledge of powers is not simply intellectual, but also essentially active:

> Attention is a voluntary act; it requires an active exertion to begin and to continue it; and it may be continued as long as we will; but consciousness is involuntary and of no continuance, changing with every thought. (EIP 59)[7]

In passing, we should also wonder whether there is an intellectual power of consciousness in the proper sense. In the passage I have just quoted from, the answer is no. However, the fact is that Reid also refers to consciousness as 'an original power of the mind' (EIP 471). In the last paragraphs of the book, he also mentions consciousness as an intellectual power (614), as he does in the preliminary (24). Here again, the correct conclusion must be that Reid sometimes uses the term 'power' in an improper sense: a capacity for... involuntary operations!

To sum up, attention and reflection are the best candidates for those operations of the understanding that involve activity, since they seem to be largely, if not fully, voluntary actions. It is significant that Reid hesitates to classify them as active or intellectual powers: he deals with reflection in *Essays on Intellectual Powers*, and with attention mainly in *Essays on Active Powers*, II, 3.

The question is: how can we make room for other operations of the understanding, which, without being voluntary, involve a lesser degree of activity? Compared with attention, in its various forms, other operations of the understanding, 'such as seeing, hearing, judging, reasoning, and the like' are actions only metaphorically. This surfaces in the following passage: 'And because the understanding is always more or less directed by the will, mankind *have ascribed* some degree of activity to the mind in its intellectual operations, as well as in those which belong to the will, and have expressed them by active verbs, such as seeing, hearing, judging, reasoning, and the like.' (EAP 64–65, my emphasis) 'Ascribing' activity to operations of the understanding may be construed, with some exaggeration, as a case of what Reid calls 'communication of attributes' (see EIP 599) – that is, metaphorical thinking – even though the unity of the mind justifies the transfer of attributes from the will to the understanding.

There are operations of my mind that are not my actions. This may be negatively inferred from Reid's claim that 'in certain motions of my body and directions of my thought, I know, not only that there must be a cause that has power to produce these effects, but that I am that cause; and I am conscious of what I do in order to the production of them' (EAP 30). For this is true of *certain* directions of my thought, not of *all* of them. There is also much to learn from the analogy with my body: just as there are parts of my body – for instance, my liver – over the operations of which I have no direct control, there are parts of the mind that operate without me.

As to the 'limited' control we have over the direction of our thoughts, it is a power, as the one we have on our body, which may be 'greatly increased by practice and habit' (EAP 41). Habit, as instinct, is 'part of our original constitution' (90), in the sense that we have the natural capacity to acquire habits; the content of each habit is a power 'acquired by use, exercise or study' (EIP 21).

Acquired power, compared with natural power, is not a second best. Most of the command we have of our thoughts is the result of training. Here there is much to learn from Reid's chapter 'Of the Train of Thought in the Mind'. He distinguishes between two kinds of succession of thoughts, spontaneous and regulated, which, 'however distinct in their nature, are for the most part mixed, in persons awake and come to years of understanding':

> They are either such as flow spontaneously, like water from a fountain, without any exertion of a governing principle to arrange them; or they are regulated and directed by an *active effort* of the mind, with some view and intention. (EIP 334, my emphasis)

It is clear that the concept of action applies to this intentional exertion by which we gain control over the stream of thought. However, this power is limited: 'I apprehend, in the best trained mind the thoughts will sometimes be restive, sometimes capricious and self-willed, when we wish to have them most under command' (334). It is important to remark that Reid also distinguishes a second kind of spontaneous presentation of thoughts: 'a train of thought, which at first was studied and composed, may by habit present itself spontaneously' (335). 'Spontaneity', then, means either that control is absent, or that the occurrence of the thought is effortless.

Reid's comments in this chapter are crucial for assessing the nature and limits of our voluntary control over our 'thought' in the most general sense of the term – which includes 'every operation of the mind, excepting those of sense' (EIP 334):

> It has been observed, very justly, that we must not ascribe to the mind the power of calling up any thought at pleasure, because such a call or volition supposes that thought to be already in the mind; for otherwise how should it be the object of volition? As this must be granted on the one hand, so it is no less certain on the other, that a man has a considerable power in regulating and disposing his own thoughts. Of this every man is conscious, and I can no more doubt of it, than I can doubt whether I think at all. (EIP 335)

Reid is well aware that the activity involved in all operations of the understanding cannot consist in 'willing' thoughts, since in order to will a thought we would need to have it beforehand – according to the *no blind agency* clause. So our limited voluntary command of our thoughts ('we have some command over our thoughts' [EIP 64]) should be construed in a different manner: Desires, affections, passions, as well as judgement, often govern the stream of thought. For instance, our thoughts on the 'stage of imagination' are often orientated by 'an innate desire of self-approbation' (EIP 337). Reid's analysis of the 'train of thought' thus illuminates his claim that there is some degree of activity in the operations of the understanding. Reid, who is a pluralist about 'active principles that influence the actions of men' and stresses their 'great number' (EAP 76), clearly ascribes mental activity to various particular active powers, animal as well as rational:

> Those active powers of the mind, which are most luxuriant by constitution, or have been most cherished by education, impatient to exert themselves, hurry the thought into scenes that give them play. (EIP 337)

A rational active power, that of attention, plays a major role in the composition of the train of thought, when it is regulated not chiefly by desires or passions, but by application and judgement (EIP 335).

Now that we are tempted to admit that there are operations of our mind that are not actions in the full sense, we need to answer two questions. The first is: why philosophers, Reid included, are biased in favour of voluntary operations of the mind, so that they say very little about exertions of intellectual powers that are not actions properly speaking? The second, which I tackle in the final section, is: how Reid can account for exertions of intellectual powers that are not actions?

As to the first question, actions are a privileged form of operations because, although we are conscious of all our mental acts, even the less voluntary, we are responsible for what we do, which coincides with the exertions of our active power we are conscious of. It is well known that, for Reid, 'from the consciousness of our own activity, seems to be derived, not only the clearest, but the only conception we can form of activity, or the exertion of active power' (EAP 30). This fact creates a bias towards actions, in the strong sense, in the philosophy of the mind. And such a bias is a hindrance to a full theoretical exploration of all the powers of the mind, although it is excellent for the ordinary practice, since it nicely fits in with the scope of our responsibility in the exertion of our powers.

Were occasionalism true, as to the correlations between our volitions and our bodily movements, it would have 'no effect on human conduct' (EAP 41), since it would not change our experience of the exertion of active powers, and thus, would not diminish our responsibility. For our concept of responsibility is entirely dependent on the consciousness of our voluntary movements (31). Indeed, 'we know not even how those immediate effects of our power are produced by our willing them' (40); but we do not need to know that in order to be the author of our voluntary actions. Interestingly, Reid mentions that the same 'endless' dispute may be also 'applied to the power of directing our thoughts'. For instance, we cannot rule out the possibility that attention requires 'the aid of other efficient causes'.[8] *A fortiori*, our less voluntary or non-voluntary operations – assent, cognitive responses to evidence, certain kinds of memory, feelings, affective responses – may be considered as dependent on the actions of other efficient causes. Were we to discover that certain intermediary operations required to connect our volitions and our exertions are actions of another agent, this would not impact our responsibility. As Lindsay (2005, 30) puts it, 'our actions can contain causal elements that we are unaware of – and not in total control of – while still being our actions'. There is a perfect match between the scope of our knowledge of powers and the extent of our responsibility.

3. Actions of another in us

Reid thus formulates the concept of action in the strong sense:

> Now it is evident, that, to constitute the relation between me and my action, my conception of the action, and will to do it, are essential. For what I never conceived, nor willed, I never did. (EAP 33)

This is action in the 'strict philosophical sense' (EAP 74). But, as we have seen, there is also a 'popular sense' of the word, in which Reid speaks of mechanical principles of action, namely instincts and habits, although instinctive and habitual actions are not voluntary as actions in the strong sense are. Here Reid draws on a scholastic tradition, which admits, not only voluntary actions, but also involuntary and 'mixed' actions.

Now we must determine to what extent the popular sense of the word *action* is correct. There are two options. First, we might consider that instinctive operations – which are involuntary – and habitual operations – which are of mixed kind – are not actions in the relevant sense: then they are just events in us, without being willed or conceived by anyone. Or, second, we might consider that instinctive and habitual operations are actions in the full sense, although they are not – or not entirely – our actions; if so, then they must be the actions of someone else, or depend on the actions of someone else. Reid prefers the second option. Why?

Because, as far as instincts are concerned, their operations manifest an intentional structure – although, like habits, instincts 'operate without will or intention' (EAP 88) – which is typical of actions in the 'strict philosophical sense'. They respond to final causes. As to habits, they obviously constitute acquired powers that deserve to be called active. As Reid puts it:

> Both seem to be parts of our original constitution. Their end and use is evident; but we can assign no cause of them, but the will of him who made us.

> With regard to instinct, which is a natural propensity, this will perhaps be easily granted; but it is no less true with regard to that power and inclination which we acquire by habit.

> No man can shew a reason why our doing a thing frequently should produce either facility or inclination to do it. (EAP 90)

The fact that we cannot assign 'physical causes' to instinct or to our capacity to develop habits, and that they suggest an intelligent will, leads Reid to view them as depending on our Maker's actions.[9] Shifting from the curiosity about obscure efficient causes to a sense of final causes, we conceive that certain operations of the mind, or rather the way in which our mind operates in general, may depend on the actions, in the 'strict philosophical sense', of someone else.

Let us get back to Reid's analysis of types of 'train of thought'. I mentioned that a succession of thoughts, first 'regulated and directed by an active effort of the mind' (EIP 334), may evolve, thanks to the power of habit, into a spontaneous stream (335). This spontaneous order in the train of thinking indicates an intelligent cause:

> It is, therefore, in itself highly probable, to say no more, that whatsoever is regular and rational in a train of thought, which presents itself spontaneously to a man's fancy, without any study, is a copy of what had been before composed by his own rational powers, or those of *some other person*. [...] Whether such a train of thinking be printed in a book, or printed, so to speak, in his mind, and issue spontaneously from his fancy, it must have been composed with judgment by himself, or by *some other rational being*. (EIP 340, my emphasis)

This shows that Reid construes involuntary and 'mixed' mental activity disjunctively either as the agent's action or as the action of another being. Reid maintains, against Hume's understanding of the association of ideas, that all spontaneous regularities in our thoughts are the product of some intelligence: 'Nothing that is regular, was ever at first conceived without design, attention, and care' (EIP 347).

Thus *all* operations of the human mind, whether actions or intellections, may be correctly viewed as actions. This does not mean that all are willed and caused by the agent or the human mind, which would be absurd. It means that some of them, which consist in the exertions of the agent's active power, are the agent's actions, and that most of them, namely all the exertions which are in the agent without being exertions of the agent's powers, are the actions of God or actions planned by God. A fuller understanding of powers requires that we move from pneumatology to natural theology. Since we are not conscious of actions that are not ours, and cannot attend to them, all we know about them is through our natural belief in an intelligent design.

That most of the operations of the human mind rest upon the actions of a divine agent might be seen as an hypothesis, which is irrelevant in the science of the human mind: 'Every conjecture we can form with regard to the works of God, has as little probability as the conjectures of a child with regard to the works of man.' (EIP 49) For all we can discover about the operations of the mind is 'by patient observation, by accurate experiments, or by conclusions drawn by strict reasoning from observations and experiments' (49). Therefore occasionalism, whether general – extended to all operations in the mental and the physical worlds – or local – extended to all physical operations, and limited to certain mental operations –, is not a serious option in the science of the mind.[10]

Nevertheless, we also have good reasons to consider that, as the vital involuntary operations of our bodies 'must be done by the power of some agent' (EAP 31), who cannot be us, so our intellectual and active powers are supported by the Supreme Being, to whom 'reason leads us to ascribe unlimited power' (31). It is not only in its origin, but also 'in its exertions', that our power is dependent on God: 'Upon the whole, human power, in its existence, in its extent, and *in its exertions*, is entirely dependent upon God, and upon the laws of nature which he has established.' (45, my emphasis) This suggests that human powers depend on God's action, or rather on God's general plan of action (expressed through the 'laws of nature'), in their inner workings. Active powers as well as intellectual powers depend on 'some person behind the curtain' (83).

What difference is there, then, between Reid's view and radical occasionalism, which does not consist only in denying the existence of physical causes, but in referring all real agency to the power of God? The difference is that Reid sticks to epistemological modesty in the science of the human mind. He does not conjecture about the content of the works of God. As Nicholas Wolterstorff (2001, 256) puts it, 'If God alone is the cause, we know only *that* God is the cause, not *how*'. We live in 'deep impenetrable darkness'.[11] Wolterstorff gives much importance to the theme of darkness.[12] However, I think that the theme applies to the search for efficient causes in the operations of nature (see EAP 35; 42). This is how we should understand Reid's declaration: 'The power of man over his own and other minds, when we trace it to its origin, is involved in darkness, no less than his power to move his own and other bodies. How far we are properly efficient causes, how far occasional causes, I cannot pretend to determine.' (44) Darkness accumulates when we do not look above the horizon of efficient causes; it dissipates when we raise our eyes to final causes.

The psychology of power is interactionist. Drawing on a constitutive sensitivity to intelligent design, human minds are able to develop their knowledge of powers in a social context. The existence of active powers in others is the object of a belief, which is not learnt, but naturally at work in social operations (EAP 17–18). This belief – the sixth principle of contingent truth, according to which the 'conviction of some degree of power' in others as well as in us is 'interwoven with the whole of human conduct' (EIP 480) –, crucial to social life, is also the core of natural theology (EIP 508–509). As our own powers cannot be the object of our consciousness or of our attention, powers in others cannot be perceived or observed. But this does not prevent us from understanding others and reacting to their powers. We know our own powers only through their exertion; we know that others have powers only as they are signified by their behaviour. Our ability to have access to others' intentions gives us a secure ground for recognising our dependence upon God.

For, although we cannot, here below, have more than an epistemological glimpse of who is behind the curtain, we are able to engage in a conversation with the one whose existence, as Berkeley saw (*Principles of Human Knowledge*, I, §148; cf. EIP 512), is not less evident than the existence of other human beings. The belief in the intelligent author of the works of nature draws on the same cognitive equipment, antecedent to all reasoning or experience, as that of the baby in its 'social intercourse' with its nurse (EIP 482–483). This tends to qualify what Wolterstorff calls the 'theme of darkness'. Our knowledge of intellectual and active powers, which appears to be quite limited when we focus on the 'philosophy of the human mind', is as complete as it needs to be, when we turn to social interactions and the commerce of spirits, which Reidian epistemology should not neglect:

> It is of the highest importance to us, as moral and accountable creatures, to know what actions are in our power, because it is for these only that we can be accountable to our Maker, or to our fellow-men in society; by these only we can merit praise or blame; in these only all our prudence, wisdom and virtue must be employed; and, therefore, with regard to them, the wise Author of nature has not left us in the dark. (EAP 30–31)[13]

Notes

1. For instance in this passage: 'Desire and will agree in this, that both must have an object, of which we must have some conception; and therefore both must be accompanied with some degree of understanding' (EAP 48; see also 29, quoted below: 'that degree of understanding which will necessarily implies').
2. For a full discussion of this, see Yaffe (2004, 31–36).
3. I think this is clear from the following passage: 'Whereas he [Locke] distinguishes power into active and passive, I conceive passive power is no power at all. He means by it, the possibility of being changed. To call this power, seems to be a misapplication of the word. [...] Perhaps he was unwarily led into it, as an opposite to active power. But I conceive we call certain powers active, to distinguish them from other powers that are called speculative. As all mankind distinguish action from speculation, it is very proper to distinguish the powers by which those different operations are performed, into active and speculative. Mr Locke indeed acknowledges that active power is more properly called power; but I see no propriety at all in passive power; it is a powerless power, and a contradiction in terms.' (EAP 21)

4. For a discussion of the distinction between exertion as activation of the power and exertion as the resulting action, see Hoffman (2006).
5. This is not an isolated claim: 'In most, perhaps in all the operations of mind for which we have names in language, both faculties are employed, and we are both intellective and active.' (EAP 60)
6. 'The attention we give to objects is for the most part voluntary.' (EAP 63)
7. On the disanalogies between consciousness and reflective attention, see Copenhaver (2007).
8. 'Were we to examine minutely into the connection between our volitions, and the direction of our thoughts which obeys these volitions; were we to consider how we are able to give attention to an object for a certain time, and turn our attention to another when we chuse, we might perhaps find it difficult to determine, whether the mind itself be the sole efficient cause of the voluntary changes in the direction of our thoughts, or whether it requires the aid of other efficient causes.' (EAP 41)
9. 'Numberless instances might be given of things done by animals without any previous conception of what they are to do; without the intention of doing it. They act by some inward blind impulse, of which the efficient cause is hid from us; and though there is an end evidently intended by the action, this intention is not in the animal, but in its Maker. Other things are done by habit, which cannot properly be called voluntary. We shut our eyes several times every minute while we are awake; no man is conscious of willing this every time he does it.' (EAP 48)
10. Here I take occasionalism to be a positive view about the omnipresent action of God, not a negative view about the absence of physical causes or powers in bodies, as some do (see Wolterstorff 2001, 54–63). Of course, Reid is a professed occasionalist in the latter sense, which is fully compatible with his 'Newtonian' rejection of hypotheses. Negative occasionalism is uncontroversial among empiricists and accepted by both an atheist, Hume, and a Christian, Berkeley.
11. Wolterstorff describes as a frustration a state of knowledge Reid explicitly considers as sufficient: 'With regard to the operations of nature, it is sufficient for us to know, that, whatever the agents may be, whatever the manner of their operation, or the extent of their power, they depend upon the first cause, and are under his control; and this indeed is all that we know; beyond this we are left in darkness.' (EAP 30) In the next sentence, which I quote below, Reid contrasts this 'sufficient', although very limited, knowledge of nature, with the indispensable knowledge of what is in our power, which we have in abundance.
12. See Rebecca Copenhaver's criticism of 'mysterian' interpretations of Reid (Copenhaver 2006).
13. I thank Rebecca Copenhaver and Patrick Rysiew, and all the participants in the New Essays on Reid Conference, for their very helpful comments, suggestions and criticisms.

References

Copenhaver, Rebecca. 2006. "Is Reid a Mysterian?" *Journal of the History of Philosophy* 44 (3): 449–466.

Copenhaver, Rebecca. 2007. "Reid on Consciousness: HOP, HOT, or FOR?" *The Philosophical Quarterly* 57 (229): 613–634.

Destutt de Tracy, Antoine-Louis-Claude. 1801. *Projet d'éléments d'idéologie*. Paris: P. Didot l'aîné, F. Didot et Debray.

Destutt de Tracy, Antoine L. C. 2012. *Eléments d'idéologie. Idéologie proprement dite*, edited by Claude Jolly. Paris: Vrin.

Hoffman, Paul. D. 2006. "Thomas Reid's Notion of Exertion." *Journal of the History of Philosophy* 44 (3): 431–447.

Huoranszki, Ferenc. 2003. "Common Sense and the Theory of Human Behaviour." In *The Philosophy of Thomas Reid*, edited by John Haldane, and Stephen L. Read, 113–130. London: Blackwell Publishing.

Lindsay, Chris. 2005. "Reid on Scepticism about Agency and the Self." *Journal of Scottish Philosophy* 3 (1): 19–33.

Reid, Thomas. 2002. *Essays on the Intellectual Powers of Man* [EIP], edited by Derek R. Brookes. Edinburgh: Edinburgh University Press.

Reid, Thomas. 2003. "Of Power." In *The Philosophy of Thomas Reid*, edited by John Haldane, and Stephen L. Read, 14–23. London: Blackwell Publishing.

Reid, Thomas. 2010. *Essays on the Active Powers of Man* [EAP], edited by Knud Haakonssen and James A. Harris. Edinburgh: Edinburgh University Press.

Wolterstorff, Nicholas. 2001. *Thomas Reid and the Story of Epistemology*. Cambridge: Cambridge University Press.

Yaffe, Gideon. 2004. *Manifest Activity. Thomas Reid's Theory of Action*. Oxford: Oxford University Press.

MIND, LANGUAGE, METAPHYSICS
Reid on the priority of natural language

John Turri

Philosophy Department, University of Waterloo, Waterloo, ON, Canada

Thomas Reid distinguished between natural and artificial language and argued that natural language has a very specific sort of priority over artificial language. This paper critically interprets Reid's discussion, extracts a Reidian explanatory argument for the priority of natural language, and places Reid's thought in the broad tradition of Cartesian linguistics.

1. Introduction

Noam Chomsky's work on human language reignited a dormant tradition of studying language as a way of revealing something important about human nature (Chomsky 1957). Chomsky traces the roots of his approach back through Wilhelm von Humboldt and Rene Descartes (Chomsky 1966). This tradition — what Chomsky calls *Cartesian linguistics* — treats the *creative* human use of language as especially noteworthy, in two senses. On the one hand, the available evidence seems woefully inadequate to account for the linguistic competence humans acquire. On the other hand, humans routinely invent novel ways of expressing themselves, which other humans have little difficulty understanding, despite the novelty.

Thomas Reid fits comfortably into this tradition. Reid thought that language ought to be studied because doing so promises 'to lay open some of the first principles of human nature' and in particular the human mind (Reid 1764, 51). One purpose of this paper is to demonstrate, through a careful analysis of Reid's central argument in this area, how naturally Reid fits into the Cartesian linguistic tradition. Another purpose is to identify the most plausible version of Reid's argument, which complements Chomsky's own important conclusions about human nature. Reid's discussion of human language, in particular his distinction between natural and artificial signs, also provides a model for his later discussion of human perception (e.g. Reid 1764, ch. 6.24, 190), and it would be fruitful to investigate how the conclusions drawn here might be extended to Reid's views on perception. But I will not attempt that task here. It's worth emphasizing at the outset that Reid's philosophy of language has received scant attention in the secondary literature,[1] and the central passages and argument I discuss at great length below have previously received no attention.

In what follows I critically interpret and evaluate a principal distinction and argument due to Reid. The distinction and argument occur in the following passage, from Chapter 4 of Reid's *Inquiry into the Human Mind*:[2]

> By language I understand all those signs which mankind use in order to communicate to others their thoughts and intentions, their purposes and desires. And such signs may be conceived to be of two kinds: First, such as have no meaning, but what is affixed to them by compact or agreement among those who use them; these are artificial signs: Secondly, such as, previous to all compact or agreement, have a meaning which every man understands by the principles of his nature. Language, so far as it consists of artificial signs, may be called *artificial*; so far as it consists of natural signs, I call it *natural*.

> Having premised these definitions, I think it is demonstrable, that if mankind had not a natural language, they could never have invented an artificial one by their reason and ingenuity. For all artificial language supposes some compact or agreement to affix a certain meaning to certain signs; therefore there must be compacts or agreements before the use of artificial signs; but there can be no compact or agreement without signs, nor without language; and therefore there must be a natural language before any artificial language can be invented: Which was to be demonstrated. (Reid 1764, section 4.2, 51)

My subsequent discussion divides into three parts. Section 2 considers Reid's distinction between artificial and natural signs in the first quoted paragraph. Section 3 considers several ways of understanding the argument in the second quoted paragraph. Section 4 advances a different interpretation of Reid's discussion, and relates it to Chomsky's views on grammar.

2. The distinction

On Reid's view, human language is the set of signs humans use 'in order to communicate to others their thoughts and intentions, their purposes and desires.' Reid divides these signs, and by extension language, into two categories: natural and artificial. Artificial signs are defined as those signs which have no meaning except for 'what is affixed to them by compact or agreement among those who use them.' The English word 'star' is an example of an artificial sign. It refers to stars because we agree that it will. The 'thumbs-up' sign in Western societies signals approval because we agree that it will. Natural signs are defined as those signs which, prior to any 'compact or agreement, have a meaning which every man understands by the principles of his nature.' Reid says natural signs come in three basic types: 'modulations of the voice, gestures, and features.' Pointing is a gesture naturally understood as calling our attention to the thing ostended. Raising one's voice while furrowing one's brow is naturally understood to signify anger.

Clearly this distinction between artificial and natural signs is mutually exclusive. That is, as defined, no sign can be both natural and artificial. Reid's discussion strongly suggests that the distinction is also jointly exhaustive. That is, we're led to believe that every sign, respectively, must be either natural or artificial. If Reid thought there were other categories, then he would have said so.

But it's doubtful that the distinction is jointly exhaustive. At least, we have no reason to suppose that all signs fall into one or the other category. The primary reason for this is that Reid defines a natural sign as one that *every* human naturally understands. But surely there might be signs whose meaning some, but not all, humans understand naturally. To use an example that Reid might have acknowledged, it is often said that identical twins have an uncanny ability to interpret one another. Perhaps this is due to experience, or perhaps it's a natural talent they have in virtue of their intimately intertwined origins. It's readily conceivable that such a pair is born with a natural ability to signal their moods and interpret one another, in virtue of their tone, gestures and features, in ways unique to them. (For example recall Poe's *Fall of the House of Usher*, where we're told that 'sympathies of a scarcely intelligible nature had always existed between' the twins Roderick and Madeline Usher. Signs unintelligible to others are perfectly intelligible to the twins.) These signs used by such twins would be neither artificial nor natural, as per Reid's definitions. Neither would such signs violate the Wittgensteinian prohibition on private language, which pertains to language that is *essentially* private. Not only would the twins' use not be essentially private, it is trivially true that it doesn't even count as contingently private, since it's used in common by two people.

Setting aside examples that Reid himself might have considered, drawing on evolutionary theory, we might even expect there to be many partially distributed natural tendencies to express states of mind in specific ways. For example suppose that touching your ear while speaking was reliably associated with *an especially sincere commitment to truth-telling*.[3] A genetic mutation, resulting in a disposition to both (a) touch your ear as an expression of such a commitment and (b) to interpret such behavior likewise in others, might confer an advantage on those with the mutation. Such a mutation would at first be unique, and then, with any luck, propagate throughout the population over time, though it might never be universally distributed. Such a sign would count as neither artificial nor natural, as per Reid's definitions, but surely it's a sign nonetheless.

Reid could respond in at least two ways. On the one hand, he might add a third category to accommodate the examples. On the other hand, he might revise the definition of 'natural sign', so as to include such signs as natural. Call this an *inclusive definition* of 'natural sign'. An inclusive definition might go like this: natural signs have a meaning prior to any agreement among those who use them, which meaning those people understand by principles of their nature. This creates space for the sort of *idiosyncratic* or *partially distributed* natural signs featured in our examples. Perhaps the difference between these two responses doesn't amount to much. But I favor the inclusive response, for two reasons. First, the people in our examples – the twins in the one case, the mutants in the other – do express and understand the signs in question 'by principles of their nature.' That makes it natural to include them as 'natural signs,' and so I shall. Second, the inclusive definition seems best suited to Reid's argument, to which we now turn.

3. The argument

Here's the heart of the relevant passage again:

> [I]t is demonstrable, that if mankind had not a natural language, they could never have invented an artificial one. All artificial language supposes some compact or agreement to affix a certain meaning to certain signs; therefore there must be compacts or agreements before the use of artificial signs; but there can be no compact or agreement without signs, nor without language; and therefore there must be a natural language before any artificial language can be invented: Which was to be demonstrated.

Reid speaks here of artificial and natural 'language.' This can be misleading, at least to modern ears, since we tend to associate 'language' with robust communication systems, replete with syntactical and semantic rules, like French or Chinese. But as we saw earlier, by 'language' Reid refers to *all* signs we use in order to communicate, not just the verbal signs associated with what we typically call a 'language.' So I will interpret his argument accordingly.

Something along roughly the following lines seems to be the most natural interpretation of Reid's argument.

Humans invented artificial signs. (Assumption)
The invention of artificial signs requires earlier agreement among those who invented them. (Premise)
There can be no agreement without the use of signs. (Premise)
So among themselves humans earlier used signs, whose meaning preceded the invention of artificial signs. (From 1–3)
Signs whose meaning precedes the use of artificial signs are natural signs. (Premise)
So among themselves humans earlier used natural signs. (From 4–5)
So if humans invented artificial signs, then among themselves they earlier used natural signs. (From 1–6)

Line 1 is an assumption for conditional proof, and so isn't subject to question. Lines 2 and 5 are supported by the definitions of 'artificial sign' and 'natural sign'. Line 3 is, I presume, supposed to be obvious. The inference to 6 is obviously valid, as is the inference to 7. By 'use' I intend 'meaningful use', which should dispel any question about the validity of the inference to 4.

Now we can see why I earlier claimed that the inclusive definition of 'natural sign' better suits Reid's argument. It's implausible that the invention of artificial signs among, say, a small group of people in South America requires these people to reach prior agreement by using signs that *all* humans naturally understand by principles of their nature. It suffices that the small group reaches prior agreement by using signs that *they* understand. It's simply irrelevant whether some other people in, say, central Asia, whom our South Americans never have and never will meet, would likewise understand those signs. Even supposing that the central Asians wouldn't understand, that doesn't prevent our South Americans from using the signs to agree among themselves.

Next I will present an objection to Reid's argument. This will be followed by a series of imagined replies, refinements and rebuttals. This process will enable a better appreciation of Reid's argument, and help us to decide whether Reid's conclusion, or something in the ballpark, is true.

We do not by a principle of our nature understand 'wolves' to refer to wolves. The word 'wolves' is not a sign in natural human language. And yet it certainly seems possible that a human, call him 'Wally', might decide to use 'wolves' in order to communicate to others his thought that wolves lurk nearby. This invention of this artificial sign didn't require prior agreement using natural signs. So premise 2 is false.

'Oh, but it did require agreement,' it might be replied. 'Wally had to agree *with himself* to use "wolves" to refer to wolves.' In response, if we're to count such a decision as an agreement with oneself, then premise 3 is false. One doesn't communicate such a decision to oneself. One doesn't use signs in order to communicate such a decision to oneself. Neither does one need to use signs to make such a decision.

Perhaps it will instead be replied, 'We should understand Reid's argument to pertain not merely to the invention of artificial signs, but the invention *and use* of them.' This reply can be met by extending the example. Suppose Wally says 'wolves' to a Stranger he encounters along the forest trail one evening, in order to communicate his thought that wolves lurk nearby. Nothing here requires prior agreement on the meaning of 'wolves' between Wally and the Stranger, or between Wally and anyone else.

Perhaps it will instead be replied, 'We should understand the argument to pertain to the invention and *effective interpersonal* use of artificial signs. The Stranger will just be confused by Wally's utterance, so it doesn't count as an effective interpersonal use of artificial signs.' This reply can be met by extending the example. Add that the Stranger hails from a community that, as it happens, uses the word 'wolves' to refer to wolves. So she isn't the least bit confused by Wally's utterance. She immediately takes him to mean precisely what he does mean. (Perhaps she falsely, but reasonably, takes Wally to be a member of her community, despite having never seen him before.)

'But notice,' it might be replied, 'that your latest extension of the case requires that the Stranger's community previously agreed to use "wolves" that way. So the example doesn't threaten a suitably modified version of Reid's argument. The invention and effective interpersonal use of artificial signs requires agreement among some people or other.' Fair enough. This reply can be met by modifying the example as follows. Instead of hailing from a community that uses 'wolves' to refer to wolves, our Stranger, like Wally, made the individual decision to use 'wolves' to refer to wolves. She is absorbed in thought when Wally abruptly says 'wolves' to her. She immediately takes him to mean precisely what he does mean, and takes precautions against the potential danger lurking nearby. None of this requires prior agreement between Wally and the Stranger.

'But the Stranger has no good reason to expect that Wally refers to wolves when he says "wolves"!' it might be objected. 'She might *unreasonably* believe him to be referring to wolves, but she doesn't *know* that he's referring to wolves. This is no *witting* and effective interpersonal use of artificial language, which is what we should take Reid to be concerned with.' This last objection gains some measure of credibility when we consider three things. In the first place, consider a later passage from the *Inquiry* where Reid recapitulates the argument already quoted:

> It appears evident from what hath been said on the subject of language, That there are natural signs, as well as artificial; and particularly, That the thoughts, purposes, and dispositions of the mind, have their natural signs in the features of the face, the modulation of the voice, and the motion and attitude of the body: That without a natural knowledge of the connection between these signs, and the things signified by them, language could never have been invented and established among men: and... this connec-tion... we may call *the natural language of mankind.* (1764, 5.3, 59)

Here Reid seems to characterize natural language in terms of *knowing* the connection between sign and signified.[4] It stands to reason, then, that he'd characterize the effective interpersonal use of artificial language in terms of knowing the connection between sign and signified.

In the second place, careful inspection reveals that the conclusion Reid ultimately draws is stronger than what he initially says he would prove. Initially he says, 'It is demonstrable, that if mankind had not a natural language, they could never have invented an artificial one *by their reason and ingenuity*.' Call this the *initial statement* of Reid's thesis. But when presenting the actual argument, he concludes, 'Therefore there must be a natural language before any artificial language can be invented: Which is what was to be demonstrated.' Call this the *final statement* of Reid's thesis. The final statement entails the initial statement, but not vice versa. (That is, the final statement is logically stronger.) If we cannot invent artificial language without an antecedent natural language, then we cannot *by our reason and ingenuity* – or, more generally, by any means whatsoever – invent artificial language without prior agreement via natural language. Perhaps Reid intended us to read the final statement of the thesis as implicitly qualified, in light of the initial statement.

In the third place, later in the same section, Reid says that we could not, by all our 'wit and ingenuity' alone, invent artificial language without a prior natural language, apparently simply reiterating what he takes himself to have proven.

In light of these three considerations, it is at least plausible that Reid intended to conclude only that we cannot wittingly invent artificial language without prior agreement via natural language. To wittingly invent an artificial sign is to invent a sign, knowing what it signifies.

This is an interesting objection, which leads us in a potentially promising direction. But first notice that it doesn't fully deliver on what our critic initially promised. Even accepting the weaker interpretation of the argument, featuring the initial statement of Reid's thesis, we may not conclude that Reid was concerned with the witting and effective interpersonal *use* of artificial language. He literally speaks only of the *invention* – the *witting* invention, if you like – of artificial language. This thesis succumbs to our initial example, wherein Wally decides to use 'wolves' to refer to wolves. Surely there's no problem supposing that he wittingly does so. Indeed, this is the natural understanding of the case. It would be odd to suggest that despite consciously deciding to use 'wolves' that way, he nevertheless doesn't know that he does so. So even taking into account the emphasis on knowledge found elsewhere, we still must substantially depart from the letter of the text in order to focus on the witting and effective interpersonal use of artificial language.

But let's set aside, for the moment at least, any concern about literal fidelity to Reid's text. Having come this far, it's worth asking whether this Reidian thesis – I don't say *Reid's thesis* – is true. I suspect that even this thesis is false. To substantiate this suspicion, we must construct a new example, involving onomatopoeia.

We do not, by a principle of our nature, understand the cry 'owooo' to mean anything. The cry 'owooo' is not a sign in natural human language. And yet it certainly seems possible that a human with some experience with wolves, call him 'Howie', might decide to use the cry 'owooo' in order to communicate to others his thought that wolves lurk nearby. The invention of this artificial sign didn't require prior agreement using natural signs. And it seems quite natural that Howie would settle on this artificial sign for wolves, having learned that wolves uniquely cry 'owooo' in that distinctive sort of way, which anyone who has heard a wolf howl would recognize.

Suppose Howie is exiting the forest along the main path at dusk, having just escaped a ravenous wolf pack, when he notices a Stranger entering the forest. Howie knows that wolves lurk nearby, and howls 'owooo' at the Stranger, in order to communicate this thought. Moreover, Howie knows that any human adult around these parts knows what a wolf howl sounds like. So it stands to reason that the Stranger would interpret Howie as referring to wolves. And the Stranger interprets him precisely that way. This certainly seems to qualify as a witting and effective interpersonal use of artificial language. But it wasn't preceded by any agreement, using natural signs or otherwise, between Howie and the Stranger.[5]

Thus, in addition to concluding that Reid's original distinction requires improvement, that Reid's original argument fails, and that Reid's original thesis is false, I also conclude that the qualified Reidian thesis under consideration is false too. The invention of artificial signs does not strictly require prior agreement via natural language, and neither does the witting and effective interpersonal use of artificial signs.

4. An explanatory hypothesis

My critique of Reid relied on possible but highly peculiar cases, some involving coincidences that we couldn't reasonably expect to occur frequently. But if we want to account for the highly systematic and stable institution that is artificial human language, it seems unlikely that we'll be satisfied with an appeal to such coincidences, especially in the quantity that would be required from a thorough accounting. It is in the spirit of Reid's original discussion, then, that I offer the following hypothesis.

Artificial human languages are frequently invented. Inventing a systematic and stable language no doubt takes time and effort, but it isn't especially difficult — as Reid puts it, 'there is no great ingenuity required' — for a group of humans to fairly quickly settle on a stable and extensible set of signs for the purposes of communicating among themselves. This is true even if they are complete strangers who initially don't share a single artificial sign in common. The best explanation for the relative ease with which such humans can invent an artificial language is that they share a natural language which they can readily implement to agree on meanings for artificial signs. For example, pointing to something and saying 'apple' in a clear, steady voice and then proceeding to do the same with several other objects that superficially resemble the first is an especially effective way to get a group of humans to understand that you're using 'apple' to refer to things of that kind.

We thus have a Reidian explanatory argument for the existence of a natural human language. This language seems an especially apt tool for establishing a common vocabulary. It thus complements Chomsky's explanatory argument for the existence of innate grammatical principles. On Chomsky's view, the best explanation of how easily human children learn the grammatical rules of artificial language is that we have innate knowledge of the most fundamental grammatical principles underlying all artificial human languages. Likewise on the Reidian view, the best explanation of how easily humans can invent, from scratch, a common vocabulary is that we share a natural tendency to interpret some gestures and expressions to signify certain things. Putting Chomsky and Reid together: the 'original constitution of our minds' equips us with the tools for acquiring both the *grammar* and *lexicon* of artificial human languages.

Not only are artificial human languages easily invented, they are effortlessly maintained. This points to a further 'original principle of the human constitution,' namely, that there is 'in the human mind an early anticipation, neither derived from experience, nor from reason, nor from any compact or promise, that our fellow-creatures will' continue using words and other signs in the same way they previously have (Reid 1764, ch. 6.24, 193). Thus we are led to posit a further fascinating feature of the human mind, if we are to account for the effortless *stability* of artificial human languages.[6]

Notes

1. As an indication of this, consider that the index to *The Cambridge Companion to Thomas Reid* doesn't even contain an entry for 'language' (though it does have one for Reid's interest in botany!), and contains only a meagre entry for 'signs'. Compare that to the multiple entries for 'language' and extensive entry for 'signs' in *The Cambridge Companion to Berkeley*, and the extensive entry for 'language' in *The Cambridge Companion to Locke's "Essay Concerning Human Understanding"*. Moreover, the Berkeley *Companion* dedicates an entire chapter to Berkeley's theory of signs, and the Locke *Companion* dedicates a chapter to Locke's philosophy of language. (But compare Jensen [1979] and Castagnetto [1992].)
2. Since Immerwahr (1978), some have accepted that Reid's views changed significantly between his early work in the *Inquiry* and his later work in the *Essays*. I reject this reading of Reid, but it isn't necessary to belabor the point here, because I am focused on Reid's interesting and neglected discussion in the *Inquiry*.
3. Suppose this commitment to be well beyond the default commitment to truth-telling embodied in Reid's 'principle of veracity.' See Reid 1764, 6.24, 193–194.
4. There is a close affinity between what Reid calls 'natural signs' and what Grice calls 'natural meaning.' To illustrate natural meaning, Grice used the example 'those spots mean measles' (1957). To illustrate natural signs, Reid used examples such as 'smoke is a natural sign of fire' and a certain countenance on a human face is 'a natural sign of anger' (1764, 177). Reid's 'natural language of mankind' might thus be regarded as a subset of Gricean natural meaning, where the signs in question are those features of human behavior and countenance that signify one's state of mind. But as I discuss in the main text, Reid might impose a further epistemic constraint on which natural signs are fit for inclusion in natural human language.
5. Earlier we noted a similarity between Reidian natural signs and Gricean natural meaning. The present example highlights a further similarity, this time in terms of Reidian 'artificial signs' and Gricean 'nonnatural meaning.' Gricean nonnatural meaning can be glossed as follows: a speaker S's utterance U means that P because of S's intention that his audience infer, based on the fact that S uttered U, that S intends them to infer that S believes that P (and perhaps also that S intends them to infer that P in part because S believes that P). See Grice 1957 and 1969. Howie has a Gricean reflexive communicative intention.
6. For helpful conversation and feedback, I thank Christian Hegele, Kevin Kuhl, Patrick Rysiew, and Nicholas Wolterstorff. Special thanks go to Angelo Turri. This research was supported by the Social Sciences and Humanities Research Council of Canada and an Ontario Early Researcher Award.

References

Castagnetto, Susan. 1992. "Reid's answer to abstract ideas." *Journal of philosophical research* 17: 39–60.

Chomsky, Noam. 1957. *Syntactic structures*. The Hague: Mouton.

Chomsky, Noam. 1966. *Cartesian linguistics: a chapter in the history of rationalist thought*. New York: Harper & Row.

Cuneo, Terrence, and Rene van Woudenberg, eds. 2004. *The Cambridge companion to Thomas Reid*. Cambridge: Cambridge University Press.

Grice, H. P. 1957. "Meaning." *The Philosophical Review* 66 (3): 377–388.

Grice, H. P. 1969. "Utterer's meaning and intention." *The Philosophical Review* 78 (2): 147–177.

Immerwahr, John. 1978. "The development of Reid's realism." *The Monist* 61: 245–256.

Jensen, Henning. 1979. "Reid and Wittgenstein on philosophy and language." *Philosophical studies* 36: 359–376.

Newman, Lex, ed. 2007. *The Cambridge companion to Locke's "essay concerning human understanding"*. Cambridge: Cambridge University Press.

Reid, Thomas. 1764 [1997]. *An inquiry into the human mind on the principles of common sense*, edited by Derek R. Brookes. University Park, PA: Pennsylvania State University.

Winkler, Kenneth P., ed. 2005. *The Cambridge companion to Berkeley*. Cambridge: Cambridge University Press.

MIND, LANGUAGE, METAPHYSICS
Disagreement, design, and Thomas Reid

René van Woudenberg

Department of Philosophy, VU University, Amsterdam, The Netherlands

This paper argues that Reid's first principle of design can be more widely accepted then one might suppose, due to the fact that it specifies no marks of design. Also it is explicated that the relation of the principle, on the one hand, and properly basic design beliefs on the other, is a relation of presupposition. It is furthermore suggested that Reid's discussion of what can be done in case of disagreement about first principles points to a position that is relevant to the current debates in the Epistemology of Disagreement literature and that merits further elaboration.

Very often we think and believe we can detect elements of design in the world. We detect design in the Eifel tower, in the killing of Franz Ferdinand in 1914, in the process of brewing beer, in guitars, in watches, in Bruckner's 9th symphony, in poems and novels, in Milo's Venus, in the waving and shaking of hands and in so many other objects, actions, processes and states of affairs. Many also think they detect design in the natural world, e.g. in the intricacies of the human body, or in the fine-tuning of the cosmos. But how, in what ways, do we come to think design thoughts, how do we come to believe design propositions (defined as thoughts/propositions of the form 'This is designed')? And do those ways give some positive epistemic status to those thoughts and beliefs? Are they, for instance, because of the ways they are formed, rational, or justified, or warranted?

This paper takes up these questions in an indirect way; it is a discussion, and in a sense a vindication, of the following principle about design that Thomas Reid endorses:

'That design and intelligence in the cause may be inferred, with certainty, from marks or signs of it in the effect.' (EIP 503[1])

This paper is organized as follows. Section 1 clarifies the content as well as the epistemic status of this principle that I shall call the Design Principle, or simply the Principle. Since design conclusions, especially if about natural objects such as plants, animals and organs are bound to be controversial, Section 2 investigates what Reid thinks can be done in case of disagreement over the truth and application of the Principle. Section 3 investigates what role, according to Reid, the Principle plays in design belief formation: is it the premise in a design inference, or does it play some other role? David Hume famously criticized one form of argument from design, such that if the critique is sound, the Principle cannot be maintained; Section 4 discusses Reid's response to Hume's critique. Finally, it is possible that disagreements about the Principle continue, even after all the moves discussed in Section 2 have been made; Section 5 discusses Reid's views about the causes of such enduring disagreement and suggests that a distinctive Reidian position can be added to the Epistemology of Disagreement literature.

1. The Design Principle clarified

First clarification: according to Reid the Design Principle is a *first* principle. First principles are propositions that have a number of interesting epistemic properties. They are believed as soon as they are understood. They are, hence, when believed, not believed on the basis of an argument of which they are the conclusion. A first principle 'has the light of truth in itself, and has no occasion to borrow it from another' (EIP 452).

But isn't this worrisome? Isn't it far more plausible that the Principle, when believed, is believed either on the basis of reasoning, or on the basis of experience? Reid discusses and rejects both of these suggestions. Belief in the Principle is not founded on reasoning, he objects, because, first, 'it is too universal to be the effect of reasoning' (EIP 504), as both philosophers and non-philosophers, both learned and illiterates, both civilized and savages take the Principle for granted without argument. Second and related, when philosophers 'who can reason excellently in subjects that admit of reasoning' (EIP 504) apply the Principle, they never catch the opportunity to offer reasons for its cogency but instead appeal to the common sense of mankind. But if such excellent reasoners as Cicero and Tillotson, whom Reid cites as illustrations of his point, don't offer reasons for the Principle, then it is very likely that their belief in it is not based on reasoning.

Reid is well aware of the fact that some of his contemporaries argue for the Principle with arguments of the following sort: 'object X is a regular arrangement of parts; such an arrangement cannot be the effect of chance; hence, X is the effect of design' (see EIP 505–506). His response is that this argument, based as it is on what was at the time called 'the doctrine of chances' (nowadays that doctrine is called probability theory), is of recent date, whereas 'the conclusion drawn from it has been held by all men from the beginning of the world'. So the conclusion was believed or taken for granted before and hence independently of the argument.

There is, however, a problem with Reid's response: the conclusion of the argument just given is not the Principle! For the conclusion of the argument is 'X is the effect of design', whereas the Principle is 'That design and intelligence in the cause may be inferred, with certainty, from marks or signs of it in the effect.' The argument doesn't conclude with the Principle, but rather assumes it as one of its premises. For the argument assumes that a regular arrangement of parts is a mark of design, and that the observed presence of such marks in an object licenses one to conclude to an intelligent and designing cause of that object. And this assumption is just an augmented version of the Principle. It is the Principle augmented with the thought that the regular arrangement of parts is a mark of design. The noted problem, of course, strengthens rather than weakens the case for the Principle's not being based on reasoning.

Could the principle then perhaps be based on experience? Reid rejects this suggestion as well because, first, the Principle, as he avers, is a necessary truth and necessary truths cannot be learned from experience, as experience can only teach us what *is* or *has been*, not what *must be*. Says Reid, 'As we cannot learn from experience that twice three must necessarily make six, so neither can we learn from experience that certain effects must proceed from a designing and intelligent cause' (EIP 507–508). Second, Reid rejects the suggestion because, if it were true, it would have the devastating implication that numerous design beliefs that are rather obviously true, should never be held. His reasoning is subtle but simple. Experience can only show that there is a connection between a mark of design and a (its) designing intelligent cause, when both the marks and the cause can be perceived in conjunction. If only marks can be perceived, but their designing causes cannot, then experience can never teach us that we must connect these marks with any designing cause. However, there are rather obvious cases in which the marks *can* be perceived and their designing causes can*not*, even though we happily and with justification trace back those marks to a designing cause. For example, we routinely and justifiably trace back thoughts, as expressed in spoken or written sentences, to a designing and intelligent cause, i.e. a mind, even though minds cannot be perceived (not in the way that the marks can be perceived, that is). And objects like watches, bulldozers and computers, so objects that display manifold marks of design, can be perceived, but the purpose and design of their makers cannot be perceived (in that way). Still, we happily, routinely and justifiably believe these objects have intelligent causes. From which it follows that we endorse the Principle on grounds other than experience. But if our acceptance of the Principle is neither based on reasoning nor on experience, then the only option left open is that the Principle is a necessarily true first principle, that 'has the light of truth in itself' (EIP 434).

Second. The Design Principle, one could think, can be understood in a weaker, internalist, and in a stronger, externalist way. Understood in the weaker way, the principle says that signs or marks of design in the effect are *evidence* for design and intelligence in the cause of the effect – evidence that the subject can be aware of by, say, reflection. Understood in the stronger way, the principle says that the perception of marks or signs in the effect elicits, in the subject, the belief that there is design and intelligence in the cause of the effect. I have two reasons for thinking that Reid intended a principle to be taken in a weaker way. First, the principle says that one thing may be *inferred* from another – and inference, it would seem, is a pretty conscious undertaking: if you infer C from P, you will have to be aware, somehow, of P. If you aren't, 'inference' is out of place. Second: as I have argued in another paper[2], Reid's epistemology is a mixture of internalist and externalist lines of thought. But it is mainly in the context of radical skepticism that he takes an externalist line; in virtually all other contexts, internalism is the main line. Since the current topic, design belief, is not a topic bordering on radical skepticism, it is most plausible that Reid intended the principle to be taken in the internalist, so in the weaker, sense.

Third clarifying remark: the Principle involves the notion of 'signs (or marks) of design/intelligence', or 'marks of design' for short. Reid nowhere enumerates such marks, but we have to think, in addition to a regular arrangement of parts, of such things as: meaningful order (e.g. of words on paper, of the parts of a watch), specific functions, interlocking functions, patterns of organization, certain sorts of purity, etc. No fast and easy list of marks of design can be made, it is long and presumably open ended.[3] Having said this, it is important to note that the Principle as such carries no entailment as to which properties are indeed marks of design! Accordingly, acceptance of the Design Principle does not commit anyone to a particular view as to which characteristics are marks of design. And this, in turn, means that its acceptance will neither foreclose nor solve disagreement about them.

A further point of clarification about the notion of 'mark of design' is that many evolutionary theorists speak of design that is due to evolution – due, that is, to natural selection working on a source of randomness such as random genetic mutation. They say, for instance, that the giraffe's long neck has been 'designed' by evolution. It bears pointing out that the 'marks of design' that Reid's Principle speaks of, may or may not be identical to what present day evolutionary theorists have their eyes on when they say that evolution has designed this or that. Now suppose there is a mark such that according to Reid his Principle can be applied to it, and that according to evolutionary theorists that mark is due to evolution. Then something of a deadlock may seem to arise, as the Principle licenses Reid to ascribe the marked feature to a designing cause that is intelligent, while the evolutionary theorist ascribes it to evolution, which is deemed 'blind' and hence most certainly not a designing cause that is intelligent. But this is a mere seeming. For, if evolution is orchestrated by an intelligent designing cause (and no empirical evidence is capable of ruling that out), then the very same feature to which the Principle might be applied can be due to evolution. Here is an analogy: the beer brewing process may be blind in the very same sense that evolution is: the process itself aims at no goals, yet the entire process itself is orchestrated by the brewer.

Finally, the Principle also involves the notion of 'design and intelligence in the cause'. What 'intelligence in a cause' comes to is perhaps obvious, but what is 'design in a cause'? I take this to be a somewhat infelicitous way of speaking about 'a designing cause'. The cause that the principle licenses one to conclude to in case of perceived marks of design, is a cause that has the properties of being intelligent and of being a designer. Reid doesn't analyze these properties but takes them at face value. And for the purposes of the paper, so will I.

2. What can be done to resolve disagreement about the Design Principle?

Not everyone will believe the Design Principle. The question to be considered in this section is whether disagreement about the truth of the Design Principle can be resolved.

As first principles have a special epistemic status (they are supposed to be believed as soon as they are understood), a special problem arises. First principles have a special epistemic status in that, as we have seen Reid maintains, they cannot be argued for. But then there is no argument available that can turn a non-believer in the Principle into a believer. (But an argument might turn a believer in the Principle into a nonbeliever.) Is there a way to tackle this special problem? According to Reid there is, as 'Nature has not left us destitute of means whereby the candid and honest part of mankind may be brought to unanimity when they happen to differ about first principles' (EIP 459). I will proceed to discuss these means, but first note that Reid explicitly states these means can only be successful in case the disagreeing parties are 'candid' and 'honest', i.e. when they satisfy certain intellectual and moral criteria, or, as we might also say, when they possess certain epistemic and moral virtues. What, then, does Reid think are the means that candid and honest people can use in order to resolve disagreements about first principles?

For starters, Reid observes that 'opinions which contradict first principles, are distinguished, from other errors, by this: they are not only false but absurd; and to discountenance absurdity, Nature hath given us a particular emotion—to wit, that of ridicule—which seems intended for this very purpose of putting out of countenance what is absurd, either in opinion or in practice' (EIP 462). With respect to the Design Principle this entails that, if it is a genuine first principle, its denial must be absurd. It entails furthermore that, in case of disagreement about it, the absurdity of the denial can, or perhaps should, be brought out in a mode of mockery: it should be ridiculed.

Both of these implications can seem worrisome. As to the ridicule part: in a discussion with candid and honest non-believers of the Design principle, it seems wrong and also ineffective to ridicule their non-belief (at least, if the goal of the discussion is to convince the interlocutor). Ridicule is at home in a discussion, or what passes for it, between persons one of whom at least lacks the aforementioned intellectual and moral virtues. The moment ridicule creeps into a discussion, one immediately fears that dishonesty or disingenuity is going on, that axes are being ground, that one of the parties isn't being taken seriously.[4] So, even if the denial of the Principle is absurd, ridicule doesn't seem to be a proper way to try to convince non-believers of the wrongness of their thought. (It should be noted, though, that if the goal of the discussion is not to convince the interlocutor, but, for instance, to confirm the Principle for ourselves, or for an audience, ridicule may very well be effective.)

But *is* the denial of the Principle absurd? Is it absurd to hold that the following principle is false: 'if X displays marks of design, then X is caused by an intelligent designing cause'? In order to assess this question, we should remind ourselves of something I pointed out earlier: Reid's Principle doesn't explicate *which* features of objects, states of affairs etc. are marks of design. And that it doesn't do this, makes the Principle in principle acceptable even for those who are skeptical or even hostile to design claims. Disagreement about design claims, so claims of the sort 'X is the product of design', need not be disagreements about the Design Principle. And if they are not, they will be disagreements about which features of objects are genuine marks of design. Design skeptics or critics such as Dawkins and Dennett deny that there are features in the natural world that are marks of design. But their denial, even if correct, doesn't entail the denial of the Principle. Even if there would be no marks of design in the natural world, the Design Principle could still be true. So, again, *is* the Design Principle true? To me it seems plausible to think that it, or some principle in the neighborhood, is true indeed. If something X has certain characteristics of which you and I and others hold that they are marks of design, then it seems right that we conclude that X has an intelligent and designing cause. I cannot really argue for the Design's Principle being true. But then again, that is to be expected if it really is a first principle (and if, moreover, what Reid says about first principles is correct).

There is a second thing candid and honest people can do when they disagree over first principles: they can reason about them, although the reasoning can never take the form of a proof. Says Reid, 'although it is contrary to the nature of first principles to admit of direct or apodictical proof, yet there are ways of reasoning about them, by which those that are just and solid may be confirmed, and those that are false may be detected' (EIP 463). These ways of reasoning can best be thought of not as confirming the truth of an alleged first principle, but as confirming that the principle at hand is indeed a *first* principle.

What ways of reasoning could confirm the *first*-ness status of an alleged principle? Reid suggests, to begin with, 'that it is a good argument *ad hominem*, if it can be shewn that a first principle which a man rejects, stands upon the same footing with others which he admits.' (ibid.) So, if you can show that your interlocutor is inconsistent in denying what you take to be a first principle, this may bring about a change of heart in her. An imperfect example, pertinent to the Design Principle, may be this: someone might be applying the Principle routinely to such artifacts as bulldozers and computers, but not to tigers and sharks, even though the features in the artifacts on the basis of which she concludes that they have an intelligent designing cause, are the same as those that tigers and sharks display, e.g. complex organization. This inconsistency, upon being noticed, may bring the interlocutor to accept the Principle as a *first* principle, and apply it consistently.

A second way of reasoning about first principles is 'a proof *ad absurdum*.' The procedure is familiar enough: drag out implications of the denial of the alleged first principle that are absurd. These absurd implications indirectly confirm the principle. Applied to the Design Principle, this could work as follows. An interlocutor denies the Principle, so he denies that being meaningfully ordered (which he takes to be a mark of design) indicates intelligence and design in the cause of what is meaningfully ordered. Then you drag out the consequence that this means that you can't conclude from noticing the following string of letters METHINKS, IT'S A WEASEL, that it has an intelligent designing cause. As this consequence is clearly absurd, it may bring the interlocutor to accept the Principle. (And he may do so without you ridiculing him! So what is correct in the first of the means that Reid mention to secure unanimity over first principles, is captured by this second way of reasoning.)

There is yet another means that Reid points to and that might help resolving disagreement about first principles, viz. an appeal to 'the consent of ages and nations' (EIP 464). Reid is well aware of the unpopularity and hazards of any appeal to such consensus. He therefore qualifies the nature and relevance of such an appeal in a number of ways. Not questioning the unalienable right to judge for oneself, the authority of the ages should nevertheless bear some weight. How? Using some apt metaphors, Reid puts his point as follows: 'Authority, though a tyrannical mistress to private judgment, may yet, on some occasions, be a useful handmaid' (EIP 464). So there is a role to be played by the conviction of the crowds. Reid's reasoning here is as follows: in matters of first principles every person must be deemed a competent judge, there being no experts on first principles. Hence, ignoring the consent of the nations and ages would amount to ignoring the verdicts of competent judges, which surely is not the path of wisdom. It is, of course, possible that the crowds are wrong. And when they can be shown to be wrong, the consent of the nations is outweighed, or undercut. But in the absence of serious reasons to doubt a presumed first principle, the consent should carry some weight.

Applied to the Design Principle this means that in case of disagreement an appeal may be made to a consensus about it – if there is one. *Is* there? This is, obviously, an empirical matter. But, given the content of the principle (and given the point I made earlier that even design deniers and design skeptics can accept the Principle), we may, I suppose, assume there *is* such a consensus. This doesn't mean there is a consensus about which items in the world have intelligent and designing cause for, as indicated, the Design Principle doesn't specify which features of objects are marks of design. But it bears noting in the present context that there is a universal consensus about artifacts like bulldozers, computers etc. having an intelligent and designing cause. It also bears noting that even when it comes to organisms, a surprisingly high percentage of people now living hold that organisms have an intelligent and designing cause – and prior to Darwin virtually everyone believed so. These facts should be noticed, even if they are, strictly speaking, irrelevant to the Design Principle as formulated.

As we saw, Reid holds that an appeal to the consensus of the nations can be undermined, namely when there is a serious reason to think that the consensus is false. Is there a reason to think that the Design Principle is false? Is the Darwinian theory of evolution such a reason? Again, it would seem not, as the Principle can be accepted even by parties that disagree about which features of organisms, if any, qualify as marks of design. The upshot of this is that an appeal to the near universal acceptance of the Design Principle in a situation of disagreement about it should carry some weight.[5]

A further consideration that Reid proposes should be given some weight in case of disagreement about first principles is at what age they are accepted or taken for granted: 'Opinions that appear so early in the minds of men that they cannot be the effect of education or of false reasoning, have a good claim to be considered as first principles' (EIP 467). Early appearance of an opinion as such doesn't make it likely that the opinion is a first principle. After all, many early opinions are clearly false. But in conjunction with the other means, especially the appeal to an uncontroverted consensus, it can do some work. *Does* the Design Principle appear early in the minds of humans? Empirical research strongly suggests this to be the case (Barrett 2009).

A fifth and final consideration that disputing parties about first principles may take into account, says Reid, is this: 'when an opinion is so necessary in the conduct of life, that, without the belief of it, a man must be led into a thousand absurdities in practice, such an opinion, when we can give no other reason for it, may safely be taken for a first principle' (EIP 467). It seems clear that the Design Principle is necessary for the conduct of life. If one would not think that at least some of the actions of one's fellows, or the results of their actions, display marks of design and hence point to an intelligent and designing cause, one would indeed be led into many gross absurdities.

3. The Design Principle: believed or taken for granted

My discussion of the Design Principle so far may give the impression that Reid's position is that when humans think design thoughts, or believe about some object, event, etc. that it has an intelligent designing cause, these thoughts and beliefs have been eventuated by a somewhat complicated train of mental events, the crucial elements of which are:

(a) noticing in an object a feature that is deemed a mark of design
(b) awareness of and belief in the Design Principle
(c) squeezing out of (a) and (b) the premises of an argument, and finally
(d) drawing from these premises the conclusion that the object has an intelligent and designing cause.

The fact is, however, that when one perceives, say, a bulldozer and believes of it that it has an intelligent designing cause, one doesn't really notice in oneself this somewhat complicated train of mental events. The formation of the belief goes far more directly. This raises the question as to the exact status of the Design Principle, and of first principles in general.

Reid also refers to first principles as 'principles of common sense'. As Nicholas Wolterstorff has convincingly argued (Wolterstorff 2001, 215–227), Reid says two quite different things about common sense principles. On the one hand he says that they are propositions that are *commonly believed*, but on the other hand he says that they are propositions that are *commonly taken for granted*. And that is a big difference, as there are many things that we take for granted without ever having formed an explicit belief about them. You take for granted that your grandfather was shorter than 7.42 meters, but before reading this sentence you never explicitly formed a belief to that effect. This raises the question whether we should best think of the Design Principle as a proposition that, in forming design beliefs, we take for granted or as a proposition that we explicitly believe?[6]

If we take Reid to be holding that design beliefs are the result of arguing from premises, more or less along the lines of the argument explicated at the beginning of this section, it seems plausible to hold that the Principle needs to be believed explicitly so that it can play the role of a premise in an argument. But if we take the Design Principle to have the former status, then it is far more plausible to think that design belief formation has the same kind of directness as perceptual belief formation.

As indicated, Reid is of two minds about the status of first principles. But I am quite confident that, when pressed, he would agree that in many cases of design belief formation the Design Principle is *taken for granted*, and does *not* function as an (explicitly believed) premise in an argument that leads up to a design conclusion.[7] The basis for my confidence is this: Reid clearly held that the formation of perceptual beliefs proceeds mostly in a direct fashion, i.e. without reasoning being involved. Yet, he also says that it is a first principle that 'Those things do really exist which we distinctly perceive by our senses, and are what we perceive them to be' (EIP 445). And he obviously doesn't intend to affirm that this first principle functions as a premise in the process of perceptual belief formation. The status of this first principle is that *we take it for granted* all the time we form, in immediate ways, beliefs about our immediate environment. Considerations of consistency make me confident that, when pressed, Reid would embrace an analogous position with respect to the relation between the Design Principle and the formation of design beliefs.

The question can be posed: what *is* it to take a first principle for granted? How shall we understand this? So far no suggestions on this have been made in the literature. But here is my proposal, proceeding from examples: when one explicitly believes that Mont Blanc is higher than the Matterhorn, one has taken for granted that Mont Blanc exists. In this case what is taken for granted is the truth of a certain proposition, viz. *that Mont Blanc exists*. The proposition that is taken for granted, furthermore, is 'related' to something else, viz. a belief (the belief that Mont Blanc is higher than the Matterhorn): the proposition taken for granted is taken for granted *relative to* a belief. Now what needs to be the case if some person S who believes that Mont Blanc is higher than the Matterhorn (= P) is *to take for granted* that Mont Blanc exists (= Q)? Here is my suggestion: S, in believing P, takes Q for granted iff

   (i) S cannot sensibly believe P and deny Q (or, which is just another way of putting the same point: in believing P, S is committed to the truth of Q),

  (ii) even if S believes Q, S did not come to believe P on the basis of an argument that includes Q among its premises.

In the Matterhorn/Mont Blanc example S cannot sensibly believe P and deny Q because P *entails* Q.

Let us run a test on this account. Suppose Sally sees a ship sailing and accordingly believes there is a sailing ship (= P). If the account offered is correct, and if the proposition that those things really exist that we distinctly perceive (= Q) is, as Reid claims, a first principle, then the following should be true: in holding her belief that P, Sally takes Q for granted, which means that (i) she cannot sensibly believe P and deny Q, (ii) even if she believes Q, she does not come to believe P on the basis of an argument that includes Q among its premises. Clause (ii), it would seem, is unproblematic. Clause (i), however, is not. For the reason why Sally cannot sensibly believe P and deny Q is not that P *entails* Q, for the entailment clearly does not hold: it isn't the case that the proposition that there is a sailing ship entails the proposition that those things really exist that we distinctly perceive. This means that the account as it stands is not correct – and that the fault lies in condition (i). But where exactly?

Here: condition (i) says that S cannot sensibly believe that P and deny Q. And we explained this by saying that this is because P *entails* Q. As our test example suggests, however, the explanation should be sought in a direction other than logical entailment. Why is it that Sally cannot sensibly believe P and deny Q? Because it is, somehow, inconsistent for Sally to form the belief that there is a sailing ship *in the way she does form it*, viz. in response to visually perceiving the ship, and deny the proposition that those things really exist that we distinctly perceive. The inconsistency is not of a logical nature. It is pragmatic: forming that belief *in the way she does*, is pragmatically inconsistent with denying the first principle: if Sally denies the latter, she would not form the former belief – at least not *in the way she does* actually form it. In order to take care of this point, I suggest we modify (i) as follows:

  (i*) S cannot sensibly form the belief that P in the way she does form it, and deny Q.

The phrase 'cannot sensibly' should be interpreted pragmatically.

Let us run a test on this improved account: suppose that Sally believes, upon finding a watch on the beach, *that this watch is designed*. If my account is correct, and if the Design Principle really is a first principle, then the following must be true: in forming her belief, Sally has presupposed the Design Principle, which means that (i) she cannot sensibly believe that this watch is designed and deny the Design Principle, i.e. the proposition that design and intelligence in the cause may be inferred with certainty from marks of design in the effect; and (ii) even if she explicitly believes the Design Principle, she did not come to believe that the watch is designed on the basis of an argument that includes that Principle among its premises. (ii) remains as unproblematic as it was. But what about (i): is it pragmatically inconsistent for Sally to believe the watch is designed, and deny that design and intelligence in the cause may be inferred, with certainty, from marks of it in the effect? If we take 'inferred' in a rather loose sense – so as not to involve reasoning from explicitly believed premises, then some form of pragmatic inconsistency seems to be involved indeed, in that it is inconsistent to deny that a perceived marks of design indicate a designing and intelligent cause, and yet maintain that the watch is designed.

What holds for beliefs is also true for actions. When one walks leisurely over the Tower Bridge, one has taken for granted that that bridge will hold. In this case what is taken for granted is the truth of the proposition *that that bridge will hold*. The proposition that is taken for granted, furthermore, is 'related' to something else, viz. an action (the action of leisurely walking over the Tower Bridge): it is taken for granted *relative* to that action. What needs to be the case in order for S, in doing A, to take for granted proposition Q? My suggestion, mirroring my previous one, is this: S, in doing A, takes Q for granted iff

    (i) S cannot sensibly do A and deny Q,

    (ii) even if S believes q, S did not come to do A on the basis of a practical argument that includes Q among its premises.

Clause (i)'s 'cannot sensibly' again has a pragmatic twist: if S denies that the Bridge will hold, S cannot sensibly leisurely walk over the Tower Bridge – as no one in his senses will leisurely walk across what he knows is a minefield.

As indicated, the account offered does not deny that some of us explicitly believe first principles, the Design Principle included. But even when we believe them, they need not and do not always enter as premises in arguments. Still, they might so enter, and sometimes do so enter, as e.g. in the famous arguments from design.

The next section takes a look at Hume's criticism of one such argument. The criticism is in fact a criticism of the Design Principle. If Hume's criticism is successful, the aim of this paper, viz. to vindicate the Design Principle, cannot be attained.

4. Reid on Hume's criticism of the argument of design

The Design Principle plays a crucial role in one version of what is known as the argument from final causes. It can be stated as follows (see EIP 509–510):

(1) Design Principle: design and intelligence in the cause may be inferred, with certainty, from marks or signs of it in the effect,

(2) there are the clearest marks of design and wisdom in the works of nature,

(3) hence, the works of nature are the effects of a wise and intelligent Cause.

Reid rightly notices that, since the argument is valid, in order to deny the conclusion, one must deny at least one of the premises. Those ancient philosophers that denied the existence of God, have rejected (2), arguing that the works of nature display no marks of design. But David Hume rejected (1). His objection against (1), in Reid's summary, is 'That the universe is a singular effect, and therefore, we can draw no conclusion from it, whether it may have been made by wisdom or not' (EIP 511). This is supposed to overthrow the Design Principle. But Reid argues that Hume's objection is unsuccessful, and hence that the Principle stands unrefuted. Now why does Reid think Hume's objection is unsuccessful, and what exactly *is* the argument anyway?

The objection, as Reid understood it, is as follows: 'if we had been accustomed to see worlds produced, some by wisdom and others without it, and had observed that such a world as this which we inhabit was always the effect of wisdom, we might then, from past experience, conclude that this world was made by wisdom; but, having no such experience, we have no means of forming any conclusions about it' (EIP 511). Spelled out a bit, Hume's objection is as follows: if we are to conclude that this world is caused by an intelligent designing cause, what we need is the following: (a) we need to have seen worlds produced by an intelligent designing cause – worlds moreover that display marks of design; (b) we need to have seen worlds produced not by an intelligent designing cause – worlds moreover that display no marks of design; (c) we need to observe that our world does display marks of design. Only with (a), (b), and (c) in place, we may draw the indicated conclusion. Or so Hume holds. And since neither (a) nor (b) are in place, he continues, the indicated conclusion doesn't follow and hence belief in it unjustified.

But Reid thinks this is all mistaken. His reasoning is the following *reductio*: if what Hume says is correct, then, by parity of reason, our belief that there exist other minds with intelligence and designing plans is also unjustified. The argument, already explicated in Section 1, is an exact parallel to Hume's objection and can be put as follows: if one is to conclude that an intelligent designing cause of action A exists, what one needs is the following: (a') one needs to have seen many instances of action A being performed by an intelligent designing cause – while action A displays, in all these instances, marks of design; (b') one needs to have seen many instances of action A performed by something that is not a designing intelligent cause – while action A displays in none of its instances marks of design; (c') one needs to observe an instance of action A that displays marks of design. Only with (a'), (b'), and (c') in place can one reach the desired conclusion that this last instance of action A has an intelligent designing cause. But (a') and (b') are not in place because we cannot directly observe intelligent designing causes. Hence the conclusion has not been established by this argument, and belief in the conclusion is therefore not justified by the argument.

This is what parity of reasons forces us to say. But since claims of the sort 'action A has an intelligent designing cause' are often obviously justified, Hume's argument against the Design Principle must be wrong.

So, the Design Principle stands: Hume's objection against it is a failure.

5.   Causes of persisting disagreement over first principles

As expounded in Section 3, Reid thinks there are several moves that can be made in case of disagreement over first principles. But suppose that the disagreement persists, how should we evaluate that situation? What should we do in such a situation?

As to the first question: we saw that the means that Reid holds can be used in order to resolve disagreement about first principles will work only in case the disagreeing parties are 'candid' and 'honest'. So, when disagreement persists, the cause could be the absence of candidness and/or honesty in one of the parties. So, if you and your neighbor disagree over a first principle, and you know yourself to be candid and honest, then that might give you some reason to believe that your neighbor is not. Now what is for someone to be 'candid'? I suggest that it is to be free from objectionable bias.

Obviously, there are many sorts of biases. In the wake of Bacon's famous treatment of the topic, Reid distinguishes four main kinds of biases that may prevent people from acknowledging a truth, even if that truth is a first principle.[8]

The first kind of biases have this in common that 'they arise from principles of the human constitution, which are highly useful and necessary in our present state; but by their excess or defect, or wrong direction, may lead us into error' (EIP 528). One instance of this bias that Reid mentions is, interestingly enough, deference to authority! Earlier on we saw that authority should pull some weight in case of disagreement over first principles. Here, as well as elsewhere, reverting to authority is useful. But people can go too far. Says Reid: 'there are many ... who may be called mere beggars with regard to their opinions. Through laziness and indifference about truth, they leave to others the drudgery of digging for this commodity.... Their concern is not to know what is true, but what is said and thought on such subjects' (EIP 528). Another bias in this class is that 'Men's judgments are often perverted by their affections and passions' (EIP 536). With respect to the Design Principle we might see these biases at work in contexts where naturalism runs high.

Another instance of this kind of bias is 'the love of simplicity, which disposes us to reduce things to few principles, and to conceive a greater simplicity in nature than there really is' (EIP 530). With respect to the Design Principle this might work as follows: love of simplicity disposes people to allow in their metaphysics only physical but no agent causes. And this may be reinforced by another bias at works in belief formation, viz. 'perversion by affections and passions' (EIP 536). It would seem that people can be passionately in the grip of a worldview that denies any design whatsoever, and this might cause them to reject the very idea that the Design Principle can ever be applied.

Not all biases have their basis in the human constitution, some are purely individual; 'some are afraid to step out of the beaten track and think it safest to go with the multitude; others are fond of singularities, and of everything that has the air of paradox' (EIP 536). There is, of course, any number of ways in which these individual biases can get in the way of the acknowledgement of first principles.

A final kind of biases arise 'from the systems or sects in which we have been trained, or which we have adopted' (EIP 540). Again, with respect to the Design Principle, many systems or sects come to mind.

Of course, the identification of biases is a sword that can be wielded by both of the disagreeing parties. Still, it can help one to understand the intellectual situation one is in when one faces disagreement over first principles.

In the current literature on peer disagreement, two positions stand center stage, the steadfast position, and the equal weight view.[9] Assuming disagreeing persons to be each other's epistemic peers, meaning roughly that they are equally intelligent, display all the same intellectual virtues such as open mindedness, and are equally informed about the evidence pertaining to the issue of disagreement, the first position says that both parties should simply go on believing what and as they did before noticing the disagreement. The second position, by contrast, says they should not. The disagreeing parties should 'move to each other', which is standardly explained in terms of degrees of belief: if A and B disagree over proposition p, and A believes p, on a scale with values between 0 and 1, with a strength of .9, and B believes p with a strength of .1 (meaning that B rather strongly believes that p is false), they should move towards each other and settle for the middle, in this case scale down and scale up respectively their belief in p to .5.

Taking up the question what to do in cases of disagreement, I should now like to suggest that Reid has his own take on this, and in fact puts a proposal on the table that has not been recognized in the current Epistemology of Disagreement literature. It seems uncontroversial that disagreement over first principles is an instance of peer disagreement, as in such controversies 'every man is a competent judge (EIP 438). Now, if you endorse a certain proposition as a first principle, and one of your peers believes that proposition is false, then, on Reid's view (and very roughly), after having examined your own judgment and having found no reason for thinking you are mistaken or biased, you should continue to believe what you believe, but only if you have an explanation as to the cause of your peer's disagreement with you – an explanation in terms of biases at work![10] This rough indication begs for further explanation, exploration and application. But that will have to await another occasion.

Notes

1. Throughout the paper, EIP is the acronym for Reid's *Essays on the Intellectual Powers of Man*. I am using the Brookes edition.
2. Van Woudenberg (2013).
3. The variety of marks of design has been in-depth discussed by Ratzsch (2001).
4. An example of the unproductiveness of ridicule in philosophy is Dennett in Dennett and Plantinga (2011).
5. *Consensus gentium* considerations are now receiving renewed attention in current social epistemology. See e.g. Kelly (2011).
6. It is also possible to widen the notion of 'belief' so as to not only comprise explicit full belief, but also dispositional and implicit belief. This expanded notion of 'belief' will, of course, not stand in such a stark opposition to 'taking for granted' (which can be deemed identical to 'implicit belief').
7. Ratzsch (2003) argued on other grounds for the same point.
8. Since not all of the biases affect belief in alleged first principles, I will single out only those that can.
9. See Feldman and Warfield (2010).
10. For comments on an earlier draft many thanks to Terence Cuneo, John Turri, and also to Patric Rysiew, Rebecca Copenhaver, Keith Lehrer, Todd Buras, Lorne Falkenstein, Esther Kroeker, and Laurent Jaffro as well as to the participants of the 19th International Philosophical Colloquium in Evian 2013, especially Georg Bertram, Robin Celikates, and David Lauer. It is gratefully acknowledged that work on this paper was made possible by a grant from the Templeton World Charity Foundation.

References

Barrett, Justin. 2009. "Cognitive Science, Religion, and Theology." In *The Believing Primate. Scientific, Philosophical, and Theological Reflections on the Origins of Religion*, edited by Jeffrey Schloss and Michael Murray, 76–99. Oxford: Oxford University Press.

Dennett, Daniel, and Alvin Plantinga. 2011. *Science and Religion. Are they Compatible?* Oxford: Oxford University Press.

Feldman, Richard, and Ted A. Warfield, eds. 2010. *Disagreement*. Oxford: Oxford University Press.

Kelly, Thomas. 2011. "Consensus Gentium: Reflections on the 'common consent' argument for the existence of God." In *Evidence and religious belief*, edited by Kelly James Clark and Ray J. Vanarragon, 135–156. Oxford: Oxford University Press.

Ratzsch, Del. 2001. *Nature, Science, Design. The Status of Design in Natural Science*. New York: SUNY Press.

Ratzsch, Del. 2003. "Perceiving Design." In *God and Design. The Teleological Argument and Modern Science*, edited by Neil A. Manson. London: Routledge.

Reid, Thomas. 1763 [2002]. *Essays on the Intellectual Powers of Man*. Edited by Derek Brookes. Edinburgh: Edinburgh University Press.

Van Woudenberg, René. 2013. "Thomas Reid Between Externalism and Internalism." *Journal of the History of Philosophy* 51: 75–92.

Wolterstorff, Nicholas. 2001. *Thomas Reid and the Story of Epistemology*. Cambridge: Cambridge University Press.

Index

Note: Page numbers followed by 'n' refer to notes